Welcome to The ABC's of Plutonium Private Club Leadership!

Let me begin by saying something that will be obvious to anyone who reads this book: Authors Michael Crandal and Gabe Aluisy really GET private clubs. Pure and simple. They also share our company's passionate belief that continuous, open-minded learning and industry specific education are the key to successful club leadership.

We are honored to have been asked to contribute to such a significant book and we congratulate them on a masterful job of compiling essential club industry wisdom that will serve as a tremendous resource for managers, officers, directors and committee members. If every club adopted a policy of incorporating this book into their board orientation, I believe the entire industry would be stronger for it.

When they set out to publish this collection, Michael and Gabe had a simple goal in mind; to prepare you, the reader, to address club governance from the perspective of the club industry. It is true that many club leaders are highly accomplished in their own areas of expertise, but the most successful and effective are able to set aside their own bias and perspective in favor of understanding and embracing the unique drivers of success in private clubs.

I believe leaders who are exposed to this book early and refer to it often during their tenure stand a much better chance of actually helping their clubs. Having been intimately involved in work with more than 600 club boards since Club Benchmarking was founded in 2009, I have seen misconceptions and lack of understanding send far too many leadership teams veering dangerously off course, making decisions that will ultimately hurt rather than help their clubs. This book has the power to prevent such problematic outcomes.

Michael and Gabe are passionate and experienced students of clubs. They have put significant effort into pulling together the knowledge you now hold in your hand. Enjoy the read and enjoy the journey of making a meaningful contribution to your club's success, today and into the future!

All the Best,

Raymond P. Cronin

Ray Cronin
Club Benchmarking - Founder & Chief Innovator

Edited by Stephen Hirst

Cover design by Richard Jibaja Interior design by Johanna Davila

ISBN: 978-0-9905832-6-4

10 9 8 7 6 5 4 3 2 1

1. Business & Economics 2. Management

First Edition

Published by Shake Creative http://shaketampa.com

Printed in the United States of America

PLUTONIUM ENDORSEMENTS

"I appreciate all that Michael has done in *assisting us in making strides to take our club to the next level.* His input and analysis have been spot-on and most appreciated. *My entire board had access to The ABC's of Private Club Leadership!"*
Tommy Brennan — President — Tchefuncta Country Club — Covington, LA

"Very compelling. Wished I had this information years ago! Easy and fun to read."
Jody Clor, GM/COO — Old Overton Club — Vestavia Hills, AL

"The ABC's of Plutonium Private Club Leadership is thought provoking, enjoyable and *a must read for volunteer directors and industry professionals* with a keen interest in gaining a deeper understanding and perspective of the Private Club Industry."
Frank Cordeiro, COO — Diablo Country Club — Diablo, CA

"This book is awesome! The 'ABC's' is a comprehensive private club leadership handbook that everyone should keep on their nightstand. I love that you thought it important to cover not only the core competencies, but touched on the nuance subjects that make club leadership the challenge it is. Thank you for believing this project was worth pursuing."
John R. Finley, CCM — Managing Partner — Paisano Performance Partners

"The expertise found in The ABC's of Private Club Leadership accurately encapsulates Michael's approach. He delivers *the highest quality member experiences* with impeccable integrity."
Jere Fonda — Past President — Thunderbird Country Club — Rancho Mirage, CA

"The ABC's of Private Club Leadership has so much useful information and hits on topics that some Clubs would rather not address and kick that can down the road. I plan on making this *book a part of Board orientations, as well as available to committee members."*
Tim Mervosh, COO/GM — Thornblade Club — Greer, SC

"A very comprehensive and fun read *with valuable information for any manager, CEO, or member involved in committees or Board of Directors.* Michael's passion and knowledge of business, organization and the critical personal touches permeates his 'A to Z' approach!"
Andy Pavlovich – Past President, Hallbrook Country Club — Leawood, KS

"*A thought provoking and insightful* book of step by step *for boards, managers,* and staff alike! This is clearly not a "one and done" read! Thank you for capturing all of this information in one area in an easy to read format!"
Steven Rosen, GM — Indian Wells Golf Resort — Indian Wells, CA

A *"must have" reference manual for Managers, Assistant Managers and Wanna-Be-Managers.* The BIG issues are addressed, insights provided and guidance given in an easy to digest, easy to reference, easy to "thumb through" and enjoy format. *"Plutonium" is a must-read because it's delivering "the meat" in a fun-to-read format that's energized with The BUZZ!!! Boring it ain't — USEFUL* it is. For anyone wanting to manage clubs, this is the one book that should be chewed on at least once-a-day, every day, forever. Good stuff!!!"
Gregg Patterson — Founder and President — "Tribal Magic!!!"

"*As a past president, as well as a current member of multiple top-tier clubs, I can say that volunteer board members should read The ABC's of Plutonium Private Club Leadership as a routine component of their orientation and that private club GM/COO's and key department heads should all have their own personal copies as well.* I have observed Michael's impact at multiple private clubs, ranging from small town country clubs to major resort clubs over a long period of time and his *"ABC's" empowers everyone to produce a higher level of member experience."*
Walt Sinclair — Boise, Idaho

"This book tackles many private club issues with unique insight, fun and superb understanding of the challenges Club leaders face. *The understanding of what Club leaders should expect from their GM and also what their fellow members should expect from the BOD's is some of the best I have seen in any business.* I worked very closely with Michael on a management transition in our Club, and he provided sound advice and leadership that we are benefitting from to this very day. However, most importantly, serving in Club leadership is fun and rewarding again."
Gary D. Smith, President — Mission Hills Country Club — Mission Hills, KS

"*This book is a 'must read'* and reference item for any private club leader that wants to understand how an excellent Club should be run. Many insights provide a road map to problem solving for executives in the Club field."
Sal V. Spano — Former Arvida/Disney CFO — President, Palm Beach Polo Golf and CC.

INTRODUCTION

The inspiration for *The ABC's Of Plutonium Private Club Leadership* came during a taped-live program on *Private Club Radio*. The featured guest that day was Michael Crandal, CNG — being interviewed by host, Gabriel Aluisy.

Just prior to closing the show, Michael asked Gabe if he'd be interested in a piping-hot bowl of "Today's Special." Gabe quickly confirmed, and here is what Michael served up.

TODAY'S SPECIAL IS ALPHABET SOUP!

Assessments are a "No – No". **B**oard members are kept in the know. **C**apital reserve plans are firmly in place. **D**epreciation funded means assets don't go to waste. **E**quity memberships need to go. **F**ood minimums — also. **G**olf is for all genders and the whole family. **H**ospitality indeed extends to the tee. **I**nitiation income is slowly on the rise, while **J**unior Programs are starting to thrive. **K**ids are kept busy while young parents exchange high-fives. **L**egacy memberships are proving a pipeline to survive. **M**embers & management are in constant harmony. The **N**ominating committee is renowned for selecting quality. **O**perations are such that all feel pride. **P**eople are in the right places — deep and wide. **Q**uality is never left to chance. **R**estaurants serve nothing but excellence. **S**acred cows are not allowed to graze. **T**raditions are respected, while simultaneously the bar is continually raised. **U**nbelievable stories abound of great staff anticipation. **V**isitors are met members extending invitations. **W**ait staff service is top-tier. **X**-tra attention is given to all members and guests. **Y**ounger members, yes they see — **Z**ee club — Zee club — Zee club! Is the place to be.

The "Special" that day proved wildly popular, as private club leaders nationwide requested hard copies to distribute at board meetings. Thus, Michael and Gabe conspired to further expand the recipe to cover from "A" to Z" many of the "secret sauce" ingredients of *PLUTONIUM PRIVATE CLUB LEADERSHIP.*

> **DISCLAIMER:** This is **NOT** a **textbook** that one would study in order to prepare for some sort of a written exam. Instead, think of this as a **handbook** of insights that bring all of that boring (yet vitally important) textbook data to life.

THE ABC'S OF PLUTONIUM PRIVATE CLUB LEADERSHIP

Many individuals in varied careers study those textbooks to pass written exams (just look at all those certificates on the wall, and the letters behind their names to prove it) And perhaps in the corporate world, book knowledge is often enough.

HOWEVER — the world of private club leadership spins on quite a different axis. Book knowledge alone, no matter how deep, is simply not enough.

Book knowledge, facts, figures, charts, SOP's and KPI's (as important as they may be) are, frankly — boring. The

THERE ARE MANY VERY CAPABLE INDIVIDUALS IN POSITIONS OF LEADERSHIP AT PRIVATE CLUBS. PRESIDENTS, BOARD AND COMMITTEE MEMBERS. GM/COO'S, DEPARTMENT HEADS AND STAFF MEMBERS. YET, THE COLLECTIVE EFFORTS OF ALL ARE OFTEN "CAPPED" AT A CERTAIN LEVEL, EVEN AT SO-CALLED TOP LEVEL CLUBS.

greatest private club leaders (volunteer and paid) bring far more to the table than that. Boredom is not allowed. It is indeed exciting to go to that next level.

So, don't forget all those **textbooks** full of knowledge sitting on the credenza behind your desk so you can cram for that next exam. But keep this little *handbook* on your nightstand to flip through frequently when it comes to bringing to life *The ABC's of Plutonium Private Club Leadership.*

HERE'S THE DEAL: Simply look through the alphabet for a subject of interest and instantly find meaningful insights. Unlike textbooks, you need not start at the front and systematically work your way through each chapter. Instead — open any page at random, and immediately pick up on a few insights to helping build your team towards PLUTONIUM CLUB LEADERSHIP status.

ABOUT THE AUTHORS

GABRIEL ALUISY

Gabriel Aluisy is the founder of The Private Club Agency, a Tampa, Florida based design, marketing and consulting firm focused on membership development and retention strategy at private clubs. He is the author of *The Definitive Guide to Membership Marketing* and the best selling book *Moving Targets: Creating Engaging Brands in an On-Demand World*. Each week, Aluisy hosts the *Private Club Radio Show*, the industry's premier podcast dedicated to private club education. Learn more at aluisy.com

MICHAEL CRANDAL, CNG

I have a great professional passion for the private club industry, and an even greater personal affection for the people that bring it to life.

There are many very capable individuals in positions of leadership at private clubs: presidents, board and committee members, GM/COO's, department heads and staff. Yet, the collective efforts of all are oftentimes "capped" at a certain level, even at so-called top-level clubs.

I am convinced that private clubs are an honorable calling, representing the highest opportunity to continually bring out the very best in people — board, committees, members, staff and management. ALL should be Plutonium Club Leaders in their own right — within their own unique sphere of authority and influence.

There are approaches to club governance (Board) or operations (Management) that exist solely for historical reasons, which are no longer relevant in today's world and lifestyles. These can keep a club locked in an orbit around a world that no longer exists. Gone are the days where all the Board had to do was make simplistic popular policy adjustments every so often, and all Management had to do was to occasionally make "low hanging operational fruit" decisions.

BUT —for those clubs proactive and confident enough to make the strategic policies (Board) and operational (Management) decisions necessary to reflect the times and build upon the rock of solid leadership — there can be plenty of good days ahead.

Yup — now we are talking The ABC's of Plutonium Private Club Leadership!

"It makes no difference whatsoever how good something sounds, looks on paper, adheres to budget or even seems logical. In an absence of Membership Satisfaction – you can forget everything else. Period.

Membership Satisfaction is "Mission Critical." It is the only reason people JOIN, the only reason they will STAY, the only reason they will INVITE others to become part of it all. Actual member experiences MUST be the focus in order to see clearly!"

Oh, and one more thing, just in case you were wondering. The letters after our author's name **Michael Crandal, CNG** stand for: Certified Nice Guy. Self-certified by the way. But, a nice guy nonetheless. *Michael can be reached directly in regard to consulting or speaking engagements.*
(760) 464-6103

MUCH APPRECIATION AND RESPECT FOR THE EXPERTISE OF OUR CONTRIBUTING PLUTONIUM CLUB LEADERS:

MARK BADO
"Fitness / Wellness in Private Clubs"
PAGE 152

PAUL MUELLER
"Capital Reserve Significance"
PAGE 59

JACKIE CARPENTER
"Employees are the Most
Important People"
PAGE 127

BILL SCHULZ
"The Evolution of F&B in
Private Clubs"
PAGE 129

RAY CRONIN
"The Balance Sheet"
PAGE 144

ROBERT SERECI
"What's In A Name"
PAGE 387

DAVE DOWNING
"Get Better NOW!"
PAGE 185

JOHN SIBBALD
Honorary Tribute
PAGE 401

DAVE DUVAL & JOE ABELY
"Debt in Private Clubs"
PAGE 88

NORM SPITZIG
"Strategic Planning in 2 Questions"
PAGE 349

JOHN EMBREE
"The Importance of Tennis Programming"
PAGE 355

HENRY WALLMEYER
"5 Myths of Private Clubs"
PAGE 279

BUD GRAVETTE
"Dual Roles of a Plutonium GM/COO"
PAGE 102

HARVEY WEINER
"This I Know"
PAGE 234

ALAN JACOBS
"It's Showtime!"
PAGE 352

GORDON WELCH
"Committee Success"
PAGE 72

CONTENTS

 ASSESSMENTS ARE A "NO – NO". 21

ATTITUDE -IN ORDER TO BE A WILDLY SUCCESSFUL PLUTONIUM CLUB LEADER — START RIGHT HERE AND NOW!

 BOARD MEMBERS ARE KEPT IN THE KNOW. 27

BOARD EXPECTATIONS — THEIR IDEAL PLUTONIUM GM/COO ROLE MODEL

BOARD OF DIRECTOR'S — THEIR RESPONSIBILITIES, ROLES AND STANDARD DECORUM

BOARD MEETINGS THAT MATTER — PLUTONIUM CLUB LEADERS PROFESSIONALLY GUIDE AND INFLUENCE

BOTTOM LINE CONTRIBUTORS ARE WHAT MATTER — NOT SO MUCH TOP LINE DEPARTMENTAL REVENUES

BRIGHT IDEAS — STARTING WITH THE FIRST DAY AT A NEW CLUB — AND 18 CONCEPTS MOVING THROUGH THE YEARS

BUDGETS — WHY ZERO-BASED IS WORTH IT

 CAPITAL RESERVE PLANS ARE FIRMLY IN PLACE. 55

CAPITAL PROJECTS — TWO BASIC KINDS AND FUNDING

CAPITAL RESERVE STUDY — FOUND IN THE TOOL BOX OF EVERY PLUTONIUM PRIVATE CLUB LEADERSHIP TEAM

CHANGES — PLUTONIUM CLUB LEADERS RESPECT THE PAST, BUT ANTIIPATE AND CREATE APPROPRIATE CHANGE.

CHARACTER IS WHAT DEFINES A PLUTONIUM CLUB LEADER

CMAA — PLUTONIUM CLUB LEADERS ARE HEAVILY INVOLVED

COMMITTEES CAN GET OUT OF HAND! — NO! REALLY?

COMMITTEE SUCCESS — PLUTONIUM GUIDELINES / MEANINGFUL REC-
OMMENDATIONS THE BOARD WILL FAVORABLY ACT UPON.

 DEPRECIATION FUNDED MEANS ASSETS DON'T GO TO WASTE. 81

DEBT IS ONLY A TOOL — NOT AN ANSWER. PLUTONIUM CLUB LEAD-
ERS KNOW THE DIFFERENCE BETWEEN THE TWO.

DECONSTRUCTING IDEAL GM/COO ROLE MODELS — VISUALLY, JUST
ABOUT ALL WE NEED TO KNOW W/ KEY DEFINITIONS.

DELIGATION SKILLS — IF YOUR TEAM DOESN'T MAKE IT
— NEITHER DO YOU!

DELINQUENT ACCOUNTS — THE SAME NAMES ALWAYS SHOW UP.

DISAPPOINTMENTS — PLUTONIUM LEADERS QUIKLY REGROUP.

DUEL ROLES OF A PLUTONIUM GM/COO — MANAGEMENT OF THE
CLUB — LEADERSHIP FOR THE CLUB.

DUES INCOME – IT FLOATS THE BOAT

 EQUITY MEMBERSHIPS NEED TO GO. 108

ELEPHANTS ARE IN THE BOARDROOM! — POSITION
DESCRIPTIONS FOR ALL NEED TO BE ESTABLISHED!

EMPLOYEE ANNUAL COMPENSATION ADJUSTMENTS —
ABSOLUTELY MUST GET THIS RIGHT FOR ALL KINDS OF RIPPLE EFFECT
REASONS.

EMPLOYEE AREAS — PLUTONIUM CLUB LEADERS ARE FIRST CLASS IN
ALL RESPECTS — NOTHING TO HIDE!

EMPLOYEES — THE PEOPLE THAT MATTER THE VERY MOST.

EXECUTIVE CHEFS — THE EVOLUTION OF FOOD SERVICE IN PRIVATE
CLUBS.

EXECUTIVE LEVEL DECISIONS NEED TO BE MADE – MAKE THEM. — THAT'S WHAT PLUTONIUM CLUB LEADERS DO.

EXECUTIVE SUMMARY — ALL PLUTONIUM GM/COO'S DISTRIBUTE ONE PRIOR TO EVERY BOARD MEETING

EXPECTATIONS ARE NOT MET, OR MERELY EXCEEDED — INSTEAD, PLUTONIUM LEADERSHIP ESTABLISHES THEM!

 FOOD MINIMUMS — ALSO. **144**

FINANCIAL SUCCESS — IS NO 'SHELL' GAME — BUT PLUTONIUM CLUB LEADERS KNOW HOW TO WIN!

F&B IN PRIVATE CLUBS — RULES THE HOSPITALITY INDUSTRY IN TERMS OF QUALITY AND SERVICE

F&B OPERATIONS — SO EVEN AVERAGE JOE'S CAN UNDERSTAND IT.

FITNESS AND WELLNESS – PLUTONIUM CLUB LEADERS CAPITALIZE ON THE BENEFITS OF A GREAT F&W CENTER

FITNESS AND WELLNESS – 5 KEY COMPONENTS FOR SUCCESS

FOOD COST OF GOODS SOLD – 10 'THINK SPOTS'

 GOLF IS FOR ALL GENDERS AND FAMILY. **185**

GET BETTER NOW! – THROUGH THE EYES OF A MASTERFUL GOLF COURSE SUPERINTENDENT.

GM/COO's FIRST 90-DAY PLAN — UPON ARRIVAL

GOLF IS THE ANSWER! — THE QUESTION IS?

GOSSIP – NEEDS TO BE STOPPED DEAD IN ITS' TRACKS

GOVERNANCE ISSUES — POLICIES, BYLAWS AND DEFINED ROLES ARE IN PLACE TO DERAIL ROGUE "BIG' AGENDAS.

HOSPITALITY INDEED EXTENDS TO THE TEE. 202

HARD WORK — THERE IS NO OTHER PATH LEADING TO PLUTONIUM CLUB LEADERSHIP

HEALTHY PLUTONIUM CLUB BASICS — 2 "MISSION CRITICAL" COMMITTEES & 3 CRITICAL LEADERSHIP FACTORS

HUMOR — FACE IT, YOU'VE ALREADY GOT A 'DREAM JOB'

HUMOR — IF YOU CAN'T LAUGH — FIND ANOTHER CAREER!

 INITIATION INCOME IS SLOWLY ON THE RISE. 219

INTANGIBLES – THE LITTLE PERFORMANCE TRAITS THAT SEPARATE PLUTONIUM LEADERS FROM ALL OTHERS.

INTERVIEW QUESTION OF BALANCE — HIRE 'REAL PEOPLE" NOT JUST RESUMES AND INTERVIEW SKILLS.

INTERVIEW SKILLS — JOHN WAYNE STYLE

 JUNIOR PROGRAMS ARE STARTING TO THRIVE. 231

JOB TITLES MEAN NOTHING — THE DIFFERENCE BETWEEN A JOB TITLE AND WHAT IT IS YOU'RE REALLY THERE TO DO.

 KIDS ARE KEPT BUSY WHILE YOUNG PARENTS GIVE HIGH-FIVES. 234

KNOWLEDGE — THINGS ALL PRIVATE CLUB PLUTONIUM CLUB LEADERS NEED TO KNOW THAT YOU WON'T LEARN IN CLASS OR FIND IN TEXTBOOKS.

 LEGACY MEMBERSHIPS ARE PROVING A PIPELINE TO SURVIVE. 244

LEADERSHIP — POP QUIZ TEST

LISTENING & SPEAKING — PLUTONIUM CLUB LEADERS MASTER EXECUTIVE LEVEL PRESENTATION SKILLS

MASTER PLAN — FOR BOTH CLUBHOUSE AND GOLF COURSE

MEETINGS — PLUTONIUM LEADERS DO NOT ALLOW THINGS TO BE RAILROAED THROUGH

MEMBER EXPERIENCES — MUST BE "STAGED" BEFORE THEY HAPPEN

MEMBERSHIP MARKETING — IS NOT A SPRINT

MEMBERSHIP MARKETING — REIMAGINED

MENU PRICING — TO PRINT OR NOT TO PRINT

MICRO-MANAGMENT — "I'VE BEEN TO THE MOUNTAIN TOP."

MISSION STATEMENT — THE CNG UNIVERSAL MISSION STATEMENT: "OUR MEMBERS VERY FAVORITE PLACE TO BE."

MONEY TALKS — PLUTONIUM CLUB LEADERS KNOW WHAT THEY ARE TALKING ABOUT!

NATIONAL CLUB ASSOCIATION — DEBUNKING THE INDUSTRY'S 5 MOST HARMFUL MYTHS / MISCONCEPTIONS

NEW IDEAS — COME BY GETTING YOUR ENTIRE TEAM TO THINK PLU-TONIUM THOUGHTS!

NEW MEMBERS — HERE'S THE MOST EFFECTIVE WAY TO ATTRACT THEM.

ONE THING THAT NO LEADER CAN AFFORD — PLUTONIUM CLUB LEADERS MAY BE ACUSSED OF MANY THINGS — THIS IS NOT ONE OF THEM!

ORIENTATION FOR NEW BOARD MEMBERS — (AKA: HOW TO AVOID DISORIENTED LEADERSHIP.)

PEOPLE ARE IN THE RIGHT PLACES — DEEP AND WIDE. **298**

PEOPLE – PLUTONIUM CLUB LEADERS MAKE SURE THE RIGHT ONES ARE ON THE BUS.

PEOPLE AND PROCESS — IT'S A BALANCING ACT

PERFORMANCE REVIEWS — CAN BE AKIN TO RATING CHICKEN WINGS.

POOR PERFORMERS — ARE NEVER UNWITTINGLY "REWARDED" BY PLUTONIUM CLUB LEADRERS

POTENTIAL FOR PERFECTION — PLUTONIUM LEADERS ARE ABLE TO SEE THINGS AS THEY ARE — AND THEN, TAKE THEM TO WHERE THEY CAN TRULY BE.

PRESIDENT ALWAYS LOOKS GOOD — PLUTONIUM CLUB LEADERSHIP KNOWS NO OTHER WAY — JOB #1.

PRIVATE CLUB RADIO — WHERE GABE INTERVIEWS THE MOST DYNAM-IC LEADERS IN THE PRIVATE CLUB INDUSTRY EVERY WEEK.

 QUALITY IS NEVER LEFT TO CHANCE. **321**

QUALITY AND SERVICE — PLUTONIUM CLUB LEADERS CONSISTENCY CREATE PERCEIVED VALUE OF MEMBERSHIP

QUESTIONS — PLUTONIUM CLUB LEADERS CONSIDER ASKING THESE OF A SEARCH COMMITTEE

 RESTAURANTS SERVE NOTHING BUT EXCELLENCE. **331**

RESPONSIBILITY CANNOT BE DELEGATED — PLUTONIUM CLUB LEAD-ERS APPROPRIATELY DELEGATE AUTHORITY — BUT ULTIMATE RESPON-SIBILITY REMAINS WITH THEM!

RETURN ON INVESTMENT OF BEING A MEMBER — "PROFIT" IS DE-FINED IN TERMS OF MEMBERSHIP SATISFACTION.

 **SACRED COWS ARE NOT ALLOWED TO GRAZE** 340

SANCTUARY COUNTY CLUB — WHERE POLITICAL CORRECTNESS RUNS AMUK.

SERVER COMPENSATION — FINDING A WAY TO LINK PERFORMANCE TO COMPENSATION.

SHAKESPERE — SURE KNOWS HIS CLUBS!

STRATEGIC PLANNING — WHAT IT IS IN TWO QUESTIONS.

 TRADITIONS ARE RESPECTED WHILE THE BAR IS CONTINUALLY RAISED. 352

TEAM BUILDING — THE "IT'S SHOWTIME" PHILOSOPHY

TENNIS, ANYONE? — PLUTONIUM PRIVATE CLUB LEADERS ANSWER WITH PROGRAMMING REACHING MEMBERS OF ALL GENERATIONS.

THREE CLUB MANAGERS — WALK INTO A BAR.

THRIVING – NOT JUST SURVIVING

TOXIC EMPLOYEES — THEY GOTTA GO! IT'S A PRIORITY.

TRAINERS TEACH — PLUTONIUM LEADERS INSPIRE

 UNBELIEVABLE STORIES ABOUND OF GREAT STAFF ANTICIPATION. 369

UNPLANNED CAREER MOVES — THE #1 REASON

 VISITORS COVET MEMBERS EXTENDING INVITATIONS. 372

VISION — HOW PLUTONIUM CLUB LEADERS SEE THINGS.

 WAIT STAFF SERVICE IS NOTHING BUT THE BEST. 374

WAIT STAFF SERVICE — SHOULD BE ORCHESTRATED BY BEING UNDER THE GRAVITATIONAL PULL OF THE CNG BLACK HOLE THEORY

WORKING YOUR WAY TO THE TOP — EXAMPLES OF HARD WORK, BUT ALSO HOW PLUTONIUM LEADERSHIP SKILLS ARE USED IN DEVELOPO-ING YOUNG TALENT WITH POTENTIAL.

 X-TRA ATTENTION IS GIVEN TO ALL MEMBERS AND GUESTS. **381**

XTRA ATTENTION AND PERSONAL CARE —THE VIBE PLUTONIUM CLUB LEADERS CREATE MEMBER EXPERIENCES

 YOUNGER MEMBERS, YES THEY SEE **385**

YOUNGER MEMBERS — LIKE POP-UP EXPERIENTIAL EVENTS

YOU'RE ON A FIRST-NAME BASIS — PLUTONIUM CLUB LEADERS LEAN TOWARDS HORIZONTAL APPROACHES TO MANAGEMENT AS APPOSED TO VERTICAL

 ZEE CLUB - ZEE CLUB - ZEE CLUB IS THE PLACE TO BE! **390**

ZEE CLUB! IS THE PLACE TO BE!

ASSESSMENTS ARE A "NO – NO".

ATTITUDE
IN ORDER TO BE A WILDLY SUCCESSFUL PLUTONIUM CLUB LEADER — START RIGHT HERE AND NOW!

YOUR ATTITUDE is the single greatest asset, or albatross, at your disposal.

While it is an intangible force – one that cannot be seen, touched, or heard—there is no question that its very existence is the most dominating factor in determining your position in life.

While you can't see it with the naked eye, your attitude has the unique ability to always be seen anyway. Run as any of us may, or hide it as we might try — our attitude lights or dims every path before us. And, in many cases, it shapes how we are viewed by those around us.

Every individual views the world through a different and unique set of filtered glasses. If you have a negative, pessimistic attitude, you will view the world as a threatening place where all your efforts are in vain.

If your attitude is negative, your world is negative.

However, if you have a healthy, optimistic attitude, then you have a rich understanding of our world as a wonderful place in which to live, learn and grow—a place where opportunities abound.

The degree of success and satisfaction you achieve is in a direct 1-to-1 ratio to your attitude toward yourself, others, and the world around you.

Your attitude is the key to *(or the lock on)* your personal door of success.

1 *THE FIRST STEP toward developing your own unique positive attitude is accepting the fact that you have a PERSONAL RESPONSIBILITY for your position in life.*

For our purposes here, "personal responsibility" means that you, and only you, are 100% in charge of who you are and what you do. Personal mediocrity and negative results can often be traced back to a lack of accepting personal responsibility.

Rationalizations	*Cop-Outs*	*Pointing Fingers*
Defenses	*Lame Excuses*	*Establishing Blame*

All are just weak attempts to justify the fear of accepting personal responsibility for the mental, spiritual and physical world in which you live. *You must accept personal responsibility for the cause-and-effect attitude in which you view the world and your role in it.*

Our weak club "leader" drives to the club complaining audibly to themselves about:

- The micro-managing president, the inept manager or grumbling members.
- Hourly staff that cannot afford to live close to the club.
- "Sacred Cows" grazing throughout the club.
- Committees out of control.
- Meetings that don't really matter.
- Unrealistic operating budget.
- No overall Master Plan in place.
- Outdated bylaws and club rules not reflecting the times.
- Artificially low dues.
- The long hours.

All these and other irritants **MAKE** time spent at the club less enjoyable than it should be, and when at home, negative thinking just seems pervasive.

At home — a non-communicative posture and a pervasive low fever of grumpiness at least take some consolation in "knowing" that this is not their fault. After all, it is all those other things that **MAKE** them that way. (Really?)

- Marge keeps a dirty house *because* her mother yelled at her too much as a child.
- Eric drinks too much *because* his wife doesn't have confidence in him.
- John goes aimlessly from job to job *because* his boss does not understand him.

- Ethel overeats and is obese **because** her parents always paid more attention to her sister.
- Eleanor continues to go into debt **because** her brother was killed in a plane crash.
- Ray is withdrawn and non-communicative **because** his friends plan activities without him.

And on and on and on and on it goes. "I am not responsible for what I am and the way I act!" — all these people are saying to themselves.

They have convinced themselves that other people and situations that they have no control over MAKE them act as they do. (Really? C'mon – really?)

As the saying goes, you really do "reap what you sow". It is impossible to plant petunias and grow potatoes. Or to do nothing, and expect a harvest.

It is equally impossible to shirk the reality of personal responsibility and expect anything more than negative results due to your attitude toward life.

Show me a weak person in a position of leadership, and I'll show you a philosopher. Show me a **PLUTONIUM LEADER**, and I'll show you someone who accepts personal responsibility for their own success or failure in life. *100% of Plutonium Club Leaders* embrace this fact! There are no exceptions.

YOU must take total personal responsibility for causing the effects in your own life!

Personal Responsibility

The vast majority of things that happen in your life are a reflection of those things that you allow your mind to linger on the most. In any business, there is no substitute for quality. So why settle for less in your attitude towards your own life? Grow up!

**YOU ARE IN THE DRIVER'S SEAT OF YOUR LIFE.
NOT THE CLUB.
NOT THE GOVERNMENT.
NOT THE DAILY HOROSCOPE.
NOT YOUR FAMILY.
NOT YOUR FRIENDS.**

2 THE SECOND STEP in developing a positive attitude is to EXPECT THE BEST from yourself

Engage in the self-talk of a winner. Expect good things from yourself — for in the long run, you will live up (or down) to your own expectations. Your own expectations of yourself should be far greater than any of those around you.

Every moment of your life, awake and sleeping, you are constantly talking to yourself, reaffirming and justifying your beliefs and attitudes toward yourself.

Your mind is like a garden, and whatever seeds you plant there will grow. So, be careful about the seeds that you are planting in the form of such phrases as:

- "I can't do this or that very well."
- "I don't have the aptitude to do that."
- "I'm not as smart as most people."
- "I make mistakes all the time."
- "I never know how to say the right things."
- "I'm not very good at doing things like that."
- "I have a poor memory."

Make a personal commitment RIGHT NOW to eliminate these types of negative assertions in your attitude toward yourself.

By continually repeating negative assertions, you are actually using a form of self-hypnosis, and perpetually reinforcing a negative attitude toward your own efforts.

Bill Bradley, an All-American basketball player and Rhodes Scholar from Princeton University, who later went on to star in the NBA and serve as a United States Senator from New Jersey, was once asked why he practiced so very many hours on the basketball court — when he was clearly already one of the very best at what he did.

He responded along the lines of, "Remember, when you are not practicing, someone, somewhere is. And, when you meet them, they will defeat you."

Keep in mind the importance of practice.

Be certain that the words and phrases you practice for hours upon hours in your mind are of a positive nature.

Develop a "can do" attitude toward the challenges of day-to-day living. Reaffirm your expectations of yourself by using positive statements such as:

- "I will be a positive mentor."
- "I can provide meaningful input."
- "I am improving in those areas I need to."
- "I feel confident in building a solid team."

And then: Practice. Practice. Practice!

However, success does not find its greatest rewards in practice alone. Now is the time to put all of your efforts into action. "Walk the Talk".

3   *THE THIRD STEP in fully developing your newly acquired positive attitude is accepting that in order to be of any real value, attitude must be transformed into ACTION!*

A large crowd at a major college basketball game was dumbfounded when a team came back from a 14-point deficit with only 3 minutes left to win in overtime by one point. Afterwards, a reporter stated how remarkable it was that the team was able to avoid losing the game.

The coach replied, "You know, that is one thing we have not covered in practice. We never practice losing."

You must put your positive attitude to work for you through your words and ACTION, in all you do.

Go out and kick up a little dust in the world. Put into action some of the very things that you may have been telling yourself for years that you were not capable of doing.

I have a close friend who, years ago, was employed in a large printing plant which mass produced Christmas cards and employed 100+ people to run the various presses. The process was a simple one, in which the heavy stock paper was loaded into a machine and all of the red-colored ink was applied. The paper was then loaded into a second machine, and the green-colored ink was applied.

This process continued for as many times as there were colors. After going through the machines, then being cut and folded, the finished Christmas cards were packaged for distribution. There were dozens of machines and each one required three operators.

One morning management called a meeting of all the machine operators to inform them that modern technology had developed a new piece of machinery — one that was capable of printing all the colors at one time and would also cut, fold and package the cards in the same operation.

This meant that a total of only three machines would be needed to get the same production as before. It also meant that only a handful of employees would be needed to operate the new machines.

Then management explained that the operation of these new machines was much more complicated and would require a highly trained technician to be at the controls.

Seizing the opportunity, one man stepped forward and announced that he was capable of operating that type of sophisticated machinery, and was looking forward to the opportunity.

This individual was one of but a few who were retained.

You must put your positive attitude to work for you through your words and ACTION, in all you do.

While the above true story may not be as dramatic as scoring the winning basket with a half-second left on the clock, it is an example of putting a positive attitude into action in real day-to-day living.

In order to "activate" your new positive attitude, you must put it into action. If you want "to be" then act "as if." If you want to be a person of high character and integrity, then start acting that way in all you say and do. If you want to be successful, then start behaving like a successful person behaves. If you want to be accepted and respected as a caring individual, then start caring and behaving in that light.

A positive attitude with great expectations of yourself frees you from all of the self-imposed limitations you have been living with, perhaps for years.

Recognize that your altitude in life is the result of your attitude towards it.

1. ACCEPT PERSONAL RESPONSIBILITY FOR YOUR LIFE.

2. PRACTICE THE POSITIVE AFFIRMATIONS THAT SHAPE YOUR ATTITUDE.

3. TRANSFORM YOUR ATTITUDE INTO ACTION.

Success is indeed an attitude.
ALL Plutonium Leaders have their's right!

BOARD MEMBERS ARE KEPT IN THE KNOW.

BOARD EXPECTATIONS
THEIR IDEAL PLUTONIUM GM/COO ROLE MODEL

BOARD EXPECTATIONS OF THEIR GM/COO
'Member Experience' Focused
- Productive Board Meetings
- Professional Guidance & Leadership
- Personal Character & Integrity
- Membership Confidence & Support

The GM/COO Role in FIDUCIARY RESPONSIBILITY
'Member Experience' Focused
- Zero Based Operating Budgets
- Capital Reserve Study / Funding Depreciation
- Strategic Plan Constantly Monitored for Progress & Relevancy
- Master Plans: Golf Course Consistency/Clubhouse Aesthetics
- Reliable 'Executive Summaries' & Proactive Mindset

The GM/COO Role in EXEMPLARY CLUB OPERATIONS
'Member Experience' Focused
- Standard Operating Procedures Throughout
- An Undeniable Palpable 'Positive Energy' Prevails
- A Dedicated, Highly Qualified Professional Staff
- Consistent/Reliable F&B Experiences
- Renowned for THE BEST Creative & Over-The-Top Club Events

The GM/COO Role in MEMBERSHIP RETENTION & RECRUITMENT
'Member Experience' Focused

Relevancy
- ENSURE the Club Remains Relevant to the Lives of All Ages
- Operating a Club Where Members are Proud to Bring Guests
- Represents Club Favorably in the Local Community. (Church/Chamber/Rotary/Etc.)
- Renowned for THE BEST Creative & Over-The-Top Club Events

Community Outreach

Would you like more details? Great! Check out: DECONSTRUCTING THE IDEAL GM/COO ROLE MODELS. Here you will find visual models as well as key definitions to all the above.

BOARD OF DIRECTORS
THEIR RESPONSIBILITIES, ROLES AND STANDARD DECORUM

THE FOLLOWING SHOULD BE COPIED AND INSERTED INTO EVERY BOARD MEMBER'S OFFICIAL "BOARD BOOK." AS PART OF THEIR ORIENTATION, ALL NEW BOARD MEMBERS SHOULD ROUTINELY GET THEIR OWN PERSONAL COPY OF THE ABC'S OF PLUTONIUM PRIVATE CLUB LEADERSHIP!

Congratulations on being asked to serve on your Club's Board of Directors!

This is an honor, just as much as it is work. The time you spend on the Board should be enjoyable, as you work in concert with other volunteer members and professional management for the betterment of the entire club.

Making decisions that are consistently in the best interests of the Club, both presently and in laying a sound foundation for the future, should always be foremost in every deliberation.

CONFIDENTIALITY

- *Directors must maintain a balance* between transparency with the membership and confidentiality within the boardroom.
- *While there is never anything to "hide"* — during early deliberations, prior to consensus being fully reached, conversations should appropriately be kept within the confines of the leadership of the Club.

- *It can be damaging* to everyone if a sensitive pending matter is "leaked" or if a potentially unpopular (yet ultimately necessary) decision is allowed to be poorly presented.
- *Respecting confidentiality* is important at times in our own homes, in business, and in charitable organizations. Your own Club is no exception.

BASIC RESPONSIBILITIES

☐ Read Bylaws

- *Be thoroughly familiar* with the Bylaws and Club Rules.
- *Make and enforce rules* for member conduct. Should serious or repetitive behavior by a member infringe on club policies, any reprimand should be administered by the Board — not the Club staff who will obviously handle any day-to-day isolated infractions.
- *Employ a GM/COO* who has the talent to accept responsibility and authority for successfully operating the entire club, and to whom all department heads report directly.
- *Utilize an annual written performance review* with the GM/COO. The President and Vice President should play the primary roles in working directly with the GM/COO after first seeking the confidential input of all other Board members. This input helps maintain continuity.
- *Examine, give input, and ultimately approve* realistic Operating and Capital Budgets that are prepared and presented by the GM/COO in tandem with your Finance Committee.
- *Establish initiation fees, dues, and assessments* that seamlessly interface with the approved budgets. NEVER "back-in" to a desired level of dues.
- *Acknowledge* that postponing needed major improvements, or deferring any needed dues increases for even a few years in a row, predictably causes "everything needing to be fixed at once," putting a heavy burden on the membership in the form of seemingly significant dues increases or assessments. This is not fair to future BOD's, management, or the members.
- *Don't "kick the can down the road."* Get done what needs to be done. Period.

APPROVING BUDGETS

- *THE OPERATING BUDGET — MUST* have sufficient Dues Income to provide the level and availability of services and facilities that are desired by the membership. PERIOD. Any cutbacks in the offering or quality of member experiences should be very carefully scrutinized if being considered necessary to "balance the budget."
- *THE CAPITAL BUDGET — MUST* reflect sufficient Initiation and Transfer fees to fund itself.

- *THE CAPITAL RESERVE FUND — MUST* be in keeping with the on-going needs of addressing depreciation and replacement of existing club assets — never to be applied to any new projects or to subsidize Club operations. Retain the professional services of an outside firm to orchestrate your Capital Reserve Plan. Any approved major new capital projects beyond the scope of any of the above must be funded by assessment and/or debt according to the Club Bylaws.

WORKING IN SUPPORT OF MANAGEMENT

- *The GM/COO has full charge and control of business operations* and of all Club personnel, subject to the Bylaws and the policies established by the Board.
- *The GM/COO attends all Board meetings* in their entirety and is expected to give a comprehensive opening report (Executive Summary) near the top of every agenda. S/he also attends all Committee meetings – and in both cases, takes (or ensures someone takes) accurate summarized minutes.
- *The GM/COO reports directly to the President* and works in tandem with the full Board.
- *Management prepares the annual budgets* and, after Finance Committee and ultimate Board approval, manages operations to attain the overall desired net result.

WORKING FOR THE MEMBERSHIP

Perspective
Reality

- *Listen to members. Keep things in perspective.* Appreciate that their perspective is their reality. Know your facts before you speak.
- *Your role is to help guide your Club.* To do this effectively, concern yourself with the major policy concerns facing the Club — not so much on daily operations.
- *Often a vocal minority's input* (top and bottom 10%) on any issue (while perhaps being well intended) *may not reflect the vast majority* that could very well be quite satisfied with the status quo, or in accepting necessary changes in policy to better prepare the club for the future. Be wary of a proclivity of some seeking the tail to wag the dog!
- *Directors MUST NOT act independently* of the Board. Criticism should be expressed in private. After thorough discussion and analysis — clear thinking always prevails, and the Board as a whole is then able to move forward with confidence after all input is heard.
- *Feel free to discuss any ideas with the GM/COO,* who is intimately familiar with the workings of the club.
- *"Vote as an informed membership would vote today."* However, the

issues of the future membership (thus the Club itself) must also be considered. The very best overall interests of the Club must always prevail.

WORKING IN SEAMLESS TANDEM WITH YOUR FELLOW BOARD MEMBERS

You have two major roles:

1. *As a Director:* Provide your own input, opinions and judgment (and ultimately your vote) on all matters that require formal Board action.
2. *As a Chairman of a Committee:* Keep your committee focused and productive. Make sure all know their role is advisory only – no authority to direct club employees. Should your committee feel strongly about any issue, request it to be on a future agenda to formally present any recommendations to the Board.

WORKING THROUGH COMMITTEES

- *If a potential issue falls within the scope of a committee you chair —* have thorough analysis and discussion at that level and if warranted, request time on the next Board meeting agenda to succinctly report and make a solid recommendation to the Board.
- *If a potential issue falls within the scope of a fellow Board members committee —* they will appreciate hearing about it, and then s/he will follow through with the same process.
- *The President is an ex officio member of all committees* and is invited to all meetings. S/he may not have time to attend every meeting during the year, and therefore relies on committee minutes and reports.
- *The President appoints chairpersons* subject to confirmation by the Board.
- *Committees have no authority to direct Club staff.* The Board has the authority to set Club Policy. The GM/COO then has the responsibility to manage the day-to-day activities of the Club in keeping with Board-approved policies.

Wondering how to make all this happen?
Check out: BOARD MEETINGS THAT MATTER.

BOTTOM LINE CONTRIBUTORS ARE WHAT MATTERS
NOT NECESSARILY TOP LINE DEPARTMENTAL REVENUES

NO CLUB GETS TO THE TOP — UNLESS THEY START LOOKING FROM THE BOTTOM UP.

Often clubs will concentrate on the least efficient business models within their departmental operations to drive GROSS top line revenue — when what floats the boat is NET bottom line contribution to margin.

Those who don't have a firm grasp on what a successful private club business model is driven by (i.e., Dues & Initiation Fees) will lose focus and spin their wheels contriving ways to drive top line F&B sales (erroneously thinking that top line revenue in this inefficient business model will contribute meaningfully to the bottom line).

And while there is this constant pressure on driving F&B sales, at the same time there are oftentimes numerous committees who unwittingly concentrate on ways to actually DECREASE net bottom line results!

They do this by conjuring up ideas such as:

1. "How can we make it cheaper to take part in the annual member/guest event?" (Translation: Let's reduce our income.)
2. "This club party MUST be the best ever. BUT we can't charge more than last year!" (Translation: Or the year before that. Or the year before that. Or …)
3. "I was a guest at XYZ Club, and we have to keep our entry price as low as theirs!" (Translation: Let's compare ourselves to others, rather than just being the best at who we are and can be.)
4. "We must book the hottest band in town! BUT we can't have a cover charge!" (Translation: Let's simply increase our costs with no offsetting income.")

And, have you noticed another inexplicable conundrum? Committees, **ANY COMMITTEE** — if allowed to talk long enough — will predictably morph into an unrelated debate about food & beverage? The names of these committees would suggest that conversations focus upon concerns such as: tri-plex mowers, wind screens, comfort stations, or maybe bocce balls. And still, if allowed to talk long enough, F&B is inevitably discussed.

Conversely — does the House/F&B Committee ever morph into elongated debates about tri-plex mowers, wind screens, comfort stations, or bocce balls? No! They are too focused on ways to lower menu prices and increase complimentary bar snacks and Arnold Palmers at the tennis courts to worry about other amenities offered at the club.

Then there is the archaic F&B Minimum Spending policy.

Basically, it is "pitched" as a means by which all those members who are not "paying their fair share" by regularly using the ala carte dining outlets will be encouraged to SPEND more there because they will be penalized if they don't! Really?

If we are indeed looking to drive the net bottom line results — why embrace punitive policies that supposedly drive members to arguably the least efficient business model in all of operations?

(That would be ala carte F&B for those of us scratching our heads.)

Aha! The fact is that F&B minimums do generate net bottom line revenue! But, in the form of "UNSPENT Minimum Income" that falls right to the bottom line.

And — that's the point.

The point is: clubs needing to stabilize their financial ship need Plutonium Leaders who understand the difference between those areas directly contributing dollars to the bottom line, and those areas that are really just amenities the club offers to its membership.

- "Amenities" are great as far as what they are. However, they are truly bad business models that you can't "grow" yourselves out of.

YOU CANNOT TAKE A BAD BUSINESS MODEL AND MAKE UP FOR IT IN VOLUME." *THE TRUE PURPOSE OF DEPARTMENTAL CLUB OPERATIONS is to create such visceral day-to-day memorable experiences that members are willing to continue paying the NECESSARY DUES to ensure these memorable experiences remain available to them.*

The most efficient source of operating revenue that falls to the net bottom line results is Dues. Followed by numerous fees. And, lastly, the dreaded "A" word — Assessments.

Just remember that members greatly dislike the feeling of being "nickel and dimed." What they really want to know is how much it is going to cost them to belong to the club — bottom line!

So — take a look at your entire club operations and consider how you might engraft the following concepts:

1. Get rid of punitive F&B minimum spending.
2. Eliminate as many fees as possible. (All of 'em?)
3. Ascertain what Dues level you really need to operate w/o the above.
4. Insist on a true "Zero Based" operating budget and then — perform!

REFOCUS ON WHAT THE BOTTOM LINE IS REALLY ALL ABOUT: CONSISTENTLY DELIVERING DAY-TO-DAY MEMORABLE EXPERIENCES FOR THE MEMBERSHIP.

If you accomplish this — the dreaded "A" word is then never necessary.

Here's looking at you — from the bottom up!

BUDGETS
WHY ZERO-BASED IS WORTH IT

Good morning everyone!

Thank you for allowing me to be your guest instructor for the day. Before we get down to work here - are there any basic questions that any of you may have?

Yes sir, right there in the middle, waving your hand. Do you have a question?

Q: I think I might be in the wrong session cuz I've already been using Zero Budgeting for years at my club. We budget and break even every year and I always make our budget. I just budget all revenue and expenses to net out to zero. In fact - I'm not bragging - but, I've earned a nice bonus every year for always achieving budget! Maybe I should be giving this seminar because that is what Zero Based Budgets are all about. Right?

A: No. Zero Based Budgeting has nothing to do with what the Net bottom line results may be (break even or otherwise).

ZBB has everything to do with the process of making sure every line in your revenue and expense reflects relevant information that is backed-up with measurable details.

Suddenly - hands are waving all over the room! And from that point on, questions came one right after the other.

Q: What do you mean "relevant and measurable?"

My club keeps very accurate historical results from the previous fiscal years and in every ensuing budget cycle we make sure that only approved percentage adjustments are made from year to year. Are you suggesting basing a budget on something other than actual historical results? Huh?

What could be more relevant than reliable historical results - and then building from there?

A: What you have just described is commonly called "Traditional Incremental Budgeting." TIB is indeed based on history. It assumes that the "baseline" for the coming fiscal year is established by prior year historical actual results.

Using this approach, the only explanations needed to be presented to gain approval for subsequent budgets relate to what variances/adjustments are deemed acceptable to last year's results.

Major focus is given to proposed variances to past results, rather than whether or not the baseline is viable or not to start with. This all but assumes that the baseline is automatically approved and deemed reflective of efficient operations. The "powers that be" may never think of it in those exact terms. But that is exactly what is happening.

Q: Yeh. So? You didn't answer my question! What could be more relevant than reliable historical results?

What is the difference between TIB and what you are suggesting, ZBB?

A: ZBB's are built upon starting from a clean slate (ZERO) every budget cycle - rather than starting from where the prior year left off. This means that every line item of the requested budget must be backed-up with measurable details and approved - rather than only variances from the previous year. ZBB requires the budget request be re-evaluated thoroughly, starting from the zero-base.

The difference is that any "hidden" operational inefficiencies or "that's the way we have always done it at our club" thinking is often, knowingly or not, engrafted into the TIB approach - while the ZBB approach quickly identifies any operational inefficiencies.   Thus, the thinking is looking forward, not backwards.

Q: This ZBB stuff sounds very time consuming - almost like building the club budget from scratch every year! Are you serious?

A: Yes. And, you are right on both counts!

1.   YES! -It is time consuming. Especially when compared to just quickly adjusting prior results by "acceptable" percentage points here and there. And...
2.   YES! - You basically are building the budget from scratch every year. However — it is seriously worth the time to root out otherwise undetectable inefficiencies that perhaps weigh down operations like an anchor in a ship.

Q: What do you mean by using the analogy of an anchor?

A: Anchoring is a common psychological predisposition where some old information can stick in our mind and is referenced to the point that it influences our thinking about incoming information - even if we are unaware of it happening.

When it comes to budgeting - becoming "anchored" in the same numbers from year to year with only minor adjustments (TIB) is easy unless you force yourself to instead start anew and do the work necessary to justify all data (ZBB).

As an example, I've read of one study where two groups of people, in separate rooms, were asked to estimate how old Confucius was when he died. But - before being allowed to answer, they were asked another question to see if their thinking could unknowingly be influenced by some other piece of basically irrelevant information.

- One group was asked if they thought Confucius was younger or older than 12 when he died.
- The other group was asked if they thought Confucius was younger or older than 130 when he died.

Keep in mind that both of these questions are really not relevant and, in fact, each of them is nonsensical. It would be logical to think that the respondents would dismiss this and then get back to giving their best estimate as to just how old Confucius actually was when he died.

However, the two groups, on average, gave estimates of his age at death that varied by a quarter of a century.

BTW — for those who just have to now know the real answer (and I KNOW you are out there) he died at the age of 72.

If people can be "anchored" by such obviously irrelevant input, imagine in the budgeting process the somewhat compelling reliance of simply accepting whatever operational inefficiencies may be unwittingly baked into prior year results and subsequently approved budgets based on TIB!

Add to this the fact that this cyclical process, if left unchecked, builds upon itself year after year after year…

ZBB, by design, rids us of any anchors, and instead encourages justifying every line item.

- ZBB starts from a "zero base" and every line item is analyzed for its justifiable needs and costs.
- Budgets are then built around what is actually needed for the upcoming period - regardless of whether the budget is higher or lower than the previous fiscal year budget or actual results.

- *All revenue and expense starts from scratch, and must be justified from the ground up.*

Q: You gotta be kidding me! The time this would take would be significant! I can see there may be some advantages to ZBB - but isn't the exorbitant time it takes significant?

A: Yes. But, it is significantly worth it! There are indeed many advantages and disadvantages in fully moving away from TIB's to totally Zero Based Budgeting.

Q: This whole thing seems ominous in scope. If we did want to move towards ZBB - where would we even start?

A: Great question! My answer is to not necessarily tackle it all at once. Instead - start specifically with your payroll and subsequent indirect expenses. Typically, 60%+ of private club expenses are directly related to payroll. That is where you start.

THE NEW GM/COO IS GIVEN A MANDATE TO CREATE AND PRESENT A TRUE ZERO BASED OPERATING BUDGET THAT ACCURATELY IDENTIFIES PROJECTED DEPARTMENTAL REVENUES, EXPENSES AND THE ELIMINATION OF ARTIFICIALLY LOW DUES. S/HE MUST BE UNDAUNTED IN THE TASK AT HAND.

Now, granted, depending upon your specific club culture, your payroll (staffing levels and rates of compensation) should reflect accurately the needs that member usage and income levels would demand. This means it is best to start your new ZBB with payroll and revenue. And, my guess is that you will quickly move towards that once you see the striking advantages of a ZBB approach to payroll.

But — you asked me where to start. My answer is if you are just beginning - start with payroll.

Then, as quickly as is possible, depending upon your particular situation, do the same ZBB approach to revenue and you will then get an even clearer payroll analysis. The sooner you do both, the better.

Ultimately, you will definitely see the benefits of ZBB and will want to take steps to have your entire chart of accounts and budget process receive the same analysis and scrutiny.

Q: Do you really think that it is possible to do an entire operating budget zero based?

A: Yes, it is possible. But, in some instances not entirely practical for everyone.

So, as I recommended - *just start with payroll and build from there.*

Also - depending upon the size and complexity of your club operations, it may not be necessary to do a detailed ZBB every year.

But, you are definitely going to want to do it at least every other year.

By doing this, it precludes the opportunity for any inefficiencies to become accepted or baked into the process.

Q: OK. We appreciate your being honest about there being both advantages and disadvantages. Can you point a few out for us?

A: There are many advantages and disadvantages. So rather than talk about them all - let me give you something in print that will summarize what they are. I've started with the disadvantages.

ZERO BASED BUDGET:
DISADVANTAGES:

- *It makes it impossible* to "back into" any predetermined desired numbers.
- *It is much more time consuming.*
- *Justifying every line item can be problematic* for those who have never been asked to do it.
- *Due to the increased complexity,* it requires department heads to really understand and take ownership of the fiscal needs of their area — rather than simply managing to a board approved budget handed to them by their GM/COO, Department Head or the accounting department.
- *In order to be successfully implemented*, managers at all levels of the organization are ultimately responsible for the management, decision-making and the budget process. In some organizations, there may be managers who have never been challenged in this manner or are incapable of understanding how budgets are created without mentoring or education.
- *In a very large club*, the amount of detailed information backing up the budgeting process may be overwhelming.
- *It may be stressful* to those who are used to establishing unrealistic expectations and then simply throwing it to management and saying, "Just make the numbers work so it supports the budget I want. Management will just have to figure things out."

ADVANTAGES:

- *It makes it impossible* to "back into" any predetermined desired numbers.
- Increases efficiency due to being rooted in specifically identified and measurable needs.
- *Stimulates analysis* where some tasks might make more sense if outsourced altogether.
- *Detects any past* (otherwise undetectable) gradually inflating historical budgets that were based on "spend it or lose it" budget mentality.
- *Requires management* to specifically identify/justify staffing levels based on approved days, hours, levels of service, and compensation rates — rather than "because that's the way we've always done it."
- *Elevates department head responsibility* because of direct engagement in the decision-making process. In other words, they truly have some degree of ownership. Translation: accountability and responsibility.
- *Identifies and eliminates* any historical staffing that is wasteful or included "ghost" employees.
- *Improves communication and coordination* between those actually responsible for operations (management) and those monitoring fiscal performance (accounting).

- *Makes it possible* to specifically identify the reasons for any actual budget variances — rather than only being able to see the resulting dollars involved.

Now, if a detailed ZBB is presented for approval and someone demands, "Just cut a lump sum of "X" dollars out!" It is completely logical to ask, "Oh really? Specifically — where?"

In the absence of a detailed, backed-up, line-by-line ZBB that was built from the ground up, it is impossible to legitimately answer the above question.

Conversely, with a ZBB you simply lay it out on the table and are able to identify specifically what positions would have to be eliminated, what rates of pay need to be reduced, what days and hours of service need to be cut back, etc. With a TIB in hand, the ability to engage in this exercise is severely compromised.

Also — a true ZBB may show that staffing and/or compensation levels have been inadequate for years and need to be increased to truly reflect the service levels the membership deserves. It is NOT all about cutting expenses! It IS all about identifying truly legitimate, essential staffing and compensation levels.

Right from the start — nothing is sacred. Every facet of operations has to be proposed, justified, and weighed on its own merits — without any support from engrafted inefficiencies, unrealistic expectations, or anchor mentality.

The entire process is totally transparent and independent of whether the total budget or specific line items are decreasing or increasing. Providing every dollar is proven justifiable — the budget simply is what it is.

It makes it impossible to "back into" any predetermined desired numbers. (Oh - have I already mentioned this before?)

> SPECIFICALLY, ANY CLUB THAT FULLY EMBRACES A ZBB PROCESS IMMEDIATELY DISTINGUISHES ITSELF. IT BECOMES A PLACE WHERE NEWER MANAGERS AND DEPARTMENT HEADS CAN TRULY LEARN, AND ULTIMATELY GROW INTO FULLY CAPABLE EXECUTIVES. IN FACT, THOSE THAT CAN'T ARE QUICKLY IDENTIFIED AND REPLACED WITH THOSE THAT CAN.

Well — we have just scratched the surface, but, we have run out of time today!

Before we end, I'd like to share with you what I personally believe is the greatest benefit of the entire ZBB process — and it has nothing to do with revenue, expenses, or even dollars.

Instead - it has to do with people.

It is a fact that a fully embraced ZBB professional environment demands people that have an understanding and believe in the process. It is easy to mindlessly "manage" within a budget handed to you that has baked-in inefficiencies from prior years. On the other hand, it is hard work to really analyze and then provide leadership in improving efficiency in operations.

Wondering how to make all this happen? Check out: BOARD MEETINGS THAT MATTER.

ZBB is an operating, planning and learning environment which requires each manager to justify their entire budget request in detail from scratch. In other words, they simply have to know what they are doing!

The burden of proof shifts from the accounting department to department heads to justify why s/he should spend any money at all — and how they might eliminate the transfer of any inefficiencies from the past into the future. (THEIR future!)

IMAGINE, IF YOU WILL, APPEARING IN THE REALITY TV SHOW "SHARK TANK" - MAKING YOUR BEST PITCH FOR FUNDING, AND THEN HAVING MR. WONDERFUL DIRECTLY ASKING YOU, "WHY DO YOU NEED THIS SPECIFIC AMOUNT OF MONEY AND WHAT ARE YOU GOING TO DO WITH IT?"

If you have a detailed ZBB where every line of projected revenue and expense reflects relevant information that is backed-up with measurable details — questions like this provide no threat whatsoever, and you would stand an excellent chance of being funded.

Without a ZBB — Mr. Wonderful, and all other Sharks, would simply look at you and say, "I'm out."

ONCE UPON A TIME, IN A LAND FAR, FAR AWAY - CLUB OPERATING BUDGETS WERE DRAWN UP ON THE BASIS OF THE PREVIOUS YEAR'S BUDGET. TO THE RESULTS FROM LAST YEAR, MANAGERS WOULD ADD OR TAKE AWAY CERTAIN POLITICALLY CORRECT PERCENTAGES. THE PERCENTAGES WOULD BE RELATED IN SOME INDETERMINATE MANNER TO THE RATE OF INFLATION, THE OVERALL STRATEGY OF THE BOSS, OR THE FRAME OF MIND THAT DAY.

Further imagine that your own real-life Finance Committee or Board of Directors all looked like Mark Cuban staring at you! Don't you think that they deserve the exact same level of confident answers that Mr. Wonderful and The Sharks got — where every line of projected revenue and expense reflects relevant information that is backed-up with measurable details?

Don't they deserve to know exactly why your proposed budget requests specific amounts of money (at clubs, we are talking about dues levels)?

Of course they do! And, *if you fail to give them the type of verifiable answers that are only justifiable via a ZBB — they will ultimately say to you, "You're out!"*

Gone are the days where the President would proudly proclaim at the annual meeting that there will be only an itsy-bitsy "X" percentage adjustment to the prior year dues, and that all-but-arbitrary performance bonuses have been approved for management, for again achieving baseless, board-approved operating budgets.

And, oh, by the way — let's not forget the applause for management for always coming in on budget! (Yeh. Right.)

Confucius say: "Those days are over."
Plutonium Private Club Leaders make sure of it!

SINCE BOARD AGENDAS ARE OFTENTIMES DRIVEN BY DECISIONS MADE AT THE COMMITTEE LEVEL ... THE ATMOSPHERE CAN GET QUITE CHILLY.

MORE CLUBS DIE A SLOW DEATH IN THE BOARD ROOM THAN IN THE DINING ROOM

Q: Is your club finally ready to energize and bring things to life during routine 90 minute focused and productive BOARD MEETINGS THAT MATTER — rather than rehashing again and again the same old dead issues for hours upon hours — with seemingly nothing ever getting fully resolved?

A: GREAT! Because if your club is truly serious about ensuring the Board of Directors are informed and positioned to address the business of establishing policy and overall direction for the club — instead of drowning in minutia — the answer is forthcoming!

PREFACE

It is worth your time to *first read through and digest the whole big picture as presented. Then — go back and strategically "tweak" the concepts and connect the dots* so that you can create an "Action Plan" within your own unique existing culture that will best position a successful starting place.

However, make no mistake about it — the goal is to ultimately arrive where ALL of the dots are fully synchronized and are actually formally approved by the board as official polices of standard procedure. It is in that environment where successful clubs ensure their committee/board/management structure is aligned to consistently create productive and meaningful meetings.

DO NOT be discouraged in thinking you could never get all this done at your club! Instead — just start where you are, make the most of it, develop your best strategy to slowly enact what you can — and go from there. The important thing is to get serious about it and get started.

BOTTOM LINE: Devise a plan that works for you. Then, get moving on that plan!

NO MORE EVENING BOARD MEETINGS! This is important!

They have a tendency to needlessly extend into the late-night hours — oftentimes facilitated by consumption of thought-provoking libations.

Instead — breakfast can be ordered at 7:15 AM — followed by every meeting starting promptly at 8 AM. (BTW - just in case you were wondering: skip the Bloody Mary's & Mimosa. I know this is a tough one. But, just try it!)

THE BOARD MEETINGS are ALL scheduled on the third or fourth Friday or Saturday of every month. Pick which day best works within your club's unique culture. All financial information should be fully complete from the prior month by the end of the first week of the following month. This allows appropriate time for analysis and a complete operational overview/executive summary to be prepared by management.

Supporting back-up exhibits, along with all committee minutes, and a meaningful agenda are packaged and distributed two days before any meeting.

Special meetings of the board may be called where a project is of a size/issue of such importance that it requires the single-minded focus of the board outside of a regular meeting.

THE PRESIDENT must be in control.
- *The president* is responsible for ensuring that discussion is orderly, focused, polite, in harmony with the agenda, and moves at the pace they desire.
- *The president* generally keeps the committee reports within the time frame requested by the committee chairs as printed on the agenda (this is explained further below). If need be, the committee chairs may request more time if it seems in the best interests of the issue at hand.
- *The president* will not allow "blind siding." It is inappropriate to expect any board member or the GM/COO to have detailed data on an item that is not on the agenda, or that they had not been specifically asked to prepare for in advance. "Blind-siding" will not be tolerated and the president has the authority to limit the questions and discussion in the unlikely event this occurs.
- *The President's goal* is to have focused, productive meetings that consistently accomplish great things for the club in an effective fashion — making the best use of everyone's time.

BUT WAIT A MINUTE! What *if none of the above describes your current president?*

Now then — *THIS IS IMPORTANT* — if you are shaking your head because you perceive you are stuck with a president who is a poor leader and you can do nothing about it — you may be dead right on the first point — but, dead wrong about the latter!

Simply by fully digesting the ABC's in this handbook and then making it YOUR business to do the behind the scenes work to orchestrate it all — your seemingly "out of control" president/board can be guided and influenced to seeing the benefits of having meetings that matter.

"SUDDENLY" — with your patience and behind the scenes support — s/he is in control and a strong leader. Hang in there!

Don't kid yourself. *It IS your job to make the club president look good!* One of the best ways to do this is to make it easy for him/her to chair meetings that matter.

And — for those who don't think it IS your job to make your president look good — ask yourself what happens if you don't. Well? What happens? Hmmm — with that dose of reality — let's move on with what you CAN do within your sphere of influence to *truly make the president look good — simply because YOU are!*

THE GM/COO attends ALL board meetings in their entirety and is expected to present a comprehensive opening report (executive summary) near the top of every agenda. The GM/COO attends ALL committee meetings and ensures accurate summarized minutes are taken.

THE GM/COO'S EXECUTIVE ASSISTANT should receive any possible policy issues and all committee reports no later than noon the Friday prior to the board meeting (a full week before).

ADVANCE PREPARATION: The office will have all information prepared for management review by Monday afternoon. After management scruti-

> "90% OF HOW WELL MEETINGS GO IS DETERMINED WELL BEFORE THEY EVEN BEGIN."

ny, a preliminary draft is discussed with the president for any final input. After presidential approval, this information is appropriately packaged and made available to the entire board two days before the meeting.

ALL BOARD MEMBERS are expected to thoroughly familiarize themselves with all handouts, committee reports, minutes from the previous meetings, and other information before the board meeting itself.

THE COMMITTEE MEETINGS all need to be scheduled during the first week of every month. This will allow appropriate time for a draft of the minutes to be prepared for the chair's approval, then discussed with the president by management, and ultimately distributed before every board meeting as scheduled below.

Give it a try to schedule them for 55 minutes each — back-to-back-to back — in the same meeting room. This all but guarantees they are direct and productive, since they know other members are waiting to use the same room for their committee meeting. Try it. It works.

- *Committee chairs (board members) must be organized.* And, they always will be — simply as a direct result of management (however subtly) behind the scenes, making it easy for them to be.
- *Committee chairs should not hesitate* to rely on management to help prepare written reports or analysis upon request. Plutonium GM/COO's orchestrate the process to the satisfaction of every committee chair.
- *Committee minutes will be emailed along with the agenda* and any supporting documents/exhibits before the board meeting. Better still if this info can be secured in a drop box.
- *It is understood and accepted* that a committee chair/board member may postpone being on the formal agenda until fully prepared to make a timely report.
- *Committee requests* that may have financial implications beyond the board approved operating or capital budget should first be reviewed by the GM/COO to determine availability of funds, cash flow implications and other considerations before being presented to the board for action.

HERE'S HOW TO HAVE A MEANINGFUL AGENDA — EVERY MEETING

Only those committee chairs that request formal Board time will be on the agenda!

Never again print out a meaningless agenda that includes an obligatory listing of every committee. It is a waste of the Board's time for any Committee Chairman to read minutes or reports that have already been provided two days earlier. *Committee discussions must take place at the committee level before board meetings — NOT during board meetings.*

THE AGENDA IS "MISSION CRITICAL": NO GM/COO CAN, OR SHOULD EVEN DESIRE, TO "CONTROL" THE MEETINGS OF THE BOARD OF DIRECTORS. DEFINITELY NOT THE PROPER ROLE.

HOWEVER — EVERY PLUTONIUM GM/COO CAN, AND SHOULD, PROFESSIONALLY "GUIDE AND INFLUENCE" THE BOARD OF DIRECTORS.

THIS IS MOST EFFECTIVELY AND PROPERLY DONE BY PERSONALLY MAKING SURE EVERY MEETING HAS A WELL-PLANNED AND MEANINGFUL AGENDA.

Early in the week before a meeting, every board member will be personally contacted by the GM/COO's office to ask whether or not they are available to attend the meeting.

IF ABLE TO ATTEND THE MEETING — they are asked several questions.

- *Do you wish to be included* on the agenda in order to offer a formal report?
- *If so, what specific items* would you like to cover in your report? If there are no specific items — there is no need to be on the agenda at all.

- *Is there anything management might do or prepare specifically for you* in advance that would be of value in your preparing for the meeting?
- *How many minutes would you like on the agenda* to fully present your report? (This number of requested minutes will actually be printed on the agenda. This is VERY important! Trust me on this one.)

IF UNABLE TO ATTED THE MEETING — they are asked just one question.

- *Is there anything that you would like the GM/COO to report on* or to make the Board aware of in your absence?

WITH ALL OF THE ABOVE INFORMATION IN HAND - The GM/COO will develop a rough draft agenda to review with the President.

At this juncture, the GM/COO is able to keep the President informed as to:

1. Specifically what Committees want to be on the Agenda.
2. Specifically what items each would like to bring before the Board.
3. Specifically how much time they estimate they will need.

The preliminary agenda items will be prioritized and developed in light of: prior minutes, committee chair reports/requests, presidential concerns, correspondence, matters that have a timeline, any bylaw requirements, etc.

It is important that the GM/COO be very near the top of every agenda to offer a comprehensive opening report (Executive Summary) that consistently helps set the tone of the rest of the meeting. When professionally executed, any minor issues are proactively and quickly addressed to full Board satisfaction that used to needlessly morph into non-productive "off the agenda" banter, gobbling up 20+ minutes per issue.

NOTE: A professionally prepared and presented GM/COO executive summary should routinely take no more than 5 to 8 minutes. Also, keep in mind that the GM/COO has already previously provided a more detailed report in the packet of information provided all Board members a few days earlier. All those items or specific Committee reports that are deemed important for this particular meeting — should be near the top of the agenda, *prioritized in a meaningful order* — immediately following the GM/COO report.

NEVER make the mistake of having housekeeping items or less important things first. It is unwise to think that minor things will be quickly addressed, then leaving the remaining time to devote to more important matters. This sounds good in theory, but has been proven faulty in practice.

Near the end of every agenda, specifically have a place for "any open discussion." Suggestion: print 10 minutes next to it, just for starters.

This provides an informal time for any matters that may not be ready for formal presentation to the board. This way, good healthy discussion will not fall between the cracks.

You may think that this leaves the barn door open for longer meetings. But if all the other pieces are in place as presented — you will be pleasantly surprised to see that this is not the case at all.

However, should any "open discussion" appear to be taking on a life of its own, yet clearly not be ready for any formal board action — the president should either direct the GM/COO to follow up, or request that an appropriate committee chair be prepared to be on the next agenda in order to make a formal presentation/recommendation.

EVERY TIME — NO MATTER WHEN — A DISCUSSION ENSUES WHERE THE BOARD IS CLEARLY FRUSTRATED AND APPEARS TO BE GOING NO-WHERE — a Plutonium GM/COO is confident and able to professionally guide and influence the process by simply getting the attention of the President at an opportune moment and offering something like this:

"Mr. President, there appears to be some genuine interest in this issue. And it deserves sufficient factual data to bring it into better focus. So, with your permission, I'd like to prepare a detailed analysis complete with back-up and supporting data that I can coordinate with the XYZ Committee. We could then put this near the top of the formal agenda next meeting. Of course, the full report will be available for you and the Board to review a few days before the meeting. Would this meet with your approval?"

By having the above type of mindset, the GM/COO is able to play an ongoing significant role (to whatever degree behind the scenes) in streamlining meeting time while at the same time routinely having meaningful agendas enabling the Board to systematically make informed decisions based on facts rather than emotions.

And, after this repeatedly happens with favorable results — a pattern emerges where the GM/COO will have to interject less and less frequently simply because it will be the President or other board member who will offer: "You know — let's just let our GM/COO coordinate with the XYZ Committee. We'll be better prepared to make a solid decision at our next meeting."

Then — at the next meeting, an informed Committee Chairman on the agenda will carry the ball.

The GM/COO will actually need to say very little if s/he has done a good job in providing solid behind-the-scenes analysis and backup support to the appropriate Committee Chairman, then the President, and ultimately to the full board in an advance Executive Summary.

What used to be vague and repetitive issues that seemed to come out of nowhere and gobbled up board time like an out of control Pac-Man, can now be orchestrated into succinct recommendations on the Agenda that take only minutes each.

THIS IS NOT EXERTING "CONTROL" THAT ANY BOARD MEMBER WILL RESENT. INSTEAD, IT IS INJECTING SOLID "PROFESSIONAL INFLUENCE AND GUIDANCE" THAT EVERY BOARD MEMBER WILL APPRECIATE AND RESPECT.

All of the detailed analysis and back-up work is orchestrated and coordinated by management behind the scenes, mostly at the committee level, BETWEEN board meetings — not DURING!

The highest and best use as a board is to thoughtfully consider policies and issues that are timely, thoroughly developed, "scrubbed down" by the appropriate committee and management in advance, and then included on the agenda for board action.

The agenda will be made available to all members of the board with appropriate supporting documentation at least two days before each board meeting.

LET'S WRAP UP WITH THREE BASIC REMINDERS:

1. *The board serves at the pleasure of the membership.* They are expected to maintain and establish prudent policies, make wise decisions, and ultimately present their club in a manner that pleases the current membership and best positions them for the future as well. Other than hire a great GM/COO — this is what a Plutonium BOD does.

2. *The GM/COO serves at the pleasure of the board.*

3. *The membership finds it a pleasure to be served by a Board who employs a GM/COO known for exhibiting professional guidance and influence* enabling them to consistently: maintain and establish

prudent policies, make wise decisions, and ultimately present their club in a manner that pleases their current needs and best positions them for the future as well. Again — this is what a Plutonium BOD does.

PLUTONIUM CLUB LEADERSHIP ORCHESTRATES MEETINGS THAT MATTER.

If all this is new to the culture of your club, it may seem harsh. But, by no means is it overly rigid and in fact, it flows effortlessly once given a trial run of 2 or 3 meetings.

The intent is to have the board truly function as a board by: (1) Not assuming the responsibility at board meetings of doing work that should more appropriately be done at the committee level between the board meetings. (2) Not becoming overly involved in actually operating the club, as this is clearly the responsibility of the GM/COO.

The highest and best use of a Plutonium Board of Directors' time and talent is to thoughtfully consider policies and issues that are timely, thoroughly developed, and "scrubbed down" by the appropriate committee and management in advance. Agendas become meaningful. Meetings streamlined and focused. The president, board and committees are all looking good — as a direct result of their collective Plutonium Private Club Leadership being great.

> Now then, it has just taken you 18 minutes to read this. How would it feel to know that if this were a board meeting — you'd only have 72 minutes to go?

BRIGHT IDEAS
PICK THOSE THAT BEST SERVE YOUR UNIQUE MEMBERSHIP
— AND MAKE THEM HAPPEN!

One of the real luminaries of the business of private clubs is HARVEY WEINER. A tremendous beacon of excellence and Plutonium Leadership long before we thought it just might be fun to use such an explosive word. Harvey has made a significant difference in the private club industry.

But – this is not about Harvey. So, we will resist the impulse to pontificate about him. Instead we'll immediately share some of the very best advice we've ever come across for anyone who has just accepted a new GM/COO position.

Harvey's advice here is so simple and basic that it is brilliant. Here it is:

When you take over as the club's new GM/COO — the first things you want to do (at little or no cost) are:

- Pressure clean the entrance monument sign.
- Plant colorful flowers at the entrance.
- Polish the brass on the entrance doors.
- Shampoo the carpets.
- Wax the floors.
- Replace all missing light bulbs in the clubhouse.
- Place a new flower arrangement in the entrance.
- Schedule a "Meet the GM" board-sponsored cocktail reception.
- Show up at the bag drop early Saturday mornings with coffee for the golfers.

MAYBE I AM EASILY IMPRESSED, BUT I WAS BLOWN AWAY BY THE WISDOM OF WHAT HARVEY OFFERED ABOVE. BUT — WHAT CLUB MEMBERSHIP WOULD NOT ALSO BE JUST AS "EASILY" IMPRESSED BY THE WISDOM OF A NEW GM/COO WHO FOLLOWED UP ON WHAT HARVEY HAS SUGGESTED?

Members WILL notice, "Wow — something is actually happening around here!"

One of the seminars I present is: BRIGHT IDEAS TO KEEP A SUCCESSFUL CLUB CAREER ON TRACK. Or better yet – simple reminders that we all need in order to keep a career path from growing dim.

In this particular presentation I offer a total of 18 points (and expand upon each) for those who have already followed Harvey's advice as a new GM/COO and are now further along in their career..

So — based on the groundwork that Harvey has laid for us — in no particular order or priority, as only YOU can establish that at your own unique club.

Here are 18 "BRIGHT IDEAS" for you to consider. Let's GO!

1. *If need be — "Reinvent" the club* by seeking professional facilitation in fine-tuning a fresh Mission Statement, Vision, and Core Values that reflect the times.

2. 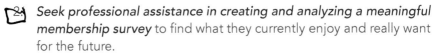 *Seek professional assistance in creating and analyzing a meaningful membership survey* to find what they currently enjoy and really want for the future.

3. *Seek professional assistance in a Capital Reserve Study* that will preclude deferred maintenance and keep your club in perpetual top condition.

4. *Professionally update Bylaws and Club Rules* with the goal of having them better reflect reality and perceptions of a new generation of members.

5. *The new generation of members doesn't write checks!* Seriously consider member online payment and member use of a pre-authorized credit card (NOT for guests!)

6. *Start looking for ways to appropriately say "YES"* to younger generation potential members (Nice denim? Ipads? Smartphones?).

7. *Look for approaches to make the club a cool place*, where kids beg their parents to take them.

8. *Forget the old standard mark-up* and create an exciting "Wine Program" that screams tremendous perceived value for members to dine at the club.

9. *Eliminate the antiquated "All the Wrong Messages" F&B minimum.* Replace it with built-in program that rewards use of the club — not punishes non-use.

10. *Eliminate any "Service Charges"* on all ala carte dining. Replace it with a new monthly, quarterly, or annual (precisely identified!) amount embedded in dues.

11. *Look for ways to eliminate any seasonal cash flow concerns* by successfully packaging "discounts" for annual dues rather than monthly.

12. *Demand from yourself a rock-solid ZERO BASED OPERATING BUDGET!* Never again just increase or reduce meaningless %'s - backing into a desired/artificial dues level.

13. *Get serious about eliminating debt!* If cash is indeed king (and it is) — then debt is an enemy. No longer tolerate kicking the can down the road — this is very important.

14. *Streamline the volunteer leadership.* Does the club really need that many Directors and Committees that may have been established decades ago? Really?

15. *Put in place "Board Approved" job descriptions* for all Committee and Board positions. Make sure, in writing, every volunteer leader knows their role.
16. *Get serious about management* providing the leadership, organization and communication, enabling productive board meetings of 90 minutes to become routine.
17. *Invest in your greatest operating assets.* In every department, have a budgeted line item for "Team Development & Motivation."
18. *Understand that the purpose of club operations* is to consistently establish the quality and service expectations of the membership to the point that they will pay dues increases when necessary. Because *— IT IS DUES INCOME THAT FLOATS THE DEPARTMENTAL OP-PERATIONS BOAT. MEMBERSHIP SATISFACTION IS PRICELESS.*

If you are brand new on the job – take Harvey's tremendous advice and get off to a great start.

Once you start getting some traction, gain more confidence/support from the board and membership — now it is time to seriously take the 18 points above, prioritize them to your own unique needs and to get the wheels turning wherever deemed most appropriate.

Perhaps you are at a club where much of the above has long since been in place. Many of them may be due to your own expertise gained over the years. But in any case, get a plan and implement it.

Why not take Harvey's points and make a habit out of them — no matter how many great years you have under your belt at your current club?

CAPITAL RESERVE PLANS ARE FIRMLY IN PLACE.

CAPITAL PROJECTS
TWO BASIC KINDS AND FUNDING

Here we will have a fly-over of the two basic kinds of capital projects and the common ways clubs tend to pay for them. We will end with a few broad-brush recommendations. Let's get started.

TWO BASIC KINDS OF CAPITAL PROJECTS

1. *MAINTAINING EXISTING ASSETS:* Here we are addressing the need to replace existing assets at the end of their useful life. Some quick examples: major repairs / replacement of a 25 year-old clubhouse roof - resurfacing of old tennis courts - patching and blacktopping of parking lot …
2. *BUILDING/PURCHASING NEW ASSETS:* Here we are addressing a confirmed need to create new assets. Some quick examples: building a facility for underground cart parking — adding new Pickleball or Padel courts — constructing a brand new "lazy river" at the pool — creation of a new short-game practice facility — adding an extension to the clubhouse to offer a fitness center to the membership …

Every club needs to establish their own reasonable definition of what types of expenses are determined as Capital or charged to Operations. Usually this is a combination of a specified dollar amount and anticipated life expectancy of what is approved to be done. Work with your outside auditors and board to establish a GAAP policy for the club and then remain consistent.

FUNDING CAPITAL NEEDS

The most common programs for funding capital needs are:

AN ESTABLISHED CAPITAL RESERVE PLAN

This approach is pro-active in nature by planning ahead and identifying future funding needs for the ongoing replacement of existing assets.
In macro terms: an outside reputable firm is retained that specializes in conducting a detailed study (inventory) of every asset of the facility. This includes buildings — HV/AC units — all grounds/kitchen/maintenance equipment — all hard surfaces — all roofs — all furnishing — everything.

A 20-year spreadsheet (Capital Reserve Plan) is created, department-by-department with extensions depicting the anticipated useful life of every component, when it will need to be replaced, and at what estimated cost while factoring in inflation.

IN THE SIMPLEST OF TERMS, WHAT WE ARE REALLY DOING HERE IS ANTICIPATING THE NEED TO ADDRESS DEPRECIATING ASSETS AND TO FUND DEPRECIATION.

Once the above is completed — leadership then looks ahead and decides on how much is needed on a year-by-year basis, as well as annual carry over from one year to the next to adequately fund future needs. Oftentimes, a decision is made to bill the membership "X" amount monthly in order to maintain an adequate Capital Reserve Fund to draw from — rather than hitting the members with large onerous capital assessments every few years to cover major costs.

Now then — a bit of politics may come into play when first establishing a Capital Reserve Fund.

Why? Three potential reasons:

1. Because some members are going to be very unhappy because they will feel all you are trying to do is mask an ASSESSMENT.
2. Others will be very unhappy because they will feel all you are trying to do is mask an increase in DUES.
3. And — most everyone will be skeptical that the "real reason" this is being done is to SUBSIDIZE CLUB OPERATIONS.

Bottom line — those that have it in their minds that it is either an Assessment or a Dues increase, are not going to change their minds. They can call it what they want. It matters not.

The fact is that funding depreciation is a necessity, and since non-members do not drive slowly by the club and throw bags of cash onto club property — funding must come from members, no matter how it might be packaged.

One thing is for sure: Capital Reserve Funds must be kept in a separate bank account and not allowed to comingle with any other Club funds for any reason. Also, all withdrawals from this fund must be strictly allocated to previously identified areas in the Capital Reserve Study.

To let the membership and Board know the seriousness of keeping the Capital Reserve Fund monies separate — it is advised that something like the following actually become a bylaw:

Article XVIII. Capital Reserve Fund.

Section 1. General.
The Club hereby creates the "Capital Reserve Fund," herein referred to as the "Fund," for the express purpose of providing funds for the replacement of existing capital items. The Fund will be shown as an isolated line item asset account reflected on the Club's balance sheet.

Section 2. Funding.
In order to provide capital for the Fund, the following amounts shall be charged to the membership of the Club payable monthly: (Fill in your various membership classes and corresponding dollar amounts.)

Section 3. Usage; Termination.
The Fund may not be allowed to commingle with operating funds or applied to any new capital projects. In essence, The Fund is for express designated purpose of funding depreciation of the Club's existing assets. This bylaw may not be amended, altered or terminated except upon the two-thirds affirmative vote of the members of the Board.

If a legitimate Capital Reserve Fund is not already in place - many members will look at the leadership of the club and wonder why, over the past 10/20 years, they have failed to plan ahead? After all, it is not as if everyone doesn't know that roofs have to be replaced, parking lots have to be rebuilt, etc. So why aren't these needs anticipated instead of hitting everyone with yet another big assessment?

If the club does not have cash on hand that is reserved to fund depreciating assets or to build new ones — then, we move to the dreaded "A" word — Assessments.

While this is the "cleanest" method on paper — in practicality, many members resent being assessed for one of several very predictable reasons:

- *Younger" members may see the need for improvements* — but think that the Club should go into debt in order to pay for some portion of them. That way, the existing members are not hit so hard all at once.

- *"Older" members have no desire to pay for improvements* that they may not be alive to fully use. They feel that they have already "paid their dues" — and built the Club that others are now enjoying, and that these younger members are the ones who should pay for any new projects or improvements! Besides — they like the Club just like it is and see no compelling reason to change it. This group will be lobbying that perhaps some project really doesn't need to be done at all and that even if it did, younger members should have to pay for it.

BUT — while neither young nor old may feel great about opening their own wallets — IF market conditions allow ...

- *Both younger and older members will unite in suggesting that future members pay more up front in the form of higher Initiation Fees.* After all - why should future members benefit from improvements that the existing members (older and younger) have already paid for in full?

HERE IS HOW FUNDING IS USUALLY PACKAGED:

In order to throw everyone a bone, major Capital Projects often wind up being packaged in any combination of four things. Here are the common recipe ingredients:

1. Some measure of an **Assessment** — where those who pay in one lump sum get a "discount" and those who opt for payment over X number of years pay the full amount. * (More on this a bit later.)
2. Some new **Debt** is assumed.
3. **Initiation Fees** are raised so that new members pay their fair share.
4. **Cash** on hand allocation.

KEEP IN MIND – if there is a lack of sufficient new members joining, and part of the equation to pay off new debt was to capture those Initiation Fees — there will HAVE to be a VERY UNPOPULAR Debt Reduction Assessment down the road. Refinancing, leasing equipment, adding debt in any form (if allowed to become a part of accepted club culture year after year after year) is nothing more than kicking the can down the road...to an ultimately dead end street.

BOTTOM LINE RECOMMENDATIONS:

- *If you do not already have in place a meaningful professional Capital Reserve Plan/Fund — immediately take the steps to get this done.* Make very sure you retain the verifiable professional expertise of a firm that specializes in the unique needs of private clubs. A professionally prepared Capital Reserve Study serves as a great leadership tool in maintaining the club in pristine appearance and working order without the need for large assessments for unanticipated needs.
- *Cash IS king.* Do not forget it. Debt, therefore, is an enemy to either be defeated or avoided. If your club has onerous debt — make it a priority to defeat it. Ahead of schedule. Going forward — avoid it. A club culture of just "kicking the can down the road" and tying the hands of a future BOD and management is folly.
- *As much as possible - stay away from allowing members to pay any capital assessment on terms.* It is a mistake to assume that all those paying on terms will still belong to the club years in the future. Trust me, you will be absorbing negative hits due to unrealized income. And remember — attaching higher interest rates on those taking terms will NEVER offset lost revenue if they are no longer members.
- *Your price of admission to the dance (Initiation Fee) should be payable in full and be routinely adjusted upward* as much as acceptable while still reflecting market value in the mind of potential new members.
- *Initiation and transfer fees income should be 100% applied* to any combination of three buckets: (#1) Striking death blows to any onerous debt. (#2) Avoiding debt altogether by properly contributing to a solid Capital Reserve Plan. (#3) Paying substantial amounts of cash to board-approved necessary capital improvements.
- *Initiation and transfer fees income should never be allowed to subsidize or 'prop up' club operations.* This is what dues are for.
- *To allow initiation or transfer fees to be co-mingled with club operations would be a capital offense.*

CAPITAL RESERVE STUDY
FOUND IN THE TOOL BOX OF EVERY
PLUTONIUM PRIVATE CLUB LEADERSHIP TEAM

INTRODUCTION

Paul Mueller has established himself over the past 20+ years as THE "go-to" guy for private clubs striving to connect all the dots between their current financial obligations, and in securing a meaningful strategic plan for the future. This is impossible to do without a professional Capital Reserve Study in place. Here, Paul maps out the entire need, process and results of doing it the right way. pmueller@clubbenchmarking.com

Capital Reserve Studies have enabled Plutonium Private Club Leaders to make the right decisions in mapping out the financial future of their clubs. I'm delighted to share the process.

In our personal lives, we make every effort in properly planning for our financial futures.

The concept of implementing the best financial practices of planning for your Club's financial future seems quite simple in concept. So why have some private Clubs still so slowly discovered the benefits of a comprehensive and objective analysis of their true capital repair and replacement needs?

I am of course speaking about Capital Reserve Studies (CRS). I have completed these studies for the past 20+ years, and am encouraged that Clubs' financial planning has evolved from that last page of the CPA's audit (listing five or six major capital projects 'to be aware of') to the state-of-the-art comprehensive financial planning tool now available to every forward-thinking private Club.

While shadows of the 2008 recession still remain for some, the majority of clubs I have worked with around the country are now renovating, expanding to add new services or even building entirely new Clubhouses.

BUT — yes, it's fun to think about new projects! However, before moving forward with new plans, Plutonium Club Leaders are first thinking about protecting their current assets — identifying when there will be a need to replace them, how much they are going to cost and how all these present liabilities integrate into future, larger-scale master planning and/or strategic planning efforts.

A DEFINITION OF WHAT WE ARE TALKING ABOUT

Let's start with a basic definition of a CRS. A professional CRS serves to formally document, organize and prioritize ALL of your identifiable Club's capital repair and replacement needs over the next 20 years. This objective and comprehensive management tool allows the Club to evaluate both near term and long-term capital requirements to maintain the Club to existing and future Member expectations.

THE SCOPE/CRITERIA OF WHAT IS INCLUDED

What do we include in the study? Most Clubs have a dollar amount cut off between an operating and a capital expense. Most use $2,500 for an individual item – I concur, as a lower amount results in 'analysis paralysis' when managing the depreciation schedule. A second criteria is to include all assets with a three-year life and greater.

Think about how many of your Club's assets fall within these criteria — a typical Club will have 400 to 600 individual assets. So yes, expenditures for repair and replacements can add up quickly.

Capital Reserve Study

THE INFORMATION/DISCOVERY PROCESS

An accurate CRS gathers, parses and confirms four different historical and current information resources.

1. *The first historical source is the Depreciation Schedule* — an oft dreaded document due to insufficient expenditure detail (i.e. NEW Clubhouse $12,500,000 2012), fully depreciated assets 'still on the books' or simple data entry inaccuracies. Still, you go to war with the army you have, so it's a start…but one that has to be vetted before it can be folded into the study.

2. *A second historical source is construction or architectural blueprints* — often jammed into the GM's office, building engineer confines, or found rolled up in a corner of a moldy attic or basement. While these may be scraps of paper or even a fire evaluation plan, good blueprints allow needed quantity determination for FFE and mechanical equipment information which may be unverifiable on site.

3. *The third source is a detailed onsite inspection of all of the Club assets.* Visual non-invasive inspection of the quality, quantity and condition of each asset allows a professional evaluation of the asset's remaining useful life. Simply put, a professional estimate on what year the Club needs be financially prepared for its replacement. Some assets such as irrigation piping or grease traps are buried— but there are ways to evaluate and fold them into the CRS.

4. *The fourth source is vitally important individual Executive Staff interviews.* From these we are able to factor in their daily challenges of operation, including of course on-going capital expenditures to meet new service trends. What Chef doesn't want a Rational? What Fitness Director doesn't want a fleet of Pelotons? These interviews assist, but do not dictate, the replacement timing and costs for specific assets.

RESULTING RECOMMENDATIONS

The gathering, organization and parsing of all of this information can result in a surprising amount of recommended expenditures to clubs that have not properly prepared for their future. The average annual needed capital expenditures for a typical Club is $750,000 to $950,000. Clubs that have not planned ahead have nowhere near this amount of cash reserved specifically for funding depreciation of existing assets. It is in these clubs where the oxygen leaves the room when I present to a Board the verifiable facts of their current assets.

Remember, this is for existing assets only. Any fun aspirational capital projects — a new video teaching facility for example — are not part of a CRS.

But when club leadership sees the needs clearly identified and they understand the solid methodology behind the CRS, they quickly resolve to identify a plan to properly fund for the needs of their club in a proactive manner.

FUNDING

Clubs derive their capital primarily from initiation fees, capital dues or periodic capital campaigns. With a (currently) strong economy, many clubs are filling their membership caps and waiting lists are returning.

1. *Initiation fees* should be (but oftentimes are not) dedicated 100% to a capital reserve fund. Any operating budget shortfall (that should be covered by regular dues, but is often not) may occasionally cull some of the initiation fee into that bucket. But this equates to kicking the can down a road of deferred maintenance that is not going away, and will only grow larger if ignored.
2. *Capital dues* — however politely worded — on member billing statements should clearly note that all funds here are specifically dedicated to pay down existing debt and/or build the reserve fund (don't even think of mixing the reserve fund with the operating accounts). This transparency demonstrates that the Club knows its fiduciary responsibility by adequately funding for the future.
3. *A capital campaign* (Assessment!) should only happen in the absence of a CRS and a plan to fund it already in place! The whole point of a CRS is to properly plan in the first place, and to avoid or minimize any capital campaigns. Further, tread lightly here as there are only so many times a Club can go to the membership for additional monies. However, through a number of circumstances, the Club may not have an alternative except for a major capital campaign. Never popular, but with careful explanation to members, capital campaigns are short term pain to solve an immediate problem.

Given the scale of a specific problem, the campaign may not fund all of the needs. Clubs are therefore breaking the once taboo notion of debt and as Club Benchmarking data demonstrates, most Clubs carry some debt typically incurred for a major Clubhouse expansion, golf course renovation or Aquatics Center. But — you also need a plan to reduce or eliminate that debt.

The methodologies above describe how to ultimately achieve the goal of a rational financial road map to fund your Club's capital requirements. Plutonium Private Club Leaders know the far reaching and overlapping benefits of establishing and maintaining a CRS.

THE BENEFITS

- *The Board of Directors* is able to communicate their fiduciary responsibility to the membership through the commission and ongoing use of the CRS. The Board has seen and acted upon the need for proper planning and while the news may not be the best, it is comprehensive and objective.
- *The Finance Committee* now has concrete information to develop the right path of funding the annual expenditure recommendations.
- *The Long-Range Planning Committee* now sees the necessary expenditures or financial foundation of the Club, and prudently acts on member or market-driven renovations or new amenities.
- *The GM/COO* now has a "go to" document to plan and track current expenditures, and have both a short term and long-term view of their various departmental capital needs.

The CRS should be seen by all of the decision makers as a living document. While a snap shot in time when developed, actual Board decisions, preventative maintenance practices and changes in technology may affect the recommended time and cost of an asset over time. Therefore, the Club should plan to update the study every three to five years to reflect historical replacements, and adjust future forecasts accordingly.

Again — in our personal lives, we make every effort in properly planning for our financial futures.

Bring important transparency and fiscal responsibility to your Club. Having a CRS in your tool box empowers the club leadership team to make the rational decisions necessary to maintain first-class physical and operational conditions expected by both existing and new Members.

CMAA
PLUTONIUM CLUB LEADERS ARE HEAVILY INVOLVED

PREFACE

This is where aspiring (and seasoned veteran) GM/COO's find their greatest source of continuing **professional** education and **personal** interaction in the industry. Using Michael Crandal, CNG as an example: Past officer of two chapters — attended 20++ national conferences — numerous workshops — served on 4 national committees — personally created and presented educational workshops approved by CMAA for educational credits at many chapters from coast to coast regarding Budgeting, Delegation Skills, Staff Motivation and Performance Appraisal Systems — Keynote speaker at CMAA Assistant Managers Conference — author of dozens of articles in leadership & management related publications. Regularly featured article in Boardroom Magazine (highly respected as the most relevant and meaningful publication in the private club industry for board members and GM/COO's).

OF NOTE: At EVERY educational session over the many years, Michael ALWAYS sits in the front row because that is where you can learn the most. Not only the **substance** of what is being offered, but also the various presentation **styles** in delivery. In either/both cases — you can always learn something, and by sitting right up front you better position yourself to do so. Try it. And — at the next CMAA annual conference, at least stop by the front row to shake hands with Michael.

CMAA PROVIDES OPPORTUNITIES TO HELP OTHERS.
Management is able to share many of their own blunders over the years with their peers — thereby sparing others from making similar mistakes at their clubs. Often, all that is needed is some sincere and meaningful mentoring. You will find that in CMAA.

CMAA PROVIDES OPPORTUNITIES TO LEARN FROM OTHERS.
Management is able to learn from the mistakes of others. A smart person learns from his or her own mistakes. But a truly wise person puts themselves in a position to be able to learn from the mistakes of others - and therefore, not have to make them themselves. My CMAA brothers and sisters have saved me countless of sometimes potentially career-threatening errors.

CMAA PROVIDES THE EDUCATION TO EFFECTIVELY LEAD.

Management is exposed to countless opportunities to learn and grow as a professional, and become empowered to serve the membership with the professionalism they deserve.

CMAA PROVIDES THE RESOURCES TO CONTINUALLY GROW.

Here is where to turn to for specific answers to the concerns that come across all of our professional radar screens from time to time. While we might think we're as creative as the next guy is - hey, why reinvent the wheel at every turn? CMAA has "been there/done that" and is available with the expertise to help navigate through what otherwise might seem like significant concerns.

CMAA PROVIDES DIRECT ACCESS TO PROVEN PROFESSIONALS.

There is a tremendous professional staff as well as many top performing GM/COO's who volunteer their time for the sole purpose of bettering the private club industry.

A PERSONAL/PROFESSIONAL NOTE FROM MICHAEL:

Yes, like most of us, I've worked my tail off and strive for the best I can be. However, if not for the education (both formal and informal) that CMAA has afforded me over the years - I know there is no way that I could have as professionally served, and provided leadership that my management peers and the members we all serve truly deserve.
I have had the opportunity to visit 100+ private clubs all over the United States.

Whether I happen to be attending the annual conference, or even just traveling on my own ⏃ all it takes from any of us is a phone call identifying yourself as a fellow CMAA member, and you will never meet more warm and caring people who are willing to share their knowledge, professional expertise, and show you their facility.

As a direct result of my early and continued involvement with CMAA:

I humbly consider myself an "expert witness" when it comes to budget preparations and overall club operations.

I do know what it takes to continually upgrade a club and to "take it to that next level" that every board has in the back of their mind.

This is not bravado in talking about myself. Not at all! I'm talking about what continued involvement CMAA can enable any of us to do. CMAA involvement definitely enhances our ability to better serve a membership and truly provide leadership to a club as a whole.

You may be a young person in the field who is sincerely wondering if an investment of your time in CMAA is worth it. Or, perhaps you're a board member wondering if an expense line supporting management with active membership in CMAA has a viable ROI.

In either case - I'll offer a resounding "YES" and all the encouragement in the world to begin utilizing the resources available through CMAA immediately and continually.

Perhaps you've been around clubs for many years, and unwittingly have morphed into thinking that, "You can't teach an old dog new tricks."

Rethink this, and share my conclusion that, "The quickest way to become an old dog is to stop learning new tricks!"

Continued involvement in CMAA will keep your professional bag of "tricks" current, refreshed, and highly marketable.

Because of CMAA — otherwise "old dogs" can always be "young pups!"

COMMITTEES CAN GET OUT OF HAND!
NO! REALLY?

A NEW AD HOC INVESTIGATIVE COMMITTEE IS APPOINTED TO IDENTIFY THE MEMBER RESPONSIBLE FOR NOT FLUSHING TOILETS AND URINALS.

PREFACE

In my communications with clubs around the country, I occasionally come across yet another "You Can't Make This Stuff Up" saga. This one is based upon the true story of a member who took pictures in the club's restrooms and then emailed them along with a complaint to management that no toilets in their club should be left unflushed. Of course, management is to blame for any variance to this and is expected to correct such unsightly situations immediately as it is an embarrassment when having guests at the club. (Horrors!) So...

A NEW AD HOC INVESTIGATIVE COMMITTEE TO IDENTIFY THOSE RE-SPONSIBLE FOR NOT FLUSHING TOILETS HAS BEEN ESTABLISHED!

"Someone in this club has been neglecting to flush after going to the bath-room," said management, "and we're gonna find out who that person is."

According to at least one member complaint, receptacles were left with evi-dence of previous use without being flushed.
In order to ascertain if this was due to widespread clubhouse mechanical/equipment failure, or instead isolated human oversight — random visual in-spections were conducted over a 2-week timeframe.

Documented results have indicated that **no such evidence was found in em-ployee areas** — thereby eliminating equipment failure, and instead conclud-ing the cause being human oversight in member-only specific areas of the property.

For further investigative analysis, tracking GPS chips were stealthily implant-ed into the employee meals in order to ascertain if employees were inap-propriately using and 'sabotaging' off-limits member-only restroom facilities. No instances of employee usage of unflushed toilets were proved germane to the investigation.

"Everyone's very curious about who's doing it," said the investigative team. "It just doesn't really make any sense. How could you forget to flush? And if the person is doing it on purpose, why? What could they possibly have to gain by intentionally doing this?"

"At first, we figured it was being left there because the plumbing was faulty — but every time it's been discovered, it's gone right down without a prob-lem. So we're not even talking about a situation where somebody clogs the plumbing and then slinks away in embarrassment."

Management has begun checking the toilets at regular one-hour intervals, but has had little luck.

At 1:38 p.m. Wednesday, it was found that all was properly flushed, but just 7 minutes and 21 seconds later, a member emailed to management the pic-tures they had just taken with their smart phone to show unflushed recepta-cles filled with bodily fluid.

"I could hang around outside the bathrooms and try to catch the culprit in the act, but I'd pretty much have to be there around the clock," the head of the investigative team proclaimed.

"Besides, everybody knows I've been assigned this task, so the guilty party probably wouldn't even use the bathroom if they saw me nearby. I've also considered directly asking everyone as they leave the bathroom — but, like, I'm, like, well, just am kind of, like, sort of, like, at a loss of words as to, like, what exactly I'd say."

A lengthy e-mail from a member, who proudly proclaims that they always flush, was received complaining that the situation is "causing huge problems" among others who also always flush and are offended by those who don't. These like-minded individuals feel it is up to management to identify the culprits and bring them to justice.

Management is considering a sternly worded sign reminding members to flush and wondering if that would be an effective measure. But, that was deemed perhaps appearing somewhat tacky when viewed by guests who really were otherwise unaware of the internal concerns of the club.

Some members sniffed at the very idea of any member actually not flushing. Their conclusion is that it is surely non-member guests who are responsible.

A petition was started to post "Members Only" signs outside all restroom facilities, but that idea didn't get far.

Soon, the various standing committees all begin offering their suggestions.

- *THE MEMBERSHIP COMMITTEE* felt it sent out wrong vibes to potential new member candidates who were being given a facility tour. So, unfortunately, signage is out.
- *THE GOLF COMMITTEE* suggested that the clubs long-standing policy of requiring guests to be accompanied by a member on the golf course could be expanded to include all restroom facilities as well. It made sense since everyone already understands that members are responsible for their guest's behavior while at the club. But, when someone pointed out that this may contribute to slow play — that ended that conversation.
- *THE SUPER SENIOR CLASS MEMBERS COMMITTEE* pointed out that, "You get what you pay for around here, and these new young millennium members just don't understand the value of a dollar." So, rather than any potential whatsoever 'unnecessary' dues increases, they are suggesting that "Pay Toilets" be reintroduced throughout the clubhouse to instill a "Pay As You Go" approach. They suggested that not only would this be a new source of revenue for the club, but that since everyone would now have to pay for the privilege of flushing — more of them actually would.

- **THE FINANCE COMMITTEE** thought this would create an accounting nightmare — but did respond in a carefully worded letter thanking them for their suggestion.
- **THE GREENS COMMITTEE** chair offered a suggestion of their own: "You know, on the golf course, we ask members to repair their own ball mark as well as one other. So, why not ask members to do the same when using the bathroom facilities? When I finish my own business and flush — I then find another toilet, and unlike some others around here, I will flush that too!" However, they quickly added, "But that doesn't change the fact that I shouldn't have to! In fact, maybe I shouldn't even have to repair my own ball marks or flush my own toilet! Why can't management do this for me?"

LET'S POST THEIR NAMES! Another member suggested that the names of those who don't flush should be posted for all to see. "I mean, we post a delinquent list of those who don't pay. So, why not post the names of those who don't flush?"

"We are not thrilled to be the ones who have to find out who's not flushing," the GM/COO said. "But sometimes you have to do these kinds of things."

The GM/COO was quick to point out their management philosophy of never asking staff to do something they would not do themselves.

This is not only an unpleasant situation for members — but, it is cutting into valuable face time, as the management team is forced to reallocate time away from other front of the house tasks in order to respond to emails regarding the ongoing investigative updates and generating progress reports.

So while it is true that more management time is now being spent in hanging around restrooms, an internet hot-spot was identified in the far northwest corner, 2nd floor restroom, 3rd stall from the right — thus enabling much work to be accomplished via laptop or optional hand-held devices by management at this remote location away from their offices.

Rumors are circulating that a dissident handful of members have suggested that the GM/COO's office be permanently relocated there.

- **THE LONG-RANGE PLANNING COMMITTEE** has recommended that in the coming fiscal year the club either request:

1. A one-time CAPITAL allocation of $183,328.46 to replace/install new automatic flush equipment in all member areas (not needed in employee areas) - or,

2. A new OPERATIONS budget line item of $86,427.41 to cover annual labor expense dedicated to the hiring of staff to do nothing but monitor potentially unflushed toilets in member areas.

Of course, the Super Senior Class would be exempt from either. But — then again, maybe we need to appoint yet another committee to look into this.

IT'S A SPECIAL BUS DESIGNED JUST FOR PRIVATE CLUBS!

Standard Committee Equipment Includes:
- 3 gas pedals
- 4 steering wheels
- 8 sets of brakes

And ZERO Emergency Exits if a REALISTIC BUDGET is not in place to operate the Club

COMMITTEE SUCCESS
PLUTONIUM CLUB LEADERS PROVIDE

OTHER COMMITTEES ARE MEETING AS WELL --- WHILE EVERY OPINION MATTERS ... THERE ARE ALWAYS THOSE WHO THINKS THEIR OPINION MATTERS MOST.

FORTUNATELY - AN INDECISIVE CHAIRMAN ALWAYS TABLES CONTENTIOUS ISSUES!

COMMITTEE SUCCESS
GUIDELINES LEADING TO MEANINGFUL RECOMMENDATIONS
THAT THE BOARD WILL FAVORABLY ACT UPON.

INTRODUCTION

Gordon Welch is a valued colleague providing Plutonium Club Leadership to the industry as President of the Association of Private Club Directors. Here is his spot-on "Guide to Making a Committee Recommendation." Also, here is a broad overview of the role of committees. We recommend every club look into all that APCD offers. www.apcd.com

BEFORE making a committee recommendation to the board of directors, consider 8 factors:

1. *Mission Statement:* Does the recommendation fit within the purpose of the organization?
2. *Strategic Plan:* What part of the strategic plan does the recommendation advance?
3. *Clarity:* Will the recommendation and rationale be clear to the board for their consideration?
4. *Committee Liaison:* If the committee has a staff or board liaison, have they been consulted?
5. *Governing Documents:* Does the recommendation fit within the governing documents (bylaws, articles, policies?)
6. *Resources:* What resources (time, money, and staff) will be required? Does the recommendation generate income?
7. *Liability:* Does the recommendation create risk or conflict with laws?
8. *Performance:* How will the recommendation be monitored for progress and success?

BUT WAIT! There's more! Gordon also provides a tremendous overview of the importance of meaningful committee structure and key points necessary to having them be productive. Buckle up — here we go!

- *Committees are an integral part of a successful club.* Their purpose includes: supplementing the work of the board and staff; engaging members and identifying future leaders.
- *Committees are an extension of the board of directors* and may appear as representatives of the club. Committees DO NOT have authority to speak for the club, expend funds nor sign contracts.
- *Committees should produce results.* They do not have authority to direct staff in any way.
- Ask the question: is this committee necessary?

- *Eliminate standing committees in favor of task forces* that can act short-term.

Committees must be aligned with the club's strategic plan and goals
Committees should interface with other committees to collaborate.
- *Most efforts of a committee will require approval by the board.*
Recommendations to the board should be in the form of a motion or resolution. A request to the board must be clear and concise so directors can fully understand and approve.

> Thank you, Gordon! Your expertise in all matters relating to private club governance is much appreciated. In the past, operations were overly scrutinized for potential solutions. Nowadays, it is recognized that governance and outdated polices need to be updated. You are on the forefront of this.

CH-CH-CH-CHANGES
PLUTONIUM CLUB LEADERS RESPECT THE PAST, BUT ANTICIPATE AND CREATE APPROPRIATE CHANGE.

It is just the way it is.

"Stop the World — I Want to Get Off" was a memorable musical in the early 60's. Every time perceived unsatisfactory change would happen to the main character — from the moment of his birth to death — he would shout out, "Stop the world!"

Fast forward a few years.

"Changes" is a song by David Bowie. The lyrics basically confirm the fact that the only thing permanent in the world is change.

Hmmm…perhaps Mr. Bowie did not have the mindset of many members belonging to the world of traditional private clubs! Many of them have faithfully paid monthly dues — FOR DECADES!

Q: Why have they continued to pay dues?

A: To a large part simply because their club represents the only place of refuge from an ever-changing world. To them — their club represents a safe haven from change. Instead, it is a comfortable place of familiarity, completely separate from the world outside of the entry gates.

THE WORLD OUTSIDE OF PRIVATE CLUBS spins on an axis that welcomes new approaches and lifestyles. In fact, the world of the general public not only accepts change — to them — it is not change at all!
It is just the way it is.

MANY TRADITIONAL CLUB MEMBERS ARE SHARP, AND ENJOY UNFETTERED SUCCESS IN THE OUTSIDE WORLD. BUT — UPON ENTERING THE INNER SANCTUM OF THEIR PRIVATE CLUB — NOW IT IS THEIR TURN TO SAY: "WELCOME TO MY WORLD!"

This private world is centered on a "comfort zone" fulcrum point that is protected from unwanted change. We all seek comfort and avoid discomfort. Do we all feel comfortable with that statement? Good. I find that comforting. How 'bout you?

Well — imagine your very favorite place to relax in your own home.

- *That special place* where once you ease in, the concerns and cares of the world are put aside — as you relax in attire that puts you completely at ease.
- *Your favorite beverage* of choice in hand — brought to you by a favorite person of yours!
- *Familiar music* is in the background.
- *Your closest friends and families* are enjoying themselves as well.
- *Soon you sense the smells* of your very favorite foods being prepared.

Whoa! Sounds too good to be true, doesn't it? Nope — it really is true. Well — at least, if you happen to be in the private club you have belonged to for many years. **It matters not what the rest of the world is doing right about now.** No need to "stop" the world —because, this, well — this is your world.

It is just the way it is.

But what happens when it seems that new people, thoughts, and ideas want to seemingly stop your world and expect you to embrace theirs instead? Ahem!

"Suddenly" — your favorite place has a new, discomforting board-approved long range plan for change — and, they want YOU to help pay for it — NOW!

Things are just not quite as relaxing any more — as now your cares and concerns are focused on what is happening to what had for years been your place of refuge from an ever-changing world.

- Suddenly, standing beside you is a stranger who has no idea what your favorite beverage has been for the past 25 years, and is trying to up-sell something you really don't want.

- You are asked for your membership number. Not even addressed by name. Pretty embarrassing right in front of your guests.
- It seems hard to have a conversation with the unfamiliar music (?) being so loud. And, whatever happened to the concept of "back-ground?"
- You look around the room and see a collection of people you have never met.
- You look at your own attire, and sense that you are somehow not in uniform.
- You decide to move where it is quieter in the dining area. You are handed a menu that is full of unfamiliar things.

And you are sharp — in great health, and only in your 60's. Yet suddenly, you just don't know if you belong here anymore. Not really.

It is just the way it is.

A new member stops by your table to politely introduce himself.

His name? David Bowie.

Within the next ten years, he may very well be the new club president.

It is just the way it is.

CHARACTER
IS WHAT DEFINES A PLUTONIUM CLUB LEADER

DO WE REALLY NEED TITLE ASSURANCE?

"Your reputation is merely what others think you are. Your character is what you really are."
John Wooden

Just for fun — way back when, for almost six full years — I focused entirely on professional speaking and writing. And, at some point, I thought it would be hilarious to put the letters CNG behind my name. I just made them up. Just for fun!

I even did a special run of business letterhead, envelopes and cards sporting metallic embossed burgundy that proudly proclaimed the letters **CNG.**

Q: Why did I do that?

A: Again, just for fun. (You gotta problem wid that, do you?) I just could not wait for people to begin asking me regularly exactly what those letters stood for. And — WOW, was I going to have fun telling people that they stood for. Ready? **Certified Nice Guy!**

Of course, I would then get to inform them that while I was a self-certified Nice Guy — I was indeed a Nice Guy nonetheless. Sound like great fun!

Right? Not so much.

In all my years of doing that - a grand total of 2 (TWO!) people even asked me about it.

I learned from this early on that people could really care less about titles and initials — instead, all that really matters is what you do for others and who you really are.

Later in my career, I accepted the GM/COO position at Thunderbird Country Club in Rancho Mirage, CA. And along with an enviable compensation package came something else: a title, and in some instances, initials.

After giving my 2-month notice, helping in the transition, and moving across country after 10+ great years as GM at Exmoor Country Club in Highland Park, IL — I arrived outside my new office, where a bronze plaque on the door marched in step with the contents of a box on my new desk.

Nicely packaged inside that box was new letterhead, envelopes, business cards and even personalized note cards — sporting metallic embossed gold beneath my full name: General Manager / Chief Operating Officer. And, in some instances, the initials: GM/COO.

Within the first week I eliminated the grandiose signage outside my office and had a smaller announcement placed on my door with only one word — Michael. That's it. Nothing else.

I did keep my full name on the rest of the business paraphernalia, but sans the title or initials.

Q: Why?

A: Because people could really care less about titles and initials — instead, all that really matters is what you actually do for others and who you really are. So, up to this very day, everyone simply refers to me as Michael. Fellow employees, from every department and level, all feel comfortable in calling me by my first name.

When at the front desk of fancy restaurants and politely asked for my last name — I just as politely respond by saying, "Michael." And, other than legal documents, I sign all my correspondence that way.

When speaking before various groups about leadership, I will ask the audience to yell out single words that best describe an attribute of the greatest positive leaders they have ever known.

The most common words offered are the likes of:

Integrity ... Honest ... Caring ... Sincere ... Focused ... Accountable ... Authentic ... Compassion ... Respect ... Transparent ... Influential ... Remarkable ... Enthusiastic ... Believable ... Trustworthy ... Responsible ...

Whatever dozen or so words are offered — they are projected on the big screen for all to see. Next, I create two "buckets" and ask everyone to drop each word into a bucket they feel that is most attributable.

The two buckets are:

1. *Formal Education.* (i.e.: MBA — PhD — etc.)
2. *Title.* (i.e.: President — King — Czar — CEO — GM/COO — etc.)

Without fail, everyone has great difficulty in finding a few words that are the direct result of either of these two buckets. Sensing their difficulty, I then create a third bucket.

3. *CHARACTER.*

Immediately smiles and affirmative nods fill the room as it becomes abundantly clear what a true leader really is. Or, better stated, what traits a Plutonium Private Club Leader exhibits in all they do. Virtually all of the words that come directly from the crowd, quickly fall directly into the third bucket. That is what it was all about.

Please! The point of all this is definitely not to devalue academic achievement or the well-deserved titles that one earns over the progressive course of a successful career.

The point is that as highly thought of buckets No. 1 and 2 may be — it is *CHARACTER* that defines a leader. It is impossible to be a Plutonium Private Club Leader in the absence of character. Impossible.

The greatest "title" that accurately reflects a fine reputation is enjoyed by those who are known by others as a man or woman of character.

And, you can trust me on that. For after all — I do have my CNG.

(BTW — please feel comfortable in calling me "Michael" just like everyone else does.)

Wondering how your staff should address you? Check out: YOU'RE ON A FIRST-NAME BASIS — PLUTONIUM CLUB LEADERS LEAN TOWARDS HORIZONTAL APPROACHES TO MANAGEMENT, AS OPPOSED TO VERTICAL.

COMMUNICATION
WHO COULD ASK FOR ANYTHING MORE?

"I Got Rhythm" is a piece composed by George Gershwin with lyrics by Ira Gershwin, and published in 1930. It has stood the test of time and become a universally accepted jazz standard.

The phrase, "who could ask for anything more?" is repeated four times in the song and Ira was initially quizzed as to why he did not title the song that — instead of being possessive of this thing called "Rhythm."

Perhaps even way back then, Ira Gershwin knew how very important this thing called rhythm is. This is true not only in music, but in everyday communications between people. And, it applies to both the spoken and written word.

We have all listened as someone wants to tell us about how they are upset or confused by what another communicated to them. Yet, when we ask them to share exactly what was communicated that seems to be bothering them so — to us it sounds like no big deal at all.
When we point that out, they look at us as if we just don't get it as they explain, "Oh — it wasn't so much WHAT s/he had to say. It was the WAY they said it!"

Maybe Ira Gershwin was right about this thing called rhythm. And, nowadays with the use of instant text responses and rushed emails, there can even be unintended tones and perceived "between the lines" implications.

Some may say, "Big deal! Who cares about rhythm, tone, or the way I communicate things?"
Well, try this exercise to see if rhythm makes a difference in what people perceive is being communicated. Say the sentences below out loud. But, as you do, make an effort to stress the upper case and bold word. Moving through this exercise, you just can't help but notice how the meaning and possible intent of each changes, however subtly, every time the rhythm and emphasis changes. Ready to give it a try? Say each out loud and emphasize the bold and capitalized word and begin to sense how it impacts an intended meaning. Let's go.

THIS is the best our team can do for the members of this club.
This **IS** the best our team can do for the members of this club.
This is **THE** best our team can do for the members of this club.
This is the **BEST** our team can do for the members of this club.
This is the best **OUR** team can do for the members of this club.
This is the best our **TEAM** can do for the members of this club.
This is the best our team **CAN** do for the members of this club.
This is the best our team can **DO** for the members of this club.
This is the best our team can do **FOR** the members of this club.
This is the best our team can do for **THE** members of this club.
This is the best our team can do for the **MEMBERS** of this club.
This is the best our team can do for the members **OF** this club.
This is the best our team can do for the members of **THIS** club.
This is the best our team can do for the members of this **CLUB**.

What is really interesting is that depending upon the rhythm of the above, not only is there an opportunity for the meaning of the SPOKEN word to be subtly altered — but so much at times to even suggest a change in the WRITTEN punctuation mark behind each statement. Go back and take a look as you read each again.

In some cases, a period just doesn't seem to cut it. Wouldn't a question mark be better?

And there are a few sentences where an exclamation point would really seem more appropriate.

Quickly typed emails intending to only zap off a few thoughts, without even a stop at spell-check before sending, can oftentimes be misconstrued.

In the absence of clear communications, recipients are quick to inject in their own punctuation marks (either mentally or emotionally) wherever there seems to be an opportunity. This can lead to multiple recipients having multiple impressions as to what was intended to be communicated.

There are "take-a-ways" from this exercise for both those transmitting and receiving communication (spoken and written).

In either case, just be aware that it is indeed not only words themselves that speak to people — but the emphasis and rhythm in which they are delivered. Like it or not — there is a natural tendency to "read between the lines" when something is not communicated well.

Do you think that last sentence should have ended with a period? Or, perhaps an exclamation point would have been best!

Before that next presentation, meeting, or even pushing the "send" key — give your thoughts and words one last run-through, through the filter of emphasis, tone and rhythm.

If we could just nail this one down — who could ask for anything more?

DEPRECIATION FUNDED MEANS ASSETS DON'T GO TO WASTE.

DELINQUENT
ACCOUNTS

THE TOP TEN REASONS

(Why the same names always show up on the delinquent list.)

#10 — Many members are named John. Johnny is a very popular name. And members, named Johnny, always come lately. And, they pay the same way too.

#9 — They were delinquent as juveniles, and old habits are hard to break.

#8 — They're protesting until the club provides postage paid return envelopes.

#7 — They receive their club mail at home - but pay from their office.

#6 — They receive their club mail at the office — but pay from their home.

#5 — They never receive their club mail - anywhere. And, don't know what email is.

#4 — They don't believe in debt! And, because of this, they have developed the lifelong habit of paying their bills in full — once every 91 days — whether they need paid or not.

#3 — Their position is that some other member is using their account number — and that the "help" just needs better training. No way could their little "Johnny" have consumed $148.53 of cokes and candy bars at the pool! NO WAY!

#2 — They are deducting last year's operating assessment from this year's bill because they had nothing to do with that deficit and therefore should not be billed for it.

And, (drum roll please) - the #1 reason the same names always show up on the delinquent list is — *THEY THINK THAT DELINQUENT FEES APPLY TO THEIR F&B MINIMUM!*

Or — maybe they were just born late, and never seemed to catch up. Who knows?

DUES INCOME
IT FLOATS THE BOAT

The only acceptable purpose of every dollar that flows into the various operating departments of the club (dues/fees/sales/etc.) is to help offset legitimate operating expenses — never to subsidize waste or mismanagement.

Having openly stated this fact — let's assume, just for a moment, that management is already orchestrating the policies established by the board and doing a fine job monitoring operating expenses in these challenging economic times. *Moving forward, the purpose here is to illustrate the importance of identifying a realistic and meaningful dues level.*

Most private clubs find that dues income represents 50+% of total operating revenue. Since no direct expenses are charged to dues income — 100 cents of every dues dollar falls right to the *bottom line.* Just try that for every dollar of increased F&B sales.

How do we increase operating revenue? The answer here seems easy, does it not?

In the mathematical equation of a private club, there are several different top-line revenue factors that could ceremoniously be adjusted in the preliminary budget spreadsheet in hopes of resulting in seemingly increased bottom-line margin. (Numbers don't lie — do they?)

Let's see, just for illustration purposes — leave everything else a constant, but for preliminary budget projections, what the heck — let's just factor in potential cherry-picked increased fees (carts/lockers/trail/F&B minimum/guest/valet/club storage/etc.). Or simply — heaven forbid — raise the dues.

Aw, what the heck — even if the dreaded "A-Word" **(Assessment!)** is dragged out of the closet — problem solved! The equation can be made to mathematically balance! Right?

Some may suggest that the way to balance the budget is to come up with ideas to encourage more F&B sales. But, by design — the least efficient departmental business model is generally found here.

> **DON'T LOOK FOR INCREASED F&B SALES TO SIGNIFICANTLY IMPACT THE BOTTOM LINE. AS SALES INCREASE, THERE ARE CORRESPONDING VARIABLE EXPENSES THAT MARCH ALONG ALMOST IN STEP.**

FOR ILLUSTRATIVE PURPOSES:

Let's arbitrarily assume a membership of 300. This would mean that a $25 monthly increase in dues generates a $90K contribution to the club's bottom line. (300 X $25 X 12 = $90K)

Now, ask yourself, how much would top line F&B sales have to increase to NET that same $90 grand? (Check, please. Guess what? It's NOT gonna happen.)

What MUST be tackled is identifying where the optimal dues level needs to be.

Increasing expenses are a constant concern.   SWoT

- *There is an on-going parade* of government environmental regulations that are focused on protecting the planet and saving wildlife.
- *State and Federal laws* relating to healthcare, pensions, and all of the taxing ramifications that come with each are nonnegotiable, expensive and highly unpredictable.
- *Insurance and utility costs* have a more predictable trend — if that helps. (It doesn't).
- *While operating expenses are increasing*, member demand and appreciation for both quantity and quality of services are not likely to be decreasing.

In fact, if indeed the net annual cost of membership were to increase, it is understandable that those remaining members who are willing to foot the bill would expect the quality of services and quantity of offerings to be perhaps further enhanced — most certainly not be compromised for them at all! Left pocket vs. right pocket

On preliminary budget spreadsheets — mathematically balancing the revenue/expense equation is simply a matter of increasing the various individual price points and fees to match the cumulative increase in expense. What could be simpler math? Just raise prices until financial security is accomplished by default, simply by pressing the "equals" key. Whah-Lah!

EVEN THE MOST LOYAL MEMBERSHIP BASE WILL NOT CONTINUALLY SHOULDER EVER-INCREASING COSTS OF BELONGING TO A CLUB ONCE THEY BEGIN TO DOUBT IN THEIR OWN MIND THE REAL VALUE OF DOING SO. IF THE TOTAL NUMBER OF MEMBERS IS IN SLOW DECLINE — EVEN IF MANAGEMENT HAS DONE A GOOD JOB OF CONTAINING EXPENSES - THE INDIVIDUAL COST OF MEMBERSHIP MAY CONTINUE TO RISE.

On the other hand — if it was this easy, the above paragraph would be the first and last on this subject. End of story. But, it's not.

This is NOT necessarily management's fault. Instead, it is simply stating a mathematical fact.

We must factor into our equation an assumption that the overall membership base may decrease at some point due to what appears to some to be out of control increasing costs.

If this mind-set proves pervasive, management may feel pressured right in mid-stream to compromise the quality of services and quantity of offerings that were originally included in the approved budget months ago. That will solve the dilemma! (No, it won't.)

At this point, it is quite possible to have the tail start wagging the dog, digging a deeper and deeper hole:

- *Ever-increasing cost* of individual membership.
- *Seemingly unmonitored expenses.*
- *Perceived compromise* of service and quality.
- *Verifiable trend* of more frustrated members slipping out the back door than excited new members marching through the front.

Here are two extreme examples of the importance of appropriate dues income:

(*For illustration purposes* — let's assume an arbitrary base of 300 full members and $300 per month Dues. As the coming FY preliminary budget nears completion, after reducing expenses by every acceptable means, the leadership of the Club clearly sees that NET results will need to increase by $500K in order to provide the quality and service levels the members want. What to do? OK - here come our two extreme examples of how generate the needed $500K.)

EXAMPLE #1)	EXAMPLE #2)
Increase the monthly dues from $300 to just under $440. Almost a 50% increase! The math works. BUT — what if all the members were so unhappy with this that they quit? *Dues income would be zero!*	Since we don't want to lose any members — what if the Club charged no dues at all to really make the 300 members so very happy that they all stayed — nobody left? *Dues income would again be zero!*

Of course, #2 would also mean that a gin & tonic after golf would cost $40, the annual locker fee would be $3,800 and Thanksgiving Dinner at the Club $350+ p/p. Hmmm — this scenario suggests yet another story, for another time!

While both of the above are obvious extremes, they do suggest two things in our imaginary budget model:

(#1) As monthly dues are incrementally raised from unacceptable depths — dues revenue will (in theory) increase from what was otherwise zero. *But, only to a certain point.*	*(#2) As monthly dues are incrementally lowered from unacceptable heights* — dues revenue will (in theory) increase from what was otherwise zero. *But, only to a certain point.*

This illustrates the importance of every club to identify the acceptable range *(between either extreme)* that will result in the greatest net dues income from the greatest number of members — NOT in theory, but in the very real unique culture that every club has.

EVERY BOARD NEEDS TO IDENTIFY 6 FACTORS:
PERCEIVED NEW MEMBERSHIP DEMAND.
THE CURRENT BALANCE SHEET.
LOCAL COMPETITION.
THE FINANCIAL LIQUIDITY OF THEIR MEMBERSHIP.
THE HISTORY, CULTURE AND TRADITIONS OF THEIR CLUB.
THE PERCEIVED VALUE OF CONTINUED MEMBERSHIP.

Taking these 6 factors into account, in tandem with a Strategic Plan, the BOD must approve policies demanding dues income necessary to deliver member experiences of the quality and service that the membership demands.

Expenses cannot be continually reduced to the extent necessary to offset a serious lack of dues income.

In these changing times in the world or private clubs, most likely all of the "low hanging fruit" has been trimmed from operating expenses — while, hopefully, not cutting into a member's delight in day-to-day experience at their club.

Let's be forthright in stating that **the purpose of departmental club operations is to create such visceral day-to-day memorable experiences that members are willing to continue paying the necessary dues to ensure these memorable experiences are not just something in the past** — but to be looked forward to next year as well.

If a serious inadequate level of funding exists from dues — in general — departmental club operations cannot and will not make up the unfavorable variance.

If a club allows dues to be short of what is truly needed (AKA: kicking the can down the road), then what should be an annual modest, gradual, insignificant SMALL dues adjustment every year instead manifests it-

THE SINGLE MOST IMPORTANT OPERATING LINE ITEM DECISION THAT THE LEADERSHIP OF ANY PRIVATE CLUB MUST GET RIGHT IN ORDER TO REMAIN FINANCIALLY VIABLE — IT IS: ESTABLISHING A REALISTIC DUES INCOME.

self as a quite significant BIG dues increase in order to make up for bad past decisions in allowing artificially low dues to prevail.

And — if that big dues increase doesn't happen — "suddenly" (yet with great predictability) the dreaded "A-word" (ASSESSMENT!) is all but mandatory. Yikes!

But wait! There's more! The tendency after a BIG operating assessment takes place is: "You know, after we just hit them with a big operating assessment, we simply can't raise the dues on top of that!"

Remember – an operating assessment only pays for past shortcomings. It does not address at all the future. The fact remains that a realistic dues line is mandatory for a financially viable private club.

> REPEAT: What MUST be tackled is identifying where the optimal dues level needs to be in creating realistic operating budgets and not slowly morphing into a "CAN KICKERS COUNTRY CLUB" marked by deferred maintenance, increasing debt and predictable excessive management changes.

WE CAN'T RAISE THE DUES HIGHER! AND OUR CURRENT MEMBERS DON'T WANT TO CHANGE. SO - LET'S PEEK INTO THE BOARD ROOM AND LISTEN IN SOME MORE!

FINALLY - A BOARD MEMBER WITH CORPORATE SENSE DEMANDS FOR BIG DATA TO BASE DECISIONS ON, RATHER THAN JUST OPINIONS AND EMOTIONS.

DEBT IS ONLY A TOOL
NOT AN ANSWER. PLUTONIUM CLUB LEADERS
KNOW THE DIFFERENCE BETWEEN THE TWO.

INTRODUCTION

Dave Duval, dduval@cbpros.com, and Joe Abely, jabely@cbpros.com, each bring CPA and MBA credentials and incredible spot-on expertise in private club financial concerns, board protocol, and operations. But what makes them truly Plutonium Leaders is their exuberance and dedication to the success of private club board of directors and management. Their firm, **Club Board Professionals,** is a respected source for expertise related to executive level strategy and decisions. We recommend their expertise with zero hesitation. Here, Dave and Joe offer their Plutonium Leader insights as it relates to club debt.

Before the great recession, approximately 20% of country clubs employed bank debt to finance capital improvements. A decade later, that number has risen to a clear majority with as many as 80% of clubs carrying debt on the books as reported by a prominent CPA firm. The reasons for that dramatic growth in the use of debt are many, but collectively they provide some interesting insights into the financial management of private country clubs.

Since debt is unforgiving and is the primary cause of club failures, it is useful to take a closer look. As a result of the recession and its impact on membership ranks, board leaders at many clubs drifted towards unwise decisions. Here are some examples:

- Deferring capital spending.
- Cutting or eliminating initiation and/or capital fees.
- Capping or limited operating dues.
- Tapping available capital income and reserves to support operations.

While these decisions may have been well-intended, they often resulted in negative situations. Here are some examples:

- Deferred maintenance piling up throughout the property.
- Constricted primary sources of capital funds.
- Artificially supported operating dues that were unsustainable.

While we can benefit from the analysis of a large number of simultaneous decisions stimulated by the recession, Club Boards across the country continue

to fall into many of the same traps.

When you couple the results of these decisions with significant changes in the requirements of younger new-member prospects looking for more expansive and family-friendly upscale amenities and facilities, many club leaders saw and continue to see debt as more palatable than requiring additional funds from current members to address rapidly growing capital needs.

With a decade of hindsight, it is now clear that embracing debt to solve a nearly insatiable need for capital is oftentimes linked to weaknesses in the planning process to start with. Here are some examples:

- *Unrealistic assumptions* about membership growth.
 Omission of normal 4-7% attrition each year in census (and financial) projections.
- *Inadequate planning* for routine capital spending in addition to debt service costs.
- *Underestimating the need* for additional transformative capital projects.
- *Overstating and including* planned operating profits as a source for debt service.
- *Failure to develop* and dedicate a separate funding source for debt service needs.

- Funding a pet project rather than an all-inclusive long-term plan.

> WHEN IT COMES TO DEBT, CLUBS OFTEN BORROW TOO MUCH, ENTER INTO UNREALISTICALLY LONG AMORTIZATION PERIODS, AND TURN TO INCUMBENT BANKS — INSTEAD OF RUNNING A COMPETITIVE PROCESS RESULTING IN SUB-OPTIMAL RATES, AND TERMS THAT ARE OFTEN NOT BEST SUITED FOR PRIVATE CLUBS.

As noted above, many of these same clubs do not adequately plan, develop and dedicate a source of funds to repay the debt. These common actions hamstring future administrations in their decision-making options and in doing so commit the club to a protracted downward spiral.

While this all sounds very dire, debt used appropriately and judiciously can be an effective financial tool if best practice guidelines are followed. Here are some guidelines:

- *Develop a long-term (10 years) financial plan* for operating and capital funds that supports strategic, facility and reserve plans.
- *Realistic assumptions* supporting long term census projections will be essential. Understand FME's – Full Member Equivalents. Seek help in planning. Update it annually.

- *Segregate and meticulously manage* distinct capital and operating funds. These are two "checkbooks" that must be planned for and managed separately.
- *Plan for funding* an all-inclusive long-term financial plan, not a project. A financial plan projects operating and capital funds simultaneously. Discuss assumptions with others who have done it before.
- *Establish and plan* capital levies (initiation fees, capital fees, special purpose fees, transfer fees, etc.) that equal or exceed annual depreciation (or the long-term needs projected in a reserve study, if available) plus transformative capital spending.
- *If debt is to be employed*, be sure there are additional provisions in the plan for a source of funds to extinguish the debt.
- *Normal annual CAPEX* needs do not go away. Members must be willing to pay more for more! The costs can't all be placed on assumed new members and inflated census counts.
- *Limit debt amortization periods* to no more than 10 years; shorter is better if manageable.
- *Anticipate* there will be another major project coming along in 7-10 years that some future administration will need to face with a clean slate.

> **UNDERSTAND DEBT CAPACITY. AS A ROUGH-CUT RULE OF THUMB AND FOR A VARIETY OF REASONS, CONSIDER TOTAL DEBT NOT EXCEEDING 1X ANNUAL OPERATING DUES AS A DISCUSSION POINT IN YOUR PLANNING.**

- *Run a competitive RFP process to acquire the best rates and most appropriate terms.* Use expert assistance. It is important to remember that capital needs are nearly insatiable and maintaining, updating and transforming the facilities to meet changing tastes and requirements of new and existing members is Job #1 of Boards.

Clubs are characterized by long days and short years. Plan ahead!

The debt package will have long term ramification to the clubs. Be sure they are well understood up front. Here are a few general recommendations:

- *Seek a fixed rate loan* without a SWAP agreement. SWAP's are complex and can increase closing costs and be difficult and expensive to unwind.
- *Avoid prepayment penalties.*
- *Minimize closing costs.*
- *Negotiate a negative pledge in lieu of a mortgage* – it will save closing costs, appraisal, legal and other fees that can otherwise reach six figures and be less contentious among members.
- *Limit the scope*, cost and ramifications of environmental reviews (beware - any surprise findings may need to be addressed whether or not you go forward with the loan).

- *Amortize the loan* over no more than 10 years, generally 5-7 years is preferred (no balloons!).
- *Be sure Debt Service Coverage Ratios* are based on changes in Members' Equity or Unrestricted Net Assets, not the more typical above-the-line operating income used by lenders in non-club settings.
- *Don't forget to consider the annual costs of the operating accounts.*
- *Avoid insurance companies* – they typically do not renegotiate down the line. Banks do.

TWO VERY IMPORTANT CLOSING POINTS:

1. *Rotating boards, officers and GM's make implementing long term plans very challenging. Sudden "lane changes" can be devastating.* While true in any club setting, these challenges are greatly exacerbated when unforgiving debt is part of the plan. Debt limits flexibility. Annual orientations of all board members that address plans in place, board and management roles, and the club's long-term financial plan are essential for achieving continuity in implementation. Perhaps most importantly, leadership succession planning will determine the fate of plans, financial vitality and ultimately the club. Embrace doing it well.

2. *Be sure Board members focus on strengthening the Balance Sheet while management implements and reports against the board-approved "P&L" budget.* Management primarily focuses on "this year" operations. Boards should primarily focus on future years, expanding the Capital Base (net fixed assets), and providing for long term capital spending, certificate/bond redemptions and debt service needs all in the context of a viable strategic plan that is embraced by the Board and membership.

> Thank you, Dave and Joe. Your informed insights are highly valued. We are INDEBTED —— to YOU!

DELEGATION SKILLS
IF YOUR TEAM DOESN'T MAKE IT, NEITHER DO YOU!

FORGET ALL ABOUT THE NICE OFFICE — the credentials on the walls, the executive swivel chair, the "impressive" brass on your door, and the nice view. Now, once all that window dressing is out of the way, focus on the bedrock truth of any enduring career. If your direct reports are not up to the job, neither are you.

A sobering reality for all of us sitting in a nice office or around a boardroom table.

Plutonium Private Club Leaders have the non-negotiable mandate of making decisions that drive expertise down and through the ranks. Appropriate responsibility and authority must be delegated at the right times, in the right places, and (most importantly) to the right people.

Over reliance on simply getting things done all by yourself works marvelously in early career stages, but those promoted to top positions of leadership had better stop doing

> **EFFECTIVE DELEGATORS ARE PROFESSIONALS — NOT TECHNICIANS. THE JOB YOU DID TO GET TO THE TOP, WILL NOT KEEP YOU THERE.**

their old job and focus on their new one of appropriately delegating important tasks and then monitoring for positive results.

You have no business doing well at something that you no longer have any business doing at all! Effective delegation frees Plutonium Leaders to focus on making the right decisions and proactively preparing the entire team for the future rather than day-to-day minutia.

Subordinates respond to not having authority delegated to them as an excuse to remain dormant. *Delegation of responsibility mandates an appropriate corresponding transfer of authority.* Responsibility without authority or authority without responsibility will fail over the long run. People do not take ownership when they feel their input doesn't factor in.

> **MANY OTHERWISE PRODUCTIVE PEOPLE DO NOT POSITION THEMSELVES TO BE PROMOTED, FIRED OR TO QUIT. INSTEAD, THEY SUPPRESS THEIR OWN CREATIVITY AND DRIVE, SEEMINGLY CONTENT TO PERFORM AT WHAT COULD BE CALLED ADEQUATE, YET NOT VERY EXCITING LEVELS.**

The two most dreaded words that can usually be found near the end of standard annual performance review forms are: ADEQUATE and SATISFACTORY. In general, no matter what else preceded in the review, if a little box next to either of these two words is checked — HEY! — this means that there is no cause for alarm because, at the end of the day, those two words virtually communicate that all is well!

Who strives to be an "adequate" friend? How many of us want a "satisfactory" marriage? When it comes to being a parent, is this level of performance OK with you? Of course not.

Plutonium Private Club Leaders are not interested in team performance being at levels that could be described as adequate or merely satisfactory. Instead, they contagiously strive for the performance of their entire team and membership experiences to be described by words like: exhilarating, motivating, creative, sensational, memorable — in other words, just consistently performing at downright exciting levels.

In order to foster a club culture of excitement, effective delegation is a mandatory component found in the makeup of every Plutonium Club Leader. People have to be involved in order to be excited.

PERSONALLY DO LESS, WHILE PROFESSIONALLY LEADING THE TEAM

IN THE ABSENCE OF DYNAMIC LEADERSHIP AND APPROPRIATE DELEGATION, MANY THINK OF THEIR ROLE IN TERMS OF ACTIVITY RATHER THAN IN ACCOMPLISHMENTS. ATTRITION CREEPS IN AND THE ORGANIZATION BEGINS TO DRIFT. YES, PEOPLE COME AND GO — BUT, IN THIS ENVIRONMENT, THE GOOD ONES ALWAYS GO FIRST!

IN ACCOMPLISHING MORE.
Throw away your old "Things to Do" list reflecting what you believe you must personally do. Instead, list the names of key direct reports, transfer those items to their proper area of responsibility and change the heading to "Things to Delegate and Monitor."

In delegating, explain the *"what"* and *"why"*, but oftentimes leave the *"how"* to the subordinate.

Hand pick those ready for further development and then involve them. Never involve someone with a problem unless you clearly see the potential of them being part of the solution.

Effective leadership allows subordinates the freedom to make an honest mistake. BUT — never the same ones twice! Those who never make a mistake are so afraid of making one (or allowing a subordinate to make one) that they fail to do anything. This is the greatest mistake of all.

Delegation is a delicate issue, as there can be problems with both over-delegation and under-delegation.

THERE ARE TWO KINDS OF PEOPLE WHO WILL NEVER DEVELOP BEYOND THEIR PRESENT STATUS: (1) THOSE WHO WILL NOT DO WHAT THEY ARE TOLD AND (2) THOSE WHO WILL DO NOTHING BUT.

- OVER DELEGATION can result when lackadaisical management assigns responsibilities and authority without first assessing the abilities of the staff — or when management delegates every last detail of every last project, but does not have any one individual who is privy to the overall picture enabling the team to know exactly where their roles fit in.

- UNDER DELEGATION is the footprint left by insecure management that refuses to relinquish authority or responsibility. Strangely, they feel their position is threatened by qualified subordinates! They are right to feel threatened, but not by their subordinates. The real threat is their own inability/refusal to develop them.
- PROPER DELEGATION of the right tasks to the right people at the right times can really help your team "make it." And, when they do, and only when they do — so do you!

Plutonium Private Club Leaders generate a club culture of excitement by involving people who are held accountable for collective performance levels that no single individual or department can attain on their own. Adequate or satisfactory levels are neither.

DISAPPOINTMENTS
PLUTONIUM CLUB LEADERS QUICKLY LEARN
REGROUP — MOVE FORWARD WITH CONFIDENCE

Many times being "rejected" is emotionally interpreted as synonymous with "failure."

But (emotions aside) keep in mind that an undeniable upward trend of overall continuous improvement is not irretrievably turned downward — cartwheeling into the abyss — by an occasional rejection.

Rejections that appear devastating to some, are just reminders to Plutonium Leaders to continually refine their efforts while never taking their eye off of the goal.

To exemplify that winning outlook --- check out this letter written by a high school senior who had just received a letter of rejection from the college she wanted to attend:

DEAR ADMISSIONS DIRECTOR:

I am in receipt of your rejection of my application. And – as much as I would like to accommodate you…well, I find I cannot accept it.

You see — I have already received four rejections from other colleges, and this number is, in fact, over my limit.

Therefore I must inform you that I reject your rejection … and will indeed, appear fully prepared for classes on September 18th.

WHAT IS COMMONLY CALLED "FAILURE" CAN TEACH US.

Failure is a teacher, and it becomes an asset to those who can learn from it.
- We may *learn* that our present strategy needs readjustment.
- We may l*earn* that our original destination is not really where we want to go.
- We may *learn* that our assumptions need to be updated.
- We may *learn* that we quit too soon.

WHATEVER IT IS: FAILURE TEACHES US, BUT ONLY IF WE LET IT!

- *In 1890* – a teacher at Harrow in England wrote on a 16 year-old's report card, "A conspicuous lack of success." That student was *Winston Churchill* – who rejected the rejection.

- *In 1902* – the poetry editor of Atlantic Monthly returned a sheaf of poems to a 28 year-old poet along with this curt note: "Our magazine has no room for your vigorous verse." The poet was *Robert Frost* – who rejected the rejection.

- *In 1907* – the University of Bern turned down a PhD dissertation as being all but "irrelevant and fanciful." The young student who wrote the dissertation was *Albert Einstein* – who rejected the rejection.

More recently …
- *In 1978* – a sophomore tried out for his high school varsity basketball team and was deemed not able to compete at that level and was demoted to the junior varsity squad –even though another sophomore classmate did make the varsity. He cried in his room that night. That young boy was Michael Jordan – who rejected the rejection.

Beyond world leaders, poets, scientists and athletes…
- *Right Here and Now — TODAY!* Career dreams and personal desires may be great, but there are times when getting emotionally "beat up" by what appears to be rejection and failure can cut deep. *That person is you!* And, by the way – just about everyone at numerous points in their professional career and personal lives feels like a punching bag.

Fear of failure is a dark state of mind that can cause paralysis and leave some with not much to smile about. But – the prognosis for a full and complete future is brighter than ever when the symptoms are diagnosed and exposed for what they really are.

FEAR = **F**alse + **E**vidence + **A**ppearing + **R**eal

So what sort of rejection and false evidence is appearing very real on your radar screen as of late? Step back from the emotions and see what there is to learn. Take to heart what lessons can teach us something. Collect our thoughts. Stay focused. Clear our mind of false evidence. Graduate at the top of the class for whatever we can be taught today.

Reject the rejection and get moving again!

And — because you are now smarter and better equipped for success than you were just a moment ago…you can now start smiling again. See? You can't kid me. You're starting to grin just a little bit at this very moment!

Reject the rejection and start smiling again!

DECONSTRUCTING THE IDEAL GM/COO ROLE MODELS
HERE, VISUALLY, JUST ABOUT ALL WE NEED TO KNOW
— WITH KEY DEFINITIONS.

MEMBER EXPERIENCED FOCUSED

IT IS NO MISTAKE THAT THIS IS INCLUDED IN EVERY MODEL - SIMPLY BECAUSE EVERY DECISION/ACTION OF PLUTONIUM PRIVATE CLUB LEADERSHIP IS BASED ON THE UNDERSTANDING THAT IN THE ABSENCE OF MEMBERSHIP SATISFACTION IT MAKES NO DIFFERENCE WHATSOEVER HOW GOOD SOMETHING SOUNDS, LOOKS ON PAPER, ADHERES TO BUDGET OR EVEN HOW LOGICAL IT SEEMS.

MEMBERSHIP SATISFACTION IS "MISSION CRITICAL."

IT IS THE ONLY REASON PEOPLE JOIN.
THE ONLY REASON THEY WILL STAY.
THE ONLY REASON THEY WILL INVITE OTHERS.

ACTUAL MEMBER EXPERIENCES MUST BE THE FOCUS IN ORDER TO SEE CLEARLY. PLUTONIUM CLUB LEADERS SEE THINGS NO OTHER WAY!

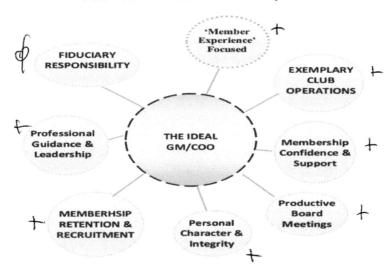

KEY DEFINITIONS

- *MEMBERSHIP CONFIDENCE & SUPPORT:* The focus of PLUTONI-UM CLUB LEADERS is not all about numbers and process, so much as it is about trusted relationships and people. People could care less about how much you know until they know how much you care.

- *PERSONAL CHARACTER & INTEGRITY:* The people who make a difference are not those with the most credentials, money, or awards. They are the ones that care and exhibit character. Remember: DWY-PYWD. (Do What You Promised You Would Do.)

- *PRODUCTIVE BOARD MEETINGS:* Meaningful agendas. No surprises. Focused. Accurate/timely data. Solves problems before they are ever allowed to even happen. Visualize possibilities, and then brings everyone into the big picture.

- *PROFESSIONAL GUIDANCE & LEADERSHIP:* Effective boards are on top of things simply because their management team is. As a working partner of the BOD, the GM/COO attends ALL meetings in their entirety and presents a comprehensive opening report (executive summary) near the top of every agenda.

97

KEY DEFINITIONS

- *A DEDICATED HIGHLY QUALIFIED PROFESSIONAL STAFF:* Identify real talent, mentor people and monitor performance with accountability for terrific results. Leadership exhibits positive support and empowerment, not fear or micro-management.

- *AN UNDENIABLE PALABLE "POSITIVE ENERGY" PREVAILS:* The entire team perpetually in a proactive mode. All the membership knows is that great experiences consistently happen at their club. There is a vibe going on all the time and everybody senses it.

- *CONSISTENT/RELIABLE F&B EXPERIENCES:* F&B provides the single greatest opportunity to touch the greatest number of members, and their guests, in personal ways that serve to enhance membership retention and encourage new member sponsorship.

- *RENOWNDED FOR THE BEST CREATIVE & OVER-THE-TOP CLUB EVENTS:* If a club has an earned reputation of throwing the greatest parties in town - the compounded ripple effects of sustained initiation and dues income dwarf the cost of subsidizing ingenious execution, outstanding food, and enthusiastic service.

- *STANDARD OPERATING PROCEDURES THROUGHOUT:* Highly personal interactions and exchanges consistently happening in EVERY department at EVERY opportunity throughout the entire club property! EVERY day. EVERY time. CONSISTENCY with quality. CONSISTENCY with service. CONSISTENCY with pride of being part of something very special. Who we are is what we consistently do.

Michael Crandal, CNG
Principles of Private Club
FIDUCIARY RESPONSIBILITY

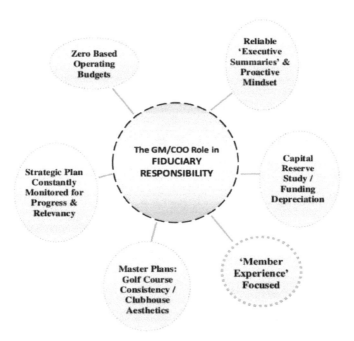

KEY DEFINITIONS

- *CAPITAL RESERVE STUDY/FUNDING DEPRECIATION:* Clear documents anticipate necessary expenditures to fund depreciation of all existing club physical assets, and empower the leadership to proactively prioritize the difficult annual capital budget choices.

- *MASTER PLANS: GOLF COURSE CONSISTENCY/CLUBHOUSE* AESTHETICS: Professionally designed master plans keep the course from becoming a mash up layout with no continuity or "signature" of its own. The clubhouse is not allowed to become a hodge-podge of various themes and intents with no clear memorable "brand" for the entire experience.

- *RELIABLE "EXECUTIVE SUMMARIES" & PROACTIVE MINDSET:* Proactively offers a succinct overview of all club operations. 90% of how well any meeting goes is determined before the meeting even takes place. Thoroughly answers any/all questions before they are asked.

- *STRATEGIC PLAN CONSTANTLY MONITORED FOR PROGRESS & RELEVANCY:* In years past, strategic plans might have been reviewed only every couple of years in efforts to keep in line with long-term goals. Today, club leaders are reviewing and making ever so slight modifications every 3 or 4 months. Forward thinking club leaders are expanding from just 'Long Range and Specific' - to 'Short Term and Broader.'

- *ZERO BASED OPERATING BUDGETS:* ZBB's are built upon starting from a clean slate (ZERO) every FY - rather than starting from where the prior year left off. The total amount of every key component of the requested budget is backed-up with measurable details and approved - rather than only variances from the previous year.

BUT WAIT, THERE'S MORE

Michael Crandal, CNG
Principles of Private Club
MEMBERSHIP RETENTION & RECRUITMENT

MAKES SURE the club remains relevant to the lives of all ages

Operating a Club Where Members are Proud to Bring Guests

The GM/COO Role in MEMBERSHIP RETENTION & RECRUITMENT

Renowned for THE BEST Creative & Over-The-Top Club Events

'Member Experience' Focused

Represents Club Favorably in the local community. (Church / Chamber / Rotary / Etc.)

- *MAKES SURE THE CLUB REMAINS RELEVANT TO THE LIVES OF ALL AGES:* Changing demographics and expectations are now a greater factor in how thriving clubs develop and execute long-range strategic planning, as well as even day to day operations.

- *OPERATING A CLUB WHERE MEMBERS ARE PROUD TO BE GUESTS:* In order to remain viable, everything possible should be done to enhance the probability of members having great confidence in inviting and entertaining their friends at the club.

- *RENOWNED FOR THE BEST CREATIVE & OVER-THE-TOP CLUB EVENTS:* If a club has an earned reputation of throwing the greatest parties in town - the compounded ripple effects of sustained initiation and dues income dwarf the cost of subsidizing ingenious execution, outstanding food, and enthusiastic service.

- *REPRESENTS CLUB FAVORABLY IN THE LOCAL COMMUNITY.* In the eyes of many, the GM/COO is the 'face' of the club. When s/he is away from the club they remain consistent: involved, proactive, caring, productive - FUN - a person of character, because they are!

BINGO!

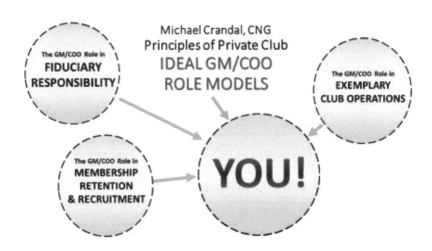

Michael Crandal, CNG
Principles of Private Club
IDEAL GM/COO
ROLE MODELS

The GM/COO Role in
FIDUCIARY
RESPONSIBILITY

The GM/COO Role in
EXEMPLARY
CLUB OPERATIONS

The GM/COO Role in
MEMBERSHIP
RETENTION
& RECRUITMENT

YOU!

DUAL ROLES OF A PUTONIUM GM/COO
PROVIDING MANAGEMENT OF THE CLUB AND LEADERSHIP FOR THE CLUB.

INTRODUCTION

Bud Gravette served as the Chief Executive Officer and Chairman of The Turner Corporation, headquartered in NYC, from 1996 to 1999. He was a member of the BOD from 1981 to 1999. During his tenure Turner had construction volume of billions of dollars, thousands of employees, dozens of offices in the USA, and activity in projects around the world.

While Chairman, he was largely credited with returning the company to profitability. Bud simply summed it up by saying, "we made a change in management philosophy; we went "back to basics," referring to the period when Turner focused its attention on its core business, construction, and its core strength: people. "This is a people business, and Turner's assets are its people. And our people have performed well."

Bud Gravette's business expertise is among the elite. His understanding of what makes private club leadership effective is equally impressive.

During the course of his career, Bud has served on committees and the BOD of several private clubs, and is a past president of three. Bud and Michael Crandal, CNG worked closely together at Thunderbird Country Club in their respective roles as president and GM/COO.

Here below, Bud masterfully explains the dual roles of an effective GM/COO in being responsible for the **management OF** the club — but also accept the responsibility for providing **leadership FOR** the club. And – his postscript at the end ties a perfect ribbon around it all!

Some of my favorite conversations and philosophies are the discussions of the differences arising between Management and Leadership of a For-Profit and Not-for-Profit corporation.

In my opinion, there are indeed substantial differences, beginning with the original concept for the organization of either one of those distinctive corporations.

The original (and on-going) concept of a For-Profit corporation is to create a sustained positive cash flow for a financial return on the capital invested.

> **THE OBVIOUS FACT IS THAT A FOR-PROFIT CORPORATION IS CREATED FOR A SINGLE REASON: FOR-PROFIT! IN OTHER WORDS, TO MAKE MONEY.**

The founders and owners invest their money, select a Board of Directors to establish and stay true to the philosophy of the organization, have a general model by which to sell a service or product at desired profit margins, and then hire Management to operate the day to day functioning of the business.

The business model of a For-Profit organization is pretty simple and straight forward:

1. Invest some money.
2. Develop a system.
3. Build a product.
4. Sell it to someone else.
5. Make a profit.
6. Distribute the profit to the investors.

Of course, they may opt to sell the resulting business, recapturing their original investment, plus a meaningful gain.

The business model for a Not-for-Profit private club is quite different, and must be adjusted slightly to reflect this fact.

There may be some similarity at the point of organization in determining what the philosophy of the Club is to be. But, going forward — that philosophy can change dramatically in the absence of an unchanging focus on profit being distributed, or earned from operations.

This is exacerbated by the fact of ever-changing ownership (members!) who feel they all have equal say in voicing their opinion in what the philosophy/direction of the club should be.

Therein lies a quite radical difference between For-Profit corporations and Not-for-Profit member-owned private clubs. This difference mandates an understanding that the necessary functions of MANAGEMENT and LEADERSHIP plays out differently within the two different structures and activities.

The investors of For-Profit companies can control every aspect of their investment. Leadership rests with the Board of Directors and the Chief Executive Officer, who have made the capital investment and control every phase of operations through the employment of a COO.

Compensation is provided for all those involved in Leadership and Management of the company, including the BOD, the CEO and COO.

Successful corporate board members (many times who come to serve on the

BOD at their private country club as it is simply "their turn" to do so) feel they "know" how things should be. But, they don't necessarily "know" that their role is different in a private club than back at their own corporate suite.

Successful private clubs "resolve the differences" by understanding that the necessary ingredients of management and leadership (applying to either For-Profit or Not-for-Profit) must be more closely melded together in the form of whomever is hired for the top compensated position in the club. S/he must provide not only day-to-day Management of the business, but also be-

UNDERSTANDING THE DIFFERENCES BETWEEN A FOR-PROFIT CORPORATION AND A NOT-FOR-PROFIT PRIVATE CLUB SHOULD BE AS EASY AS DAY AND NIGHT. UNFORTUNATELY, IN THE WORLD OF PRIVATE CLUBS, IT OFTENTIMES IS NOT.

come the spearhead of Leadership, whether so designated or not. The individual executive (GM/COO) responsible for the management of the club must also accept the responsibility for providing leadership for the club. In my experience, that Club, without this happening, is either destined to failure or limited to mediocre success.

I have come to this opinion for three basic reasons:

1. A lack of continuity on the Board. Not-for-Profit organizations routinely require a change in the makeup of a BOD every year. Changing shifts of wind in the sails can cause sudden changes in direction.
2. A lack of continuity in the office of President: Private clubs routinely change every year, because it is someone else's "turn" to be President. Changing volunteer leadership frequently can cause the wind to shift.
3. No lack of a slightly ever-changing membership: Normal attrition means many of those who have been around for years are gone, while new members with perhaps different expectations come aboard.

Faced with a condition of equality of a wide cross section of Not-for-Profit private club members, versus the financial strength of individual For-Profit investors — the Not-for-Profit corporation is at a distinct disadvantage of staying the course (UNLESS the private club has a GM/COO who brings to the table the ability to both manage and lead).

This Leadership role by a GM/COO must be handled judiciously so that the BOD, while perhaps not outwardly recognizing "they are being led" — are at the same time, inwardly, appreciating the appropriate lead-

A TALENTED GM/COO WHO PROVIDES MANAGEMENT TO THE COMPENSATED STAFF AND LEADERSHIP TO THE UNCOMPENSATED BOD AND CLUB MEMBERS CAN ACHIEVE THE SUCCESS DESIRED FOR THE ENTIRE MEMBERSHIP.

ership being provided. I believe that this is necessary for a member-owned, Not-for-Profit, private club to maintain the continuity of direction in which the organization is headed.

It is imperative that a private club hire and properly compensate a competent executive to provide leadership that is otherwise inherently missing in a Not-for-Profit — while not in a For-Profit organization.

Unless the hired GM/COO for a Not-for-Profit club assumes the dual role of providing both management and leadership — the stage is set for frequent changes of direction of the organization at the whim of every new board member, or new president.

Most of the time, a lack of continuity or frequent change blossoms into an exercise of irritation for Members, and a cause of concern for the club's viability.

By design, the members of a Private Club hold equal ownership and "take turns" to some degree in fulfilling the uncompensated role as members of the board.

The members (in general) and the BOD (specifically) need to make certain they fill the compensated role of GM/COO with an individual capable of providing operational supervision (Management) as well as continuity of direction (Leadership). This keeps the club either on the straight and narrow path of purpose, or provides for the new direction in order for the club to achieve the purpose of positive change.

None of this, by the way, is to suggest in any manner, way, shape or form that the most highly compensated employee does not report directly to the club president or is not fully accountable to the BOD. This chain of command is firmly in place!

However, what I am suggesting is that the lines of accountability, responsibility, authority, management and leadership heavily lean in the direction of a competent GM/COO.

The acronym "GM/COO" must not simply be meaningless letters after an individual's name in the club newsletter.

By truly putting all the letters together, "GM/COO" — the result is a successful balance of both the responsi-

THE LETTERS "GM" (GENERAL MANAGER) SPEAKS TO THE ROLE OF MANGEMENT.

THE LETTERS "COO" (CHIEF OPERATING OFFICER) SPEAKS TO THE ROLE OF LEADERSHIP.

bility and authority this dual role provides towards the success and viability of a member-owned — Not-for-Profit — private club.

I've enjoyed sharing my thoughts with you as they apply to private clubs and wish you great success at yours.

POSTSCRIPT FROM BUD:

I have a very definite opinion that top-tier clubs are the result of there being in place long-standing board-approved policies requiring the hiring of a GM who is not simply a manager. Instead, they hire a true "Plutonium Club **Leader**" who, as their GM/COO, is professionally capable of providing the direction and leadership necessary for their sustained success. Such a professional knows, by experience: best industry practices, what works best, what has been tried and what doesn't work at all.

You don't get that kind of leadership from a rotating, non-professional group of people (in terms of private club management) who are taking their "turn" at being a president, or board member, or committee member, of a private club that they happen to be a member of.

It is very unusual to have members of clubs who join for varied reasons and uses (social, fitness, golf, skeet shooting, dining, tennis, yachting, dancing, etc.) who can also provide the necessary expertise and experience needed to truly professionally lead a private club *(even if it is their turn to serve as president, be on the board, or serve on a committee).*

> A COMPELLING REASON WHY A PROFESSIONAL AND EXPERIENCED GM/COO SHOULD BE EXPECTED TO NOT ONLY PROVIDE CAPABLE MANAGEMENT, BUT TO ALSO PROVIDE COMPETENT LEADERSHIP TO THE CLUB.

Club members tend to be very professional and successful people — owners of hardware stores, realtors, merchants, car dealers, lawyers, doctors, accountants or an officer of the gas company, the telephone company…a multitude of other diversified professions. But most don't know diddily—darn about how to lead and manage a private club. Not really.

I'm going to offer a few examples (obviously somewhat tongue in cheek) of the necessity of expecting professionals, rather than amateurs, to do the heavy lifting —you will get the point.

In order to provide a viable culinary program for a deserving membership, a "Plutonium Leadership Board of Directors" hires a professional GM/COO who, in turn, hires a qualified Executive Chef — instead of a backyard BBQ guy who feels compelled to dictate menus and provide 3x5 recipe cards.

S/he hires a professional Director of Golf and Director of Racquet Sports — rather than expecting club members (amateur golf/tennis players) to head up dynamic departments.

CLUB MEMBERS, WHO MAY LIKE TO DABBLE IN COURSE DESIGN OR FEEL THEIR LOW HANDICAP QUALIFIES THEM TO DECIPHER THE IDEAL SPEED OF GREENS, ARE OUT OF BOUNDS AND NOT IN PLAY.

This same level of professional performance/expertise is required when it comes to both the art and science of golf course design and agronomy.

A capable GM/COO makes certain that highly qualified professionals are in constant play.

The member who is taking their turn as President-for-a-Year, and happens to be the owner of a hardware company, may provide the necessary leadership for screwing in a light bulb — but, in all likelihood s/he knows nothing about what to do with the many intricacies of leading a Not-for-Profit private membership club. No —private club leadership comes better from professional management than from a bunch of amateurs trying to become experts in club management in their spare time.

IN CLOSING — The Board of Directors still retains the greatest responsibility and sole authority necessary to be exercised towards the success of their club. Specifically, hiring just the right capable executive to serve as GM/COO with just the right blend of management and leadership skills to serve the members and staff well. Hold that individual accountable for what they were hired for in the first place, and enjoy your club.

Thank you, Bud! You remain the greatest single career mentor for Michael Crandal, CNG. Admired, respected & loved for a lifetime.

107

~~A X~~ EQUITY MEMBERSHIPS NEED TO GO.

EXPECTATIONS ARE NOT MET, OR MERELY EXCEEDED
— INSTEAD, PLUTONIUM LEADERSHIP ESTABLISHES THEM!

It is so very simple when you think about it. It really does not matter what business it applies to! It doesn't matter if you are selling tires, toothbrushes, or ice cream cones.

There is ONLY ONE thing you can give your customers (Members!) if you want to stay in business — and that is: what they want.

If someone insists on giving them what they don't want, guess what?

Now - let's not be silly here! Taking things to extremes someone may exclaim, "Are you kidding? All my members want is MORE! And all they want to pay is LESS! So, it is impossible to give them what they want! What am I supposed to do if they have unreasonable expectations?"

 Of course, to be sure, comments such as the above may be more reflective of the discouraged individual making them rather than the actual challenge at hand. But, for illustrative purposes, it does drive home the point that part of a leader's role is in projecting a proactive vision to help cast and mold the expectations of the membership in a positive, yet realistic, direction.

In other words - *"Wants and expectations can be somewhat professionally guided and influenced by effective leadership from the top."*

Much of this comes from the board level via general policies that accurately reflect the culture, changing times, and purpose of the club.

However, much of this also MUST come from the operation side of the equation - specifically - where actual membership day-to-day experiences take place.

More than anything else, it is the manner and spirit in which member experiences are proactively and seamlessly orchestrated in a professionally prepared "pre-flight plan" before ever leaving the runway at every point of contact, that establish expectations.

A common phrase is that in order to be successful it is necessary to **meet** expectations. OK. Let's take that as a given (as weak as it is).

But it is really a superficial phrase in that it assumes that whatever expectations are allowed to gain traction on their own are realistic. And, that may be very far from being true if left to simply fly in the breeze of the latest whim that seems to have the loudest voice at the moment.

In the mass market, customers may come and go — depending upon their desire of various expectations of quality/price points/service, etc. With most businesses, their real intent is to increase their share of the universal market pie.

But, in the club business – the pie does not get any bigger than the size of a limited membership. The name of the game is NOT necessarily increasing the size of the "pie" - but, instead making sure that the existing "captive market" is delighted with what they are getting.

In the corporate world - if customers are left feeling less than delighted, they go somewhere else. However...

In the world of private clubs - if members are left feeling less than delighted, the management goes somewhere else.

Check the math. Simple, isn't it?

Of course, EVERYONE has expectations! But keep this in mind:

If the primary focus is on meeting (or even exceeding) the expectations of the membership - fact is, there is a very strong undercurrent perpetually pulling the team into a reactive (if not outright defensive) mode. Always responding to the latest expectation. "Gee, what do they want now? And, what about now? Now? And, now? And now..."

Who likes to fly by the seat of their pants? Nonsense - for crying out loud, we are the professionals here!

The expectations of Plutonium Club Leaders should actually be flying higher than those of the members! waaaaaay higher! (BTW: If not, the stage is set for Micro-Management.)

> PLUTONIUM CLUB LEADERS ARE PER-
> PETUALLY IN A PROACTIVE MODE -
> ESTABLISHING EXPECTATIONS
> THAT THE MEMBERSHIP IS ALWAYS
> AMAZED AT EXPERIENCING. BEFORE
> THEY EVEN KNOW THEY ARE GOING
> TO EXPERIENCE IT!"

> PLUTONIUM CLUB LEADERS FOSTER
> A CULTURE WHERE THE PROFES-
> SIONAL STAFF ACTUALLY ESTAB-
> LISHES THE EXPECTATIONS OF
> THE MEMBERSHIP RATHER THAN
> MEETING, RESPONDING TO, OR EVEN
> EXCEEDING THEM. WHILE THIS
> MAY SEEM DAUNTING TO OTHERS,
> PLUTONIUM CLUB LEADERS PRO-
> ACTIVELY CREATE DAILY FLIGHT
> PLANS WHERE EXPECTATIONS ARE
> ESTABLISHED.

All the membership needs to anticipate is the knowledge that great experiences always seem to happen at their club.

They may not know specifically what it might be this particular time. Or what "little" thing will blow their mind today. Whatever it is - they know it is coming.

The expectations of their professional club staff are, quite frankly, out in front leading, guiding and influencing expectations in a very exciting proactive way.

There is a very subtle difference here, but a dramatic one. In fact — a pivotal one.

Flying, itself, was an impossible idea, but a great one!

Team productivity is similar to a computer in that if you change the input, you automatically change the output.

Of course, any input from any member is warmly accepted and immediately addressed. BUT - don't wait to simply respond to their input. Instead, get the team together on a regular basis and proactively go through EVERY potential member point of contact before there is any chance for input.

Before ever heading towards the runway — go over EVERY check point of potential member experience, and proactively put everything through the team filter of, "Let's make this easier, faster, more engaging, more fun, and more delightful for our members."

And remember that a great flight plan is perpetually updated and in play at every point of contact.

Plutonium Club Leaders ESTABLISH great expectations, not just meeting, or merely exceeding them.

- *evaluate* where you are now.
- *envision* where you want to be.
- *think* about creative IDEAS, and ultimately
- *transfer* your team's great ideas into an action flight plan.

Create a flight plan and then take to the skies!

Bing! The captain has just turned on the creative thinking light. Your Plutonium team is now free to establish expectations higher and more delightful than ever before.

Again - a very subtle difference here, but a dramatic one indeed. Happy flying!

ELEPHANTS ARE IN THE BOARDROOM!
POSITION DESCRIPTIONS FOR ALL NEED TO BE ESTABLISHED, INCLUDING BOARD MEMBERS, COMMITTEES & MANAGEMENT.

If you were starting a **BRAND NEW** club from scratch, creating position descriptions for key roles would be quite straightforward, with no emotions attached.

You'd begin by CREATING very specific documents that (if ultimately approved as policy) map out an interwoven relationship and clear lines of areas of both responsibility and authority to ensure success in delivering the quality and service levels of a deserving membership.
You'd map this all out by design, *before* the positions would actually be filled with top performing candidates who were interviewed, deemed both professionally qualified and personally prepared to successfully fill those roles.

This approach may be more difficult when looking at an *EXISTING* club that may be decades old and full of traditions.   In this case, oftentimes new management finds a lack of clear lines of responsibility and authority to consistently deliver truly great member experiences. There can be a hesitancy to not truly create the documents as above.

Oftentimes, quite unwittingly, new management - with the very best of intentions - winds up authoring individual documents (position descriptions) here and there that simply MIRROR the existing jobs that individual current employees (perhaps with emotional attachments) are already doing.

The above approach is not necessarily conducive to member satisfaction.

A mandatory component of Plutonium Leadership is making sure that when position descriptions are looked upon as a whole, they create truly interwoven departmental relationships with clear lines of responsibility and authority to ensure the overall consistent delivery of great member experiences.

Once the ideal organizational model is created, it then needs to be formally (as a whole) presented to the board of directors and ultimately approved as club policy.

From that point forward - club operations will be executed as designed with ideal candidates filling every role. Anything short of that would be operating outside the lines of club policy.

And – we may as well quickly address what is in the back of your mind if you are now managing a club that has been around for a few decades. You know the question, so no need to restate it here. Here is the answer:

A: UNLESS YOU HAVE A CLUB POLICY THAT EMBRACES A FORMAL POSITION DESCRIPTION OF "SACRED COW" - YOU ARE NOT ADHERING TO APPROVED CLUB POLICY IF SUCH POSITIONS ARE ALLOWED TO EXIST ON YOUR WATCH. ANY MORE QUESTIONS?

All future hires go thru this filter. All current employees must do so as well. Mandated adjustments must be made where necessary. Otherwise, again - board approved club policy is not being adhered to. Very simple.

BTW – the exact same process applies to creation and ultimate board approval (policy) of job descriptions for all board members, committee chairs, and the committees themselves.

The board & committee roles must be very clear to ensure no one is coloring outside the lines.

Personalities, or individuals with an agenda, are ALWAYS trumped by club-approved, documented policies and position descriptions.

Some may wonder if getting the board involved with basics like staff job descriptions is inviting over-involvement in operations, which is clearly the responsibility of management. Much to the contrary. In fact, just the opposite. Why? Because

- *Every department head position* description ultimately leads directly to the authority of the GM/COO.
- *Every committee* job description directly states their role is an advisory one only, with no authority to direct any department head in any manner.
- *Every committee chair* job description mandates their role to keep their committee coloring within the lines.
- *Every board member's* position description succinctly draws straight lines to their role of making policy with no role whatsoever in daily operations.

Which brings us back to the position description of the GM/COO who reports directly to the president and is responsible for managing the entire operation within the policies established/approved by the board.

Oftentimes the elephant in the board rooms of many otherwise fine clubs is the absence of the above structure and approved policies as outlined. MANY of the so-called "problems" of a club are merely "symptoms" of an absence of meaningful board-approved club policies. That MUST include position descriptions FOR ALL.

It is impossible to separate sound club policies and board-approved position descriptions (FOR ALL) and expect anything other than elephants grazing in your board room from time to time.

Elephants in board rooms tend to bring along all sorts of excess baggage:

- *Micro-Management* seeds are needlessly sown.
- *Over-Involved Committees* demand management time away from leading operations.
- *Under-Qualified hires* result from pressure to put out fires.
- *Sacred Cows* are unwittingly allowed to graze for far too long.
- *Desperately needed department head expertise* is rationalized away for budget reasons.
- *Departmental Silos.* Isolated decisions. Inconsistency in member experiences.

All are just symptoms of problems for which there is an appropriate remedy.

It's about time that all excess baggage be checked.

If a vacuum exists where solid policies and position descriptions should be in place - the dog just keeps on chasing its tail. And, just about everyone from time to time colors outside the lines that really do not even exist.

Clueless board members who may not know what they don't know. Micro-managed GM's are searching for a clue to give them what they need to know.

Looking for clues? We just gave you some!

Start from where you are. Remember to compare where you are to what position descriptions you would be working on if starting a brand club from the ground up.

In this light — creating position descriptions for key staff (and Board members & Committees!) is quite straightforward, and hardly an emotional experience. It's just business.

For the entire club staff, think about creating very specific documents that, if followed, would map out interwoven departmental relationships and clear lines of communication regarding both responsibility and authority to ensure the overall success of club operations.

Then, do the same with all committees, chairs, and board members. This is critical.

As you create the first draft of preliminary position descriptions for both paid staff and volunteer leaders, occasionally step back from the canvas. Look at the big picture. Then, since every club is uniquely different and one size definitely does not fit all - "tweak" things as need be towards working best in ultimately serving your staff and membership.

Plan on this process taking a month or two. It is worth it. During your "discovery" phase, touch bases now and then with the appropriate people (board and department heads) and keep right on "tweaking" as you learn more and keep moving forward with more and more confidence.

Ultimately you will emerge with an entire professionally prepared package that is nailed down and ready to be presented for the full board to consider, act upon, and approve as official club policy.

Do your homework. Build prior consensus/support from all concerned. Send it all out ahead of time. Include it again in your executive summary sent to the board before the meeting. Get it on the agenda. Present it as a total package. Ask for the board to approve it as club policy going forward. Get it done.

Once the board approves the package as official club policy, send the elephants packing and eliminate all of the excess baggage in the form of: micro-management, over-involved committees, under qualified hires, sacred cows grazing, and departmental silos — all resulting in inconsistency in member experiences.

You will now have board-approved policies mandating *everyone* colors within the lines.

Management also has a clear directive to have qualified individuals as department heads — anything less would not be in keeping with policy.

Plutonium Private Club Leaders get this done!

THE BOARD OF DIRECTORS
Their Four Key Functions

BOARD: *(Establishes Club Policies)*

#1) **What does it take to get into our Club?**
(The Initiation Fee & the people we want as members.)

#2) **What is the annual cost of belonging?**
(Dues and any mandatory fees.)

#3) **Approval of Operating and Capital budgets.**

#4) **Hire/Fire the GM/COO**

Marco

Does the BoD agree w/ the numbers?

GENERAL OVERVIEW OF SEPARATION OF DUTIES

THE GM/COO
Four Key Functions

MANAGEMENT: *(Operates According to the Board's Policies)*

#1) **Maintains the level of Club services expected.**

#2) **Operates at proper level of staffing and monitors revenue / expenses.**

Prepares the annual Operating and Capital budgets for Board review.

#4) **Hire/Fire all Department Heads.**

While the above is just a general overview, here is a great summation offered by two exemplary fellow PLUTONIUM PRIVATE CLUB LEADERS:

"Many private club boards devote too much time discussing operations — that's the job of the management team. Instead, focus on satisfying current members, modernizing and expanding facilities, anticipating the requirements of the next generation and devoting the bulk of time to strategic issues such as: increasing membership, member satisfaction, dues, initiation fees and capital levies, long-term strategy & capital planning, maintaining/increasing the club's capital base, planning and funding aspirational capital projects, including the judicious use of debt, succession planning for board and management, and Risk Management."

Joe Abely And Dave Duval —Co-Founders/Club Board Professionals

EXECUTIVE LEVEL DECISIONS NEED TO BE MADE
MAKE THEM. THAT'S WHAT PLUTONIUM CLUB LEADERS DO.

A "Mission Critical" non-negotiable trait of effective and efficient leaders is their inner confidence of being comfortable in their own skin in making decisions that only comes with years of meaningful experience.

No — we're not talking about the occasional inexperienced "loose cannon" that somehow slips between the cracks and believes that their every casual remark becomes a verdict cast in stone.

An inexperienced "shot-gun" or "machine gun" approach to throwing out edicts is a far cry from the seasoned Plutonium Club Leader who instead deliberately pulls the trigger of a high-powered rifle with a laser scope in making decisions.

OBVIOUSLY, THE BEST INFORMATION AT HAND IS FIRST PROCESSED — BUT, ULTIMATELY, EXECUTIVE DECISIONS MUST BE MADE IN A TIMELY FASHION AND THEN COMMUNICATED IN A COMPELLING MANNER. DECISIONS ARE INITIALLY SHARED WITH THOSE WITHIN THE IMMEDIATE SPHERE OF DIRECT INFLUENCE - AND THEN EXECUTED DOWN AND THROUGHOUT THE ENTIRE CLUB ORGANIZATION.

Plutonium Private Club decision makers aren't necessarily identifiable by:

- *The size* of a box or where that box may be positioned on an organizational chart.
- *A position* description in a file cabinet in HR.
- *Their picture* on a wall in a club hallway.
- *An article* with their byline in the club newsletter.
- *A title* embossed on a business card or their name on a bronze plaque.

All Plutonium Leaders are both effective and efficient decision makers. They are easily distinguishable by the following traits:

1. *Their ability* to make decisions in the first place.
2. *Their willingness* to shoulder responsibility for any corrections necessary for their decisions.
3. *Their sense* of urgency in making any necessary adjustments to previous decisions.
4. *Their willingness* to repeat 1, 2 & 3 above as often as necessary.
5. *Their humility* in giving the team credit for implementing any ultimate correct decisions.
6. *Their ability* to move on to the next vital area requiring decisions to be made.

In early career development, many individuals may move up the ladder in convincing fashion. But, often this is understandably the result of them dutifully following and executing well the decisions of those above them.

There is nothing wrong whatsoever with this normal early progression towards occupying bigger boxes that are positioned higher up the ladder on an organizational chart.

Every club definitely needs an entry and intermediate cadre of aspiring men and women who are fully capable of enthusiastically carrying out the decisions of those above them. The best slowly distinguish themselves as those who are gaining viable experience every step of the way.

When asked out of the blue how long they have worked at their profession, many will proudly respond with a numerical answer of (let's just say for illustrative purposes) 10 years of experience. They may even highlight this on their LinkedIn profile and underline it within the first paragraph of a cover letter.

We need to understand that the preponderance of folks may truly only have 4 years of actual experience - and another 6 years of duplication!

Yes, early career progression has roots in being able to follow the decisions of those higher than you (just try the opposite approach and see how far that one gets you).

But that is where the line is drawn.

At some point in career development, successful executives/leaders distinguish themselves by transforming genuine experience into being able to make effective and efficient decisions of their own.

While not wanting to sound overly simplistic, that is what they pay you for: to make decisions.

Some may argue by wincing a bit and then saying, "Oh I have to correct you. Isn't my job to make correct decisions?"

My response is to ask how will you ever know if any decision might be ultimately correct or otherwise, unless a decision is made to start with? No matter what, in every situation — at some juncture — there is a starting point where a decision must be made.

Then, some might again cower a bit and defend their position by asking, "But what, what, I mean, what if heaven forbid, like, uh, what if a wrong decision is made?"

The answer is that you then reevaluate the situation, and guess what? You now have more information than before and now have to make another decision!

"Bottom line — any person in a position of leadership is there to make decisions."

Imagine the Board of Directors in executive session contemplating who to hire as the next COO. Assuming that all issues of fine character and exemplary industry knowledge are a given - it is an immediate "knock-out punch" to hear any variation of a comment that conveys:

"You know, s/he is so very strong in many ways. BUT — I sense that s/he has difficulty in making decisions."

Pssst — guess what? The line has just been drawn.

Every decision made is a small thread that impacts the whole fabric of who we are. Over time, we are defined by the decisions we make.

Don't Major in the Minors: There is no sense in making decisions to stomp on ants if a herd of stampeding elephants is approaching.

Early on, just as soon as you are aware that your decisions have consequences, make the conscious decision to only allow your mind to dwell on quality.

> **REMEMBER THAT THE MOST IMPORTANT DECISIONS YOU MAKE ARE DECIDING WHO YOU ARE GOING TO RUN WITH.**

Make the right decisions as to who your friends, neighbors, employers, coworkers, direct reports, etc. are. Sound decisions in this arena lead to a more productive and enjoyable life (both at the Club and in your own skin).

Make the decision that you are not going to be overly impressed by "success" - even your own! Strangely, at least on the surface: failure itself is NOT always our greatest enemy. Rather, it is allowing ourselves to succeed, but at the wrong things.

MAKE THE DECISION TO FOCUS ON WHAT REALLY MATTERS.

There is a so-called "law of attraction" that purports if you think about something long and hard enough, you will ultimately draw what your mind focuses on into your life. Hmmm — if that really were true, why waste your lifetime focusing on perishable goals like cars, jewelry and houses? C'mon now, is that the best you can do? Is this the stuff that really defines you? Give yourself more credit than being defined by what you drive, the sparkle of your bling, or how many square feet you think you need.

How about instead focusing on meaningful goals like:

- Being a great friend.
- Being a man or woman of integrity and character.
- Being a great spouse and parent.
- Being a quality employer.
- Being a quality employee.
- Seeking God's will for your life!

These are the things that make a life worth living.

Make the decision NOW to get rid of negative thoughts and embrace the positive. Start really thinking about things that truly matter. The important thing is:

YOU MUST MAKE DECISIONS!

Life is not just something that happens to you. There are no such things as victims, only volunteers. Your life is F-U-L-L of opportunities for decisions. We all know in our hearts that a bad life is just as easy, or hard, to lead as a good one. The difference between the two all depends on the choices and decisions you make.

Don't Drift Off Course: Your decisions should be made with the knowledge that you are always headed in the direction of those positive goals you have set for yourself. Proper decisions keep us headed in the right direction.

It makes little sense for us to take our eye off the ball, going off at the speed of light in the wrong direction rationalizing, "So what — just look at the great time I'm making!" Years later you wind up wondering, "How did I ever get so far off course?"

In the decision-making process, remember there is a big difference between being "efficient" and being "effective."

GET THE RIGHT THINGS DONE, THE RIGHT WAY!

Making the decision to dig a foundation for a new home with a soupspoon is effective. It will work. BUT it isn't very efficient. Right thing. Wrong way!

The key is to look at every event of your life as a choice, but not as an isolated one.

So, if you want to dig that foundation for a new house (or a great career) go right ahead. But make the decision to operate a backhoe and not a soup-spoon.

EMPLOYEE ANNUAL COMPENSATION ADJUSTMENTS
YOU ABSOLUTELY MUST GET THIS RIGHT

In any club there are lots of moving parts on both the revenue and expense side of the equation. And while there is usually some room for error or budgeted contingencies — there is one area that is "Mission Critical" in getting it right: *EMPLOYEE COMPENSATION & RELATED EXPENSES!*

> **A PRIVATE CLUB BUSINESS MODEL IS BASED ON CONSISTENTLY DELIVERING GREAT MEMBER EXPERIENCES. SERVICE IS HOW WE DELIVER. SERVICE IS PROVIDED BY PEOPLE.**
> **THEREFORE, THE SINGLE GREATEST EXPENSE A CLUB HAS IS FOUND IN EMPLOYEE PAYROLL AND ASSOCIATED BENEFITS. IN FACT — THESE COSTS ALONE USUALLY REPRESENT 60%+ OF COMBINED OPERATING EXPENSES.**

If you've got it wrong here or even if a casual approach is taken - unfavorable "ripple effects" can cause long lasting waves of unfavorable net results.
To name just a few:

1. *Your very best performers* may just decide it is not worth it to them to stay.
2. *Your poorest performers* decide that it is. (YIKES!)
3. *If annual "blanket" percentage increases* are used as a basis rather than performance — many employees will use this as a basis to annually expect a raise simply by limping through years of delivering "satisfactory" or "adequate" service. That's when you hear, "Honey - I'm home! And, look! I made it through another year without being fired and here is my annual raise! Aren't you proud of me?"
4. *Do we really need any more reasons* to get this one right? No.

A serious approach and professional analysis is imperative prior to making payroll adjustments. This applies to any "as needed" individual employee review as well as the overall annual budgeting process.

It is irresponsible or "lazy management" to rely on simplistic blanket percentage increases from the prior year. Such an approach suggests that (as if by magic!) all employees become more productive the day new budgets are approved. Really? C'mon.

The simplistic approval of any percent increase is nonsensical when applied in a vacuum.

For instance, what sense does it make to apply a so-called Cost of Living Index percentage to a base number that is perhaps already too high or way too low to start with?

Mindless percentage increases (or even decreases or freezing) without first knowing what they are being applied to makes *zero* sense. And that, BTW, is NOT the *zero*-based type of budgeting we aspire towards.

When it comes to how to best handle employee compensation it can start to get pretty hot. So, we need some "Firewall" protection.

I have prepared two guidelines for you that are intended to work in tandem. They are the CNG Universal Compensation Guide and The Five Firewalls. Keep reading, there are more details for each to follow after a short intro.

Take the time to digest the explanation of each as it fully factors in meaningful points that are all relative in getting it right.

Here you will see four fixed overall performance levels where every individual employee will find an appropriate home - and a "fact-based" potential % adjustment.

Please keep in mind that the %'s shown here are simply for illustrative purposes. They can/should be adjusted up or down by YOU to best reflect your unique situation in relation to the FIREWALLS suggested below.

Percentages don't mean much. OK. I admit it. They are useless…IF we don't simply use some common sense regarding unique situations that must be factored in order to getting it right.

Here are the details for both of the above. Remember — they are to work in tandem together.

THE CNG UNIVERSAL COMPENSATION GUIDE.
To refer to when considering potential % adjustments.

0% Potential Adjustment:

This could (surprisingly to some) apply to employees who may very well be doing *outstanding* work! Huh? BUT — whom are already being compensated in an equally appropriate *outstanding* manner for what the position demands in the marketplace.

In this situation, perhaps some sort of a one-time bonus may be indicated rather than a further increase in base salary. OR, IN SEVERE ECONOMIC DOWNTURNS, ALL PAYROLLS MAY BE APPROPRIATELY FROZEN.

2 - 3% Potential Adjustment:

This range applies to employees who are clearly doing their job in a satisfactory manner and who **ARE** already being paid in the range of what their job calls for.

4 - 5% Potential Adjustment:

This range applies to employees who are clearly and consistently performing at a level that exceeds normal expectations and <presently compensated at "market value" for that position.

6 - 10% + Potential Adjustment:

This range is reserved for those employees who clearly and consistently perform in an outstanding manner and ARE NOT presently at a level of compensation that recognizes this fact.

This range might also apply to those who are clearly performing well, but were hired at a lower starting rate for what their position calls for in the market place, and in order to stay in pace with the competition we must bring it in line.

THE FIVE FIREWALLS

To go through in any consideration of compensation adjustments.

1. The present rate of compensation. Is it viable? Stand up to scrutiny?
2. The market value for the position. Plutonium Leaders demand being competitive.
3. The economy (exterior) of the geographical area.
4. The economy (interior) of the club itself. Cash flow, reserves, projections, etc.
5. ABOVE ALL --- Job performance! Increases are based on Merit. NOT longevity.

EMPLOYEE AREAS
PLUTONIUM CLUB LEADERS MAKE SURE
THEY ARE FIRST CLASS IN ALL RESPECTS — NOTHING TO HIDE!

MEMBERS AND STAFF SHOULD BOTH TAKE PRIDE IN THEIR SURROUNDINGS!

Many clubs would be well served by taking a fresh look behind the scenes and making sure all employee areas are reflective of the same upkeep and pride as the rest of their club.

If employee areas are allowed to become dated, in disrepair or are simply areas of the club that you would not be proud to include in a New Board Member Orientation tour — as if you have something to hide — this should be a wake-up call to exhibit leadership and get something done.

It is easy to allocate club dollars to areas where members frequent and take pride in having guests see. But what about maintaining and improving areas where employees frequent, and where members and guests, by design, never see?

Employee areas may be out of sight, but should never be out of mind.
It's unrealistic and impractical to expect employee locker rooms, dining area,

CLUB EMPLOYEES ARE DISHEART-ENED TO SEE ONGOING MAJOR CAPITAL IMPROVEMENTS ALL AROUND THEM - WHILE BEHIND THE SCENES, THEIR EMPLOYEE AREAS REMAIN SOMEWHAT DINGY AND ALL BUT FORGOTTEN.

and restrooms to be exact replicas of member and guest areas. However, these areas should still be in keeping with the manner in which members expect to be served.

Is your employee dining area full of mismatched stacking banquet chairs and old folding tables? Are metal lockers bent and rusted? Is lighting provided by flickering fluorescents with an annoying hum? Do restroom plumbing fixtures show their age? Is the tile flooring discolored? Are temperatures and humidity not all that different than outdoors, no matter the season?

Are the walls of employee break areas adorned with "motivational" posters that the staff is supposed to find inspirational? You know — all those posters highlighting words like: Quality, Respect and Service? These posters are all but insulting to a team where none of the words on them seem to be meant for the staff at all. To prove it — just look around.

The easy takeaway here is unless you know FOR SURE that none of the above applies to employee areas at your club - make it your business to tour all of these areas and then take appropriate action. *NOW!*

It could provide an opportunity to earn tremendous appreciation by staff and instill genuine pride in being a part of such a great club.

Perceived major improvements in the eyes of employees don't have to be major capital expense items. Fresh paint. New flooring. Updated lighting. Comfortable tables and chairs (that ALL match!) can usually be accomplished simply by just going ahead and getting it done.

Start immediately by doing two things:

1. GET RID OF ALL THOSE GENERIC TACKY MOTIVATINAL POSTERS!
2. REPLACE WITH PHOTOS OF THE STAFF IN ACTION THROUGH-OUT THE PROPERTY!

Blow up the pictures to various larger poster sizes, have them put on canvas and hung nicely covering the walls of employee areas.

Swap out with new staff pics every 3 months. Then present the ones that are taken down to those individual employees who were featured before. They are thrilled to be able to have these. Oftentimes, grateful staff will tell stories of thanks as their pictures at work became great gifts to appreciative parents.

There will be an all but immediate boost in employee morale and attitudes. And, while that is a great thing — that is NOT why you make sure all employee areas are first class. NO! You do it simply because it is the right thing to do.

Now — go do the right thing.

And, don't forget to include this area in your next New Board Member Orientation tour of the facility. After all — Private Club Plutonium Leaders have nothing to hide.

EMPLOYEES
THE PEOPLE THAT MATTER THE VERY MOST TO YOUR CLUB! YES — EVEN MORE THAN MEMBERS.

INTRODUCTION

Jackie Carpenter is a respected Plutonium Private Club Leader and Editor of one of the most powerful resources available to private club decision makers: The Private Club Advisor. The PCA is a concise monthly 4-page business letter that captures industry current best practices, trends, governmental regulations and cutting-edge insights. Individual editions of The PCA are routinely included in board books as a source of relevant and meaningful information to ensure a more effective decision-making process. The PCA is a "must read" for every Plutonium Private Club Leader! www.privateclubadvisor.com Here, Jackie hits the nail on the head in identifying the most important people in your club.

Community is a word that perfectly encapsulates everything a club is trying to create. It is defined as "a group of people living in the same place or having a particular characteristic in common; a feeling of fellowship with others as a result of sharing common attitudes, interests and goals."

Clubs are founded to bring people together. Creating a community feeling is the secret sauce that transforms a club from being just a building into a genuine "Third Place" — a place where people want to go when they aren't at home or at work/school.

A "Third Place" goes beyond just the facilities and amenities; it's about a feeling, a vibe, and a culture that makes it a place where people want to be. Sure, the facilities are important, but it's the community feeling that makes it welcoming, interesting and exciting to be part of.

A community at its core is made up of PEOPLE. While buildings, amenities, and programs are important — if you want to create a true community at your club, you've got to focus on the PEOPLE! But here is where many clubs get it wrong — *the people that matter most to your club are the employees — not the members.*

Hear me out. Yes, members are the entire reason a club exists and they are, of course, significant beneficiaries to the community that is created. But it's the employees — yes, the staff — who actually create, protect and cultivate a club community. The members just show up and enjoy it.

> **WITHOUT THE RIGHT TEAM OF PEOPLE TO IMPLEMENT THE PROCESSES, EXECUTE THE PROGRAMMING AND NURTURE THE CLUB CULTURE, A CLUB WILL NEVER BE GREAT.**

The team of people who live and breathe the club mission, who "touch" the members on a daily basis and who passionately foster the club culture, are the people on which we should be focusing.

In my 15+ years of experience in the club industry, through my extensive education and Master's Degree in Hospitality, throughout my continuous research as the editor of The Private Club Advisor, I have learned that all the knowledge and experience in the world are secondary.

When the focus and the priority are placed on the employees, they go above and beyond to create and enhance the community.

When people are fulfilled in their jobs, they feel part of something bigger. They have a purpose, they make a difference and they see that their jobs matter in the lives of others. Employees with a purpose become a team of people collaborating and working together to constantly innovate and anticipate the future.

When employees are prioritized as valuable assets, they remain passionate, committed, loyal and enthusiastic about their jobs. Work doesn't feel like work and the entire member experience is elevated because the team is genuinely excited about what they do. They are happy, motivated leaders and the energy they create is infectious to all those around them. This lively, uplifting community becomes so attractive to members that they bring guests, tell others about their experiences and choose the club over almost every other place.

> **WHEN CARRIED TO AN EXTREME, THE "MEMBERS FIRST" MIND-SET CAN CREATE A TOXIC WORK CULTURE THAT LEADS TO DETERIORATING SERVICE, INCREASED TURNOVER, A LACKING COMMUNITY AND ULTIMATELY A STRUGGLING CLUB.**

Too many clubs put all the focus on the members and what usually ends up happening is that the same people who are entrusted with nurturing the club's sacred community, are de-energized, knocked down and forced to make sacrifices repeatedly.

Employees' jobs become more difficult when in the design stages of club construction or renovation service stations and kitchen areas are cut in half to make room for the new or expanded member bar and lounge. When money is tight staff bonuses are reduced, raises are eliminated, education is cut back and other employee benefits are scrutinized.

Additional pressure is placed on employees to reduce labor (which just means fewer employees have to do the same amount of work) and they are constantly forced to do more with less. Work becomes stressful and the opposite of fun.

Without the talented, energetic and hardworking people who plan, execute, anticipate and create on daily basis, the club would just be a boring building with a restaurant, golf course and swimming pool.

It's the PEOPLE — *the employees* — who make members feel special, who are the keepers of the culture, who are the builders of community and who ensure the members are engaged, excited and continuously coming back to the club.

Thank you, Jackie, for sharing your spot-on Plutonium Private Club Leadership expertise in our ABC's as well as in every issue of the Private Club Advisor.

EXECUTIVE CHEFS
THE EVOLUTION OF FOOD SERVICE IN PRIVATE CLUBS.

INTRODUCTION

David Meyers Associates, Ltd. is the premier retained search firm specializing solely in the needs of private clubs and their need for top-tier Executive Chefs and support team. Further, one of the most respected individuals in the world of private clubs is **BILL SCHULZ**, who serves as Senior Culinary Associate and graciously penned this great piece. Bill is a past president of CMAA, a great personal/professional friend and most certainly a Plutonium Private Club Leader of Leaders. https://meyersassociates.com

For Chefs who work in clubs and Chefs considering switching their career to clubs, there is something you all should know. Club food service operations are unique; sometimes fickle and often very unpredictable. They are complicated and diverse and can be frustrating at times.

WHY THEN ARE CLUBS SO DIFFICULT?

They sound pretty good! So, what's up? The answer is twofold:

1. *Members pay dues for the privilege of belonging to a Club and enjoying the amenities, which include eating in the dining room.* This creates very high expectations, including the feeling that because of those dues and the fact that it is "their club," menu prices should be a little less than every other restaurant in town. Sounds crazy, but it's the truth. That is what a Club is all about. There is not much you can do about this – it is just the way it is, and it will never change.
2. *Members are captive in their own Club.* The Chef needs to create menus and programing that appeal to all tastes, all ages of members, all moods, and with availability whenever the member wants it. Consider the Club's demographics and you will find members representing all ages and generations. When at the Club, members are not visiting a specific public restaurant to accommodate their taste and desire at the time. Within the club's facilities, they are basically eating in an extension of their own home — and expect that whatever they want will be available to them.

HOW DID WE GET TO THIS POINT?

Let's consider the generational / age differences that make up the membership.

The 60+ aged members:
- They have tastes shaped within a more formal yet, in many ways, simpler era.
- The traditional role of the housewife was changing as convenience and processed foods ruled.
- Swanson invented the frozen TV dinner and the Betty Crocker Cookbook was the culinary bible.
- Adding another layer to an already complex food operation is that these members also now have more dietary restrictions.
- Overall — let's call them the "less adventurous" members.

The 40 to 59 aged members:
- They are more adventurous.
- But: still connected to more traditional culinary rules.
- They've witnessed a transition from independents to chain restaurants.

The 25 to 39 aged members:
- There are no rules for the 40 and younger member.
- Forget about formality - get real, they prefer to eat on the fly.

- "Farm to Table" (local harvest).
- Sushi rising to prominence.
- Nutrition and a "Prepared Food to Go" mentality shaped the new Millennium.

Beyond just the age differences that make up the membership at private clubs — we must take a look at how the very ways we look at food, menus and dining has evolved over the decades. So what better time than right now to travel back in time and enjoy the ride over the past 60+ years in the light of *THE EVOLUTION OF FOOD IN AMERICA.*

THE 1950's: Glimpses of "Fast Food" concepts were introduced.
An entrepreneur named Ray Kroc opened a McDonald's franchise in Des Plaines, IL. Popular dinner foods included fried chicken, tuna noodle casserole and meatloaf. Relish trays were visible on all restaurant tables.

THE 1960's: European chefs began having an influence.
Jet travel shrank the world and great international chefs like Julia Child introduced Americans to the luxuries of French cooking. There was a sudden emergence of "new choices" of food.

THE 1970's: Food, menus and dining habits started changing.
Tastes were becoming more eclectic. Gadgets and gimmickry became prevalent in our kitchens, and fast food took off while at the same time families were splintering.

THE 1980's: Chefs began to get recognized as something akin to celebrities.
Two early chefs of influence were Wolfgang Puck and Paul Prudhomme.

- *Wolfgang Puck* opened Spago in 1982 and suddenly California Cuisine was on the map. He later opened Chinois on Main in Santa Monica. His early exposure to Southern California's multicultural population intrigued him, inspiring him to fuse the Asian flavors and products of Koreatown, Chinatown, and Thai Town with his French and California-based cuisine, in a fine dining setting. Chinois brought diners a fresh and imaginative Asian-fusion menu that laid the groundwork for fusion cooking in America.

- *Paul Prudhomme* was the Chef who put the cooking of Louisiana (especially the Cajun gumbos, jambalayas and dirty rice he grew up with) on the American culinary map. He will be forever known for his famous Blackened Redfish.

THE 1990's: "Lite" and heart healthy options emerge. ♥
The infamous " " appears on more and more menus — with many diners actually looking for them. Americans had grown fat from all of the overindulgence and processed food. Naturally, healthy cuisines (notably Pacific Rim and Mediterranean) emerged. Fusion cooking prospered and the influence of the internet and Food Network began to bring food to the forefront.

Aside from being responsive to the dining desires of members of different demographics and members being captive in their own club — there are other particularities that influence Club culinary operations. Fasten your seat belts!

- *Personalization* — each member wants to feel that the Chef is cooking for them personally. Active Chef/Member interaction has become expected.
- *The disassociation between "What is Served and Pricing"* (i.e., lobster at chicken prices). Clubs are known for providing value for their members.
- *Full vs. Empty Dining Room Effect.* Members don't want to eat alone. They all want to eat together and at the same time, which challenges the kitchen daily.
- *"I Want What I Want, When I Want it!"* An egg white omelet with anchovies for dinner anyone?
- *The "Chaos Effect" of Special Orders.* This has only compounded in recent years with gluten free, peanut allergies, and other dietary restrictions.
- *The bottom line is - it's the "Best Meal" I've ever had!* OR it's the "Worst Meal" I've ever had! Members are just plain "fickle!"

So, there you have it. Clubs are a great career choice, but they are what they are. Successful Club Chefs understand this; they thrive in this environment, are flexible and enjoy the diversity and challenge found in clubs.

Bill would like to recognize Michael Masson, CCM - the General Manager at Baton Rouge Country Club, Louisiana for inspiring him to both understand and present this fascinating Evolution of Club Food Service.

> *Thank you, Bill! Your inspiration offered by Michael Masson took flight. Thank you both for your "Plutonium Chef Insights" that are portrayed here as a valuable addition to our "ABC's."*

EXECUTIVE SUMMARY
ALL PLUTONIUM GM/COO'S DISTRIBUTE ONE
PRIOR TO EVERY BOARD MEETING

PREFACE

With zero pride of authorship — here is an actual Executive Summary format that I prepared and sent to the BOD prior to the next meeting. It is very typical of those I prepared and made available to every board member prior to every meeting for over 15 years.

DON'T "micro-manage" the numbers here! They are from a different time and place. But, DO augment the concept/presentation to best reflect your unique leadership style and club culture.

A meaningful Executive Summary highlights major key points without getting into the minutia of details that the BOD can oftentimes start focusing — needlessly so.

Note in the example how the words "Favorable" and "Unfavorable" are used. Also — any of those "Unfavorable" may deserve some sort of a quick explanation or a proactive statement as to what management is going to do about it.

Once the BOD sees a verifiable consistent pattern of the GM/COO's Executive Summary being a consistent source of concise, spot-on and 100% reliable information — I've learned at the very best club's nationwide — the BOD feels no compulsion to "micro-manage" the monthly operating statement at all.

They instead much prefer to receive the GM/COO's Executive Summary in advance so that the meeting itself can focus on more long-range vision for the club as a whole and any necessary tweaking of policies. Suddenly - as if by magic — meetings last 45 to 90+ minutes LESS than ever before, yet are MORE productive at the same time.

After the exhibits, yellow notecards are provided to offer insights to each. Whether or not each is 100% applicable to your own unique club is up to you. Nonetheless, each is served up and can be modified to best suit the culture and needs of any club.

As a general guideline — a meaningful Executive Summary will primarily focus on actual YTD results and 12-month projections. There is seldom reason to delve deeply into the most recent 30-day results unless there are significant ramifications that are going to impact the entire FY.

BTW – this sample was reflective of times right in the vortex of the past recession. I could have easily shared a far greater favorable example of an Executive Summary. However, I feel it is more helpful to share an example of how to communicate even unfavorable results in difficult times.

BOARD OF DIRECTORS
EXECUTIVE SUMMARY — MARCH 19, 2010

FY 2010 CLUB OPERATIONS
7 Mos. Ending / Aug. ~ Feb.

	Actual	Budget	Variance		FY 09 Act.
INCOME					
Dues	3,299,300	3,541,600	242,300	Unfavorable	3,503,800
All Other	1,440,200	1,535,600	95,400	Unfavorable	1,555,700
TOTAL	**4,739,500**	**5,077,200**	**337,700**	Unfavorable	5,059,500
EXPENSES					
Payroll	2,107,600	2,110,500	2,900	Favorable	2,125,100
All Other	2,823,700	2,964,000	140,300	Favorable	3,146,800
TOTAL	**4,931,300**	**5,074,500**	**143,200**	Favorable	5,271,900
NET	**-191,800**	**2,700**	**-194,500**	Unfavorable Rounded	-212,400

WHY THIS EXHIBIT IS IMPORTANT TO INCLUDE IN AN EXECUTIVE SUMMARY:
The two areas that most significantly impact the overall NET bottom-line operating results are DUES INCOME and PAYROLL EXPENSE.

So — create an exhibit like this that makes it easy for board members to quickly see what is going on in these two critical areas.

Typically there is a line item for Dues, but payroll is oftentimes found spread throughout the Operating Statement by department and NOT shown as a single cumulative number.

This simple exhibit give the BOD's a quick and easy picture to digest.

Also include the prior year actual YDT results to give the BOD's some perspective.

NEXT: Having now seen this, the BOD's will want to know how the lump sum payroll numbers breakout by department. So – we give it to them in the next exhibit.

YTD BASE PAYROLL

DEPT.	FY 10 Actual	FY 10 Budget	Variance	FY 09 Actual	FY 08 Actual
F & B	540,000	553,300	-13,300	555,000	587,100
Grnds. Maint	517,400	497,300	20,100	497,700	492,600
Admin.	325,100	327,800	-2,700	326,600	307,300
Golf	299,200	280,200	19,000	293,300	292,700
Cottages	100,500	103,100	-2,600	102,300	104,100
Lockers	87,600	97,600	-10,000	97,800	100,000
R & M	81,600	92,400	-10,800	91,900	87,800
Hskpg.	73,300	78,200	-4,900	79,900	73,000
Fitness	82,900	80,600	2,300	80,600	67,800
TOTAL	**2,107,600**	**2,110,500**	**-2,900**	**2,125,100**	**2,112,400**

NOW THE BOD MAY WANT TO DIVE INTO DUES IN GREATER DETAIL:

Note how the numbers tie-in to those in the previous exhibit.

Yes — the departmental payroll numbers are shown throughout the pages of a typical operating statement. However, this exhibit makes it unnecessary to flip through pages to get this information.

Again — we've created an exhibit that gives the BOD a convenient picture that is quick and easy to digest.

Note that, again, prior YTD results are given for the BOD perspective.

THE NEXT EXHIBIT: *The most important single page in the entire Executive Summary. We are going to create a NET DEPARTMENTAL CLUB OPERATIONS snapshot.*

A typical summary page of an operating statement will list all sources of REVENUE at the top, followed by all sources of EXPENSE at the bottom. The BOD then has to mentally do the math by looking at a department revenue and then subtracting the expenses at the bottom to get the NET of each department. Or, they can flip through pages where each department is broken down. It needs to be much easier! Take note of the column that uses the words "Unfavorable" and "Favorable." This single page eliminates having to flip through page after page. Make it easy for the BOD to quickly see the info they really want.

	Actual	Budget	Variance		2009
GOLF					
Operations	-216,500	-186,400	-30,100	Unfavorable	-220,700
Course Maintenance	-1,014,100	-1,025,600	11,500	Favorable	-1,068,100
Golf Shop	-13,900	3,800	-17,700	Unfavorable	-1,200
Tournaments	0	0	0	n a	0
NET GOLF	**-1,244,500**	**-1,208,200**	**-36,300**	**Unfavorable**	**-1,290,000**
FOOD & BEVERAGE					
Dining Room	-357,100	-375,900	18,800	Favorable	-377,700
Halfway House	-10,500	-15,100	4,600	Favorable	-13,000
NET F&B	**-367,600**	**-391,000**	**23,400**	**Favorable**	**-390,700**
OTHER					
Cottages	-25,600	-19,300	-6,300	Unfavorable	-4,900
Locker Rooms	-82,800	-100,000	17,200	Favorable	-98,100
Tennis Courts	-42,400	-43,900	1,500	Favorable	-45,400
Fitness Center	-108,000	-92,500	-15,500	Unfavorable	-107,100
Adm. & Gen.	-662,500	-643,200	-19,300	Unfavorable	-688,600
Housekeeping	-123,400	-134,800	11,400	Favorable	-147,700
Entertainment	-90,500	-126,400	35,900	Favorable	-132,000
Grounds Maint.	-144,900	-145,200	300	Favorable	-157,800
R & M	-199,800	-215,800	16,000	Favorable	-220,400
Utilities	-174,200	-196,000	21,800	Favorable	-189,900
NET OTHER	**-1,654,100**	**-1,717,100**	**63,000**	**Favorable**	**-1,791,900**
FIXED					
Property Taxes	-155,600	-153,100	-2,500	Unfavorable	-159,400
Liability Insurance	-80,700	-78,900	-1,800	Unfavorable	-80,800
TOTAL FIXED	**-236,300**	**-232,000**	**-4,300**	**Unfavorable**	**-240,200**
NET OPERATING	**-3,502,500**	**-3,548,300**	**45,800**	**Favorable**	**-3,712,800**
INCOME					
Member Dues	3,299,300	3,541,600	-242,300	Unfavorable	3,503,800
Mail Box Rentals	6,300	7,100	-800	Unfavorable	7,300
Other	5,300	2,600	2,700	Favorable	5,700
TOTAL	**3,310,900**	**3,551,300**	**-240,400**	**Unfavorable**	**3,516,800**
NET	**-191,600**	**3,000**	**-194,600**	**Unfavorable**	**-196,000**

*NOW THE BOD MAY WANT TO DIVE INTO DUES
IN GREATER DETAIL:*

Note how the numbers tie-in to those in the very first exhibit.

Here we break down Dues Income by membership class.

A column using the words UNFAVORABLE and FAVORABLE is recommended.

NEXT: Since Dues Income is generated by the number of members in each class, we then create an exhibit that captures this data.

YTD DUES INCOME

CLASS	ACTUAL	BUDGET	VARIANCE	
Regular	2,627,700	2,800,800	173,100	*Unfavorable*
Associate	10,100	20,300	10,200	*Unfavorable*
Exec. & Jr.	148,000	195,300	47,300	*Unfavorable*
Social	494,300	501,600	7,300	*Unfavorable*
Social Exec.	15,400	20,500	5,100	*Unfavorable*
International	3,800	3,000	-800	*Favorable*
TOTAL	**3,299,300**	**3,541,500**	**242,200**	*Unfavorable*

MEMBERSHIP COUNT BY CLASS

CLASS	CURRENT ACT	FY 2010 BUD	2009	2008
Regular	241	254	266	281
Associate	2	2	2	3
Legacy >60	3	4	2	1
Legacy <60	14	15	12	8
Exec. & Jr.	14	21	21	21
Social	53	58	69	69
Social Exec.	6	8	6	6
Social Prop.	43	41	35	30
International	5	4	4	4
TOTAL	**381**	**407**	**417**	**423**

IN THIS SPECIFIC EXAMPLE:
Just by skimming all prior exhibits, it becomes quickly apparent that bottom line NET operating concerns are primarily due to UNFAVORABLE DUES INCOME — not so much payroll or departmental operations.)

Note the use of the "Red Flag." It is recommended to use this visual image in any areas that the BOD should be made aware as to unfavorably impact the full 12-Mos. results.

It is important to identify YTD concerns. Plutonium Club Leaders don't stop there.

NEXT: The following exhibit breaks down the number of members in each class and resulting YTD dues income, but also projects a revised forecast for the full 12-Mos. results if nothing is done to correct the situation.

DUES INCOME PROJECTIONS FOR FY 2010

CURRENT FISCAL YEAR DUES INCOME

BUDGET / UPDATED FORECAST / PROJECTED VARIANCE

	FYE 7-31-10 Budget		FYE 7-31-10 Forecast		Variance	
	Mbrs.	Dues	Mbrs.	Dues	Mbrs.	Dues
Reg.	255	4,733,700	241	4,482,600	(14)	(251,000)
Leg. >60	4	74,400	3	55,800	(1)	(18,600)
Assoc.	2	34,800	1	17,400	(1)	(17,400)
Junior	1	9,300	1	9,300	0	0
Exec.	20	186,000	13	120,900	(7)	(65,100)
Leg. <60	15	139,500	14	130,200	(1)	(9,300)
Social	100	868,300	97	853,600	(3)	(14,700)
Soc. Exec.	8	35,200	5	22,000	(3)	(13,200)
International	4	5,200	5	6,500	1	1,300
TOTALS	409	6,086,400	380	5,698,300	(29)	(388,000)

THE FOLLOWING IS A LETTER SENT TO THE MEMBERSHIP EXPLAINING THE SITUATION DEPICTED IN THE ABOVE EXECUTIVE SUMMARY EXHIBIT. THIS ACTUAL EXHIBIT WAS ATTACHED TO THE LETTER IN ORDER FOR THE MEMBERS TO BETTER UNDERSTAND THE SITUATION.

CURRENT FY 2010
BOARD APPROVED DUES ADJUSTMENT

DATE: March 8, 2010
TO: All Members
FROM: Board of Directors and Management

THIS YEAR'S Dues Shortfall of $388,000:

As reported at our Annual Meeting on March 6, 2010, the current year's budget was prepared with the most accurate forecasts available. In anticipation of a minor decline in membership and a minimal number of new applications for membership, the dues income was estimated to be as described in the attached DUES INCOME PROJECTIONS FOR FY 2010.

The mid-season updated forecast reflects what has occurred with the Club's total membership. As described, the total membership is 29 less than planned in the budget process and the total dues income is now projected to be a shortfall of $388,000.

LAST YEAR'S Net Operating Surplus of $221,000:

After the dues shortfall adjustment for the previous fiscal year, dues income was $19,800 unfavorable to budget. However, overall club operations performed at a very favorable level allowing us to finish with a net $221,000 surplus. The dues adjustment shortfall for this year is partially offset by last year's operating surplus for a net shortfall for the current year of $167,000. ($388 - $221 = $167)

THIS YEAR'S Dues Shortfall Adjustment of Net $167,000:

In order to generate this amount, the Board of Directors has unanimously approved the recommendation of the Finance Committee resulting in the following adjustment to the 2009/2010 dues as follows:

Membership Class	3 Payments Ea: Apr / May / June
Regular, Legacy>60, Associate	$180
Executive, Junior, Legacy<60, Social	$ 90
Social Executive, International	$ 45

NEXT YEAR'S Budget Process:

The shortfall dues adjustment is only for the purpose of achieving parity each year with the dues budgeting process. As the budget is prepared for the ensuing year every effort will be made to anticipate as close to reality what will occur with the number and classes of membership the Club will sustain. It is extremely important that our membership recognize the importance of introducing friends and relatives to the opportunity for enjoyment with a membership in our club that we all enjoy so much.

On the expense side of the equation, Management remains diligent in continued efficient operations and will be coordinating with all Committee Chairmen to factor in their input.

Also factored into the equation is the continued level of quality services that our membership has come to appreciate and expect. Anticipated utilization of the Club's facilities is considered as well.

After receiving and reviewing all projections and recommendations, the Board of Directors will act upon an Operating and Capital budget for fiscal year 2010 / 2011 at either its upcoming April or May meeting. Once ultimately approved, the results will be promptly reported to the membership. *While there are always many potential variables, we remain fixed on never compromising the fact that our club will continue to serve its members and their guests as a high quality, full service country club.*

G. Washington
President

Michael Crandal
Gen. Mgr. / Chief Operating Officer

MISC. ODDS & ENDS

In no particular order of importance or priority.
- The new Golf **Course Maintenance Facility** is complete. An occupancy permit is the forthcoming. We anticipate this happening with a week or so. Once a firm occupancy date is established, we will identify a good date for a membership "Open House" to tour the new facility.
- A new **Kid's Spring Break Camp** was hoped to be introduced this April 2nd and 3rd. However, we were not able to pull every detail into place to the point where a truly "Highest Quality" stamp of approval could be awarded. But sufficient pre-planning has already been done so that this annual program will be launched next year and will include supervised programs involving Tennis, Golf, Art & Crafts, and games. The Fitness Center will coordinate all the activities. We plan to have this be an annual tradition offered to the membership w/o additional charges.

- A *safety handrail* has been added to steps leading to/from stage in Ballroom.
- *Two outsourced laborers on the golf course* have been added by Roger in order to better tend to the "little things" that help elevate the golfing experience at Thunderbird. This is working out great and Roger is pleased with the subtle improvements made.
- Access to The Bridge will be restricted during the busy Spring Break period while negotiations are still in process.

TIMELINE — FY '10-'11 OPERATING BUDGET

MARCH 12 — 7:30 AM - FINANCE COMMITTEE MEETING
Basic timeline was shared with committee.

MARCH 19 — 7:30 AM - BOARD MEETING
Timeline shared with Board and request for each Committee Chairman to share their input at any time as work continues.

MARCH 26 — 10:00 AM - FIRST PRELIMINARY ROUGH DRAFT
The GM/COO and Club Controller will meet. Controller will factor in as much hard input as possible regarding things like: Property Taxes … Insurance Rates … p/r tax rates … Employee Healthcare bump … etc. … etc.… Major Assumptions seen on next page will simply serve as a starting place until more input/information is received.

Informal interaction with President/Vice President, & Treasurer will be ongoing through the entirety of this timeline.)

APRIL 1 — PRESENTATION TO PRESIDENT/VICE PRESIDENT AND TREASURER
At this meeting we will present where we are to date … get their insights … directives … share ideas --- all in order to prepare for FINANCE COMMITTEE 4/12.

APRIL 6 — PRESENTATION TO EXECUTIVE COMMITTEE
At this meeting we will present where we are to date after getting input from the Officers a few days ago. Fine tune further in preparation for 4/12 FINANCE meeting.

APRIL 12 — PRESENTATION TO THE FINANCE COMMITTEE
At this meeting we will present what should be very near a final budget recommendation. From input at this meeting, contingent upon final blessings from the Finance Committee, we will then prepare a final recommendation to be presented to the Board. Exact date is tentative to Committee availability --- but will be very close to this date.)

APRIL 14 — PRESENTATION TO BOARD (Possible Approval.)
At this meeting a recommended Operating Budget will be formally presented to the Board for their consideration. The Board will opt to approve the
Operating Budget at this meeting … or, may request further refinement and
wait until the May meeting to act.

PRELIMINARY MAJOR ASSUMPTIONS

*All subject to modification as more information becomes available during
the budget process.*
To start with, use the following assumptions of membership levels:

An overall net loss of 8 members. From 381 to 373.

Reg.	241	= 230	(Net reduction of 11 after 2 Exec & 1 Jr. transfers.)
Assoc.	2	= 2	(Flat)
Leg. >60	3	= 3	(Flat)
Leg. <60	14	= 20	(Net gain of 6.)
Exec.	13	= 13	(Net flat after 2 transfers to Reg. & 2 new.)
Jr.	1	= 0	(Eliminated Class. 1 transfer to Reg.)
Social	53	= 50	(Net reduction of 3.)
Soc. Prop.	43	= 43	(Net flat after deaths & transfers from Regular.)
Soc. Exec.	6	= 6	(Flat)
Intrntnl.	5	= 6	(Gain of 1.)

The above preliminary assumptions have NOT yet been reviewed by the
Membership Committee. This is simply a starting place that will be potentially adjusted as we move forward.

- *To start with, leave unchanged individual Annual Dues* for each class
  of membership. After we move forward analyzing income & expenses, we will take a look at what general range dues levels must be set
  at various assumed number of members.
- *Assume payroll still frozen.* Assume zero pension contribution.
- *Factor in an assumption of F&B sales remaining flat*…and the COGS
  reduced in both food & beverage by 1% due to increased pricing.
  We can analyze this together to see what price points may be ac-
  ceptable and see where we land.
- *For budget purposes, assume employee healthcare expenses* are in-
  creased 10% after we negotiate new rates when current rates expire
- *For budget purposes, for the time being…leave all fees unchanged.*
  Afterwards, we will take a look to see if any adjustments are warranted.
- *Assume Cottage revenues remain flat.*
- *From there, we will obviously take a still harder look at Operating
  Income/Expenses* as well as learn a ballpark amount as to what our
  new Annual Dues would have to be in order to break even using

the above assumptions at the above suggested level of members in each class.

CLOSING:

This Executive Summary serves to bring you up-to-speed on events at the club and should enable us to hit the ground running at the upcoming board meeting. The agenda for the meetings is attached.

As always — should you have any questions or would appreciate any further details prior to the meeting, please let me know and we will follow up immediately.

Thank you for all your support and service to the club.

FOOD MINIMUMS — ALSO.

FINANCIAL SUCCESS
IT'S NOT A 'SHELL' GAME
BUT IF IT WERE, PLUTONIUM CLUB LEADERS KNOW HOW TO WIN!

INTRODUCTION

Ray Cronin and his Club Benchmarking team have brought more meaningful input into the business side of the private club industry than anyone in the past 10 years. Ray "pioneered" the importance of solid data and cut through the haze of club leadership focusing way too much on monthly operations rather than the balance sheet — where the viable future of a member-owned private club truly resides. Ray is a tremendous Plutonium Club Leader whose legacy is private clubs basing financial decisions upon verifiable factual data, rather than opinions or emotions. The ABC's of Plutonium Private Club Leadership would not be complete without him. www.clubbenchmarking.com

> A FINANCIAL "SHELL GAME" IS BEING PLAYED ACROSS THE CLUB INDUSTRY. FINANCE COMMITTEES, BOARDS AND MEMBERS ARE SEARCHING FOR FINANCIAL SUCCESS UNDER THE CLUB'S OPERATING INCOME STATEMENT "SHELL" — WHILE CLUB BENCHMARKING DATA PROVES SUSTAINABLE FINANCIAL SUCCESS IS FOUND UNDER THE BALANCE SHEET "SHELL."

FINANCIAL SUCCESS OVER TIME

The clubs embracing Best Financial Practices segregate the Operating Ledger from the Capital Ledger.

The Operating Ledger accounts for the operating revenue and expenses associated with operating the club – the obvious purpose of which (as passionately advocated throughout this book) is delivering *Plutonium* services and amenities to members.

The Plutonium experience is the magnet for attracting new members and retaining them, as well as the current members.

The Capital Ledger accounts for Capital Income and Capital Expenses – depreciation is a capital expense.

THE KEY IS TO REALIZE THAT CLUBS SET THE OPERATING LEDGER TO BREAK-EVEN. BY DEFINITION, A BREAK-EVEN OUTCOME IS NOT A FINANCIAL OUTCOME. THE OPERATING LEDGER WAS NEVER INTENDED TO, DOES NOT AND WILL NEVER PRODUCE THE MONEY TO DRIVE A CLUB FORWARD FINANCIALLY.

Members of the club "consume" the Operating Ledger enjoying the club every year – exactly as it is meant to be! And yet, finance committees, Boards and even members are constantly scrutinizing the Operating Ledger, looking to "cut costs and save money" or find inefficiencies, while neglecting the Balance Sheet which is directly related to Capital Income and Capital Investment.

It is Capital Income that provides the money to drive a club forward financially. Club Benchmarking data PROVES this.

To any Board or Finance committee members reading this — please rest assured the data proves that if you are aiming to improve your club's financial outcome, the focus must be on future capital needs and the resources to meet those needs.

Figure 1 below shows the Operating Margin across the industry in relation to Capital Income, both framed in relation to Operating Revenue.

The figure shows the Operating Ledger is a break-even proposition while the money to invest in the club is related to Capital Income.

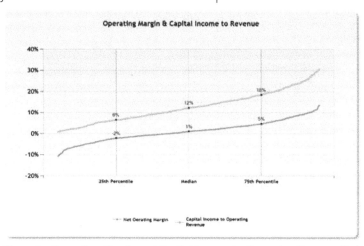

Figure 1 - Operating Margin and Capital Income to Operating Revenue Ratios

Our research shows nearly 75% of clubs are undercapitalized.

OUR DIRECT INVOLVEMENT WITH OVER 1,000 CLUBS OVER THE LAST TEN YEARS LEADS US TO CONCLUDE THAT MISPLACED FOCUS AND FINANCIAL DIALOGUE ARE THE CAUSE – IN OTHER WORDS, CLUBS ARE LOOKING UNDER THE WRONG SHELL. WE NEED TO FOCUS THE FINANCIAL DIALOGUE ON CAPITAL INCOME AND INVESTMENT – NOT THE OPERATING LEDGER.

We have benchmarked the Balance Sheets of more than 500 clubs, and in the process discovered four Balance Sheet Key Performance Indicators (KPIs) that accurately depict how well your club has fared financially over-time. These KPIs include:

1. Net Worth Over Time
2. Net-to-Gross Property, Plant & Equipment Ratio
3. Equity-to-Assets Ratio
4. Debt-to-Equity Ratio

It takes no more than 30 minutes to pull together the measurement of these metrics and compare them to the industry (as of October 2018). Let's take a look – you can do the calculations for your club as you follow along.

THE CLUB BALANCE SHEET

The Balance Sheet Benchmark will yield insight immediately. Figure 2 below shows the average club's Balance Sheet. The key insight is:

- *Equity is money contributed by the members over time*, mainly in the form of Capital generated through Initiation Fees, Capital Dues and Capital Assessments.
- *Liabilities is the money garnered from others* – most of which is bank debt.
- *The average club is 70% Equity, 30% Liabilities.*
- *On the other side of the Balance Sheet*, the criticality of Equity from Members becomes clear – 80% of the Assets end up as a single line item which is Net Book Value of Property, Plant & Equipment (PP&E). Net PP&E is the current book value of the physical asset base after accounting for all depreciation over time.
- *The key to understanding a club Balance Sheet* is simply this — members contribute equity to maintain, expand and keep relevant (meaning fresh and up to date) the physical plant of the club. In addition to member equity, clubs also rely on banks to help fund that capital.

Use the table below to benchmark your own club – fill in the blanks using

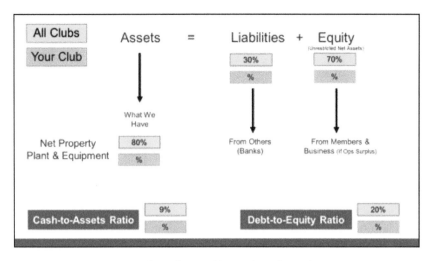

Figure 2 -Balance Sheet Benchmark

your own audited financial statements. It will take less than five minutes.

NET WORTH OVER TIME

We define Net Worth as the Equity section of your Balance Sheet, often termed Unrestricted Net Assets in a member-owned, not-for-profit club. It may also be termed Member's Equity or Shareholder's Equity. It is the club's "Net Worth or Book Value".

- Thirty-five percent (35%) of clubs are worth less in October 2018 than they were in December 2006.
- Considering inflation, fifty-percent (50%) are worth less in real terms in 2018 than they were in 2006.

Incredibly, half the industry is going backwards. Obviously, any business (whether for-profit and not-for-profit) must increase its net worth over time if is to be a going concern.

Measuring this KPI for your club is simple: take your audited financial statements since 2006 (so the picture includes timeframe prior to the economic meltdown) and chart the year-end Equity for each of the years. Calculate the Compounded Annual Growth Rate (CAGR) using excel formulas and compare them to the

> HOW DOES A CLUB INCREASE ITS NET WORTH? GIVEN CLUBS SET THE OPERATING LEDGER TO BREAK-EVEN EXCLUDING DEPRECIATION EXPENSE, THE ONLY WAY TO INCREASE NET WORTH IS FOR CAPITAL INCOME TO BE GREATER THAN DEPRE-CIATION EXPENSE. GROWTH OVER TIME IS A RESULT OF CAPITAL INCOME.

Capital Income > Deprec Expense

147

25th Percentile	Median	75th Percentile
(0.8%)	2.0%	4.9%
Clubs with negative CAGR are literally consuming themselves. They have decided to focus on cutting expenses instead of on the member experience. They have also cut or eliminated initiation fees.	Clubs with less than 2% CAGR are not keeping up with inflation. They are thus not generating adequate money to fund future capital replacements and improvements.	The upper quartile represents Capital Rich clubs able to generate the necessary capital to re-invest and re-invent consistently over time. They have the highest initiation fees and the highest member retention rates.

industry rates below.

Our research leads to the conclusion that financial sustainability requires minimum CAGR of Net Worth of 3.5%. Only 38% of clubs reach that threshold.

THE MINIMUM OF 3.5% GROWTH IS NECESSARY FOR THE FOLLOWING THREE REASONS:

1. *Depreciation is a backward-looking expense* reflecting what assets cost to procure in the past, not what they will cost to replace in the future.
2. *Every club has assets in use that are fully depreciated* and will eventually need to be replaced, thus the depreciation expense does not capture or reflect the needs of the entire asset base. The only way to properly reflect future capital needs is to commission a third party, objective and professional Capital Reserve Study.
3. *Our research shows that clubs have significant (in the 20% range) inaccuracies in their fixed asset schedules in relation to the actual assets in use.* Another indicator that depreciation does not reflect accurately is the full inventory of assets in use.

Net Worth decreasing over time manifests on the assets side of the Balance Sheet as declining value of PP&E which means physical assets are showing wear-and-tear and are not fresh and up-to-date.

IF YOU ARE A BOARD OR FINANCE COMMITTEE MEMBER AND YOU HAVE DETERMINED YOUR CLUB'S NET WORTH IS DECREASING OVER TIME, YOU ARE LIKELY IN A CLUB OVERLY FOCUSED ON THE OPERATING LEDGER AND MISSING THE CRITICAL NEED FOR CAPITAL INCOME AND INVESTMENT. IT IS A VERY SIMPLE METRIC TO PROVE, WHICH WE ADDRESS BELOW.

NET TO GROSS PP&E RATIO

All audited financial statements have a paragraph in the notes section addressing PP&E. That section enumerates the Gross PP&E, the accumulated depreciation and the resulting Net PP&E.

A very simple and eye-opening metric is the Ratio of Net-to-Gross PP&E. How depreciated (read as worn, depleted) the asset base is will be reflected in this ratio.

Figure 3 below presents the Net-to-Gross PP&E Ratio for more than 500 clubs. The median is 46% which means the club at the median has an asset base a bit more than halfway through its book life. Our analysis indicates a ratio of 60% or higher is ideal.

This ratio is very simple to understand and embrace. Clubs with a lower ratio have assets that are worn and depleted. Clubs at or above 60% have assets that are fresher and up to date, aka more relevant.

Calculate your club's ratio and place it on the chart below.

If your club turns up below the median, you have work to do. That work should begin with enlisting a third party to complete an objective, profes-sional assessment of the assets via a Capital Reserve Study (CRS).

THE CRS (ONE OF THE PLUTONIUM PRIVATE CLUB LEADER'S ABC'S!) IS THE CORE DATA AT THE HEART OF ANY CLUB'S FINANCIAL FUTURE. WITHOUT AN UP-TO-DATE STUDY (NO MORE THAN FIVE YEARS OLD) IT IS IMPOSSIBLE TO PROPERLY PLAN FOR THE FINANCIAL FUTURE.

The time currently spent focusing on the operating ledger searching for financial success with no answer in sight needs to be turned toward pro-jecting your club's future capital needs and assuring you have the capital resources to meet those needs.

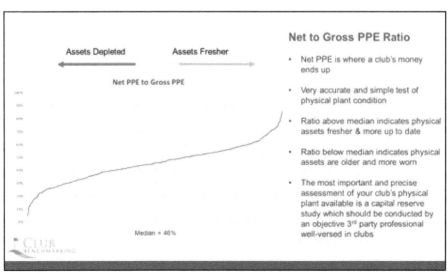

Figure 3 — Net to Gross PP&E Ratio

EQUITY TO ASSETS AND DEBT TO EQUITY RATIOS

Money generated from either member equity infusions or bank debt inevitably ends up in the club's PP&E. The Equity-to-Assets Ratio indicates how much of your physical plant has been paid for through debt as opposed to member equity. Debt is just a bridge in time which eventually must be repaid through members' infusion of equity. Interest on debt is the tax paid on insufficient member equity. *The average club is 70% Equity and 30% Liabilities with a Debt-to-Equity Ratio of 20%.*

In the end, a healthy, financially sustainable club requires member equity. *There is no way to generate meaningful equity other than from members contributing via Initiation Fees, Capital Dues or Capital Assessments.* Calculate your own club's position using your last audited balance sheet and insert your ratios on the balance sheet benchmark in Figure 2. That will clearly communicate how your club has been doing in terms of increasing the member investment in the club.

ALL RATIOS TAKEN TOGETHER

Certain patterns have emerged in our benchmark of 500 clubs and they are summarized below.

Determine where your club fits from the calculations you have completed during your study of this section and consider the proposed corrective action. Turning the tide in a club going in the wrong direction or continuing positive momentum in successful clubs both require the same action – Member contribution to capital over time.

That is the secret to the shell game: Focus on Capital Income and on investing that capital to keep your club relevant, fresh and up to date.

Net Worth Negative or Less than 2% CAGR

If your Net Worth is flat/declining or growing at less than 2% and you have a relatively low Net-to-Gross PP&E ratio, you have an urgent situation to confront.

The sooner the club embraces the need for increased Capital Income, the sooner the ship will be righted.

Clubs in this situation are likely suffering from an inability to recruit new members and also likely suffering from stagnating or declining initiation fee.

If the Net Worth issue is complemented by a relatively healthy Net-to-Gross PP&E ratio, your club has funded investment with debt which eventually needs to be repaid by members contributing equity.

It is critical the clubs in this category have a Capital Reserve Study done and begin to plan forward. Time is of the essence and increasing Net Worth is the only answer.

Net Worth between 2% and 3.5% CAGR

Your club likely needs more Capital Income from your members. The suggested form is recurring Capital Dues.

Assure you have an up to date Capital Reserve Study and develop a long-term (10 year) Capital Plan to meet deferred capital needs.

Net Worth Increasing at over 3.5% CAGR

Clubs in this category should have Net-to-Gross PP&E ratio above 50%. If it isn't, and your Cash-to-Assets Ratio is more than 10%, you are hoarding cash that should be invested to drive your club forward.

Assure you have an up to date Capital Reserve Study and develop a long-term (10 year) Capital Plan to assure your health continues.

SUMMARY

Sustainable financial success is rooted in Capital Income and Investment and manifests itself in certain Balance Sheet KPIs which are easily calculated:

- Net Worth Over Time
- Net-to-Gross PP&E Ratio
- Equity-to-Assets Ratio
- Debt-to-Equity Ratio

Taken in context with the presentation of other club benchmarks, these KPIs will provide strategic context for your club's outcome through today.

The Operating Ledger (set to break-even at over 80% of clubs excluding depreciation expense) is not the financial driver of a club. It is the vehicle for delivering the club experience members enjoy.

Scrutinizing it for financial outcomes is looking for success in the wrong place. Search for financial success and sustainability by planning your club's capital future.

Play the shell game to win!

> *Thank you, Ray for your continued PLUTONIUM PRIVATE CLUB LEADERSHIP and the significant positive legacy that the industry will continue to benefit from in the years ahead.*

FITNESS AND WELLNESS
THE ENTIRE CLUB BENEFITS

Mark Bado, MCM, CCE (General Manager at Myers Park Country Club) is undoubtedly amongst the most respected leaders in the industry. He's taken every club he has served to that "next level." Mark graciously offers his Plutonium Leadership insights on the significant ramifications of a vibrant Fitness and Wellness program.

From general managers to spa and fitness directors, from club members to club financials, all aspects of the private club structure can enjoy and capitalize on the benefits from the marketing and development of a Fitness and Wellness center.

As private clubs continue to evolve and attempt to attract an increasingly selective "buyer", country clubs are no longer viewed as "Dad's Golf Club" – a place where Dad could go, play a round of golf with the boys, go and have drinks, and then, six hours later, meet up with the wives for dinner. That concept is a relic of the past.

In order to remain fiscally viable, clubs now need to offer a broader range of services and amenities that cater to the entire family. They are looking for a club that offers well-rounded programming that can satisfy their recreational, entertainment, and dining needs.

As golf rounds played per year level off, and tennis and pool operations remain homeostatic, wellness centers are the new frontier – a blue sky – available to be molded and shaped by those innovative clubs who want to offer new, relevant services to their membership to continue to grow their census and their bottom lines.

As members' lifestyles, incomes and priorities change, so too must the club that services them. To offer the maximum amenities and touch points to its membership, clubs must evolve, and that evolution includes the creation, operation, and marketing of a wellness center within the confines of the club.

While many clubs have balked at the idea of expanding this "non-revenue" department, those who have ventured into the wellness program arena have been rewarded with higher member satisfaction, increased repeat visits, increased awareness of club events and programs, and higher member usage in the other areas of the club operations, specifically dining.

> THE MORE WELCOME AND SATISFIED A MEMBER FEELS WITH THE SERVICES BEING OFFERED AT THEIR CLUB, THE MORE LIKELY THEY ARE TO CONTINUE TO USE THEIR CLUB, TO FEEL COMFORTABLE WITH PAYING THEIR DUES IN PROPORTION TO THE BENEFITS THEY RECEIVE, AND THE BETTER WORD OF MOUTH THAT WILL BE CONVEYED TO POTENTIAL MEMBERS BY THE CLUB'S SATISFIED USER BASE.

The additional revenue in other areas of the club is a direct by-product of the members' desire to be at the club for the wellness programs.

Recent statistics indicate that more people in any given day will visit a club's wellness center than will be on the golf course. That fact alone indicates the growing need to make the wellness center a point of destination for the membership.

For the club, this also translates directly to the bottom line since after completing their spinning class, or their yoga session, or receiving their deep tissue massage and blood pressure check-up, they have the option of staying at the club — or sharing a meal or drink with a fellow member.

Every time a member walks through the entry to the club with each of these "moments of truth," it is an opportunity to introduce them to potentially new services and offerings at the club. By offering activities at the wellness center that encourage them to visit the club more often, the potential for increased revenue generation magnifies.

Ancillary benefits also arise from the inclusion of a wellness center in a private club's operations. These benefits include increased usage in the other departments of the club.

An additional benefit to clubs who include a wellness center among its operations is improved health of its staff. For example, at The Kansas City Country Club, various programs are offered to staff free of charge that will promote increased health awareness as well as provide pre-screenings for certain diseases and conditions. Among the wellness programs offered to all members of the Club's staff are blood pressure checks, skin cancer screenings, pulse and heart rate checks, flu shots, and nutritional and exercise clinics.

In the long run, these types of benefits make your staff more aware of their physical health, thereby creating a healthier workforce and decreased insurance premiums for the Club that directly impact the bottom line of the club's operations.

Besides the economic benefits to members who will receive "more bang for their buck" with the addition of a wellness center to the amenities offered by the club, there are also physical and mental benefits to be gained by taking advantage of the array of services offered through a wellness center.

Known as the "Elements of Wellness" and detailed by the Mayo Clinic in its 2013 report detailing the benefits of regular exercise, these benefits include:

- *Physical Well-Being:* regular exercise has been found to not only control weight but aid in the prevention of certain diseases including coronary, vascular, and mental diseases as well as certain cancers and arthritis.

- *Intellectual Growth:* physical activity has been noted to lead to the development of new nerve cells within the brain along with increased learning capacity and increased memory functions.

- *Social Interaction:* participating in group classes or wellness programs provides the membership with an additional chance to be with old friends and meet some new ones as everyone comes together to improve their bodies, their minds, and their spirits. Nothing makes a spin class or Pilates workout go faster or encourages you to work harder than sweating among friends.

- *Spiritual Fulfillment and Emotional Well-Being:* this benefit does not indicate a religious based experience per se; instead it speaks to the sense of self-fulfillment, pride, self-confidence and contentment within oneself that is derived from regular exercise. Yoga, meditation techniques, and tai chi are all examples of the type of classes offered through wellness centers that help heal the mind, body and spirit through increased relaxation, stress reduction, and inner peace.

When promoting a new wellness center to the membership, a club must emphasize not only the added value for their dollar that they will be receiving by availing themselves of this new facility, but also the personal benefits that everyone can receive by participating in a structured, supervised exercise program tailored by a well-educated, professionally trained staff that understands the physical, mental and nutritional needs of a diversified membership base.

Change is never easy but is almost always necessary in order to stay relevant, to continue to add real and perceived value, and to continue to challenge staff and members to reach their full potential and personal fulfillment.

> WHILE THE DECISIONS REGARDING SPACING, LOCATION, FEE STRUCTURE, STAFFING, AND EQUIPMENT MAY BE DIFFICULT AND TIME CONSUMING, ONE DECISION IS EASY – THE DECISION TO CREATE A WELLNESS CENTER TO MEET THE GROWING NEEDS AND DESIRES OF A CLUB'S MEMBERSHIP.

If private clubs hope to remain fiscally viable and continue to attract and retain members, they must continue to offer innovative programs and amenities including such options as wellness centers.

When clubs create a true wellness/fitness center, one that goes beyond the treadmill and stationary bike to offer programs and classes geared to a variety of ages and physical abilities, they will create a renewed vitality and interest in their club, making it the destination of choice for their members to meet all the needs of their bodies, minds, and spirits.

Thank you, Mark! Your passion for offering tremendous Fitness/Wellness programs is deeply respected and much appreciated. Thank you for your continued PLUTONIUM PRIVATE CLUB LEADERSHIP.

FITNESS AND WELLNESS
FIVE KEY COMPONENTS TO GREAT MEMBER EXPERIENCES

A highly qualified candidate for Director of Fitness and Wellness offered five components of great membership experiences. While every club needs to address their own unique needs, this is a good blueprint to reflect upon.

THE GOAL: A Fitness and Wellness center marked by growing engagement of the entire membership regardless of age or gender.

1. THE DIRECTOR:

 *Establishes a close relationship* with the golf, tennis, and aquatic professionals to implement fitness programs that encourage participation in these sports and enhances better play and injury prevention.

- *Carefully evaluate the balance* between outside contractors vs. employees.
- *Highly involved* with ALL new member orientation/tours.

 *Personally offer* a few "complimentary" classes each week to build participation. However – their primary focus must be directing the entire department towards success.

2. STAFF

- *Consistently* very professional, yet warmly personal.
- *ALL identified* with sharp, clean attire keeping with the look and vibe of the facility.
- *Consistently* very professional, yet warmly personal.
- *The entire team*: personal trainers, class instructors, front desk and housekeeping project positive energy at all times.
- *Knowledge* of the operation and available adjustments for each piece of exercise equipment.

3. CLASSES/PROGRAMING

- *Something for the entire family.* Strength. Balance. Cardiac. Flexibility. Nutrition. Weight.
- *Continued introduction* of new class formats such as "On the Ball," Hybrid Stretch, BARRE, combo classes, small group specialized six-week classes, yoga for men, yoga for golf, balance specific classes,

senior specific classes, disco dancing, etc.
- **Provide** wellness/fitness educational workshops and lectures.
- **Offer** off-campus wellness excursions such as kayak adventures, group hikes, and fun social-based activities.

4. FACILITIES/EQUIPMENT

- A long-term capital reserve/replacement plan keeping all equipment in top condition.
- **Flawless cleaning schedule** and a proactive preventive maintenance plan.
- **Carefully evaluate** the balance between leasing vs. purchase.

5. DON'T FORGET:

- Promote!
- Promote!
- Promote — via every media that the club has at its disposal!

FOOD & WINE
IN PRIVATE CLUBS RULES THE HOSPITALITY INDUSTRY IN TERMS OF QUALITY AND SERVICE

DATE: Today & Every Day Going Forward
TO: All Private Club Management, Staff, Board, Committees, and Members
FROM: Michael Crandal, CNG
RE: It does not get any better. You are the best of the best.

Any successful enterprise is simply a mirror image of the degree to which the owners and employees of that business consistently deliver what their customers want. Does that sound too simplistic?

If so, ask yourself, "What happens to any business endeavor that fails to consistently give customers what they want or — worse yet — tries to give them something they don't want at all?" The short answer is that they miss the target and become irrelevant in the marketplace.

It's all about the world of the consumers — who they are and what they want.

In the absence of a clear mission, hitting the bulls-eye is, at best, fraught with inconsistency. Knowing that inconsistency is akin to the end of the world — major corporations pay major dollars to consulting firms that specialize in doing nothing more than bringing specific focus to helping clients know who their customers really are, and what they want.

Interesting contrast —strikingly so — between the corporate world and the world of member-owned private membership clubs!

Private clubs already know — with crystal clear clarity — precisely who their members are and specifically what they want. However – in order to remain relevant to the lifestyles of potential younger members, Plutonium Leaders are PERPETUALLY open-minded as to what different expectations they may have, and adjust appropriately.

In the world of private clubs — let's tee-up a great news headline:

From The Consumer's Standpoint: Private clubs are at the top of the Food & Beverage Industry in terms of consistent QUALITY & SERVICE.

My background work and research gathered in (ultimately coming to the above conclusion) encompassed a myriad of components. Initially it appeared that the plethora of various interviews, case studies, personal comments from presidents of formidable clubs, and the professional insights from Executive Chefs, F&B Directors, Membership Directors, and GM/COOs was creating a broad-brush spattering of dots on the canvas before me. These dots ultimately connected into a very clear and compelling picture.

While there are many thumbnail sketches of the undeniable advantages private clubs enjoy over those in the public arena, the BIG PICTURE is this: *Private Clubs are outrageously successful in consistently delivering to those they serve exactly what they want.*

This BIG PICTURE presents big opportunities — for the entire club leadership team — to contribute towards the retention of existing members, ensuring member satisfaction, driving member growth, and being very relevant in the marketplace. Period.

Of all departmental operations at a private club, F&B provides the single greatest opportunity to touch the greatest number of members, and their guests, in personal ways that serve to enhance membership retention and encourage new member sponsorship.

Private clubs (simply by the nature of being private) are singularly focused on consistently delivering to their membership exactly what they want. Club members represent a truly "captive audience" who are themselves the greatest source of potential new members.

The on-going success of the entire operation is a mirror image of the unwavering focus of the entire club staff on member satisfaction.
The great news is that:

1. Private Clubs are at the top of the F&B Industry in terms of consistent quality & service.
2. Private Clubs are outrageously successful in consistently delivering to those they serve exactly what they want.

Now, it's time to get a bit more formal in substantiating the above headlines.

Reading further is not going to be so formal that "Black Tie is Optional"— but, what follows will indeed touch upon the major factors leading to the conclusion that Private Clubs do indeed have a tremendous "unfair" advantage in the marketplace.

I've gathered for you some meaningful quotes from club presidents —insightful comments from membership directors, consultants, executive chefs, and GM/COO's. We will also have a few final recommendations and will conclude with "Take Out Orders" — are you ready?

LET'S HAVE SOME FUN!

Can you imagine a business where the board of directors, shareholders, and customers were the exact same people? Imagine no further than a private club! In clubs we see:

1. THE FOCUS of the board of directors — *(Members!)* Make sure that the right policies are in place that reflect the current times and that the customers *(Members!)* are consistently satisfied
2. THE FOCUS of the customers — *(Members!)* Enjoying their club and expecting the elected volunteer board members to employ qualified professionals to deliver, within the established policies, the QUALITY and SERVICE that they *(Members!)* want. Pssssst: Members — they just wanna have fun!
3. THE FOCUS of the professional staff, board, and customers — *(Members!)* Make sure that the shareholders *(Members!)* consistently enjoy a great return on their investment of membership.

PUBLIC OFFERINGS UNDERSTANDABLY EXIST FOR ONE REASON — TO MAKE THE OWNERS MONEY.

THE CLUB EXISTS FOR ONE REASON — TO MAKE THE MEMBERS HAPPY.

This clarity of focus defines the difference between "benefit-oriented" pursuits within the world of private membership-owned clubs and the financially "profit-oriented" businesses world.

The shareholders (Members!) define "Return on Investment" in terms of membership satisfaction where profit accrues in the form of increased satisfaction and perceived higher quality — in both the products and services offered.

Shooting a shotgun randomly into the night sky just might hit something now and then. However, it is much more productive to use a high-powered rifle with a scope while focusing directly on a specific target.

Being focused on members whose names and individual requirements and expectations you have learned makes everyday decisions easy for those paying attention. It is also a lot more fun than dealing every day with come-and-go consumers who may in fact be nameless/faceless individuals, seen but once in any given lifetime.

> "IT COMES DOWN TO THE PERSONALIZATION THAT OCCURS AT THE BEST PRIVATE CLUBS. THE SERVER KNOWS THE NAMES OF EVERYONE IN THE FAMILY AND THEIR PREFERENCES. THE CHEF KNOWS THEIR FAVORITE ENTREES AND SPECIAL LIKES. BOTTOM LINE: PERSONALIZATION THROUGHOUT THE CLUB IS THE POINT OF DIFFERENTIATION."
> RICK COFFEY, VP GLOBAL CLUB PARTNERSHIPS MOBICOM COMMUNE PTE LTD

Everyday decisions are made regarding operations, policies, and capital improvement considerations while looking through the lens of how to consistently deliver to the members exactly what they want. Private club operations are highly personal and routinely present opportunities to favorably distinguish themselves from what can be found elsewhere.

Yup — private clubs are focused. Viva la difference!

Market Force Information is the largest mystery shopping and merchandising company in the world. They help their clients understand what is most important to consumers, and to identify what encourages them to return again and again and again.

They recently polled 6,100+ consumers on what their favorite restaurant brands are based on their best experiences. The research identified the difference between "OK" dining experiences and those that truly "delighted" them.

Their two top "findings" enabling corporate brands to effectively compete:

1. Know what matters most to your consumers.
2. Train your teams to consistently give the consumers what matters most to them.

They wrapped up their "findings" by noting that every research study they've done over the past several years in the F&B industry has consistently confirmed that the best way to ensure that consumers come back again and again is to delight them every time.

So it seems that in this most recent study, 6,100+ consumers confirmed, yet again, the very real advantages that private clubs have.

- *Club members definitely know what matters to them most.*
- *Club staffs definitely know what it is, and their job is to deliver it.*

And, oh yeah — about that "every time" concept — yes it does indeed encourage members to return again and again and again.

FiveStars is a nationally respected marketing firm that is retained by some of the most recognized brands in the hospitality industry. They released a "White Paper" directed at restaurateurs pinpointing top reasons their customers might be looking to going elsewhere. The following 10 weaknesses were amongst those highlighted:

1. You don't know who your customer is.
2. Your customer service is less than perfect.
3. You haven't walked in your customers' shoes.
4. You don't engage with your customers.
5. Your brand doesn't tell a story.
6. Your brand image is inconsistent.
7. Your wait times are inconsistent.
8. You haven't made good on a promise.
9. You are overly promotional.
10. You haven't given them a reason to return.

The same document then adds a push encouraging the creation of "Customer Loyalty Programs" to encourage repeat customers. The point is that customers need to be loyal to **THEM** in order to be encouraged to come again.

Ironically — private clubs flex their muscles in stark contrast to all of the above! In a private club — it is the club that is loyal to its members!

In fact, all decisions are made and the entire concept, organization, and staff exist for one reason: to provide quality and service to the members. Period.

Q: Doesn't this fact encourage loyal members?

A: Absolutely! And, consistently so. *But only as a byproduct of what private clubs are focused on: giving the membership exactly what it wants in terms of consistent quality and service.*

These factors identified by FiveStars that cause customers to go elsewhere are telling ones. Conversely, these same reasons may be what compel John Q. Public to consider joining a private club. And, once there — members are routinely given great reasons to return again and again and again and. Loyalty, quality, and service are just 3 that quickly come to mind.

BRANDING is all about consistency.

A casual stroll down a few grocery store aisles can be confusing when hoping to find a favorite brand. Every other product seems to boldly proclaim: "NEW-LITE-IMPROVED." Even if you do find what you thought was a favored brand, the packaging has changed.

It seems that the public marketplace is driven by whatever winds may be blowing out of the minds of marketing and advertising gurus on Madison Avenue.

- *Some* must think it is important to stay in step with the latest exit polls.
- *Others* seem to routinely alter who they are and what they do in response to their competition doing the same.
- *Others* just seem to change for the sake of change.

Many brands act like politicians in packaged attempts to appear trendy and cutting edge. They stick their finger in the air to check the direction of the prevailing wind, and then race to the front of the line with print, electronic, and sales pitches proclaiming themselves as leaders.

Private Clubs are all but the last bastion of organizations that strategically embrace change — while at the same time consistently approaching things with an unwavering long-range commitment not to compromise what they offer (Quality) and how they go about delivering it (Service). In essence, this defines who they are.

Club tradition, culture, and values are factored into every decision. You can't establish a track record if you are constantly shifting gears or trying new tactics on a whim.

Private clubs are somewhat "hard-wired" not to compromise what their membership expects in terms of quality and service — as it is they, themselves, who define these things. Yet at the very same time, as newer and younger generations are warmly welcomed as members — clubs evolve with the times and will always reflect the desires of the membership.

In the public world, there are great financial pressures to lower standards of quality to "acceptable" levels and to grade service levels on the curve when compared to the lowest benchmark down the street. As a result, even with a discount "Customer Loyalty" coupon in hand — there is a lingering sense of something lacking in the entire equation.

The term "brand" brings to mind well-recognized players such as Coca-Cola, Tiffany, Ferrari, Nike, and

> **PRIVATE FIRST CLASS**
>
> "WHILE THERE MAY BE DIFFERENT CLASSES OF MEMBERSHIP AT PRIVATE CLUBS — EVERY GREAT CLUB HAS ONLY ONE CLASS WHEN IT COMES TO CLUB OPERATIONS. FIRST CLASS. THAT DOESN'T MEAN THAT IF A CLUB THROWS A "WEENIE ROAST" IT HAS SOMEHOW LOWERED ITS STANDARDS. IT JUST MEANS THEY KNOW HOW TO THROW A FIRST CLASS WEENIE ROAST! EVERYTHING SHOULD BE PUT THROUGH THAT FILTER: "WE DO THINGS AROUND HERE FIRST CLASS, OR WE DON'T DO THEM AT ALL."
>
> **WALTER G. STERN,**
> **PAST PRESIDENT**
> **WESTWOOD COUNTRY CLUB**
> **ST. LOUIS, MO**

Disney. These brands immediately arouse expectations. Corporations work hard to raise the power and status of their brands and guard them carefully against unlicensed use or unfair imitation. In the public arena, advertising can help create or re-shape an image, but personal experiences confirm the reality behind the image and, as such, are the most powerful.

STYLE: Publicly traded corporations work very hard to create brand identities

QUALITY
SERVICE

163

FIRST-CLASS
OPERATIONS

that promise consistency in regard to their products, logos, company uni-forms, and (yes) quality and services.

- *BUT* — in the public world – quality and service are defined by those retained on Madison Avenue, exit polls, competition, and what is deemed "acceptable" when graded on a curve. All of the above changes, in a New York minute — given a chance of improving profit.

SUBSTANCE: Great private clubs work very hard to create a brand identity that delivers consistency in regard to EVERYTHING they do.

- *BUT* — in the world of private clubs — quality and service are defined by the members. Nothing is going to divert members' focus from the "profit" in the areas of personal enrichment, cultural growth, good health, making new friends, creating lasting memories, and enjoying their family. Simply put — your brand is your promise to your cus-tomers. (Members!) It tells them what they can expect from you. It differentiates you from whatever else is out there.

F&B IS CENTER STAGE

While every facet of a club has a direct impact on those members utilizing that particular department at any given time, Food & Beverage operations represent the only place where 100% of the membership is served. Not all members golf, play tennis, visit the spa, shoot skeet, go to yoga, swim, or attend club events. However, all members do indeed eat and drink.

All departments are "Mission Critical!" But it must be acknowledged that the F&B department is the most visible, utilized, and often most scrutinized area of the entire club. Turn this fact into your advantage. Look upon this as great news!

The entire leadership team must, at every appropriate opportunity, share the news of the club's great Food & Beverage program focusing on quality and service. This is the area where the greatest return on investment can be lever-aged toward: Increasing retention levels — Encouraging guests — Creating new member referrals.

Dining at the club is a personal experience.

- We are selective in our physical surroundings. Every form of life must ingest food in one form or another in order to maintain life. But we humans are the only form of life that somehow derives pleasure not only from the act of eating but also from the environment/ambience of where we decide to eat. Where better than a familiar clubhouse?

- We care about the people around us. Our enjoyment is further enhanced by surrounding ourselves with family, friends, and like-minded people to share the time with us. Where better than at the club?

- We like what we see. How our food is presented adds further enjoyment. The saying that people "eat with their eyes" is proven by the great appreciation we have for a culinary presentation that immediately makes us stop just to enjoy the visual stimulation before even taking a first bite. It matters not whether it is a full-blown holiday buffet, a classical dish, or simply a half sandwich and a cup of soup. Nobody does it better than the club's culinary team.

> **PRIORITY #1**
>
> "YOU CANNOT PRIORITIZE THE VARIOUS OPERATING DEPARTMENTS OF A PRIVATE CLUB. WHY? JUST ASK ANY MEMBER WHAT THE MOST IMPORTANT AREA OF THEIR CLUB MIGHT BE AT ANY GIVEN POINT IN TIME, AND THEY WILL BE HAPPY TO TELL YOU THAT IT IS THE ONE THAT THEY ARE EXPERIENCING AT THAT VERY MOMENT! EVERYTHING THAT HAPPENS AT ANY MOMENT AT THE CLUB IS PRIORITY #1 TO SOMEONE — AND EVERY ONE OF THEM MUST BE TREATED AS SUCH."
>
> **BUD GRAVETTE, PAST PRESIDENT THUNDERBIRD COUNTRY CLUB RANCHO MIRAGE, CA**

- We appreciate the manner and spirit in which we are served. Equally important to quality food preparation, plate presentation, and accompanying beverage of choice is the manner and spirit in which service delivers every component of an enjoyable meal to the table. We are not only aware of those around us, but we also care about those who serve us. Many of the club's loyal service staff have been there for years, and care deeply for the members.

THE FOOD

The Private Club Culinary Team: Professional and deeply talented.

It is no secret that many chain restaurants rely upon, to a very high degree, part-time "cooks" that are trained to prepare a few unchanging things from a very limited menu. Standard recipes are never deviated from, and there is no premium on individual creativity. And the corporate executive chef? Oh, s/he is back at corporate headquarters. Restaurants may be quite limited in what they do for their patrons.

Conversely, to consistently deliver quality and service to a diversified private club membership, great expertise is needed.

In order to seamlessly orchestrate diversified membership dining experiences all at the same time (casual, formal, private parties, and club events to rival the Four Seasons or the finest luxury cruise ships), a club demands a qualified executive chef with a sprinkling of aspiring chefs who have graduated from solid culinary schools.

Private clubs rely upon truly talented executive chefs who are not only exceptional talents, but are also very strong in developing talent and building great teams.

Club members are familiar with the very best restaurants in town and away from home. It is understandable that they would want their club to offer the same quality and depth of experiences they've had elsewhere. But, at the club it all takes place at the same time, under the same roof, often out of the same kitchen.

Having a truly great executive chef and culinary team with the professional ability to consistently provide quality and service is greatly appreciated and serves as a source of pride for members.

FOOD FADS — not the "bread & butter" of a club's menu.

Some restaurants seem to want to be the "first" to feature every new food fad. It is not unusual to be handed a "menu menagerie" of: Foams — Bacon Flavored Chocolate —Sriracha Sauce —Deep Fried Twinkies — Wild Boar Burgers — "Edible Wood" — Egg-White Chips — Chia — and Kale Ice Pops!

It seems there's always a new "it" food or presentation. But soon the fad fades, and the "flavor of the week" settles into obscurity.

A scoop of rocky road with your mud pie — literally! For those who really like to live on the cutting edge of culinary trends, "edible soil" is predicted to catch on in the United States! Yup. Soon you may be eating dirt! The renowned Japanese restaurant Ne Quittex Pas recently unveiled a $110 prefix soil-based menu, including dirt and potato soup, dirt risotto with sea bass and dirt ice-cream. According to Yoshihiro Narisawa, a chef from another respected Tokyo restaurant, soil is rich in umami (oh, so that explains it).

A PERSONAL NOTE: And to think, my mother would have grounded me (no pun intended) if I fed my little sister mud pies as a kid. Heck, I wasn't such a bad kid after all! Just a culinary genius, years ahead of my time!

Digesting new information — for real! Then there is Harney Sushi, a restaurant in San Diego.

Because more than half of Californian seafood is supposedly mislabeled, this restaurant has devised edible rice paper QR codes. By using their smart phones, diners can literally scan and pull up detailed information about the provenance of a fish while eating it. You can't make this stuff up.

Executive chefs of private clubs do not usually spend hours on the Internet googling the latest global food fads or blogs of local self-proclaimed food "experts." They are way too busy focusing on consistently preparing and creatively presenting exactly what their members enjoy ordering.

Q: Do private club chefs avoid new ideas in preparation and presentation?

A: Absolutely not! In fact, they make it their business to stay abreast of the new combinations of fresh ingredients and ideas to prepare and present innovative appetizers, salads, entrees, and desserts. Because club members enjoy having some variety on their menus, culinary teams delight in routinely offering variety in the form of menu specials that (contrary to just about everywhere else) truly are special.

The Future of Private Club Menus?

You never see the headline: "Psychic wins lottery!" However, it is safe to predict that club menus will reflect ongoing adjustments, additions, deletions, preparation methods, and presentation angles. You can also bet that there will be continued interest in healthy eating for all family members of all ages and gender (oops... you don't mean to say that your club is still featuring deep fried Hostess Twinkies?).

Private club culinary efforts are not aimlessly drifting along in an ocean of change, subject to whatever breeze happens to come along. Instead, private clubs chart their course through an ocean of change in this manner:

- *FOOD FADS* make a bit of a splash and then quickly settle as if they were never there.

- *FOOD TRENDS* can indeed slowly build into waves suggesting the sails be adjusted a bit.

> THE SERVICE: UNEQUIVOCALLY THE BEST IN THE HOSPITALITY INDUSTRY. THIS IS AN AREA WHERE PRIVATE CLUBS HAVE A DEVASTATINGLY UNFAIR ADVANTAGE!

- *FOOD QUALITY & SERVICE* consistently raise the tide and call out, "All hands on deck!"

Quality and service are not fads or trends. They are status quo at private clubs. Private club executive chefs are taking advantage of locally sourced products that work "farm to table." Buying local fruits, vegetables, meat, and poultry is far easier for local private clubs than for corporate restaurants. Sustainability for both food and beverages will be embraced. Healthful kid's meals/menus will continue to be regularly available. Clubs have always been way ahead of the public on this one and will continue to make sure food & snacks that are fresh, healthy, and appealing to kids are always available.

Without great detail, here are other things that private club executive chefs are enthused about offering: organic and natural ingredients, appetizers & entrees that lend themselves to Take-Home, increased fresh salad entrees with optional protein toppers, sous vide cooking, and flatbread with a great array of toppings.

Restaurants have some of the highest turnover rates of any business. This, coupled with the low requirements for entry level front of the house staff, creates a scenario not conducive to memorable dining experiences for guests — at least not consistently favorable ones.

Figuratively speaking, if one were to make a point of monthly visits to a cross-section of restaurants within a 10-mile radius of home, quality in staffing would vary wildly. As a result, John Q. Public stands an excellent chance of experiencing variable and ever-changing dining experiences at the same restaurants over the course of a year.

Private clubs are committed to maintaining a loyal professional staff. The professional service staff at almost all private clubs has a reliable core of employees who have been with the club for many years. They know the names, likes/dislikes, favorite drinks, etc., of the members. Private clubs attain consistency by retaining a reliable staff that is capable of developing appropriate personal/professional relationships with the membership.

They are scheduled full time, compensated well, and universally provided excellent employee benefits. Seldom are any of these true for those working in restaurants. Service at private clubs showcases the fact that there is more to serving food than merely putting it on a plate or in a bowl and placing it on a table. What brings an enjoyable meal to life is the manner and spirit in which it is done.

Staffing levels at private clubs are generally more adequate than restaurants simply because the staff takes pride in being ready to serve when the members desire to be served — instead of the Maitre d' deciding when the staff is ready to serve

THE PUBLIC F&B SERVICE INDUSTRY HAS A SCREW LOOSE

Patrons of "sit-down" restaurants usually take a quick look at what the menu offers and become comfortable in their seats a bit before the server arrives. When the server does arrive, what should be a solid 3-legged stool of the restaurant industry is now shaky, at best. One of the legs has a screw loose.

Yes, FOOD is still being offered. Yes, BEVERAGES as well. But it seems that **SERVICE** has all but universally been taken off the menu.

Just listen to what the "servers" have to say. As you do, hold on to your wobbly seats!

- *"HOW ARE Y'ALL GUYS DOIN'?"* Guys and Dolls was a great stage play that was selected as the 1951 Pulitzer Prize for Drama. But, referring to all guests dining as "guys" doesn't play well and wins no prizes for anything.

Perhaps the whole table should respond in unison: "Oh, a wise guy – eh? Nyuk — Nyuk — Nyuk!"

Family Guys — Bad Guys — Good Guys — Those Guys — These Guys — You Guys — may all be roaming the streets (and if I'm at the table, even a Certified Nice Guy). BUT — for crying out loud, no "guys "should be found at all in a dining situation. Just ladies and gentlemen. Please and thank you, very much!

- *"MY NAME IS ANASTASIA AND LIKE, I'M YOUR SERVER."* Brace yourself. You are about to hear a 60-second life-like story. Like, it goes like this: "I mean like, I am really not like a server. Like I am really like studying theatre at the community drama college and like I am just doin' this stuff to make like some money. Like I'm minoring in Philosophy, so like, if the actress stuff doesn't like sorta work out — I mean then like maybe then I can like explain it to my parents. But — anyway, like 'nuff about me. Like, how are all you guys doin'?"

- *"IS EVERYTHING ALL RIGHT HERE?"* This is made complete with a deer in the headlights stare that seems to be pleading, "Oh puullllleeeeeeaazzzze have just this one table be OK! Table #4 is upset. I forgot to take the wine to #6. And Anastasia is in the kitchen crying because she mixed up and the guy that wanted steak got salmon. And the doll with him got the guy's steak!"

- *"HOW IS EVERYTHING TASTING SO FAR?"* What kind of question is this? And, it is being asked by the same person who earlier took your order and then placed it before you. Steak tastes like steak. Salmon like salmon. And so on. Don't they know that? Evidently s/he has a short memory as s/he returns 5 minutes later to ask how it is tasting — and then quickly throws in the qualifier: "… so far." Could everything start tasting like something else in the next few moments?

Will s/he come back every 2 or 3 bites to re-check, "How is it tasting… now?"

- *"ARE YOU STILL WORKIN' ON THAT?"* Didn't their mother teach them not to point? Being asked if you are still workin' implies that they think you look like you should be retired. That is bad manners enough — but it gets even worse when accompanied by a pointing index finger hovering 6 inches above your plate. First, stop pointing. Second, guests are not "workin'"" on anything. They are there to en-joy a meal and conversation. Third, if anybody there is "workin'" — it is the staff not guests!
- *"I'LL TAKE THAT WHEN YOU ARE READY."* Really? No kidding? You didn't think you were going to get it before I was ready, did you? Thanks for letting us know, though — just in case there was any doubt on your part.

- *"WILL YOU BE NEEDING ANY CHANGE WITH THAT?"* The dinner bill for two is $68 and you lay a $100 on it. Then say (just to keep things on the up and up) — "I'm done workin'. You can take this now. I'm ready." Next, just for effect — point your index finger and hover it about 6 inches above the check presenter. And — it matters not the dollars involved — count on hearing, "Will you be needing any change with that?" Most of us have no hesitancy to leave an appropriate tip to acknowledge good service, but little desire helping to fund the server's second home in Sun Valley, or top off the gas tank in the Lamborghini parked out in the employee lot.

- *"NO PROBLEM."* These two words seem to universally be offered in response to any comment or request offered by any guest at any time for any reason. Servers these days in public restaurants don't have to have a big vocabulary or at least one that includes common phrases such as: You're welcome. My pleasure. Right away. Thank you. Go ahead right now in your mind. Just think at random any four or five comments or requests you might verbalize to your server during the course of a typical dining experience. I dare you to not smile as you realize that the universal response to any of them is now, "No problem."

THE END: This is all in good humor. But it's pretty hard to smile and wince at the same time.

THE TRUTH: None of this happens within the confines of private clubs. Not a bit of it. Ever.

HERE ARE SOME QUICK CONCEPTUAL IDEAS that ALL departments can use to "leverage" F&B creativity towards membership growth, usage, retention, & satisfaction.

The executive chef is truly the star of the show! It is s/he that personifies the culinary operation wherever members and guests may be found within the friendly confines of the entire club.

Something undeniably "special" happens when an executive chef makes an appearance in brilliant and crisp full whites! Nowadays many chef uniforms are sporting all kinds of "novelty" pants, shirts, and hats that offer colors, themes, and great eye-catching styles that are in great fashion. Go for it!
The culinary team can indeed stand the "heat" – BUT, from a "marketing" viewpoint — they need to get out of the kitchen and in front of the members as much as reasonably possible.

Consciously make an effort to seek out and proactively create appropriate opportunities to showcase the culinary team throughout the entire club.

Here are several ideas that have proved wildly successful in generating F&B excitement:

IN THE SPA/FITNESS CENTER? Just take an activity and "amp it up" a bit by featuring your executive chef and/or culinary team by occasionally having an action station, located front and center — where healthy mini-smoothies are prepared in sight from scratch. Perhaps offer 3 different ones and let members vote for their favorite. Share that the most popular will be offered as a complimentary "taste" with every lunch in the informal Grille next month.

AT THE TURN? Particularly during your annual member/guest events, delete the skirted table offering the same-old-same-old for the last quarter century. Get 'em out of the kitchen and into great coordinated uniforms complimented with color- coordinated pipe & drape and/or a small tent. Do something fun! Gazpacho soup from scratch? Chilled fresh fruit mini-balls carved in sight? Quick mini-tacos assembled on the fly? Hand-dipped mini gelato cones? Jumbo frozen strawberries hand-dipped in warm white chocolate and served on a stick?

HOT DAY ON THE COURSE OR COURTS? Order some special canary yellow chef's hats, and strategically place a few team members making and shaking fresh lemonade from scratch! Make a show of it!

EVEN HOTTER DAYS? Sure, routinely you offer bottled water. This time you prepare the night before by rolling moistened hand towels and storing them in the walk-in freezer. Take them out so the timing is perfect and then distribute them from a roving cart. Guess who is driving the cart? Let the chef tell them that it works like a charm in a 100+ degree kitchen — so s/he thought it would work today for the members as well!

EVEN IN THE LOCAL COMMUNITY? Concepts like: Farm to Table – Sustainable – Locally Grown – Fresh – are becoming increasingly desired and, yes, marketable! So *get your culinary team not only out of the kitchen, but away from the club altogether and out into the community!*

Scout out local farmer's markets within a-30 minute drive and have your culinary team routinely frequent these outlets in search of great "finds" for the club! *And – oh, yes – make sure they are in their full kitchen uniforms with the club logo in plain sight!*

You will be AMAZED at the proud smiles from any of your club members and the excited spontaneous conversations started by non-members who are incredibly impressed by actually talking with the executive chef or culinary team members from your club. Trust me on this one!

Members will feel proud of their club and their guests will be very intrigued by the obvious F&B creativity and fun ideas you come up with. Local folks who have never been to the club will start talking to their friends about how they talked to the executive chef of an exclusive club.

The intent here is not to offer a tiny list of old things that OTHER clubs have done. Instead — the major thrust is to inspire ALL Plutonium department leaders to be creative in coming up with NEW FUN IDEAS of your own that YOUR club can use to leverage the sphere of influence your F&B department has in membership growth, usage, retention, & satisfaction.

Are you wondering how to rally your team to come up with great ideas? Try this…

First - keep in mind that the answers on how to grow and improve anything are NOT found in file cabinets in H/R. Sure, all clubs need policy manuals, employee handbooks, new employee orientations, organizational charts, job descriptions, SOPs, performance reviews, bonus systems, mission statements, core values, etc.

BUT — *great ideas for enhancing membership growth, usage, retention, & satisfaction are inside the hearts and minds of creative people who are encouraged to take all of the available information and:*

- *Evaluate* where we are now.
- *Envision* where we want to be.
- *Think* about creative IDEAS, and ultimately…
- *Transfer* ideas into action!

Plutonium Private Club Leaders convey (in a very compelling manner) the reasons none of us should be overly content about "HERE" and light a fire in the minds and hearts of everyone to unceasingly think about creative ideas to propel us "THERE."

Knowing that it is impossible for people to be creative and defensive at the same time, Plutonium Leaders establish a culture in which everyone breathes the same air in a positive atmosphere of sharing thoughts and ideas.

THE RESULT?
Everyone is always THINKING about creative IDEAS to continually drive things toward being Easier — Healthier — Faster — Error Free — Worry Free — Understandable — Agreeable — Efficient — Organized — Professional — Personable — FUN! – FUN! – FUN!

The collective knowledge and experiences of an entire team, if not applied, are no better than an individual with a total lack of knowledge. What you don't know can hurt you. What you do know and don't apply hurts as well.

THE JOB OF A LEADER IS TO MAKE EVERYONE ELSE SUCCESSFUL.

A leader's success is measured in the ability to use knowledge and ability to motivate others to put their knowledge to work for the entire team in driving incredible membership experiences.

THERE ARE NO BUDGET RESTRAINTS! Thinking is even for the frugal, as it costs nothing. BUT —not thinking can get pretty pricey. It does not necessarily take money to make money. What it does take is ideas. And ideas only come from those who are thinking.

And, never forget that no team grows any bigger than the size of its ideas. IDEAS MAKE THE WORLD GO 'ROUND! As you begin to think about the things around the club, you will find that the ideas begin to come. Many situations that you thought were out of control will now have not one but several solutions that may put them very much in control.

GREAT NEWS TRAVELS FAST

"CLUBS CAN BE CREATIVE AND MEMBERS PLACE A HIGH PRIORITY ON A TOTAL CLUB EXPERIENCE FOR THE ENTIRE FAMILY. MEMORABLE MOMENTS...GREAT FOOD AND FUN...TRAVELS FAST WITH THE YOUNGER GENERATION BEING QUICK TO SHARE THEIR EXPERIENCES THROUGH SOCIAL MEDIA."

JANET COLLINS
SAWGRASS COUNTRY CLUB
PONTE VEDRA BEACH, FL

Do not be discouraged when told new ideas are impossible. This can be one of the first positive signs of a truly great idea. Really great ideas are impossible. That is what makes them such great ideas to start with. Flying was an impossible idea, but a great one. Handheld devices were impossible ideas once, too.

It is much better to come up with new ideas and to fail occasionally, than to think about nothing and succeed all the time.

Team productivity is similar to a computer in that if you change the input you automatically change the output. Don't react to the very real challenges your club faces with no more than "knee-jerk" responses. Develop you team with the ability and freedom to THINK — for from thinking comes new ideas. With these new ideas comes the need for further thinking.

Now then, don't simply read these thoughts and file them away for future reference. Instead: send this to your entire team — call a meeting — throw it in the middle of the table — and establish a culture where everyone breathes the same air in a positive atmosphere of sharing thoughts and ideas.

YOUR "TO GO" ORDERS:

Private clubs will surely face more changes in the years to come, and some are wholly unpredictable. However, Plutonium Club Leaders (YOU!) willfully determine that they are definitely NOT going to be routinely reacting to change, but instead being proactive in actually initiating positive change.
The future success of private clubs is 100% contingent upon the success of the people (members and employees) that lead it.

- *Successful leaders* are not people who do not need change in their lives.
- *Successful leaders* are people who both respond to and initiate positive change.

Some folks seem to be waiting for change to stop happening (good luck with that one). Here are some quick facts that Plutonium Leaders do not ignore.

- *During 2013:* 650,000 men quit golf, while almost 260,000 women took it up.
- *The majority of decisions* as to whether or not to join any private club is made by a female.
- *81% of decisions* of where to dine are heavily influenced by children.
- In all reputable F&B surveys: the word "casual" is one of the 4 most common requests.
- *In all reputable F&B surveys*: the words quality and service are always predominant.

While some of the "changes" have weakened the overall marketplace, many of them play right into the strengths of a private club. When looking change right in the eye we should not blink in leading with our strengths. This is particularly true when it comes to Food & Beverage!

1. Evaluate where you are now.
2. Envision where you want to be.
3. THINK about creative IDEAS, and ultimately...
4. Transfer your team's great ideas into an action plan!

SOMEONE ALWAYS THINKS THAT, "IF ONLY THE F&B STAFF HAD MORE TRAINING!" --- THAT UPSELLING DRINKS, APPETIZERS, AND DESSERTS WOULD CAPTURE REVENUE THAT THE CLUB IS MISSING!
(THUS - LOWERING DUES?) SOOO ... STAFF FOLLOWS ORDERS.
SOON - MEMBERS REVERT BACK TO JUST ASKING STAFF TO PROVIDE WARM AND CARING SERVICE AND NOT BE SELLING THINGS.

Get a plan and then get moving on that plan. You'll not only gain traction on the challenges of today, but also advantages over whatever new challenges the days ahead may bring.

It won't be easy because the task of being awesome is always harder than just being average.
However, it is also a great deal more fun!

Be mindful that *the primary reason given to join a club these days is to have fun. Lots of fun — with friends and the entire family creating lasting memories.* These things should be happening all the time at the club. Everywhere! People will "invest" themselves in belonging to a place like this!

Your Food & Beverage operation represents a means by which to communicate and extend Quality, Service and FUN throughout the entire club property.

FOOD & BEVERAGE OPERATIONS
SO EVEN AVERAGE JOE'S CAN UNDERSTAND IT

INCOME IS LIMITED

Private clubs have a limited membership with only so many dining opportunities (providing they are even in town).

Additionally, it is unrealistic to expect anyone to come to the same place night after night for dinner. Often when clubs successfully promote a particular day of the week, other days become slower.

With a plethora of public options — how many times will anyone eat at the same location during a given month?

Public restaurants specialize because it's unprofitable to be unfocused. Yet, private clubs attempt to be: ALL things, to ALL members, ALL the time.

Therefore, by default...unfocused and unprofitable.

However, if a club specialized in only one form of dining, then a large percentage of members would be alienated.

MULTIPLE OUTLETS MULTIPLY EXPENSES

To satisfy multiple member expectations, multiple outlets are offered. This built-in inefficiency requires: MORE staff, supervision. MORE perishable food inventory. MORE menus than the size of the user population justifies.

Rather than serving a total of 100 members from one menu, in one outlet — a Club serves:

- 12 in a formal environment.
- 26 with a themed buffet.
- 52 in a casual room.
- 10 more that dropped in asking "their" Chef to prepare something special just for them.

The same 100 guests are served — but at dramatically different costs.

FOOD & LABOR COSTS

It may appear that routine staffing demands at a public restaurant mirror those of a private club. Wrong.
In order to seamlessly orchestrate diversified membership dining experiences all at the same time (casual, formal, private parties and club events to rival the finest luxury cruise ships) — a club demands a qualified executive chef with a sprinkling of aspiring chefs who have graduated from solid culinary schools.

Successful public restaurants utilize p/t "cooks" that can prepare a few unchanging things from a limited menu. Standard recipes are never deviated from.

When the general public is looking for that exact experience, they know exactly where to go.

- Great Lasagna - An Italian restaurant
- Great Fish - A seafood restaurant
- Great Steak - A steakhouse
- Great Breakfast - A local cafe
- Bargain Price - A family buffet restaurant
- General Tso's Chicken - A Chinese restaurant

Why go to a BBQ rib joint for Veal Lemone? If looking for fresh seafood, who goes to a short-order café? No one craving a great steak drives through a fast food take out. Fine diners avoid buffets. Great breakfasts are not found at your favorite Chinese restaurant.

Yet – members visit public restaurants and expect to meet these expectations – and often expect their club to offer the same specialized experiences, all at the same time, under the same roof, out of the same kitchen. I dare you to tell me I am wrong!

STAFFING LEVELS — BY NECESSITY — "HIGH"

Restaurants have the highest turnover rate of any business.

This fact (and low expertise requirements) keep labor & benefit costs down. The "norm" for costs in these environments is vastly different from that of a quality private club.

Private clubs attain consistency by retaining a fulltime service staff for many years, that is capable of developing personal/professional appropriate relationships with the membership.

For consistency, public restaurants "train" ever changing service staff with memorized scripts and up-selling pitches.

But members understandably expect and deserve to be greeted by name, seated at "their" table, and brought their favorite drink with no mindless memorized script or up-selling.
Public restaurants seat you when the staff is ready to seat you — not when you are ready to be seated. This is why, even with reservations, you are told there will be a 20-minute wait, though there are empty tables within plain sight.

Public restaurant staffing is kept to a minimum for three reasons:

1. Less staff means less expense.
2. Guests are directed to the bar where profit margins are greater.
3. The staff likes this because the fewer servers there are the greater their cash tips.

Quality private clubs justify "overstaffing" so that members can be seated WHEN they want and to be served by WHO they want.

TYPICALLY - ONLY 'LEFT OVER' DOLLARS ARE CREDITEDTO THE CLUB ITSELF.

Members unwittingly think of the club itself LAST when it comes to allocating revenue from events.

Event pricing is always wanted to be kept low and is improperly established PRIOR to identifying what the expenses are ("we can't charge more than last year").

Typically, a committee has three meetings and has yet to seriously discuss how much the club should be compensated.

Meetings center on: **MORE** unique prizes — **MORE** attention getting invitations — **MORE** creative decorations — and how the band needs to play longer and have MORE musicians than in the past. **MORE! MORE! MORE!**

Then, after all these "**MORE**" arrangements — as an afterthought...

"Oh, the club will just have to figure it out. Our remaining budget has $12.95 for cocktails/hors d'oeuvres and a steak & lobster dinner." Inclusive – of course!

There is also a tendency to want various areas staffed at special club events (to greet at the front door — the registration table — arrange centerpieces — tour the course with complimentary iced tea ...) while assuming that the club can simply "make available" employees who aren't doing anything else — unlikely.

If there were nothing for them to do — they would not be scheduled. Nonetheless, F&B staff is added to the payroll with no offsetting income.

It is very easy to have events appear to be on budget — simply because the real costs are "buried" elsewhere in F&B.

UNPROFITABLE DAYS/HOURS OF OPERATIONS

Public establishments have firm closing times.

They also measure their drinks into thimbles rather than free pour into decent sized rocks glasses, but that's another bar story. Again – tell me I'm wrong.

Your club will stay open beyond the "usual" closing time if only one member is sitting in the lounge, or only one group wants to play cards.

"It's quarter to three. There's no one in the place 'cept you and me. So set 'em up Joe. I got a little story I think you ought to know. We're drinking my friend, to the end of a brief episode. So make it one for my baby. And one more for the road."

A public business opens its doors during days and hours that are profitable for the owners.

A private club opens its doors at any and all unprofitable times that are convenient for the members.

A club offers menus and days/hours of operation that, while making a great deal of sense in terms of attempting to be all things to all members, are appropriately deemed nonsensical by F&B professionals.

THE CHEF POINTS OUT THAT COGS WOULD BE DRAMATICALLY REDUCED IF THERE WERE NOT SO MANY MODIFIERS, SUBSTITUTIONS AND SPECIAL REQUESTS FOR UNPROFITABLE ITEMS. SOOOOO ... A WRITTEN DOCUMENT IS PREPARED AND HANDED TO EVERY MEMBER DINING AT THE CLUB. IT PROVES TO MEAN LITTLE.

CONSIDERATIONS

- Does the club need to be open almost every day for breakfast, lunch & dinner? Every month the Clubhouse is open? Really?
- Does the club need buffets for less than 50 guests?
- Should costs be "buried" in F&B rather than charged to club events?
- Does the club need to keep ala carte dining open during major club events?
- Do multiple rooms need to be staffed when a grille room is already available for service?

The answers to these and other questions depend solely upon the desires of the membership and unique culture that every club has the right to establish. There is no right or wrong answers. Just remember two things...

"Well, that's how it goes. And Joe I know you're gettin' anxious to close. So thanks for the cheer. I hope you didn't mind, my bending your ear. But this torch that I found, it's gotta be drowned.

Or it soon might explode. So make it one for my baby ... And one more for the road."

FOOD COST
OF GOODS SOLD

10 SPOTS TO KEEP IN MIND.

If you are like me, many times we just need to be reminded of things, rather than informed. In that spirit, here are some friendly reminders.

1) PRIOR TO ORDERING

- Are we getting the best possible price for the quality? Prove it.
- Have we truly analyzed the benefits of pre-cut steaks or butchering our own?

2) RECEIVING

- Do we confirm quality, quantity, and price? Really?
- Was everything we ordered actually delivered?
- Was everything delivered actually ordered by us?
- Do we physically weigh things? Are our scales accurate?

3) STORAGE

- Poor refrigeration/gaskets lead to spoilage.
- Uncovered or poorly ventilated food ends up in the trash.
- Is fish on crushed ice with excellent drainage?
- Does "par stock" mean something? Or, just a "That's the way we've always done it?"
- Does anyone know what's in the bottom of those chest freezers?

4) SECURITY

- Does the master key on the corner of the Chef's desk provide security?
- Who has access to keys after hours?
- Is the time clock located in our kitchen? Does every employee really need to be in the kitchen area?
- Are walk-in doors propped open during peak times?

5) DISTRIBUTION

- Does the kitchen get credit for food sent to the bar? i.e.: lemons, limes, oranges, olives, etc.?
- Why is the bar-back always running in and out of the walk-in?
- What are the service attendants doing in the produce box?

6) THE KITCHEN

- Do all entrees have standard recipes & portion sizes? Really?
- Are standard scoop sizes monitored in the pantry?
- Are gallons of coffee down the drain because the urns are full at closing time?
- Is our prime rib being slow-cooked?
- Are sheet pans of bacon thrown out?
- Creative uses of tenderloin "tails"?

7) OUTLETS

- What happens to excess: butter, cream, salad dressings, breads, desert cart items?
- Does every order represent a meal for guests? Or — for employees who don't care for the employee meal that day?

8) THE MENU

- Is our menu properly "engineered"?
- Is there a proper balance between popular and profitable items?
- Are the popular items priced appropriately?
- Do the number and complexity of items reflect the expertise of the Chef, staff, the size of the kitchen and equipment?
- Do daily "Specials" utilize the "odds & ends" already in inventory?
- When there are multiple banquets — as much as possible — are their menus coordinated to "streamline" inventory and preparation?
- Do servers know the most profitable items?
- Is our pricing (or inclusion) of coffee and "sides" appropriate?

9) ADMINISTRATIVE

- Are identical meals priced the same for ala carte vs. banquet? Should they be?
- Which department pays for soda tanks and where is revenue credited?
- Are employee meals accurately accounted for or is an arbitrary figure or percentage being used for tax purposes or habit?
- Do our employees routinely leave with "to go" bags?
- How is wine tracked from beverage to kitchen?
- Do we purchase "jug" wine for cooking, or does kitchen staff just ask the bartender for a bottle of Brunelli di Montalcino?
- Where is the cost of all those complimentary hors d'oeuvres reflected?

10) BILLING

- Are we paid for the products we serve? Every time? Really?
- Does our service staff have the authority to make adjustments? Are they documented?
- Can servers bypass the POS and place verbal or handwritten orders?
- Were those extra 300 shrimp added to the bill? Buffets can run low, and the host may appropriately ask for more. But – do we KNOW it was added to the bill?

A forgetful mind is a terrible thing to waste…or something like that.

GOLF IS FOR ALL GENDERS AND FAMILY.

GET BETTER NOW!
THROUGH THE EYES OF A MASTERFUL GOLF COURSE SUPERINTENDENT

INTRODUCTION

Dave Downing has served as a Golf Course Superintendent at private clubs, Director of Golf Course Operations for 72 hole facilities, Vice President of Golf Course Operations and Construction, Golf Course Consultant, Director of Golf and President of a golf course management company. He has prepared courses for 11 televised professional events and has successfully produced superior conditions in nearly every region of the USA. Dave is a past President of the GCSAA, served on local chapter boards and is a past President of the Carolinas Chapter of GCSAA. Beyond his impeccable professional stature, Dave is a man of strong Christian faith and values that leaves no stone unturned in being of service to others. We are fortunate to have Dave share his incredible *Get Better NOW!* way of looking at all we do that Plutonium Club Leaders will immediately embrace. dave.d@golfmsolutions.com

Get Better NOW!

I was interviewing for a job and was corresponding with the Sr. Director of Properties. In his email tag line was the phrase *Get Better NOW!* At first, I thought it was a phrase about improving your golf game. However, it finally dawned on me it was instead a more far-reaching philosophy of continuous improvement.

I bought in hook, line and sinker.

I was ultimately hired for the position and everything we did in our department was based on the Get Better NOW! philosophy. It was easy for me to buy in because, over the course of my career, this encompassed how I approached being a golf course superintendent, a manager, a leader, a husband, a parent and a Christian.

When I was going through the Penn State Turf Grass Management program our professors Duich, Watshcke and Waddington emphasized that they were only providing the very basics of being a good Golf Course Superintendent. Part of their teaching style and grading was to get you to either learn or admit you needed help. The way they accomplished this was ingenious.

When taking tests every incorrect answer would immediately deduct 10 points from the test results. But if we answered with, "I don't know", rather than taking a guess — it would only be a 5-point reduction.

> **THE FIRST LESSON LEARNED TO GET BETTER NOW! — WAS DO NOT BE AFRAID TO ASK QUESTIONS OR SEEK OUT HELP FROM MENTORS, OR PEERS.**

This scoring technique was used in the field as we toured the campus learning to identify grasses. So, we learned quickly to admit we did not know and ask for help in the identification. We were being taught not to be afraid of asking for help — even though we got a point reduction.

> **THE SECOND LESSON WAS TO WRITE UP AN AFTER-ACTION REPORT.**

I learned this while working for the PGA TOUR at the TPC of Connecticut in Cromwell, CT. Following my first Greater Hartford Open, my Director of Golf required each of the department heads to write up an After-Action Report. What he wanted us to do was identify the good things that happened as part of the lead-up and through the event, and memorize them to make sure we did the same things again in preparation.

He challenged us to look at each facet of the preparation and — even if it had gone well — ask if there¬ was any lesson learned that would have made more sense. He asked that we identify challenges we faced that were unexpected, and also what would we have done differently looking back on them. Finally, he asked us to identify where we made mistakes, what we learned, and again to identify what we would do to insure we did not do it in the future.

> **IT WAS INCREDIBLE MENTORING THAT ENABLED ME TO ADMIT I MESSED UP AND SHOW WHAT I LEARNED FROM THE SITUATION. WHILE THIS WAS A REQUIRED ACTIVITY, I HAVE CONTINUED DOING THE SAME TYPE OF ANALYSIS FOR THE ENTIRETY OF MY CAREER.**

To me the hard part is being able to admit that as I have looked back over an event, an aerification, an over-seeding or some other project — that I could have planned for it better, made better decisions during the execution, etc. Being able to be truthful about it and learning by looking back has been a huge help for me to **Get Better Now!**

There are a couple of phrases over my career that I have learned to love, and those I abhor. One of my favorites is, "If you don't have the time to do the job correctly, how will you find the time to do it again?" The simple statement embodies the full meaning of **Get Better Now!**

Do it right. It is the most efficient and effective way to get things done!

The ones that I really abhor are, "This is how we have always done it" and "If it ain't broke, don't fix it." These are the total opposite of Get Better Now!

We should **ALWAYS** be looking at each task and determining if we are doing it correctly, is there a way that will take less time, less effort, etc. Will it help our Club be successful? The first one about how it has always been done a certain way, has nothing to do with the result. I see it so often where the results are far from satisfactory. Yet, it becomes accepted because "We've always done it that way."

These leads me to this final part of **Get Better Now!**
In my 40+ years in the golf business, the people, the facilities, the manufacturers, distributors that have worked to improve, grow, learn, adapt and make any needed changes — these are the ones who always prove to be the most successful people and companies.

Fear of the "What If" can be very powerful in keeping each of us from being the leader we need to be. This is often because we have a fear of change.

I have told those that have worked for me, my kids and even recently my 7-year-old granddaughters, that the only constant in life is change. I have certainly seen in my time in the golf business the changes that have occurred.

As golf is in a state of change, what does that mean to private club leaders? Are we looking at everything we do with an attitude of **Get Better Now?** Do we know our current and prospective members and what it is that makes them choose to hold membership in high esteem?

Are our courses too hard? Are they too expensive to maintain?

Due to dedicated hard work and advanced technology, the private club industry has generally created outstanding conditions that many members now take for granted and anything less is difficult to back off from.

Q: So how can we continue to produce the product and be successful?

A: We must take on the **Get Better NOW!** approach towards every aspect of what we do and how we do it.

We must be willing to admit that the course may need to be altered to make it more player friendly. We may have to admit that we need help in taking a look at our operations and see if there are ways we can save time and labor, reduce inputs, yet still produce memorable membership experiences.

> PLUTONIUM LEADERS ARE OPEN TO LEARNING. THEY ARE OPEN TO CHANGE. THEY ARE WILLING TO ASK OTHERS FOR HELP. THEY ARE MENTORS IN HELPING OTHERS TO GET BETTER NOW!

> WHEN THE RECESSION HIT IN 2007/2008, WE AS A PROFESSION WERE LOUDLY PRAISED FOR DILIGENCE AND CREATIVITY IN DEALING WITH BUDGET CRUNCHES. BUT AS WE HAVE MOVED FORWARD AND AS WE ARE GAINING TRACTION, ARE WE STILL BEING AS CREATIVE?

Golf Course Superintendents tend to be introverted and just want to do their job. However, they play a vitally important role on a team that must run a successful business in order to be a sustainable enterprise.

As a consultant in nationwide demand, I see a large range of operations and I'm asked what opportunities for savings or improvements might be considered. Because of my experience I am often able to make suggestions about savings in terms of products, staffing, water usage, etc.

But often the recommendations are not fully followed through with. Why would that be?

In my view the reason is the fear of change. Fear overcomes the desire to **Get Better NOW!** We may have been hired to be **mere managers**. But, instead, we need to be **Plutonium Leaders** —proactively focused on doing all we can to make the business aspect of private club operations sustainable and member experiences memorable.

Over the past few years many great golf courses have closed. Many highly conditioned golf courses have closed. Reduced revenues, increasing costs, debt service, there are many reasons — but, we as Golf Course Superintendents need to be part of a leadership team that is making decisions every day that will help the club succeed.

For me, my career has been marked by the desire to improve, learn, get more bang for the buck, ask questions, seek help, look internally and externally to drive to an honest evaluation of how can we continually do better on the business aspects, as well as enhance member experiences.

I've been fortunate to work with people that were also looking to improve and grow, and were willing to challenge me to look at other options.

Plutonium Private Club Leaders inspire the entire team by letting them know that they are trusted enough to let them **Get Better Now!** Plutonium Leaders encourage and challenge the team to become more creative, to learn, to look at all aspects of club operations and be open and accepting of change.

If you can do this — I know you will create Plutonium Leadership teams that will help you and your club be successful.

Thank you, Dave! Your great insights and encouragement towards Get Better Now! is greatly appreciated and valued by all your fellow Plutonium Leaders.

GOLF
IS THE ANSWER

The question is:

"Can you think of any activity that people enjoy so much that it can border on an addiction --- is completely legal --- is based upon fair play and honesty --- encourages proper etiquette and consideration for all participants --- involves fresh air and beautiful surroundings --- that between periods of actual activity provides opportunity for interaction between participants --- that can be shared with another couple, or done all by yourself, or with others of the same gender, and even with your children --- that produces no carbon emissions --- AND YET --- IN SPITE OF ALL THIS --- The #1 complaint about this compelling activity is that whenever we do it, it takes us too long to get it over with?"

GOSSIP
NEEDS TO BE STOPPED DEAD IN ITS TRACKS

Even its' name hissssssses.

It TOPPLES — Governments. It WRECKS — Marriages. It RUINS — Careers. It DESTROYS — Reputations. It COMPROMISES — Friendships. It CAUSES — Heartaches, Nightmares & Indigestion. It SPAWNS – Suspicion. It GENERATES — Grief. It DISPATCHES — Innocent people to cry in their pillows.

It's called GOSSSSSSSIP.

Office GOSSSSSSSIP. Shop GOSSSSSSSIP. Locker Room GOSSSSSSSSIP. Club GOSSSSSSIPPPP.

It makes emotional headlines and causes mental headaches.

The Rotary Club has a very simple, yet marvelously effective approach to stopping gossip, rumors and innuendo dead in their tracks. It is called the 4-Way Test.

Before YOU repeat a story— or within your responsibility or sphere of influence even allow it to circulate at all — establish this type of "firewall" for the team.

"The Four-Way Test of the things we think, say or do"

1. Is it the TRUTH?
2. Is it FAIR to all concerned?
3. Will it build GOODWILL and BETTER FRIENDSHIPS?
4. Will it be BENEFICIAL to all concerned?

Profound in its simplicity, if the answer is not YES to every question — be wise, don't even go there.

Take heed from the advice given by the wisest man who ever lived: "A gossip goes around spreading rumors, while a trustworthy man tries to quiet them." Proverbs 11:13

GOVERNANCE ISSUES
PLUTONIUM CLUB LEADERS MAKE SURE POLICIES, BYLAWS AND DEFINED ROLES ARE IN PLACE TO DERAIL ROGUE "BIG" AGENDAS BEFORE IT IS TOO LATE

HOW DO SOME CLUBS DEAL WITH MAKING BIG DECISIONS?

PREFACE: OK…from the get-go — the two biggest decisions any private club has on their plate are in the laps of two committees:

1.   *THE NOMINATING COMMITTEE* – that identifies top caliber volunteer leadership.

2.   *THE SEARCH COMMITTEE* – that identifies top professional managerial talent.

•   Unwise decisions by either of these will trigger unfortunate "ripple effects" throughout the club that can linger for years. Conversely…excellent choices will establish a winning culture lasting perhaps decades.

Moving on — assuming both of the above are in good shape — occasionally a dissident "rogue" handful of members, or even a strong-willed departmental committee chair (that is hell-bent on pursuing a personal agenda or project) can slowly start beating the drums in attempts to cause the board to address what is suddenly deemed a necessary "BIG DECISION."

Let's talk a bit about how to put in place a process that all but precludes so-called "BIG DECISION" issues to somehow disrupt the entire membership, board and management. Let's get started.

When it comes to making "Big Decisions" at a private club — the first thing that each club needs to identify is what potential factors combine to even refer to a pending decision as a BIG one in the first place? In other words — a myriad of decisions are made on a daily basis in running any business. So, why are some decisions deemed bigger that others?

WHAT QUALIFIES AS A BIG DECISION?

There is no "Silver Bullet/One Size Fits All" answer to this question. Basically, there are going to be 3 firewalls to consider before arriving at the answer that best reflects each unique club. Here they are:

1) Club Culture: Every club has a major focus or overriding sense amongst the membership of "This is who we are." It is here where things like tradition, the mission statement and core values converge. And it varies wildly from club to club.

A club that has a very golf-centric focus, prides itself on low-handicappers, and a course designed by a renowned architect, may feel that ANY change to the course itself is a very BIG deal. So, no decisions are made without an overwhelming full vote of the membership. At clubs like this, even the removal of a single tree may be viewed as a BIG decision and take many months prior to any actual action taken.

A club that prides itself in being a home away from home, where the focus is definitely on having the entire family spending leisure hours at the club— here, a resort-type of pool with many features and extensive fitness facilities may be deemed as really BIG deals! Even making a change of Swim Meet dates can cause a major rift at the club.

More examples could be made, but you get the point. What is considered very important to one club is all but insignificant to another. Sure, every club wants theirs to be the best it can be, but every club has a slightly different slant/idea as to what that even means.

2) Club Governance Model: If the club has a strong tradition of the board having no direct role at all in club operations and giving full authority and responsibility to their GM/COO — then there are no decisions to be made at the board level. Other than the very biggest of all: hiring and holding the GM/COO fully accountable to the board for adhering to all approved club policies, and consistently providing exemplary member experiences within approved budgets. Other than that, the board has no decisions to make, at least regarding club operations.

However, when it comes to making policies or decisions relating to the expenditure of large funding for capital projects, there may indeed be some quite BIG decisions that need to be made. While management may make recommendations or provide the board with meaningful data to assist them in coming to a decision, these types of decisions are the responsibility of the board.

While we've briefly touched upon Club Culture and Governance considerations — we still don't have any real "handle" on what truly constitutes a BIG decision and how to go about making them.

So, just like in many issues in business and politics, let's "follow the money" and perhaps it can be here where a club can adapt a firm policy in identifying what a BIG decision may or may not be for them. By the way — I defy anyone to suggest that a private club is NOT a business oftentimes rife with internal politics.

The culture of a club (as well as governance) can perhaps be construed/spun by any particular group of members with an "agenda' to ramrod or railroad a particular project they hold dear. However, the numbers don't lie. So, let's see if we can set up a reliable 3rd firewall that is not up to negotiation or end-arounds.

3) Club Annual Gross Revenue: This amount includes the total dollars that the club generates from initiation fees, transfer fees, dues, operations and any other source of revenue.

If the club is smart, net club operations (including dues income) will be budgeted at a break-even. This obviously means that contributions to margin via gross profit of operations is zero.

NOTE: If a club budgets a significant surplus, the members would have every right to complain that their dues are too high! If a club budgets a significant deficit, the dues level is artificially low and what is truly being built into the budget is an operating deficit assessment to offset this shortfall. Bottom line — operations should, by design, break even.

Now then, if the above is true (and it is), and since day-to-day operation decisions are the responsibility of management — it only follows that the board should be spending the vast majority of its time focusing on decisions relating to those areas where potential significant net variances can result in the clubs overall financial viability and future.

Loosely speaking *(VERY loosely)* clubs fall into 5 different annual gross revenue groups:

1. <$4Million to <$9Million
2. $9Million to <$12Million
3. $12Million to <$16Million
4. $16Million to <20Million
5. $20Million +

To each of the above, adequate reserve funding for depreciation as well as for desired new capital projects would vary greatly. However, each needs to closely dissect and analyze their own unique current cash position, as well as the variable projections of cash flow over at least the next 5 years.

BIG decisions are those that impact the balance sheet. Thus, depending upon current cash position and future projections — *one of the greatest*

BIG decisions that can impact a balance sheet is debt. Any decision that does not include a viable plan to work towards systematically reducing or eliminating debt totally is a BIG decision. And a very bad one.

ACTIONABLE RECOMMENDATIONS

When it comes to making decisions at the board level, the following 7 considerations are relevant as you move forward:

1. View the culture of your club as a factor. And, yes…

2. Acknowledge that your club governance model is also a factor. But also, realize…

3. BIG decisions tend to have major impact to the balance sheet. That is where you find them!

4. Every club should look at their annual gross revenue, have your very best financial/numbers-minded members (small, focused, ad hoc committee) look at the big picture, make data-based projections, and identify either a set dollar amount or a set % of annual gross revenue that is not to be exceeded annually for any new project. This should ultimately be engrafted into the working of a proposed bylaw.

5. Have this small ad hoc committee make a special presentation and recommendation to the finance committee. The finance committee work closely with the executive committee in conveying the projections and recommendation of the ad hoc committee. If need be – go back to the original ad hoc committee for any necessary clarifications or tweaking.

6. After all this homework is complete, provide the full board with an 'Executive Summary' of what will be presented and why at the next meeting. Have prepared a formal recommendation of the exact wording of a new bylaw that makes sense for your own unique club and situation. In essence, this bylaw will convey what a "BIG" decision is, set monetary parameters, and cover the procedure the board must follow in making these decisions.

7.   Remember that club operations should not enter into the equation because, by design, this is net neutral — not a contributor to gross profit and nothing more than an amenity. Yes – a "Mission Critical" amenity. But, NOT a collection of profit centers at all.

In order to keep any wayward board, rogue committee or overzealous group of members from ramrodding increased debt or pirating reserves earmarked for funding depreciation so they can get a pet project underway — IT IS GOING TO REQUIRE A FIRM BYLAW THAT CLEARLY DRAWS THE LINE ON WHAT AUTHORITY THE BOARD HAS IN ULTIMATELY APPROVING WHAT IS DEEMED A BIG DECSION.

Also — for what is deemed a BIG decision, included in the new bylaw there may be a required 'super majority' approval vote of the board to be passed. Or, depending upon club culture/governance and exiting bylaws, it may have to be presented to the full membership via an annual meeting. In any regard, each club simply needs to figure it all out for what best reflects the overall health and viability of the club as a whole.

EVERY CLUB IS A UNIQUE "RUBIK'S CUBE" ALL TO ITSELF

Keep in mind, also, that your bylaws need to clearly convey that committees are empowered to make recommendations to the board…but, ultimate decision authority rests solely with the board operating within approved bylaws (no committee "end arounds" condoned).

My recommendation is that a healthy club always maintain in the neighborhood of 10% of their annual gross revenue as a cash reserve. This is NOT to be considered a 'slush fund' or cash to be used for discretionary allocations. NO! Instead, simply kept in reserve at all times.

Granted, all the above is NOT a specific recommendation simply because every club is different with various moving parts. And arriving at the exact wording of a meaningful bylaw may prove somewhat of a "Rubik's Cube" along the way. However, ultimately, every club should be able to land on what is best for them in answering the question of how BIG decisions should be made at their club.

HERE IS A SAMPLING FROM ACTUAL PRIVATE CLUB BYLAWS

The following is provided simply to show literal examples of how different clubs approach many of the aspects we've touched upon here. Some give the BOD greater authority, while others require a full vote of the member-ship. As you will see, different percentages are required for approval from one club to another. Many clubs limit the scope on what kinds of changes can be made at all.

Keep in mind that this is a random sampling with different levels of annual gross revenue. The purpose is simply to give you some ideas as to what might be the best adaptation for your own unique club. It's unlikely that you can simply use any of the exact wordings, but you can alter the details to what reflects your club culture, governance and balance sheet.

Here we go:

ALTERING COURSE DESIGN: Our golf course is a place of history, and its character should always reflect its 1896 and turn-of-the-century design and atmosphere. No modifications, alterations or changes to the existing golf course design or layout shall be made without approval by a seventy-five (75%) percent vote of the entire Board of Governors, nor shall any approved modification, alteration or change be made without incorporating the histor-ic appearance and design of a Midwest Donald Ross golf course.

LIMITATION ON INCURRING DEBT: The Board shall have no power, except as authorized by vote of the Regular Members of the Club, to make the Club liable for any debt or debts, other than for the ordinary/routine operating or maintenance capital expenses of the Club, in excess of a maximum of one million dollars ($1,000,000).

STANDING COMMITTEES have no authority to implement changes, but only to make recommendations to the Board of Governors which is then responsible for determining whether those recommendations are approved.

STANDING COMMITTEES shall act in an advisory capacity to the Board and be responsible for the execution of such programs and recommendations as are approved by the Board.

AD HOC COMMITTEES may be appointed by the President, with the ap-proval of the Board, for a specific and focused task of thoroughly looking at any issue and reporting back to the President their findings and subsequent recommendations. Ad Hoc Committees shall be dissolved upon completion of the assigned task.

DEBT/LOANS in excess of $100,000 during any fiscal year requires a 2/3 ma-jority vote by the members of the Club at a duly constituted meeting. For the purpose of this requirement, a lease of kitchen or golf course equipment for five (5) years of less shall not be considered debt. The Board has the authority to authorize a seasonal Line of Credit (Bridge Loan) for normal club operations (Cash Flow) provided the loan is utilized for no more than 120 days.

ASSESSMENTS for capital expenditures in excess of $100,000 within any year shall require two-thirds (2/3) favorable votes cast by the members responsible for paying the assessment. An assessment of less than $100,000 in the aggregate within any year, whereby the funds are to be used or set aside for capital expenditures, may be done at the discretion of the Board and shall not require member approval. This assessment shall be prorated equally among all members of the Club.

OPPERATING AND CAPITAL ASSESSMENTS: The Board of Directors has the authority to establish the monthly operating dues necessary to support the coming approved fiscal year budget. Any fiscal year shortfall is subject to an Operating Deficit Assessment not to exceed an amount equal to one month of the then current operating dues. The Board of Directors has the authority to approve such. Any proposed Capital Assessments greater than the current monthly regular capital dues, must have the approval of the majority of voting members of the entire club.

THE GENERAL MANAGER shall serve as the Chief Operating Officer of the Club. The GM/COO shall (1) manage the affairs and direct the operation of the Club subject to the direction of the President and the BOD's; (2) hire, supervise, evaluate and discharge all other Club employees; (3) prepare budgets of revenues, expenses and capital refurbishment and replacement for submission to the Finance Committee and for approval by the BOD's; (4) be authorized to incur expenses and capital expenditures in accordance with the approved budgets, or as directed by the BOD's; (5) direct the administrative affairs of the Club; (6) attend all meetings of the BOD's; (7) make reports of the affairs of the Club to the President, the BOD's, and Stockholders, as requested by the President or the BOD's; and (8) be a non-voting member of all Committees formed by the BOD's. The GM/COO shall assume such other responsibilities as maybe delegated by the President and shall report to the President on a day-to-day basis.

THE GENERAL MANAGER shall manage the affairs, and direct the work and employees, of the Club. The GM shall work with the Finance Committee to prepare annual operating and capital budgets for approval by the Board, and shall be authorized to incur expenses and capital expenditures in accordance with the approved budgets, or as directed by the Board. The GM shall be responsible for hiring and terminating employees of the Club.

GENERAL MANAGER'S
FIRST 90-DAY PLAN UPON ARRIVAL

When considering a career opportunity moving to a new club, it is good to have an overall Executive Plan of Action for your first 90 days on the job. In fact, oftentimes, a search committee may even ask potential candidates for something akin to this. (i.e.: "If you were our new GM/COO — what would be your approach to the first 90 days? What could we expect to see you doing?")

While being generic in approach, every GM/COO is fully capable of tweaking the below to specifically target the unique needs set before you when either considering a move or — what the heck — even if you have been at the same club for a number of years, why not take a fresh look and go through the same exercise to re-energize and focus on what really needs to be done where you are right now.

 Below is a "model" in 30-day increments that is broken into 3 distinct components:

1. Identifying the overall GOALS.
2. Stating what the RESULTS of achieving these Goals would be.
3. The ACTION PLAN that will enable the Goals and Results to be brought to life.

 Ready? Let's get started!

UPON ARRIVAL/FIRST 30 DAYS EXECUTIVE PLAN

GOAL

- *Become thoroughly familiar with the culture* and traditions of the club.
- *Plant seeds of genuine mutual trust and respect* with staff and membership.

RESULTS

- *Better prepare yourself to offer recommendations* that are specific to the club, rather than generic.
- *Better position yourself to later make management/leadership decisions* based upon who the club really is now and where they might want to go in the future.

ACTION PLAN

- *From day #1 – maintain a highly visible presence* throughout the entire footprint of the property.
- *Spend majority of your time personally meeting staff and membership* – where they are! NOT at your desk.
- *Focus first on ALL the people involved.* NOT so much on numbers, dollars, strategic plans, SOP's, etc. – all of that will follow.
- *The Action Plan "Mission Critical" priority* is to first establish relationships with members and staff.
- *Within first 30 days* – consider promoting once a week a very casual hour for members to meet and greet the new GM/COO over coffee in the "Whatever Room" – limit to 10 at a time. Perhaps joined by a board member.

ON-GOING/SECOND 30 DAYS

GOAL

- *Build upon the above* and move forward while diving deep into club operations.
- *Become thoroughly familiar* with existing club SOP's.
- *Become thoroughly familiar* with existing club business model.

RESULTS

- *A new GM* who will very soon become an informed and valuable "working partner" with the BOD's in offering meaningful constructive ideas and new perspectives toward both short and long-range goals.
- *A new GM fully prepared* to add polish to SOP's that serve the membership well --- and to introduce new procedures to further enhance member experiences.

ACTION PLAN

- *Spend time behind the scenes* with the CFO and club treasurer to fully grasp the complete financial condition of the business side of the club.
- *Become thoroughly familiar* with the club's strategic plan, bylaws, rules and policies as approved by the Board of Directors.
- *All budgets will be "tested"* to ensure that they are supported by appropriate back up. Every department's methods for producing each line item will be checked for accuracy and justification with all other areas of the operating and capital budget.

- *Provide visible leadership* to maintain employee morale and membership confidence during transitional time.

ON-GOING/THIRD 30 DAYS

Before moving forward, it must be acknowledged that all the above is NOT something that is accomplished and then set aside as if on a "To Do List" that is checked off and can then be forgotten before moving on to the next task. Hardly. Instead - these things are basically on-going and built upon daily. Not just in 30-day increments, but over many years…day after day…month after month…year after year.

GOAL

- *Keep the Strategic Plan alive and moving forward* (not something that sits in a 3-ring binder collecting dust in GM/COO's office).
- *Maintains club positioned as THE premier club* that consistently attracts quality new members.
- *Establish board-approved SOP's* based upon continuous improvement.
- *Retain top "best of the best"* department head talent/leadership throughout.

RESULTS

- *A GM who stridently supports the vision of the board* and keeps moving the ball down the field toward all strategic goals.
- *A membership that takes pride* in entertaining family, guests and business associates — often predictably leading to new-member sponsorship.
- *A staff that takes pride* in being part of something very special.
- *A board focused on a clear vision for the club* — approving relevant and timely policies, "tweaking" the Strategic Plan — and, NOT being overly concerned/involved in operations.

ACTION PLAN

- *Schedule meetings with the Strategic Planning Committee* to make sure everyone is fully invested in a vision for the club.
- *Work with Club President* to have once every quarter, at the top of the board meeting agenda, a 30-minute update on any/all things related to progress in moving the approved Strategic Plan forward.
- *Prepare meaningful KPI's* for board approval that will enable consistent measurement of management performance.

- *Prepare a meaningful bonus plan* for all key department heads that supports and encourages absolute excellence in professional performance centered clearly on membership satisfaction.

Nothing changes from where we started on day #1 – maintain a highly visible presence throughout the entire footprint of the property.

The above general outline can be of value to both those considering a career move, as well as those just looking to take a fresh look at how they might better their performance right where they are after even many years. Repeat as many times as need be.

TIME PASSES AND THE GOLF CHAIRMAN BECOMES PRESIDENT. HIS GOAL IS TO SHORTEN BOARD MEETINGS. SO, THURSDAY EVENINGS WITH DINNER TO FOLLOW IS OUT. INSTEAD EARLY SATURDAY BREAKFAST MEETINGS. IT SEEMS TO BE WORKING. SOMEONE ALWAYS MAKES AN EARLY MOTION TO ADJOURN.

HOSPITALITY INDEED EXTENDS TO THE TEE.

HARD WORK
THERE IS NO OTHER PATH LEADING TO PLUTONIUM CLUB LEADERSHIP

THE HARDER YOU WORK — THE LUCKIER YOU BECOME

My first management job was with a major hotel brand. My position was that of Restaurant Manager, and my responsibilities included the supervision of three very different and distinct F&B outlets in a nine-story hotel.

Approximately 60 employees were in my jurisdiction and I reported directly to the F&B Director of the hotel and indirectly to the property GM.

My normal workday was from 5:00 PM to approximately 1:00 AM.

I mention the number of employees and the size of the hotel only to emphasize that there was really a lot of work to do. Believe me, I had my hands full.

There were times when I knew that I was in over my head — however, by determination and hard work I was learning and succeeding at the same time.

But — even though I was doing well and working very hard at it, I knew that this was not enough. I sensed that if I were to develop only my restaurant management skills, but do nothing more rather than becoming one of the best restaurant managers at an early age, then as the years passed, I would become and remain an adequate restaurant manager at an older age.

I knew that I had to do more; I knew that I had to draw attention to myself.

In order to positively gain attention — and to expose myself to the opportunity of learning new and different skills — I made a point of coming to work at 2:00 or 3:00 rather than the expected 5:00 PM. I also made a point of being available around the hotel until 2:00 or 3:00 AM.

Don't think I'm NUTS! Let me explain, will ya?

I spent those extra hours on the job for a very specific reason.

During my normal shift, my time was completely taken up by those duties that directly related to my current position. I was, therefore, limiting my ability to expand and add depth to my hospitality industry areas of knowledge.

Gradually, as things would come up at various other departments in the hotel — many of them began to fall my direction. The word was out, "Hey – why don't you talk to Michael about that? After all, he is available and willing to help!"

By simply "marketing" my availability and the quality of my work, I was able to help out in other departments and learn new skills.

Soon, I was gathering knowledge about:

- How to manage the front desk of a hotel.
- How a centralized storeroom operates.
- How to use forecasting and trends in budgeting and scheduling.

In order to be upwardly marketable, you must have some set of skills or services that are ready for the market place.

> I WAS EXPOSED TO A GREAT DEAL OF USEFUL, MARKETABLE SKILLS THAT I WOULD NEVER HAVE HAD THE OPPORTUNITY TO LEARN HAD I BEEN CONTENT TO SIMPLY JUST REFER TO THE WRITTEN JOB DESCRIPTION THAT I HAD TO SIGN IN H/R AND TO DO ONLY THE JOB AS DESCRIBED (NO MATTER HOW WELL I MAY HAVE DONE THAT SINGLE JOB ALONE).

After skills and services have been accumulated to a high degree, you will find that the actual hours spent working may decline. This is not to suggest that contentment and lack of motivation have set in. Hardly.

As a result of hard work throughout a career, you will ultimately position yourself to start working smarter and smarter rather than just continually harder and harder.

There are, of course, those who scoff at working so hard since they themselves feel it necessary to do only enough to get by without drawing any attention.

The high points of those just looking to get by are: Break time. Lunch time. Quitting time.

> **THE HARDER YOU WORK —THE LUCKIER YOU BECOME! HARD WORK WILL NOT KILL YOU AND CAN BE ONE OF YOUR GREATEST CALLING CARDS, SEPARATING YOU FROM THE GREAT MANY AL-SO- RANS.**

They foolishly mock those who begin to move ahead by making trivial rationalizations like, "Pooh-pooh. They were just lucky."

Hmmm — ALL Plutonium Club Leaders just seem to be "lucky," do they not?

A few years later I had a similar experience as my career path began to take shape. I became aware that there was a need for an experienced person to prepare the weekly payroll and quarterly tax reports for the first private membership club where I was then employed.

 I was only one of about 120 employees and — I knew nothing about payroll preparation or tax reports. BUT — I did know that *if I did not concern myself with anything other than accomplishing what I was directly responsible for at that time, I never would learn these skills that could better prepare me for greater career success down the road.*

So I contacted the club's General Manager and secured an appointment in his office. After a minute or so of obligatory pleasantries, I told him that I wanted to talk about the need to find an experienced person to prepare the payroll and tax reports.

He seemed pleased, and asked if I knew anyone who could fill the position. I told him as a matter of fact I did — ME!

I quickly and honestly admitted that I had no skills that qualified me for the job, other than my desire to learn and my willingness to work hard.

I further explained that I would be happy to do the job with no increase in salary, and that in no way would I allow this added responsibility to affect the performance of my other duties that I greatly enjoyed.

I made it very clear that I would consider the opportunity to learn as my total compensation for doing the work. The only real "cost" would be that my proposition would require the company to invest the time to teach me the needed skills to do the job.

You have got to create "WIN-WIN" situations! My employer could WIN by filling a need to have the payroll and taxes done. I could WIN by creating the opportunity to develop new professional skills. Marketable ones!

I soon found myself preparing weekly payroll and quarterly tax reports.

LET'S PUT WORK IN OUR VOCABULARY!

I'd like to close with an excerpt from a quote by Bob Burdette that is included in a wonderful collection called Elbert Hubbard's Scrap Book:

"Remember you have to work. Whether you handle pick or wheelbarrow or a set of books, digging ditches or editing a newspaper, ringing an auction bell or writing funny things, you must work. Don't be afraid of killing yourself. Men die sometimes, but it is because they quit work at 9:00 p.m. and don't go home until 2:00 a.m. It's the intervals that kill you! Work gives you appetite for your meals; it lends solidity to your slumber and gives you perfect appreciation for a holiday. So, find out what you want to be and do, take off your coat and make dust in the world. The busier you are: the less harm you are apt to get into, the sweeter will be your sleep, the brighter your holidays, and the better satisfied the whole world will be with you."

THERE IS AN UNMISTAKABLE DIRECT LINK: The desire to win is important. BUT — the willingness to prepare is mandatory. And, the greatest single factor in getting to the top is simply being prepared to work hard in creating opportunities and positioning yourself in getting there.

HEALTHY PLUTONIUM CLUB BASICS
2 "MISSION CRITICAL" COMMITEES & 3 CRITICAL LEADERSHIP FACTORS

THERE ARE TWO MISSION CRITICAL COMMITTEES IN YOUR CLUB:

#1) THE NOMINATING COMMITTEE -
WHERE TOP CALIBER VOLUNTEER LEADERS ARE SELECTED.

#2) THE SEARCH COMMITTEE -
WHERE TOP PROFESSIONAL TALENT IS ULTIMATELY SECURED.

Unwise decisions by either of these will trigger unfortunate "ripple effects" throughout the club that can linger for years. Conversely — excellent choices will establish a winning culture lasting perhaps decades.

The leadership (volunteer and professional) MUST interact with the membership and staff – resulting in being deemed worthy of their ongoing confidence and support.

In contrast — while having changed the name to *"Can Kickers Country Club"* — here are actual excerpts (you just can't make this stuff up) from the president in a letter sent to the entire membership and posted for all club staff to see.

YIKES! Reading between the lines, it is easy to ascertain that unwise "MISSION CRITICAL" decisions were made at some point — and the residual lingering effects are being felt. This type of scenario easily points to three very critical missing Leadership factors that have resulted in causing the membership to cringe and the staff to shake their heads when reading the president's closing: "See you at the club!"

Dear Fellow Members:

It has been a frustrating year for the board and the membership. We have to raise credibility of the board and improve harmony within the membership.

In my 24 years here, I have made many friends and I am planning on keeping it that way. We should be having fun here. While there will be different opinions and opposing perspectives, I'm asking for your support and cooperation in making this a friendlier place.

See you at Can Kickers!

3 CRITICAL LEADERSHIP FACTORS OF HEALTHY PLUTONIUM CLUBS

1) TRUST & CONFIDENCE:

- *All healthy clubs* have leadership teams whose oars are all rowing in the same direction. Otherwise, it is impossible to earn the trust and confidence of the membership.

- *Confident Board and management leadership* is based on trust and a deeply rooted, mutually supportive commitment that all discussions and recommendations are placed face up, fully transparent, on top of the table, with no hidden agendas allowed to bring dissention into the clubhouse.
- *Everyone trusts each other* as various viewpoints are shared in a team spirit that helps clarify and bring issues into focus. It is this trust that allows consistently credible policy decisions to emerge from a board that has confidence in a management team to make things happen.
- *This type of collective synergy* of trust and confidence filters down throughout the entire club membership and staff.

2) COOPERATION & SOLIDARITY:

- *Once the board ultimately makes a decision*, all individual and personal slants are voluntarily put aside. Differing viewpoints shared inside the board room are productive. But — if leaked outside of the board room — they can prove unnecessarily counterproductive.
- *Clubs renowned for their excellence* have board rooms where confidentiality is deeply respected by all. It is akin to a huddle at a crucial time in a football game.
- *While various positions may have their own ideas — once a play is called — everyone cooperates as a unit*, moves forward in solidarity, and plays their part towards doing what was decided on as our next winning move.

3) FAIRNESS & CONSISTENCY:

- *Making solely popular decisions* (or failure to make any at all) — without routinely being first put through "firewalls and filters" of common sense — is a frequent residual effect of a lackadaisical approach to "MISSION CRITICAL" tasks.
- *Often, the most difficult (unpopular) decisions* are the most necessary.
- *Top clubs always take time* to ask themselves, "OK, this decision looks difficult. But — is this ultimately fair and is it truly consistent with who we are as a club?" The answers here help clarify what decision needs to be made. Good clubs make them.
- *Effective leadership is not afraid* to do what needs to be done — popular or not.

Clubs that are able to look at all the 3 areas above and consistently say, "MISSION ACCOMPLISHED" — are where quality people want to:

1. Become Members.
2. Stay Members.
3. Become Employed.
4. Stay Employed.
5. TAKE PRIDE IN ALL THE ABOVE!

We've just described what makes for a HEALTHY PLUTONIUM CLUB!

HUMOR
IF YOU CAN'T LAUGH — FIND ANOTHER CAREER!

You just can't make this stuff up! But - if you've been in club management long enough, you are well aware that you don't have to.

F&B MINIMALISTIC RATIONALE

It was the last night of the minimum billing cycle. Dining room packed. A powerful storm knocked out the electricity for miles around the club. So, everyone makes the best of it. Staff brings in every candle from every corner, basement, attic, storeroom of the clubhouse and brilliantly illuminates the dining rooms in a festive manner.

But – obviously, the kitchen cannot honor the ala carte orders already turned in, or accept new orders from the floor. So – we've got to make the best out of a difficult situation.

Ahhh - the Chef comes to the rescue by pointing out that his signature beef stroganoff special is hot and ready to dish up — and, there is enough for every table yet to be served.

So – to turn what could have been a very bad situation into a good one -the service staff is told to happily announce to every table waiting that the chef's wonderful beef stroganoff is going to be served COMPLIMENTARY to everyone!

But, wait! There's more! We are even going to serve those remaining in synchronized service style. The entire room erupts in happy smiles and applause from an otherwise distraught room full of disappointed members.
That is, all except for one table of 4 ladies who are demanding to see the General Manager!

One of the ladies seems to be spokesperson for the other three as she raises her voice in complete disdain, "But if you don't charge us, then how are we going to get in our minimum?"

I'm tellin' y'all — you can't make this stuff up. Just can't.

TIME FOR A BOARD MEETING MICROPHONE CHECK

"Check. Check. 1-2. 1-2. Check. Check. Can anybody hear me out there? Is this thing working? 1-2. 1-2. Can you hear me?"

The board is going around and around in beating up an issue where your professional experience suggests a very simple, yet effective solution.

However, you know that there is no reason for you to jump in prematurely - as it often is best if a solution comes from a board member, thus enabling them to take "ownership" of an idea, and then you really get behind it and make it work.

So, you wait patiently in hopes that they will migrate slowly to where you know they need to go.

 Only in this case, that does not look like it is going to happen any time soon. Instead, the board seems frustrated and just keeps beating up the same issue with seemingly no meaningful closure in sight.

So you keep listening, but ultimately decide that it is indeed time for you to recommend what you know to be the appropriate solution to the entire issue at hand. You wait for an appropriate opportunity and ask the president if you might offer a suggestion. The room grows quiet — as if frozen in time, all eyes are now fixed are on you.

Then, in less than 15 seconds you offer a spot-on summary of the absolute perfect decision to remedy the issue at hand.

You are feeling good that you were able to provide valuable professional insight to solve what the board somehow felt was a real conundrum — enabling them to move on in the agenda. But no. Noooooooooo!

After you speak, they return immediately to exactly where they had left off prior to your speaking. It is as if a "pause" button had been pushed, allowing you to speak, then it is pushed again and it appears that you never spoke at all. Wait, what?

For the next ten minutes you sit in silence, wondering if you are having an out of body experience, just watching and listening to the seemingly endless debate to nowhere - but you might not even really be in the room.

Then it happens.

One of the board members slaps their forehead and suddenly announces that it just came to him!

The room grows quiet again, and in less than 15 seconds a board member offers a spot-on summary of the absolute perfect decision to remedy the issue at hand.

WOW! The solution offered seems vaguely familiar to you because — well, it was all but word-for-word the exact same one that you offered just ten minutes earlier.

But this time, it's all smiles as the board gives high-fives around the table for their great idea.

Tell me that this doesn't happen in club board rooms across the country. Not that it makes any difference. Really. But just tell me it doesn't happen. Go ahead. I dare you.

PARKING LOT DINGS & DENTS

The head of the Valet team tells you that one of the members is waiting out front and wants to see you immediately. It seems that they are very upset that their car was just damaged at the club, surely by one of the valet parkers. Of course, the club should be responsible for the auto body repair work!

You arrive with hat in hand to assess the damage, offer an apology, and to of course cover any damage caused by the club.

The member is quite irate, wondering how such a thing could ever happen at their club!

And the damage just happened that very day - between the time they dropped off their car in the care of the club, and when the valet just now delivered it.

Even worse, the damage is so obvious and severe, they not only question the apparent negligence of the valet staff, but their very character as well — because they should have immediately reported the damage they caused.

You ask to take a look at the damage, and to take a picture for insurance purposes. You are taken to the driver's side where the member defiantly waves their arms and then points to an obvious 6-inch crease in the door.

OMG! There really is some damage here!

You bend over to look closely and, sure enough…there is rust in the full length of that crease that took weeks, maybe months, to accumulate.

Oh, what the heck. You finish this story.

Makes you wonder — who comes away with more dings and dents: The cars in the parking lot, or the GM/COO? I'm just askin'?

NOT MY LITTLE JOHNNY!

Mrs. Member comes to the accounting office saying that there is some kind of a mistake in their monthly billing. Actually, something this big is more like gross negligence!

There is simply no way, I mean – NO WAY - that they spent an extra $183.97 in F&B charges over the past month.

This is obviously an indication that the "help" needs more training in making sure that the correct member account number is on each transaction.

They have been a member for "X" years and even the new staff should know their names, make sure a member signs each check, and that the proper account number is there. YIKES!

The Controller quickly apologizes for any errors, agrees that every effort should be made by even new staff to know the names of members, to make sure members sign each check, and that the proper account number is used. Mrs. Member is not interested in seeing a detailed account pulled up electronically. No. Prove to me that these transactions are mine!

So, the hard file is brought out.

And - there we produce 28 different chits - sometimes 3 to 5 transactions on the same day - all signed - all clearly with Mrs. Member's account number. All generated at the pool snack bar. All signed by her little son, Johnny. Everybody in the pool! Johnny be good!

IS YOUR COMMON AREA SHOE ROOM A PRIVATE LOCKER FOR A FEW?

The shoe room started looking like a storeroom, slowly morphing into a state of visual disarray. Why?

It was found that a handful of members had a half-dozen or so shoes always left there.

MLR staff was informed of the policy that when shoes, either golf or street, were done being cleaned and made to look like new, they should be placed in a shoe-bag and left in the member's private locker for their convenience.

Hmmmm — what problem could there be with that?

Well, it seemed that members who opted to not incur the expense of securing a locker, were instead "tipping" the staff to keep their shoes available at all times right there from the shoe room drop-off window.

This effectively negated somewhat their need to pay for a locker, yet...oh you get it! Why bore you with the details?

The end of this particular story?

All these shoes were tagged and put in a large garbage bag, accompanied by the appropriate letter informing them that private lockers were available, that professional shoe service was included in the member locker fees, and were prompted to contact the Accounting Office to make arrangements for a locker. Otherwise...

We all like happy endings don't we.

HOW A FIRST INTERVIEW BECAME AN EXIT INTERVIEW

No kidding. This one is true as well.

A candidate is being interviewed for a new job. Things seem to be progressing well. Nearing the end, one of the board members asks something along the lines of: "Thank you for your time visiting with us today. Your background is very interesting. Tell me, if we were to ultimately offer the position to you, how soon could you start?"

The candidate quickly answered, "I've got my clubs in the trunk of the rental car out front."

And — he was serious about that. FORE!

This is NOT a joke.

KNOW WHEN TO HOLD 'EM & KNOW WHEN TO FOLD 'EM

In CMAA, some of the most revered names of GM's are those belonging to "The 25 Year Club." These are managers who have served their same club for 25 years or more.

WOW! Congratulations!

Yet, there also those in the industry who seeming could belong to the "25 Clubs in 25 Years" club.

Somehow…they just seem incapable of holding a job! Yet they always seem to get interviews, and somehow get hired. At seemingly good clubs as well!

Go figure!

Here is a true story of one of the members of the tongue-in-cheek, "25 Clubs in 25 Years" club.

Two GM's were attending the same 3-day CMAA educational opportunity. In order to save their respective clubs money, many attendees opted to share lodging.

On the last night they were each talking about the experience before retiring for the day.

Seemingly out of the blue, with whatsoever no prior indication of such subject matter before - our aspiring inductee into the "25 Clubs in 25 Years Club" announces,

"Well - I guess it is time for me to polish up the old resume again."

"What? Huh? What makes you say that?"

"My president told me so."

"Oh."

Yup. True story. End of true story. Nothing else to say but, "Oh."

HOW TO GET CAPITAL REQUESTS FOR NEW KITCHEN EQUIPMENT APPROVED

Let's be frank about seeking approval for annual Capital Budget line items.

GM's who have been in the business for many years will confirm that recommendations for major "Big Ticket" golf-related capital requests are generally easily approved.

Not necessarily always. But, generally so.

They will also confirm that even minor "Small Ticket" kitchen-related capital requests are generally not so easily approved.

Not necessarily always. But, generally so. Tell me I am wrong about this. I dare you.

The solution?

Just show a picture of any/all highly desired new kitchen equipment with grass-catchers bolted on the sides.

Ah, that should do the trick. Pictures do speak a thousand words!

HUMOR
FACE IT, YOU'VE ALREADY GOT A "DREAM JOB"

It is 1:30 in the morning and I can't sleep. Ever since the Board meeting, which ended four hours earlier, I find myself unable to quiet my mind enough to catch a few z's.

Instead, I casually sip a Cabernet and flip through the sea of infomercials that run rampant in early morning television programming. My hopes are that the mind-numbing viewing will make me drowsy. And, you know what — I think it is starting to work just a little bit. Am I dreaming, or what?

Soon, I'm drifting off and dreaming of a career change — since, as these infomercials purport — it's a "piece of cake" to earn any number of advanced educational degrees, for only three easy payments. And the final exam can be taken right from the comfort of my La-Z-Boy recliner.

Get A Medical Degree in Less Than Three Weeks!

For my final exam, I'm provided a razor blade, a piece of gauze, and a bottle of scotch, with which I will be able to remove my own appendix in under 15 minutes.

Get a Degree in History Today!

All I need to do here is describe the history of the papacy from its origins to the present day, concentrating especially (but, not exclusively) on its social, political, economic, religious, and philosophical impact on Europe, Asia, the Americas, and Africa. Sure, piece of cake.

I have to laugh as I contemplate the fact that earning a degree in ANY field is a bit of a cakewalk compared to what it takes every day to "make the grade" in a successful career in club management. A successful club management career mandates maintaining a straight "A" average in the following daily pop quizzes, tests, and final exams:

MINIMUM SPENDING 101

It is 7:43 pm on the last day of the Minimum Spending accounting cycle. The point-of-sale system has inexplicably stopped printing in the kitchen a half hour before. It's the middle of your dinner rush. The dining room is packed with members who rarely use the facility, because it seems the only time they do, it is always too packed, and the service is too slow. This is your single annual opportunity to show them otherwise.

YOUR ASSIGNMENT: Casually stop at every table and enthrall them with your charm.

(BTW – In preparation for tonight's exam it is mandatory that earlier this day you spend two hours on the phone repeatedly explaining exactly why stopping by the club to pick up 15 raw steaks and seven bottles of wine to go doesn't count against their minimum.)

TIME MANAGEMENT 101

Obtain a 10-Ton truck. Then, without dropping even a single grain of sand or having the truck break down, load it with 12 tons of varied expectations. **YOUR ASSIGNMENT:** Using the above analogy, successfully schedule your average workday.

(Hint: Providing you forego sleep, you have 24 hours to complete this assignment on a daily basis.)

DIPLOMACY 101

It is a beautiful Saturday morning at 7:43 in the middle of peak season. You've just been informed that there is some kind of big commotion at the first tee and your presence is required immediately! Upon arrival, you see a foursome wanting to tee off. They are: Hillary Rodham Clinton — Attorney Gloria Allred — Anderson Cooper from CNN, and — the president of your club's ladies golf program.

YOUR ASSIGNMENT: Without causing a scene or backing up play — convince them that Tuesdays before noon is really the best time to play golf. It really is. Really. It is! No, really.

MEMBER EXPECTATIONS 101

At the direction of the Vice President (who, by the way, will be your boss next year, or at least somebody's boss) create a menu that includes everything but the kitchen sink. You are to do this at price points at least 15% less than the least expensive restaurants in town (that those vocal members who never spend their minimums refer to as benchmarks).

YOUR ASSIGNMENT: Personally visit every "benchmark" and while there: (1) Thoroughly convince the servers that the $150+ they pull down every night in cash tips is perhaps a bit overly self-indulgent on their parts. (2) With your powers of persuasion and logic, prove that in their heart they really would rather work at your club for an average of $15 per hour, including a service charge that is, of course — fully taxed. (Trust me — some day they will thank you for having provided this teachable moment that enabled them to sleep better knowing that they are paying their fair share in taxes.)

STRESS MANAGEMENT 101

You're at your desk. The new House Committee chairman sticks his head in your office and asks if you have a moment to meet his sister-in-law who is visiting from out of state. She looks vaguely familiar. Her name is Martha Stewart. It turns out that she will be visiting on a regular basis, and hopes that you don't mind her "helping out" from time to time in a few areas of the club she has heard might be in need of just a little sprucing up.

YOUR ASSIGNMENT: Have them both leave your office believing that you are genuinely excited about this. (Of course, it matters not that you see the two of them sharing a "fist bump" as they walk 15 feet from your office door.)

CLUB BORED MEETING MANAGEMENT 101

You are seated in the hot seat surrounded by a dozen successful individuals who have positioned themselves to enjoy the country club life by achieving status as doctors, lawyers, stockbrokers, realtors, or independent entrepreneurs. Few, if any, of these distinguished individuals have directly supervised or depended upon hourly employees, many who make slightly more than minimum wage, to produce a product or deliver a service.

YOUR ASSIGNMENT: By means of delivering a compelling opening Executive Summary — enable them to have complete empathy and understanding of the complexity of maintaining and leading a diversified team of employees to consistently exhibit pride and a dedication to each of their tasks.

Of course, do so while: (1) Not at any time appearing to be defensive or pandering. (2) Always valuing the input and insights offered from every Board member. (3) Constantly nurturing a mutual respect that permeates the entire operation. (4) Never allowing your mind to wander while looking forward to a cabernet at home after the meeting.

CLUB MANAGEMENT GENERATIONAL DIVIDE 101

The Men's Bar/Card Room is full of the club's elder statesmen who enjoy playing gin rummy while ingesting conversation-provoking libations. For weeks the "drums have been beating" with the focus of the conversations revolving around how the current Board is a bunch of young, suspender-snapping, big spenders who don't understand the value of a dollar or what the club is all about. It sounds as if the club has slowly ebbed into the abyss ever since their respective terms on the Board were over, some 15 to 40 years ago.

YOUR ASSIGNMENT:
Walk into the room with a John Wayne swagger of confidence. Repeatedly tap on the side of an empty rocks glass with a teaspoon. After gaining their attention, allow 5 seconds of complete silence. You now have 78 seconds to convince them that they are wrong.

TENNIS MANAGEMENT 101

YOUR ASSIGNMENT: Have the tennis players skip the free lemonade & iced tea at courtside and actually come into the clubhouse and sign a chit — for anything.

WEEKLY LADIES BRIDGE CLUB MANAGEMENT 101

YOUR ASSIGNMENT: Satisfy their requests for an ever changing three-course luncheon menu for $6.95 — inclusive. (Oh, and don't forget to include the one glass of white wine, nor the separate checks.)
Who needs a career change or another degree when you already have a dream job that is rewarding to the n'th degree!

I went to bed looking forward to adding this Cabernet to the club's wine list. And I could really care less if Martha Stewart thinks it is a good vintage or not!

INITIATION INCOME IS SLOWLY ON THE RISE.

INTERVIEW SKILLS
JOHN WAYNE STYLE

Q: So, tell us, Mr. Crandal — just how do you relate to the Boards you've worked with in the past?

A: "I won't be wronged, I won't be insulted, and I won't be laid a hand on. I don't do these things to other people, and I require the same from them."
-THE SHOOTIST (1976)

Q: How do you respond to pressure situations?

A: "I haven't lost my temper in 40 years; but, Pilgrim, you caused a lot of trouble this morning; might have got somebody killed; and somebody ought to belt you in the mouth. But I won't. I won't. The hell I won't!"
-McCLINTOCK (1963)

Q: Mr. Crandal, in checking your background, it appears that all speak very highly of you. Why is that?

A: "Well, there are some things a man just can't run away from."
- STAGECOACH (1939)

Q: Why did you leave your last job?

A: "All battles are fought by scared men who'd rather be someplace else."
- IN HARM'S WAY (1965)

Q: It seems that there must have been some problems at your last position. How were those problems addressed?

A: *"Out here a man settles his own problems."*
- THE MAN WHO SHOT LIBERTY VALENCE (1962)

Q: Oh, we are sorry to hear that things have been difficult for you since your last job.

A: *"Don't apologize — it's a sign of weakness."*
- SHE WORE A YELLOW RIBBON (1949)

Q: No — we really are sorry!

A: *"Sorry don't get it done, Dude."*
- RIO BRAVO (1959)

Q: OK. We'll draw up a formal offer and have a contract for you to sign tomorrow!

A: *"That'll be the day!"*
- THE SEARCHERS (1956)

Q: Mr. Crandal, we are very excited to offer you the job!

A: *"Now you understand. Anything goes wrong, anything at all - your fault, my fault, nobody's fault - it don't matter - I'm gonna blow your head off. It's as simple as that."*
- BIG JAKE (1971)

FINALLY - A VERY SMALL MINORITY OF MEMBERS' WAG THE TAIL OF THE DOG BY RANTING THAT ALL FINANCIAL PROBLEMS ARE CAUSED BY MEDIOCRE F&B OPERATIONS THAT SHOULD BE MAKING MONEY IN ORDER TO LOWER DUES. SOOOO ... A SEARCH COMMITTEE STARTS INTERVIEWING IDEAL CANDIDATES FOR A NEW GM/COO! THEY WANT AN F&B BACKGROUND AND SOMEONE THEY CAN WORK WITH.

INTERVIEWS
SUCCESSFUL ONES ARE OFTEN JUST A QUESTION OF BALANCE

"It's not the way that you say it/when you do those things to me/It's more the way that you mean it/when you tell me what will be."

The Moody Blues are an English rock band. Among their early innovations was a dynamically orchestrated fusion of classical music, rock, and thought-provoking lyrics. Their breakthrough album Days of Future Passed is critically acclaimed to this very day.

One of their most renowned works is their 1970 album, A Question of Balance, that featured the lead track, "Question."

The song alternates between two different melodies:

1. A fast-paced section with the lyrics, "Why do we never get an answer…"
2. A slower one, "It's not the way that you say it when you do those things to me…"

What does any of this have to do with the business world of a meaningful interviewing and hiring process? Plenty. It sets the tone for understanding the importance of balance in identifying really serious talent with very real people.

I admit it. I want more than just the right answers to technical skill interview questions. Much more.

While I know that in order for a business model to look good framed on an office wall, or printed on glossy paper in the Annual Report under the header, "Our Team" — the right talent must be matched to the right boxes within any particular organization chart deemed worthy of the task at hand.

And yes, a good portion of any interview/hiring process had darn well better zero-in and focus on identifying serious talent to fill those boxes. That's non-negotiable.

However, even if a candidate gives all the right answers, I want more. We've got to be sure we are asking the right questions as well.

Questions that succeed in identifying serious professional talent is not enough. I also want seriously fun people that don't take themselves too seriously.

Some of the stodgier amongst us may immediately sniff and proclaim, "Just what the heck does the word "FUN" have to do with getting "WORK" done!"

Please note that the above doesn't even end with a question mark. Nope. To stodgy folks an emphatic exclamation point is the only suitable punctuation after what they believe to be an absolute, rather than a question at all!

I would submit that the most serious work (both quantity AND quality) is best accomplished by very serious talent, that is delivered by very seriously fun people.

FIRST - (Let's start with classical.)
- The "routine" relevant questions are asked in a somewhat fast-paced manner in order to identify serious professional talent. Then, and only then, if they are still left standing…

SECOND - (OK. Now ~ let's rock!)
- I hit 'em, seemingly out of the blue - with an abruptly slower-paced, highly personal question that on the surface seems borderline irrelevant and out of tune with what has been going on up to this point.

Often a candidate will appear to be on automatic cruise control as they methodically, correctly answer every technical question and theoretical scenario thrown their direction.

Then suddenly that zinger "Question of Balance" comes from out of nowhere that makes them pause in hopes of regaining their equilibrium.

What is that "Question of Balance" that tells me if a candidate offers me that "more, much more" that I am really looking for? Here it is:

"So - tell me. What is the funniest thing that has ever happened to you?"

KA-BOOM!

A show-stopper.

Suddenly they realize that all of the coaching, outplacement training and current articles in the WSJ, Fortune, Business Insider and INC. Magazine never prepared them for this one!

Their degrees, credentials, and past titles are of no help now.

Suddenly it is just two people, sitting with intent eye contact in silence.

"No. Really. Tell me. What's the funniest thing that has ever happened to you?"

And, you know what - in some ways I suppose that the actual answer itself is not really what I am looking for. Because, perhaps, that "something" they slowly recall may not be funny to me at all. (You know, one of those things where you just had to have been there?)

What I am really looking for as their mind slowly remembers that funny incident or story, as one of their funniest life experiences now unexpectedly dominates their current thought process... I'm looking to see -

- their eyes start to sparkle —
- their head beginning to unconsciously nod this way or that —
- their hands starting to gesture, and —
- a smile coming to their face.

Here we are, in what — up to now, has been a pretty much serious moment in life - a formal job interview! Suddenly there is laughter, smiles, and life.

If it gets to this point, I know I've got a live one! A real person. Someone who, if they have gotten this far along the formal interview process, I already knew was seriously talented.

Now I also know that they are a fun person, who will do well in working as part of a team of highly talented folks, in an energy-charged fun environment.

Over the years I've seen a plethora of responses to the Question of Balance:

- One fellow impressively passed the classic questions with flying colors. However, when it came time to rock - he sat in silence for a full 5 seconds (try it, it's a long interlude in an interview situation) and then just said, "Uh, I guess nothing really all that funny has ever happened to me...what's that have to do with working here!"

Oops. There is that exclamation point again where it should have been a question. Stodgy folks need not apply. Even talented ones!

- Another, as if a breaker switch were thrown, instantaneously went into LOL mode and was unable to even finish a complete sentence as that special funny moment came flooding back, complete with tears of laughter! They had to plead for forgiveness as they simply could not finish the story without having unbridled laughter stop them cold every 4 or 5 words.

Soon we are both laughing! Between laughs, I'm slightly tempted to offer them a job on the spot! Yesssss! I mean we are already laughing and crying! Let's just shake hands right now and really give both of us something to celebrate! Yup - you gotta have talent. But whatever talent within truly blossoms when smiles and laughter comes easy.

- One of my favorites was the person who hesitated just a smidge, smiled coyly, got that sparkle in their eye - but then said warmly, with a smug sort of confidence, something along the lines of, "You know what, a lot of funny things have happened to me in my lifetime, I mean a ton - and, I'm not telling you any of them!"

I almost felt compelled to hire them immediately - just so down the line I could find out what they were! In any regard, here was a person who had the confidence to look me in the eye and simply convey that they were a very balanced person who had no intention of sharing personal insights. At least not just right now! The smile. That sparkle. Both blew their cover. Love it!

- One got that "deer in the headlights" glazed-over look before, in just above a whisper, saying the words, "Will you repeat the question, please?"

(Uh. In a word - "No".)

The point here is that even if a candidate seems to answer all the classical questions with flawless accuracy - to identify a truly great hire, we need to stop a beat and think, "OK. You are saying all the right things so far. But now it's time to change the melody a bit. Let's rock!"

Good hires are all about a Question of Balance.

INTANGIBLES
THE LITTLE PERFORMANCE TRAITS THAT SEPARATE PLUTONIUM LEADERS FROM ALL OTHERS

"Whatcha See is Whatcha Get" is a great song from the early 1970's by The Dramatics. However, all great business leaders know that things run much deeper than what is merely seen at the surface level.

There are deeply rooted "invisible to the naked eye" intangibles that reflect professional consistency and personal character that maintain greatness.

Others may have careers that languish in the minor leagues, and never really understand why.

The resumes of achievers in executive leadership and professional sports both document their outward "stats." But if we were able to personally know them — we would slowly uncover a common thread of intangibles that ultimately separate those who make it to the "bigs" and thrive ⏃ and others who pine away as career minor leaguers.

MUST get the most out of ability. Their own ability AND that of the entire team.

It is a big mistake to evaluate executives (or athletes) only by the apparent skill level portrayed on paper. All the ability in the world will never get any lasting traction if lacking the intangibles.

- Common sense
- Emotional control
- Focus
- A driving will to never compromise best efforts, and…
- Some skill — are what lead to positive results.

It's the things you can't see that get you to that next level. Let's take a look at some of the intangibles that go beyond the stats.

MUST HAVE POSITIVE INFLUENCE ON TEAMMATES

Is it just me, or have you also ever noticed that things do not always go according to plan?

Original plans, like the sails of a great ship, may from time to time need to be adjusted slightly to reflect unforeseeable new prevailing winds. Should the ship start drifting slightly off course, it is easy for some to become hesitant in making difficult (yet appropriate) decisions that could avoid wandering unnecessarily into the vortex of a storm.

These isolated times of necessary course corrections are viewed as opportunities for those who are prepared to step up their performance another notch.

Successful leaders (or an entire company for that matter) are NOT those who have no problems on their plate, or challenges of navigating through changing times. They ARE those who consistently handle them well, and rally the entire team to believe they can collectively prevail.

MUST HAVE A "NOSE" FOR THE BALL:

If a trend is not going in favor of the team — look for those who are still not afraid to handle the ball, and you will be looking at a professional who possesses a mandatory intangible.

Keep in mind that generals do not earn their stars in tranquil times of peace. It is in times of duress that they distinguish themselves.

MUST ROUTINELY MAKE BIG PLAYS:

Irrespective of how much time and skill was devoted to drawing up game plans, organizational charts, and standard operating procedures — victory is determined by those who consistently make big plays. They are the ones who actually want the ball when the game is on the line, and who then calmly produce in the clutch.

"BIG PLAYS" should be routine occurrences that the entire team prides itself in making day after day. The result is an undeniable, palpable, consistent "winning streak" of great consumer experiences.

A LITTLE DIFFERENCE IS ALL THE DIFFERENCE

- *A horse* can win a race by "a nose".
- *A boxer* can win a fight with just one punch.
- *The difference* between a major league baseball player and a career minor leaguer is only about 3 hits a week.
- *A football game* can be won when the wide receiver beats his man by just half a step — just one time.

The difference between "often good" and "consistently great" has little to do with potential. It has everything to do with the degree of focus given to the little intangibles that loom so big in overall performance.

A little difference is all the difference when it comes to making big plays.

It is the little things that matter in striving to continually add polish to ultimately great consumer experiences, like particles of sand – compressed into a massive rock.

MUST HAVE THEIR OWN STYLE WHILE STILL BEING A GREAT TEAMMATE:

While individual styles may be variable, creating an atmosphere that constantly moves the entire team in a positive direction must be an intangible fixed asset that proves contagious.

Some bring to the team energy and enthusiasm. Some a calming, statesmanlike presence. Some carry themselves in a dynamic way that others want to emulate. Mission Statements and Core Values may look good when printed in the annual report. But they're D.O.A. if not brought to life by leadership that confidently stirs the pot in a positive way, toward that unique team chemistry that maintains pride of being a part of it all.

TEAM CHEMISTRY IS AS IMPORANT AS IT IS HARD TO DEFINE. Every successful "major league" endeavor has a unique winning culture, one that is generated by the team chemistry of those entrusted to successfully lead and operate it.

MUST ANTICIPATE AND PROACTIVELY SET THE STAGE FOR TEAM SUCCESS.

A genius is: "Someone who sees a target that no one else sees yet — and hits it!"

An essential intangible is having the sense of being able to anticipate what just might happen before anyone else does. Anticipate the needs of consumers. Anticipate the desires of all those around you. Anticipate potential economic challenges and how to best respond to them. Anticipate where the ball is going to be thrown next.

Achievers are always looking downfield and anticipating what needs to be done to achieve success, and they are prepared to offer support and insight in order to get the needed policies in place. Then, they are prepared to lead the entire team within those meaningful policies towards making great things happen every day in the field — not just once on the drawing board, during an annual strategic planning meeting.

Leadership that is able to anticipate equates to being able to solve potential problems before they ever have a chance to happen and to create - in advance - the best-case scenarios for successfully navigating economic challenges and changing times.

Change is inevitable. Those who are successful initiate positive change, rather than reacting negatively to it.

MUST BE COACHABLE:

Yes, there is some merit in "doing your own thing." But if carried to an extreme, this single trait can score a knockout punch on any hope for hall of fame status.

> **THERE ARE 2 KINDS OF PEOPLE WHO ARE GOING NOWHERE:**
>
> **SOMEONE WHO WILL NOT DO WHAT THEY ARE TOLD. AND, SOMEONE WHO WILL DO NOTHING BUT.**

When errors are pointed out and suggested corrective action ignored, some otherwise very noted executives can find themselves on the end of the bench very quickly.

Nothing will sit you down quicker than a reputation as being un-coachable. There is a wealth of business experience and insight to be gained from board members, effective peers, proven department heads, and fellow teammates who can all potentially serve as great mentors. Listen up! Be wise and seek their input.

We all need mentors. There is no such thing as a "self-made" leader - regardless of whatever title may be on their office door or how many gatekeepers they have. We all need mentors!

No one will work alongside a "know-it-all" for very long. Why? Because this is a person who has stopped learning. After all - they already know it all. Don't they?

Those not willing to be coached today, by default, are unwilling to prepare for the changes that tomorrow will surely bring.

So, statistically speaking — find a comfortable chair in the clubhouse and ask yourself: how are the stats looking these days? Do you like what you see?

Taking a closer look at the intangibles can manifest visible results — favorable ones.

WHEN INTERVIEWING FOR THAT GM/COO POSITION ... CANDIDATES HAD BETTER BE READY FOR SOME "TRICK" QUESTIONS THAT NEED TO BE ANSWERED ... YET, IN A VERY POLITICALLY CORRECT WAY.

NOTE - IF THE CANDIDATE IS SMARTER THAN THE AVERAGE BEAR, S/HE WILL ANSWER, "WELL - THAT DEPENDS, OF COURSE, ON WHICH OF YOU IS ACTUALLY ON THE MENU.

JUNIOR PROGRAMS ARE STARTING TO THRIVE.

JOB TITLES MEAN NOTHING
PLUTONIUM CLUB LEADERS KNOW THE DIFFERENCE BETWEEN WHAT THEIR JOB TITLE IS, AND WHAT IT IS THAT THEY REALLY DO

When meeting new people in a social environment, after just a few moments of obligatory personal pleasantries, it is inevitable that our minds quickly try to "size up" the person in front of us. Don't take it personally — they are doing the same thing to you!

It's now only a matter seconds before one of you will inevitably ask what both of you really want to know of the other.

And - because we all see the world through our own unique set of filtered glasses, the answers offered to that question will prove pivotal as to how each views the other from that point on.

The answer instantly transforms what may have been only a polite exchange of small talk while glancing around the room, into some real eye contact as their story comes out.

What is that pivotal question? We all ask it of others and we all get it asked of us.

Here it comes, "What do you do?"

Well — "What exactly is it that you do?"

On the surface it seems like such a simple question that could be simply answered, "Well – I get up - brush my teeth – have a cup of coffee," etc.

We all know the question goes deeper than that.

What is really being asked is: what is your job?

That, too, seems like such a simple question that could be answered with little explanation. Just say the words "I am _____" and then fill in the blank with a NOUN (…a CPA…a chef…an astronaut…an editor…a banker…an attorney…a pastor…a general manager… etc.).

When the question, "What do you do?" is responded to by offering an occupation or position title — the question itself has really not been answered. The word "do" is a VERB - thus, a proper response would describe activity.

Executives need to clarify the difference between their job title and what they really should be doing.

Regardless of whatever job title or lofty position — what leaders MUST be doing is:

1. Selecting the right people, identifying talent, and putting them in the right places.
2. Developing, motivating and mentoring them.
3. Culling the herd when necessary.

- *That is what you do! That IS your job.*

Every introspective leader should look in the mirror, have some real eye contact, and pointedly ask themselves the question, "What do you do?"

A meaningful answer would be something along the lines of:

"My profession is that of a Chief Operating Officer, who knows that my real job is all about selecting the right people and providing great leadership as a positive mentor of a great team. That is my real job. And, that is what I do."

If an executive realizes what their real job is, focuses on that job, and is committed to really making it happen — career success is a highly predictable byproduct of just going about the business of doing the same job every day. This is true regardless of what industry or title may be under your name on your business card.

BUT — NEVER FORGET: Your boss or board of directors has their own set of filtered glasses as well!

And when they get you in their sights, they're not impressed by looking at the title beneath your name on your business card, or office door.

All they want to see is:

1. How successful are you in identifying top talent?
2. What is your ability to manage/lead that talent?
3. Will I look good as a direct result of having you on my team?

NEVER FORGET: What THEY see - is what YOU get!

BUT – APPROACHES CARVED IN STONE ARE OBLIVIOUS TO RELEVANT LIFESTYLES OF POTENTIAL YOUNGER MEMBERS. IT SEEMS AS IF SOMETHING JUST FLIES IN FROM RIGHT FIELD OUT OF NOWHERE.

KIDS ARE KEPT BUSY WHILE YOUNG PARENTS GIVE HIGH-FIVES.

KNOWLEDGE

HARVEY CALLED THE FOLLOWING, "THIS I KNOW" — WELL, IT'S NOT ALL HE KNOWS! BUT IT HIGHLIGHTS WHAT ALL PRIVATE CLUB PLUTONIUM CLUB LEADERS NEED TO KNOW.

www.searchamericanow.com

HARVEY WEINER
IS LEGENDARY WITHIN THE PRIVATE CLUB INDUSTRY

IF A LIST WERE CREATED OF THOSE ACTIVELY PROVIDING EXECUTIVE SEARCH, LEADERSHIP, AND GOVERNANCE EXPERTISE FOR 40+ YEARS — THE LIST WOULD BE A SMALL ONE. HARVEY WEINER — FOUNDER, IN 1974, OF SEARCH AMERICA.

THE WISDOM HERE IS AKIN TO A YOUNG ADULT GOING THROUGH 4 YEARS OF INTENSE SEMINARY IN HOPES OF BECOMING A GREAT SPIRITUAL LEADER. BUT — AFTER GRADUATING, OVER TIME THEY LEARN THAT THERE ARE MANY (TONS) OF THINGS SIMPLY NOT FOUND IN TEXTBOOKS, THAT THEIR ENTIRE EFFECTIVENESS HINGES UPON.

A PRIVATE CLUB BOARD POSITION OR MANAGEMENT CAREER ARE SIMILAR. ONCE YOU ATTAIN THE POSITION — YOU QUICKLY LEARN THAT THERE ARE TONS OF THINGS THAT WERE NOT LEARNED IN YOUR CHOSEN FIELD OR OFFERED IN FORMAL CLASSES.

"KNOWLEDGE COMES FROM EDUCATION; WISDOM COMES FROM EXPERIENCE; ARROGANCE FROM FEAR AND INSECURITY."

THANK YOU, HARVEY — FOR SHARING WISDOM THAT WAS NEVER TAUGHT IN SCHOOL OR TO BE FOUND IN TEXTBOOKS.

General Wisdom for Plutonium Private Club Leaders
(Includes the Volunteer Board AND Professional Management Team)

- Attitude: Control it, or it will control *and* define you.

- BOD role within a private club is **STRATEGIC**. Management is **TACTI-CAL.** Translation: The board decides the *right thing* to do. Management decides **the right way** to do it.

- Breakfast BOD meetings tend to be more focused and productive. Evening meetings too often include adult beverages.

- Club leadership endeavors to drive the narrative in a positive direction. People can see or hear the same thing and come away with totally different recollections.

- Competing effectively may mean *rallying* the crew, t*acking* against a headwind and current, and *maintaining* focus on the finishing line.

- Compliment selectively and deservedly. "Good job" diminishes in value when overused.

- Convene a President's & Manager's Roundtable Lunch, once a month or so, either in the middle of the dining room or in a private room. Open the invitation to any Member by RSVP on a first call basis, capped at ten Members. Don't have the same Members attending most of these lunches, and don't have just your supporters or chronic complainers. The purpose is to preserve the perception of transparency, provide an opportunity for Members to speak frankly on any relevant topic, and to foster relationships between all participants.

> CREATE A PAST PRESIDENTS' COUNCIL AND ENCOURAGE THEM TO MEET PERIODICALLY. THE CURRENT PRESIDENT AND/OR MANAGER MIGHT ATTEND THESE MEETINGS, AS A RESOURCE. ACCESS EACH PAST PRESIDENT'S INDIVIDUAL SILOS OF INFLUENCE, CULTIVATING INPUT AND ADVOCACY FOR BOARD DECISIONS. IF THEY FEEL LEFT OUT, FORMER CLUB LEADERS MAY BECOME COUNTERPRODUCTIVE.

- Does your club have a designated CFO? I refer of course to a Chief Fun Officer! Delegate this enjoyable gig to either a staff member or to the right club Member.

- Don't bother comparing yourself to the best of the others. But are you the best of which you are capable of being?

- Never ignore a Member who needs to talk to you. Always return a Member's call.

- Never send an irretrievable e-mail, voicemail, text, letter, or social media post without considering the consequences (remember how simple this was before the Internet?).
- Forgiveness takes practice. Hurtful or inappropriately selected words can be forever.

- Encourage civil debate. People may argue. That doesn't mean they don't care about or respect each other. Imagine the influence of those two putting forth a joint recommendation.

- A lack of argument may indicate low respect for the other's opinion. Encourage civil debate.

- People we might expect to help in a time of need can disappoint us, while those least expected may come to our aid without even being asked.

- Respect is not an entitlement. Club leaders can't make someone respect them. But they can always be respectful of others, behave as worthy of respect and continually earn it. Whether they respect you or not is up to them.

- Keep earlier leadership in the loop. Respect the foundation on which the club stands to this day. Decisions made by you now may send the club on an irreversible path. Likewise, decisions made by former board members and prior management help define the club as it now exists. Wouldn't it be helpful to know the rationale of days gone by?

- Respect tradition, but courageously, yet tactfully, challenge inappropriate practices.
- Success comes in a can, failure comes in a can't. Whether you think you can or can't —you're right.

- Thinking takes more effort than reacting.

- Treat people with respect. All people. All the time.

- When seeking solutions — no matter how thin you slice it, there's still two sides.

- A career in private club leadership is like riding a bicycle. Uphill it's difficult and slow. A rapid downhill ride demands attentiveness and control. But, as a rule, if you don't keep moving, you'll fall over.

- Avoid becoming a lightning rod. When a private club board seems split on an issue, they may ask the manager for an opinion. Take sides at your peril. Provide facts, benchmarks and projected consequences of every option. Assure them that you will support whatever decision they make, reminding them that no decision is also a decision.

- *Burn no bridges!* There are many ways to leave a job but only one way to do it properly.

- Character is revealed by how you treat those who can do you absolutely no good.

- *The board's avocation is your vocation.* Their success in a legal or medical practice, or as a fast food franchisee, or as a real estate agent or developer, does not guarantee understanding private club, much less 501(c)7 governance. Paraphrasing the Broadway show, The King & I, "They must be Properly Taught". We recommend board orientation, shortly after elections, as critical to effective governance.

- Cultivate and nurture trusted friendships and professional collegiality, even over long distances. We, in the club industry, are each other's best resources.

- Dependability: No matter how drained you feel, when called upon to help — you do.

- If something must be done first thing today, tape a reminder note to the car's radio dial or to your cellphone.
- Detest dealing with strong personalities and micromanagement? Change professions.

- Drive the club's staff hard, and sooner or later they'll drive you out.

- From time-to-time eat lunch in the employee's break room, or with the grounds crew.

- Enjoy golf? Play with staff, when the club is closed. Don't join a regular foursome of Members. If you're golfing while a Member's burger was overcooked, you may be cooked also. No matter who you're playing with there will always be Members who resent that (#1) you're playing at all, and that (#2) you never play with them. Be wise and arrange mutual reciprocity with a nearby manager to play each other's course. (This advice applies to everyone in your family)

DON'T EVER FORGET — THE BOD'S WON'T EVER BE NICER TO THE GM/COO THAN THEY WERE DURING THE INTERVIEW, AND ALL OF THOSE WHO HIRED YOU ARE LIKELY OFF THE BOARD IN THREE YEARS.

- Build and nurture advocates but remember your place, the board didn't intend hiring a buddy.

- Enjoy your work or find something else to do with your time on Earth.

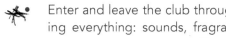• Enter and leave the club through a different door each day, observing everything: sounds, fragrances, lighting, housekeeping, maintenance, temperature, staff activity, and your own sense of arrival. Note your impressions while still fresh.

- Everybody needs a hug sometimes (but, better to first check with HR).

- Forget about creating a vanity wall in your office, replete with your degrees and certificates, photos of you with Arnold Palmer, you with the President, you on a magazine cover, you and colleagues at a conference, you, you, you and more of you. None of this defines you as a decent human.

FROM TIME-TO-TIME, SHOW UP ON THE FIRST TEE OR BAG DROP OR DOCK ON SATURDAY MORNINGS. BRING A COFFEE URN AND PASTRIES.

- Get over yourself. Develop bench-depth. Train your successor. No matter how many direct reports, if you are constantly the controlling, go-to authority, they'll never grow, and you'll get no rest. Think of yourself as indispensable? You may be, until you are not.

- Know where to draw the line between needing to be liked and being the leader that your staff wants and needs. Some of the most likeable people in the club business spend lots of time between jobs.

- Leading a large club, say over $15MM, is more about managing managers than everyday issues. At a small club, say under 350 Members and $1MM in F&B, every small mistake shows up.

- Live far enough away from the club so that Members can't look over your fence, drop their almost-late monthly payment in your personal mailbox, join you in your morning jog, drop by for a chat or a drink, or stop your spouse in the local market to ask why the club's coffee price was increased. It's painful when Member's children, at school, treat your kid as "their club's manager's kid." At least try to live in another school district.

- Mistakes happen. No matter the training efforts, how you react to their mistake will have lasting impact. If this is a teaching opportunity, then help them learn. If the same person often repeats the same mistake, then perhaps that person will do better elsewhere or in a different position.

NEVER, EVER PARK YOUR VEHICLE CLOSE TO THE CLUBHOUSE WHEN IT IS OPEN.

- Never promote to management an employee who ably performs a function (i.e., serving, cooking, bartending, marketing, golf, tennis, pro-shop sales, accounting, etc.) without first investing in their management or supervisory training. Anything less is a set-up for failure.

- Consider the consequences of promoting someone beyond their skill level and, should they fail, offering to put them back where they were. No way! They're gone, and their career path is unalterably, negatively affected. The club loses a previously productive worker who will now, still untrained, apply for positions at or above the level to which you promoted them. The cycle of failure will be painfully repeated elsewhere until someone invests more than blind confidence that s/he is capable of leading others.

- Never ridicule an employee's idea, a child's dreams, or an artist's vision. Imagine the tragedy if they believed you.

- Professionals are true to their craft and can be counted on to do right in the right way.

- Staff development is an investment. Yes, it can be expensive, particularly if, after being trained, the person leaves your club for another position. But, imagine the expense of not training, particularly if the untrained are those who choose to remain at your club.

- Terminating an employee must not be done impulsively but following deliberation, documentation and ultimately with kindness. Even when you've got the authority to do so, when considering terminating a popular or long-term employee, seek input from board members or, at minimum, the impacted chairperson. Treat the employee with the same dignity you'd like when your time comes, as it may one day.

- The club cannot compete with every local restaurant, nor should you try. But, find out where Members dine when not dining at the club. Deliver something which those restaurants cannot.

- Unemployed? Account for resume date-gaps. Go to work — even short-term consulting for a colleague is preferable to moping around the house, waiting for the phone to ring. Stay in the game.

VISIBILITY IS THE NUMBER ONE EXPECTATION OF BOARDS, MEMBERS, CLUB EMPLOYEES AND SEARCH COMMITTEES.

- When entering the club repeat, to yourself, *"It's Showtime!"*

- We are responsible for what we say and do, no matter how we feel.

- When seeking a new job, family and friends (though well-intentioned) can't be objective. They care about you and worry over your circumstances, but they lack the expertise to be of real help and often become a serious "time-suck" as you try to assure **them**. Get referrals to a professional, trusted resource, capable of being your GPS through an otherwise daunting maze. Reach out to those whom you've helped through the years.

- You **ARE** in a fishbowl. The clothes you wear, how you present yourself inside the club, and while out-and-about in the community, send a message about who you are. Avoid publicly compromising your image or that of the club which, at all times, you represent.

YOU DON'T HAVE TO CHANGE JOBS. BUT — YOU MAY BE ABLE TO CHANGE THIS JOB. THERE IS NO PERFECT CLUB, NO PERFECT JOB, NO PERFECT COMMUNITY, NO PERFECT BOARD, AND NO PERFECT HUMAN. GET OVER IT!

- You may be able to get by on charisma for a day or two (STYLE). Then, you'd better know something. Regardless of how supportive the board/management relationship is at first, as it fades there had better be something else to take its place (SUBSTANCE).

Guidelines for Successful Clubs

- A vibrant and successful private club is not its physical structure. A club succeeds because of what goes on within those walls: service, recognition, relationships, fun.

- Acquire the names of every guest and consider adding them to the newsletter e-mail blast for a few months. The membership department might drop them a personal note in case they have any questions or observations about the club.

- Cash tipping is simply not a good idea. Sure, the rules may prohibit cash tipping, but try stopping the Member whose generous tips assure him that his vodka-tonic is 20% ice, 5% tonic, and 75% Grey Goose Ducasse. How do other Members feel about subsidizing special treatment for the select few?

- First Impressions: Get rid of the weeds at the entrance, plant and maintain seasonal color in the beds. Make sure the brass entry door handles are clean and polished and the doors aren't sticky. Select an understated but distinctive scent for the club entrance and use it consistently.

- It is passé to simply promote your club as a home-away-from-home. If your club isn't distinctively superior and delivering a special experience, why should someone join? A private club must deliver value — not to be confused with a bargain — and a unique Member experience. Otherwise prospective Members may just stay home and pay-for-play at a muni. Why be a member?

- Manage-by-Seduction: Give Members just a taste of quality furnishings, service, food, art, sense-of-arrival, and they'll want to keep that and more. Then – keep it going!

- Members generally trend towards not making reservations except, maybe, for a customarily sold-out event. Successful clubs set up their staff for success when a culture exists where the membership routinely make reservations, which guide efficient planning.

MEMBERSHIP IN A PRIVATE CLUB IS A PRIVILEGE, NOT AN ENTITLEMENT. CLUB RULES MUST BE CONSISTENTLY ENFORCED. STAFF INFORMS. BOARD ENFORCES.

- Members may have joined the club for its amenities such as golf, tennis, swimming, dining, etc. However, the thousands of private club Members who've participated in our popular focus groups over four decades, almost universally state they've kept their membership because of friends, most of whom they've met at the club. It's not the physical place, but what goes on around the club that builds loyalty.

- Never do anything which may cheapen your club's brand. Many clubs, during the recent economic downturn, cut costs, reduced services and quality, slashed, waived or deferred initiation fees and dues, kept low dues despite smaller membership. They often deferred essential maintenance and invaded capital reserves to supplement revenue shortfall and maxed out their credit line. Those clubs today suffer the consequences: typically struggling with inadequate capital reserves, equipment that now must be replaced because it wasn't properly repaired, brand deterioration, and bargain-oriented members who may now serve on the board. We've all heard of clubs being auctioned on the courthouse steps, sold to housing developers, converting to semiprivate or selling to daily fee operators. Some have been abandoned to seed and weed. Equity refunds? Fuhgeddaboudit!

- Publish lots of Member photographs in the newsletter and e-mail blasts. Use these to share information and promote events, but don't overlook their value as ego publications.

- Seeing Members having fun at the club produces more Members attending and doing the same at the next event.

- Resist slashing expenses and cutting ingredient quality and service staff. As an alternative, consider improving quality and announcing a likely increase in initiation fees sometime soon, to stimulate a decision among the demographic sought by the club.

- Something that you don't ever want to overhear: "What a great place to work, if only we didn't have to deal with all these demanding Members".

- Always capitalize the word Members. Without whom there would be no club!

- Struggling clubs oftentimes do not fully empower a true General Manager/Chief Operating Officer with the authority and responsibility to effectively lead and be held fully accountable for leading the entire operating team. Clubs that have operated under the club manager, clubhouse manager or committee-run concept are accident prone as they transition from driving on one side of the road to the other. The turnover rate of those signing-on as a club's first GM/COO is cause for concern as substantiated by our firm's interim management services being frequently called upon to get things right.

- What's your club's signature dish: sticky buns, pretzel rolls, a long-gone but beloved chef's special entrée or secret sauce, Aunt Mable's seasonal berry cobbler, locally sourced seafood chowder, house-made ice cream, smoked bluefish spread, club-grown produce? What do your Members call attention to when they say to their guests: "You've just gotta try our chefs' _____ ?"

Guidelines for Life in General

- A reputation, built over a lifetime, can be ruined in a day by individuals who don't even know you.

- Genetics, upbringing, experience, environment and circumstances have influenced who you are, but you are responsible for who you become.

- It takes a long time to become the person you want to be. Be reasonably patient with yourself.

- It's not **what** you have in your life, but **who** you have in your life that counts.

- Money and stuff are worthless criteria for a successful life.

- Some people may care for and about you, but just don't know how to show it.

- Those who are honest with themselves accomplish more in life.

- True friends can do anything or nothing, and still enjoy their time together.

- Trust may take years to build but can be destroyed in minutes.

- We can keep going long after we think we can't.

- We each are able to replace the negative narrative of that still, small voice in our head.

- We must separate the person from their actions. However, we often judge ourselves by what we think and what we feel, while others tend to judge us by what we do.

- What happens to you is less significant than what you do about it.

- When angry we tell ourselves that we've got the right to be. But we don't have permission to be cruel.

- When times get tough, before speaking without thinking, write a venting note-to-self, set it aside, read it later, then throw it away.

- Wisdom reflects lessons learned from various experiences — it has less to do with years lived.

AND – VERY IMPORTANTLY...

"YOU SHOULD NEVER LEAVE THOSE YOU CARE ABOUT WITHOUT A KIND PARTING WORD. YOU MAY NEVER SEE EACH OTHER AGAIN."

Thank you, Professor Weiner! Sitting in the front row of your class
"WISDOM THAT ONLY COMES WITH EXPERIENCE"
(40+ years of it!) is deeply appreciated!

LEGACY MEMBERSHIPS ARE PROVING
A PIPELINE TO SURVIVE.

LEADERSHIP
POP QUIZ TEST

THIS IS A TEST. A TONGUE IN CHEEK TEST.

To prepare yourself for the final exam. You don't actually have to take this quiz. Just read it straight through and you'll get the point.

Q: What are the names of —
- The 5 wealthiest people in the world?
- The last 3 Heisman trophy winners?
- The last 2 winners of the America's Got Talent contest?
- 4 people who have won the Nobel or Pulitzer Prize?
- The last 3 Academy Award winners for best picture?
- The last 3 teams who won the World Series?

How did you do?

The point is that none of us remembers the headliners of yesterday for very long. And these are no second-rate achievers. They are the best in their fields.

But the applause dies. Awards tarnish. Achievements are forgotten. Accolades and certificates are buried with their owners.

Here's another quiz. See how you do on this one.

Q: What are the names of —

- 3 teachers who aided your journey through school!
- 2 friends who encouraged you through a difficult time!
- 5 people who taught you something worthwhile!
- 4 people who made you feel appreciated!
- 2 people you enjoy spending time with!

THE LESSON

The people who make a difference in your life are not the ones with the most credentials, the most money, or the most awards. They are the ones that care and exhibit character.

THE INTROSPECTION

What kind of difference are we making in the lives of the people we interact with?

And, if they were asked to "name names" — for what would we be remembered, if at all?

Deeper still — what types of quiz questions would our names immediately bring to mind if asked of our peers, employees, and members of our own family?

THE FINAL EXAM

By the way, there are no letter grades here — just a simple Pass/Fail.

Q: Name an individual who wants to be remembered by their peers, employees and members of their own family as a person who cares and exhibits character.

- A: Let's all just fill in our name right here! And, for "Extra Credit" you can add mine, as I am right along with you.

Like to explore character traits a bit more? Check out: CHARACTER IS WHAT DEFINES A PLUTONIUM CLUB LEADER

LISTENING & SPEAKING
PLUTONIUM CLUB LEADERSMASTER EXECUTIVE LEVEL PRESENTATION SKILLS — KNOWING WHEN TO SIMPLY BE STILL AND OBSERVE

I have had a chair at dozens upon dozens upon dozens of Board of Directors meetings, and have personally seen the following listening and speaking techniques used with great skill by proven executives from many professions (even me).

WE BASICALLY USE 500 WORDS TO COMMUNICATE ALL OF OUR FEELINGS. These same 500 words have over 150,000 different meanings.

How many times have you found yourself unwittingly painted into a corner because of something that you said and, then when challenged, were unable to substantiate the very premise of your statement? YIKES!

I am not in any way referring to lying. But rather, allowing yourself to become caught up in an emotional issue that tempts you to feel compelled to needlessly throw in your own two cents, in an emotionally charged manner.

Suddenly, you find yourself saying something that seems very logical, quite plausible, and does indeed make some degree of sense – but then you realize that you have no means to even remotely substantiate your position.

Suddenly, everyone else in the room is mute – you are wondering how this seemingly out of control dialogue with everyone talking at once could become so alarmingly quiet. All eyes and ears slowly turn to you – when you actually had nothing to say in the first place, not really.

- Sometimes – the less you say, results in the less you have to apologize for later on.

- Sometimes – we forget that while talking, we are not in a great position to learn anything.

- Sometimes – the desire to speak is a compulsion so strong that you feel it must be acted upon.

Those who cannot keep silent when they should, are the very same people who usually cannot speak when they should. You must learn the difference between those two points.

Many of us know WHAT to say, and HOW to say it. The problem is that, in either case, few of us listen long enough to know precisely WHEN.

Work on developing the talent of being able to listen closely.

You must depend upon receiving new information to be able to continually expand and deepen your knowledge and understanding of the world and everything in it. (Not to mention yourself!).

It really is true that our actions do speak louder than our words. Because of this, sometimes WHO we are speaks with such a deafening roar that people can't hear what it is that we are trying to say.

An example of this is the person who is so opinionated on every subject and is "always flapping his jaws" or someone who talks "just to hear her head rattle." They are not likely to find a receptive audience, no matter how well thought out and intelligent their input on any issue.

This is sad, but true. It is a bit like the story of "The Boy Who Cried Wolf" in that WHO he was spoke so much louder than WHAT he was trying to say, no one would hear him.

The importance of being prepared and organized before you speak cannot be over emphasized. There is little sense in having to recover after you have spoken.

If you are preparing for a meeting with your staff, a full-scale board of directors meeting, a small committee meeting or just an informal conference over lunch – be prepared and organized before you ever enter the room. Have the framework of the pertinent issues at hand and be ready to move in the direction you wish to head – but, only at the appropriate time.

One of the most important elements of preparedness lies in being ready to do more listening than talking. By developing your ability to really listen, you will be taking a GIANT step in dealing with either of these two situations:

1. *When you are dealing with people who really have nothing to say* and would be better off listening; let them do the talking. The fastest way to silence someone is to let him or her do all the talking.

2. *When dealing with someone who does indeed have some valuable thoughts* that are well prepared and of significance, listen closely. You will then be in a perfect position to encourage them and help them to further clarify and expand upon their thinking. This is someone you want to encourage to keep talking.

Notice that the common denominator in both instances is LISTENING!

Make certain that the speaker is aware that you are taking notes from their statements. This lets them know that not only are you interested in what they have to say, but that you do not plan to interrupt them. This can accomplish two things directly with an indirect bonus.

FIRST: If the person speaking is NOT prepared and fully able to verify their statements, nothing will silence them faster than observing their audience, in apparent rapt attention, taking notes of every word they have to say.

SECOND: If you feel the speaker really has something significant to convey and a sound presentation, this is a good opportunity for you to get his or her ideas down in writing. It would be foolish for you to attempt to commit all of their ideas and insights to memory.

THE BONUS in either case is that you will be able to learn and grow as a result of your having developed the skill of really listening and taking intelligent notes at a meeting. Let's face it; even the very worst presentations definitely serve as examples for us to take notes with the intent of improving our own performance.

Yes, we all know that a smart person learns from his or her own mistakes. But a truly wise person is able to carefully observe, think about, and learn from the mistakes of others.

As you take your notes while observing the person who doesn't have a sound presentation, be aware of not only what they are trying to say, but also HOW they are going about it.

- What body posture does s/he exhibit?
- How does s/he gesture with their hands?
- What is the tone & volume of voice?
- Is there eye contact?
- Does input seem to flow naturally, or come in contrived sentences?
- What does attire communicate about the speaker?
- Is there any humor? If so, was it appropriate or distracting?

While listening to someone speaking poorly – you should be able to consider all the above and identify the reasons why they do not convey confidence. This way, you will learn how not to handle yourself when in a similar position.

PLUTONIUM CLUB LEADERS ALWAYS COMMUNICATES

Politely.
Respectfully.
Encouragingly.
Efficiently.
Effectively.
And At All Times — With:

HUMILITY.

While listening to someone who is confident and convincing, make notes in relation to the questions posed earlier. You can learn much from them on how to enhance your own performance.

This, then, is truly a WIN-WIN situation for you. But it's only true IF you develop the basic skill of listening, and speaking only when there is a basis to do so.

Be precise and as brief as may be appropriate in any given situation.

Let your "yes" be yes and, your "no" be no.

Here is a way to be sure that others will listen to you once you are certain that you really have something of value to contribute. Be sure that you have the general attention of the group — but — then do not begin to speak immediately.

An occasional outburst of TOTAL SILENCE can be one of your greatest tools and adds credibility to whatever is said after it.

Get their attention, and then pause for a full three or four seconds before beginning to share your thoughts. This is a particularly strong move to use when a meeting has gotten out of hand and everyone else seems to want to talk all at once.

For some strange reason some people are not in the least bit hesitant in interrupting others, but balk when it comes to interrupting an outburst of silence.

The longer the pause before speaking, when accompanied by effective eye contact — I promise you, the greater the level of anticipation will be from all the attendees at the meeting. It will reach the point that they will be really anxious to hear what you have to say.

The confirmed "good" news is that now you have their undivided attention. However, the potential "bad" news is you had better know what you are talking about!

Make sure, make sure — oh, for crying out loud —*make very sure* you know what you are talking about!

Be very careful using this little hint that I share with you. Do not use it unless you really have something significant to say. The truth is if you don't, then perhaps you shouldn't be speaking at all.

The less you speak; the more people are inclined to listen when you do. If you are 100% sure of your facts, then you can afford to keep quiet until the appropriate time.

> **THOSE WHO ARE THE BEST PREPARED WITH THE MOST TO CONTRIBUTE ARE THOSE WHO SPEAK ONLY WHEN THEY HAVE SOMETHING TO SAY. THE REST ONLY WANT TO SAY SOMETHING. THERS SPEAK.**

Meetings can sometimes run way too long. Not because everything that needs to be said has not been said yet. Simply because the unprepared and unorganized have not yet had a chance to say it yet.

DON'T SPEAK HASTILY: *"My dear brothers and sisters, take note of this: Everyone should be quick to listen, slow to speak, and slow to become angry." JAMES 1:19*

And … "That's all I have to say about that." – Forest Gump

MEMBERS & MANAGEMENT ARE
IN CONSTANT HARMONY.

MASTER PLAN
FOR BOTH CLUBHOUSE AND GOLF COURSE

Have you ever noticed how some clubs simultaneously portray a deceptive early American/Mediterranean/southwestern/18th century/French country house/high-tech/Spanish Colonial look throughout their clubhouse?

Without a board-approved professional interior design master plan, a clubhouse slowly morphs into a hodge-podge of various themes and intents (ditto with the golf course, but we'll tie that in later).

Imagine our own homes if different family members had free reign:

- Your college-aged son does the living room.
- Great Aunt Meltha, the dining room.
- Cousin Bobby, the front entry.
- Your master bedroom? Your mother-in-law!

After years of however well-intended "Band-Aid" approaches, someone predictably proclaims that there is no need to allocate more money into the house for a couple of years (AKA: "deferred maintenance").

In this case...looks are NOT deceiving!

Great clubs have policies (ideally in the form of a bylaw) that preclude members (family or otherwise) being allowed to meddle in clubhouse décor—much less in redesigning the golf course. They also have an approved professional master plan that is reviewed and monitored annually.

There are outstanding national design firms that specialize in high quality design for private clubs. Have a few of these take a look, and then prepare a "first impressions" report.

A club is wise in retaining the professional services of an interior design firm with proven expertise in developing all-encompassing master plans, broken down into phases over time.

A professional design firm will create detailed layouts specifically indicating where each piece of furniture is to be placed, artwork is to be hung, at what height, and where every lamp is to be placed, etc.

- No more having bus boys making these weighty decisions!

Once a thorough search process is complete and you have identified the firm that best reflects your unique club traditions and culture— plan on retaining their services for at least 3 to 5 plus years in order to ensure continuity and constant adherence to the board approved master plan.

You should have two professional "walk-throughs" done routinely every year.

Prior to the time of annual club closing for maintenance and employee vacations:

1. YOUR DESIGN FIRM WILL IDENTIFY FURNITURE THAT NEEDS REPAIR/REPLACEMENT. THEY WILL:

- *Select colors and types of paint* to be used to touch-up needed areas
- *Indicate specific lighting* for all areas of the club -
- *Identify wall coverings* that need repair —
- *Select appropriate carpet and tile* -recommend fabrics, textures, styles, and colors, of window treatments.

Amateurs, no matter how well-intended, should do NONE of these things.

BTW --- It is STRONGLY recommended that every club routinely close down completely major portions of their clubhouse for the specific purpose of annual repairs/maintenance/general upkeep. Make it a policy of the club to get this done. Close 2 or 3 weeks every year.

2. ROUTINELY SCHEDULE A SECOND WALK THROUGH 7 OR 8 MONTHS DEEP INTO YOUR FISCAL YEAR:

This allows time to identify areas, get competitive bids, and prepare a written report that serves as a blueprint for management to professionally guide the recommendations that the board will ultimately consider in approving various repairs and/or improvements into the next year's fiscal operating and capital budgets.

With the discipline of at least two annual professional walk-throughs and detailed written documentation, you know in advance exactly:

- *WHAT* you are going to do.
- *WHEN* you are going to do it.
- *HOW* much it is going to cost.
- *WHO* is going to do it.
- *WHY* it should be done at all.

The mandatory "ABC's" of having a clubhouse the members are proud of:

A. Dedicated housekeeping staff.
B. Systematic preventative maintenance program.
C. Relationship with the right professional interior design firm.

No matter how great a master design plan may look on paper — it is wasted if daily housekeeping is lacking and areas of the clubhouse are allowed to become soiled or in premature disrepair. The same applies if corroded pipes leak above your brand-new ceiling onto your brand-new furnishings, sitting on your brand-new flooring.

(Similar truths are inescapable on the golf course as well. Hold on - it's coming.)

With a dedicated approach to housekeeping, a systematic approach to preventative maintenance, and a professional approach to clubhouse décor, your clubhouse will reflect stability, quality and continuity for many years.

(Again - these very same concepts apply to the golf course. Spot on. Mirror image.)

But what about the golf course?

The analogy of interviewing several professional interior design firms for the clubhouse is exactly the same intent and process as doing so with golf course architects in order to create a master plan for the course.

In a member owned private club — there are always a few (you think?) members who fancy themselves to be golf course architects and are qualified to decide:

- Location of bunkers.
- Size/shape of greens and water hazards.
- Placement of tee boxes.
- Types and placement of trees.
- Removal of trees.
- Where cart paths should be created.
- Length of the rough, etc.

Board/committee opinions change over the years.

If ever-changing amateur decisions are allowed simply based on: (A) who has the strongest personality — (B) who is in a position of influence at any point in time, or — (C) an absence of any overall, board approved master plan to guide these decisions —— the course will indeed slowly morph into a mash up layout with no continuity, flow, or "personality" of its own.

Every club wants their golf course to be a "memorable" experience that differentiates itself from others. Indeed, it may become "memorable" — but in the absence of a board approved Master Plan...for all the WRONG reasons.

To circumvent all this — reputable golf course architectural firms are interviewed and asked to make presentations as to their vision for a master plan for the course. Then, based upon budget considerations, phasing, priorities, and the perceived wants/needs of the membership — a master plan is approved and becomes policy.

Never forget:

Whether on the golf course or in the clubhouse — GREAT club experiences are memorable in the mind and heart of members and their guests — for all the RIGHT reasons.

MEETINGS
PLUTONIUM LEADERS DO NOT ALLOW THINGS TO BE RAILROADED THROUGH!

PREFACE

Most executives will say that they generally don't care for meetings. But the fact is that ALL meetings are not a waste of time — but weak leadership allows meetings with no meaningful agenda at all...or, instead, often a hidden one. Here is an example.

In the beginning was — *"THE PLAN."*
And then came — *"THE ASSUMPTIONS."*
And darkness was upon the faces of **The Employees.**
And they spoke among themselves, saying, "It is a crock of _____, and it stinketh!"

The employees went to their **Department Heads** and said, "It is a pail of dung and none may abide the odor thereof."

And, the Department Heads went unto The General Manager and said, "It is a Container of Excrement. Its foul odor is very strong. None may abide by it."

(And, all the while, a Committee filled its nostrils with the aroma of "THE PLAN." They hired an Outside Consultant who provided a written report conveying what they wanted to hear.)

And lo, the General Manager went before **The Board** and suggested, "Ahem — ladies and gentlemen, ahem — this does indeed appear to be a Vessel of Fertilizer. May I respectfully just kind of, well, ah — recommend that we consider that none may abide by its strength? I mean —I'm just sayin'?"

And, the Board went into closed sessions — speaking in hushed tones amongst themselves — saying to one another, "What does s/he really know? This Plan contains that which aids plant growth. It is very powerful! And, we have a written report to prove it!"

A small **(but vocal)** group armed with a petition from a **self-appointed ad hoc Committee** with its roots in **The Men's Bar at the Club** — went to T**he Executive Committee** and said, "Behold! It promotes growth and is very powerful!"

And the Executive Committee went unto T**he President** and presented with fervent voices, "This **NEW PLAN** will actively promote growth and in these areas in particular!"

And — the President looked upon "THE PLAN" — and proclaimed it good! And, "THE PLAN" — became: *"POLICY."*

And, this — *just in case you were wondering* — is how #*%? happens!

If all the above seems humorous (albeit painfully so) it is only because we've all seen it unfold in one form or another.

> **PLUTONIUM CLUB LEADERS STOP POTENTIAL OUT OF CONTROL TRAIN WRECKS DEAD IN THEIR TRACKS. WITHIN THEIR SPHERE OF INFLUENCE, PLUTONIUM CLUB LEADERS DO NOT ALLOW THINGS TO BE RAILROADED THROUGH AND BYPASS MEANINGFUL SCRUTINY AND INPUT.**

MEMBERSHIP MARKETING
IS NOT A SPRINT

When it comes to private club membership, sales are not a sprint. Most people will agree with that simple and trite statement. You've probably heard it before from a board member or even a general manager.

The problem is, the advice that comes next is often wrong, too. The classic follow-up to "it's not a sprint," is usually "it's a marathon."

I'm going to show you why it's not a marathon either. In fact, effective membership sales are actually a series of short sprints, more like a relay. Just like a relay, you need to have a strong team from beginning to end and you need to maximize every leg of the race.

The overwhelming majority of private club marketing directors I've met treat the sales process like a sprint.

Here's the classic scenario I've seen played out over and over.

The prospective member is referred to the club or finds the club through some marketing channel. — The membership director schedules a tour and in about an hour will briskly shuffle them from one area of the club to another. — They'll probably hop in a golf cart and see a few holes, stop by the pool or fitness facility, have a peek at the tennis courts, tour the dining rooms and banquet facilities and arrive back at the clubhouse and in the MD's office. — The prospect will then be handed some pamphlets about the club and talk numbers.

The savvy membership director will ask for the sale because that's what they've been trained to do at some point in their career. After all, good salespeople close, right?

The problem is, that tried and true membership sales process isn't working like it used to.

But why is it getting harder and harder to sell a private club membership? I've heard a number of theories posed from industry experts who talk about more competition, changing value systems, time-constraints, aging populations and so on.

All of those have some truth to them. But I think there's something right under our noses that's even more important to recognize, and it has to do with the methodology of how we're selling.

A few months back I had the pleasure of speaking with Susan Greene on my show, *Private Club Radio*. Susan is the current PCMA President and membership director at The Oaks Club near Sarasota, Florida. If you have the pleasure of meeting Susan, you'll be instantly struck by her bubbly personality and bright floral outfits. She's a Florida gal, after all.

But beyond her famously welcoming personality lies a very sharp salesperson. She's keenly aware of her market, and the strengths and selling points of her offering. Suffice it to say, if she got you in a room for an hour, she could sell you just about anything.

However, instead of sharing her tips for getting a prospect to put pen to paper, she made a statement that caught me by surprise. "Your goal as a membership director shouldn't be to make the sale, it should be to move the sale forward," she told me.

I'd love to tell you how when that line hit me, the clouds parted and the trumpets sounded. Except it didn't happen that way at all. In fact, I said something mundane like, "Great advice, Susan," and moved on to my next question in the interview.

In the days and weeks that transpired I let that statement marinate.

I knew this simple truth had something profound behind it, but I didn't know how it all fit in just yet. It took me talking to psychologists to figure out why it was so important.

KEY CONCEPTS FOR A DISRUPTIVE IDEA

I regularly chat with psychologists. Not to clear my head or work through a deep-seated issue, but to pick their brains on my marketing ideas. You see, I firmly believe if we can understand how our market thinks and how they will instinctively react, we can better position ourselves for optimal results. Who better than a psychologist to tell us what our prospects are thinking?
During one of these conversations I focused my questioning around creating desires. What does it take to create a desire in the mind of a consumer?

The discussion naturally wove its way through a number of concepts, but eventually landed on the notion of habit formation. It made a lot of sense to me.

We desire things for which we have built a habit. Conversely, habits can be built by associating experiences or things with a desirable outcome. It's a simple concept and it was my first key. It only takes a quick glance at modern technology success stories to realize why habit-forming behavior is the Holy Grail for brands. The very mobile device in your pocket or purse right now is the best evidence I can present.

Surveys have shown that nearly a third of folks would prefer to give up sex before they gave up their mobile device. Why is this? Because our phones have become our biggest habit. Everything that is contained in them has been designed with habit formation in mind.

Every time you see a little red circle around one of your apps it's a trigger that leads to a behavior. You see the notification icon, you want to press the button, and you get rewarded with something. Maybe it's an important email, maybe it's a cute picture of your friend's baby on Facebook, or maybe it's the next episode of that podcast you're really into.

Nir Eyal's brilliant book, Hooked: How to Build Habit Forming Products, explains the process of how habits are formed with our everyday tech. It's a four-step process of triggers, actions, variable rewards and investment.

Using our example above, that little icon on your phone's screen is the trigger. That trigger causes the action of you opening the app. The reward is what you see or experience, like that cute picture of a baby. You're then asked to make an investment, whether that's filling out your profile, responding or leaving a comment, sharing something yourself, etc.

Now, it's critical to note that rewards must be variable for these habits to form — otherwise the monotony would cause boredom and use would drop. If I just saw cute babies all the time, I'd get bored. I need to see links to informative articles, photos of my friends, or a funny video sometimes, to keep me guessing and keep me interested. Once this four-step process is repeated a few times, habits get formed.

As the conversation progressed, I found the second key that would unlock Susan's statement: habits take *30 days to form.* A month's worth of electrons firing and dopamine spreading and all that other good brain stuff causes those synapses to build and eventually a habit is made.

MEMBERSHIP MARKETING REIMAGINED

Armed with this knowledge on how habits are formed and how long they take, I once again contemplated the sage words of Susan Greene.

As I alluded to earlier, the problem of private club membership isn't the offer, it's the process. It's the way we're going about trying to sell something.

If we can think of the sales process as a 30-day habit-forming process, instead of that proverbial "three-hour tour", I think success will come more easily.

Those close ratios will go up. You'll turn more prospects into members. It's science.

My challenge to boards, GM/COOs, and membership directors is to begin to treat the membership sales process as a relay race spread out over 30 days. Break that down into a 4-week period where you can get a prospect immersed in your club. Give those prospects variable rewards and let them begin to associate the time spent at your club with the "good times".

Get them in that habit. In practice, this is a 40,000-foot view of how it might look.

- *Week 1:* prospects tour your facility and are introduced to key staff.

- *Week 2:* prospects are invited back to play a round of golf or hit some tennis balls or sail around your harbor so they see what it's like to decompress after a tough day at work.

- *Week 3:* invite them to have a meal at the club so they can have a sensual experience that equates your club with delight.

- *Week 4:* invite them to one of your affinity groups, like a wine club, so they can interact with folks that they can see themselves relaxing with.

All the while, it's important for the membership director to follow up and make sure they are "moving the process forward," as Susan so eloquently said.

After those 30 days of experiencing what it might actually be like to be a member of your club, that prospect is going to be in a much better state of mind to pull the trigger. That's the time to ask for the close.

They'll have built those neural pathways that associate your club with pleasurable moments. They'll have made your club their habit!
This is a disruptive concept. This is outside the box.
Some boards and management will be opposed to this idea. I understand that.

But it takes something disruptive and scary to affect change. It's going to take a mindset shift to turn the tide and revitalize this industry we all love.

This isn't the only answer, but I think it's a strong one that will help many of your clubs out there. If it's not right for yours, that's ok too.

Please keep searching and remember that it's when we think we've got it all figured out that we're in the most danger.

MENU PRICES
TO PRINT OR NOT TO PRINT — THAT IS THE QUESTION

Oftentimes members want prices printed on their menus — but priceless for guests? Why?

Is the host planning to first check out all the prices and then convince their guests on the wisdom of ordering a Cornish hen instead of a veal chop? Really?

Or - lean over to the guest on their left and whisper, "It's OK - you can have a cup of coffee - it's included in the price of the meal." Wink – Wink.

Then lean to the right, "The canned mixed vegetables served on a bed of nails is much better than the fresh white asparagus. Trust me — I've been a member here for years."

Having sticker prices on cars makes a bit more sense. But even in the showroom, at a Chevy dealer, you pretty much know the price range of the products they sell. And, if you go to the Porsche dealer, you have that same sense of where you are.

But many members drive a Porsche to their club, and then expect to be handed a menu with Chevy prices.
I'd suggest that:

- Priced menus be available on the "members only" portal of your website.
- And ALL menus used in the ala carte dining areas of the club be priceless.

OK. Let's sum up what we've just covered:

- A new Chevy? Oh — say $18 to $46 grand.
- A new Porsche? Ah - let's go with $68 to $180+ grand.

Menus at the Club? - *PRICELESS!*

PREFACE:

Gabe recently interviewed Michael for the third time on *Private Club Radio*. The programs that have featured Michael are consistently the most downloaded of 150+ shows (and counting). The subject this time: what it takes to turn a club around. Here is a transcript of that interview.

GABE: Michael, you're an expert at turning clubs around. What are some common problems you see clubs facing these days?

MICHAEL: Many clubs have somewhat unknowingly strayed from their own Mission Statements. Or, conversely, held too closely to them. There has to be a conscious commitment to balance between these two extremes. Here are a few thoughts that come to mind.

1. Club traditions and unique culture is very important. But — keep in mind: the past is valuable as a guide post — but, very dangerous if used as a hitching post. Staying in, or longing for, the past does not necessarily help run the business of the club today or to attract tomorrow's potential members.

2. Over the past decade the definition of remaining relevant to the lifestyle to a new generation of potential members has evolved and changed dramatically.

3. Approaches to club governance (Board) or operations (Management) that exist solely for historical reasons, which are no longer relevant in today's world and lifestyles — keep you locked in an orbit around a world that no longer exists.

Understand that the future of a club is based upon consistent member experiences that satisfy the quality and service expectations of an ever-changing marketplace to the point that they will excitedly recommend their club to their business associates, family and friends.

Those who ask if the private club industry is changing are way behind the curve. Why? Because it already has changed. And it will never return to what it was in the days where all the Board had to do was make simplistic popular policy adjustments every so often, and all Management had to do was to occasionally make "low hanging operational fruit" decisions. Those days are gone.

But for those clubs resourceful enough to make the strategic policies (Board) and operational (Management) decisions necessary to reflect the times — there can be plenty of good days ahead.

GABE: I have to imagine that very often the problem a club THINKS they have is not exactly the problem they DO have. When you walk into a club that needs help, how do you go about finding where the problems and inefficiencies lay?

MICHAEL: Answers are found by listening. I do lots of that. I've never learned one single thing while I am talking. Therefore, I first listen to what people have to say. What is on their mind? Where is their heart at? What concerns to they have?

ALL problems in any business model, ultimately have a direct link to "people problems." Also, keep in mind that virtually every member-owned private club (when it comes to Net departmental operations) does not have a viable business model. To prove it – that's why members have to pay dues!

Nonetheless, prior to my arrival on site, before having the opportunity to personally interact with all the key people (staff/management/board/committees) — I thoroughly review current and historical financial data, digest the minutes for the past year of all board/committee meetings and become familiar with their bylaws and club rules. I digest the past year of club newsletters and review their web site content and appearance.

This enables me to "hit the ground running" in preparation, before getting down to what truly matters. What matters is listening and then earning the confidence of all the people involved.

Financial data, minutes from meetings, and club newsletters don't change things. PEOPLE change things.

So, to answer your direct question as to how I go about finding where any problems and inefficiencies are — while I do my homework ahead of time — my focus is on the people at the club. All of them!

Why? Just ask yourself this question: "If - by magic ▢ I had all the right people in all the right places, who were all really focused and all excited about what they do - what then would happen to all those "problems" of ours?" The short answer is that they would ALL go away.

GABE: Can you share any warning signs that boards should look for?

MICHAEL: Yes. Here is just a random sampling. To all board members out there — if you find your meetings:

- Rehashing again and again the same old dead issues for hours upon hours…with seemingly nothing ever getting fully resolved.
- Finding a need to spend time in "Executive Session" in order to delve deeper into "operations" while the GM/COO is out of the room.
- Committee chairs coming woefully unprepared to truly present actionable (fully vetted at the committee level) recommendations that the board can confidently act upon.
- A GM/COO either not expected (or not qualified) to be near the top of every agenda, who consistently provides proactive meaningful input that sets the tone for the rest of the meeting. And that Includes a succinct "Executive Summary" emailed prior to every meeting.
- Agendas that are truly redundant, and all but meaningless.
- Far too much time spent dissecting the past 30-day operating data (particularly F&B) rather than focusing on the long-range future of the club, the best polices to protect club traditions while still reflecting the times, and in supporting top management talent.

Now then – having pointed out just a few things above — all are directly related to having (or not) — the right people in the right places.

- I often find clubs allowing onerous debt to be kicked down the road for far too long. This is particularly true when initiation fee income is no longer what it was years ago. Add this to repetitive annual Board decisions approving what amounts to "artificially" low dues levels and high levels of deferred maintenance (a potential death spiral if not addressed).

Quite often, potentially strong board and/or management performance is compromised because they "don't know what they don't know."

By working together, light is shed on a viable plan moving forward. It is all about the people. Not financial data. Charts. Reports. Graphs. Projections. It is having people know their roles in getting results. Favorable data, etc. is a byproduct of knowing what you are doing, and ensuring the right people are in the right places. I create an environment where this happens.

GABE: Once you've identified any problems, what comes next?

MICHAEL: Let me first share *"The CNG Universal Mission Statement"* that I believe every club can use as an inspiration. Just seven words: *"Our member's very favorite place to be."*

Imagine if the entire leadership team buys into a Mission Statement like that and then retools itself where every policy and operating decision is put through the filter of enhancing the success of the mission or not! Every SOP, leadership and staff roles, rules, bylaws — EVERYTHING — needs to contribute to a master plan of being: *"Our member's very favorite place to be."* That's the plan moving forward. Here are the two specific areas where people bring it to life:

1) Staff/Management/Operations: Positive leadership must consistently steer in the direction of:

- Making sure we have the right people and putting them in the right places. Developing, motivating and mentoring them. Culling the herd when necessary.

- Building and maintaining exemplarily management teams is accomplished by identifying talent, mentoring them, and monitoring accountability for terrific results — with a style of leadership based upon positive support and empowerment, rather than fear or micro-management.

2) Board/Policy/Governance: Here we get into:

- Updating bylaws and club rules to reflect the times and being relevant.
- Recasting lines of communication, authority and accountability.
- Creating position descriptions for board officers and committee chairs.

Behind the scenes stuff that REALLY matters and oftentimes needs to be cleaned up in order for the leadership team (Board and Management) to truly deliver day-to-day member experiences that fuel retention and recruitment to solidify the future of the club.

GABE: What's the "secret sauce" of getting staff and members to buy into your plan as an interim GM?

MICHAEL: It's not my plan. It's theirs! I just provide the professional expertise and personal care in helping them identify what their mission is and their plan to get there.

I simply do not believe in having a bad day and instead engage everyone on a personal level while consistently bringing sound business savvy & financial acumen to the table.

I revere the fact that the business world spins on an axis of accountability. Therefore, I demand from myself the expertise necessary to create, present, gain ultimate approval — and then monitor unwavering adherence to both Operating and Capital budgets. It's just the way I roll.

I quickly assess the level of talent available and then focus on creating an all but palpable positive energy that sets everyone up for success. Sure, I create reports, organization charts, flow charts and PowerPoint presentations. But what I really do is spend time with people, build relationships and set up the team for success.

And by the way — every situation is unique in what specific factors really would make the club their member's very favorite place to be. One size does NOT fit all. However, once the board and executive level management agree on the mission at hand — we simply map out their plan, gain momentum and don't look back.

Secret sauce? Here are the ingredients that, when mixed with expertise and care, creates the recipe for a successful mission:

Staff Management / Operations / Board / Policy / Governance.

Gabe, I'm flattered that you began by suggesting that I am an expert at turning clubs around. But the truth is that I don't turn any of them around. Instead, my expertise is more in listening, filling voids where "not knowing what they don't know" is an obstacle, creating an environment conducive to success, and then getting out of the way. It is the rejuvenated board / management team that turns things around.

MEMBER EXPERIENCES
MUST BE STAGED BY MANAGEMENT

Just as any great Realtor will "stage" a fine home in showcasing it for an "Open House" event — the same holds true with member experiences.

Contrary to a piece of real estate being presented on a specific weekend date during limited hours — favorable member experiences must not only be "showcased" — but delivered consistently every day all day...every day all day...every day all day...

In the public business world, "scores" are ordinarily kept in data reflected in numbers/dollars/percentages, etc...

We are talking about a vibe that the entire staff enjoys delivering to a deserving membership to the extent that both the staff and membership just can't help but to be proud of being part of something very special.

Oh, to be sure...there are plenty of membership surveys, KPI's and suggestion box responses that can help club leadership monitor, to some degree, how perceived membership experiences just might translate into numbers/dollars/percentages, etc....

However, to be sure...private clubs that truly differentiate themselves are those whose leadership focuses in real time, delivering incredible experiences to their members. This is firmly rooted in real eye contact, genuine

> **IN THE PRIVATE WORLD OF EXEMPLARY CLUBS, THE ONLY "SCORE" THAT ULTIMATELY MATTERS IS MEMBER EXPERIENCES THAT CONSISTENTLY DELIVER AN ALL BUT PALATABLE POSITIVE ENERGY VIBE THROUGHOUT THE ENTIRE CLUB.**

smiles and a joyful "Can Do – Will Do" attitude delivered by staff from top to bottom consistently every day all day...every day all day...every day all day...

The above paragraph simply does not happen if management time is overly spent in offices creating reports, reviewing data, blah, blah, blah.

Consistent exemplary membership experiences are proactively "staged" to be consistently delivered. Not in theory or reviewed in data after the fact.

ON BEING DIFFERENT

You have to be able to fill in the blanks with the very special things that really makes your club different.

You just have to believe with conviction:
"Our club is the only club that consistently delivers _____!"

Take the above open-ended statement and ask it as many times as your team is able to fill in the blank with a member experience. Then, take the steps every day in making

> **THE ENTIRE TEAM HAS TO EMBRACE, WITH CONVICTION, THAT THERE IS SOMETHING TRULY "DIFFERENT" ABOUT THE EXPERIENCES YOUR CLUB DELIVERS — AND, THEN CONSISTENTLY PROVE IT.**

sure that this is not just rhetoric...but, actually experienced at your club.

The entire team, top to bottom, must be able to fill in the blanks. Otherwise – what makes you think you are any different from all the others?

ON BEING FAMOUS:

Like it or not — every club is "famous" for something!

You MUST compellingly answer the question, "What are we famous for?"

Imagine major network broadcast news anchors and grocery store check-out magazines boldly splashing your answer to this question with the subheading: "XYZ CLUB MEMBER EXPEREINCES ARE TRULY DIFFERENT!"
Keep in mind:
Slogans and taglines that employees recite at team meetings, or printed on the back of little laminated cards they were given after orientation, mean nothing if the actual experiences of those you serve don't consistently prove it.

So what things do you want your club to be famous for?

STOP! Don't just read that last sentence and move on. No. Really stop and come up with your answers. Write them down. Now — then read on.

The entire team, top to bottom, must be able to take confident pride in their answers.

> **"IF YOU DON'T KNOW WHAT YOU ARE FAMOUS FOR — GUESS WHO DOES? EVERYBODY ELSE!"**

Not to be negative, but simply telling the truth — there are clubs out there who are "famous" for all the wrong things. Those who spend too much time in their office may not know it — but, again, guess who does? Hint: Maybe your members!

ON MEMBER EXPERIENCES

- CLUB GOODS – are produced and kept ready to go.
- STAFF SERVICES – are delivered on the spot.
- MEMBER EXPERIENCES – are staged ahead of time.

Your team MUST be dialed-in to the outcome of member experiences BEFORE any of them actually happens!

In other words, there should really be no need to ask members a silly rhetorical question like, "Did you experience everything you were hoping for at your club today?" We are routinely asked departing questions like this from bored employees at big box retail stores.

In the outside retail word, our consumer satisfaction experiences hover around the following:

- 70% are totally forgettable.
- 25% are so bad, we wish we could forget them.
- 5% are so great that we cherish the experience.

Why is the above so deplorable? I suggest that it is a predictable by-product of any business model that focuses on numbers/dollars/percentages, etc. — rather than staging great consumer experiences. Examples of glowing exceptions are the likes of Southwest Airlines, Disney, Nordstrom's, Chick-fil-et-A, and Costco.

It ALL comes down to selecting and maintaining a professional club staff that takes things personally.

Outside of private clubs, we are all so used to impersonal experiences that we've become desensitized to them. It has become what we expect and don't even know it!

OBSERVING THE STYLE OF THE OUTSIDE WORLD:

- "So-called" quality and service are defined by those retained on Madison Avenue, exit polls, competition, and what is deemed "acceptable" when graded on a curve.

- Changes to ad campaigns will be made in a New York minute if believed to move the dial in terms of numbers/dollars/percentages, etc...

- Advertising can help create or re-shape an image, but it is our actual personal experience that confirms the reality behind the image.

EXPERIENCING THE SUBSTANCE INSIDE THE WORLD OF PLUTONIUM PRIVATE CLUB LEADERS:

- Quality and service are defined by the members. There is no "grading on the curve."

- Nothing is going to divert members' focus from their actual experience in the areas of personal enrichment, cultural growth, good health, making new friends, creating lasting memories, and being proud of their membership every day all day…every day all day… every day all day …

- Members don't care about data and stats when they come to the club. They only care about their actual experiences. Save all the data for the annual meeting.

Simply put — it is the membership experiences that are staged in advance — and then **consistently** delivered —that makes a club "famous" and what differentiates you from whatever else is out there.

MOVING FORWARD:
Routinely fill in the blanks:

- "Our club is the only club that consistently delivers _____!"
- "Our club is famous for _____!"

GET THE TEAM TOGETHER ON A REGULAR BASIS AND PROACTIVELY GO THROUGH EVERY POTENTIAL MEMBER POINT OF CONTACT BEFORE IT EVEN HAS A CHANCE OF HAPPENING. THEN, JUST LIKE THAT GREAT REALTOR — "STAGE" THE ENTIRETY OF OPERATIONS BEFORE MEMBERS EVEN ARRIVE.

Then create on-going SOP's and Action Plans that proactively STAGE every member experience to be: more personal, more engaging, more fun, more delightful and simply unforgettable.

Your club is on stage every day — every day all day — every day all day — every day all day…

Would you like a deeper dive in what needs to be staged? Check out: EXPECTATIONS ARE NOT MET, OR MERELY EXCEEDED — INSTEAD, PLUTONIUM LEADERSHIP ESTABLISHES THEM!

MICRO-MANAGMENT
(I'VE BEEN TO THE MOUNTAIN TOP!)

In regard to board members "meddling" in operations — I'll share a personal story.

I have no recommendation as to what YOU might/could/ought to do in your specific situation. I'll just share how it one time went down with ME.

I was GM at a wonderful club in Chicago that our team had built to Platinum Club of America recognition while I was there (I loved my role there for 10+ years before being recruited to a great opportunity in CA).

It was into my 5th or 6th year in Chicago that I experienced the most controlling, type-A personality, micro-managing president I had ever worked for. VERY sharp business-minded guy with also a caring and warm heart. But when it came to business...he was ALL business. And he was used to controlling his business with a finger firmly planted in every piece of the pie.

He owned his own family business and was crazy successful. In the family biz he was used to making all decisions, just like his dad before him probably did, and most likely just like he may have been grooming his children to do.

This president (who I like very much, still keep contact, greatly respect and personally enjoy) was in my office, on my email, on my phone — and felt he had to be involved in any and all decisions...no matter how routine or large. The very face of micro-managing.

So, I began inundating him with reports and detailed back up on every little thing — naively thinking this would give me some breathing room.

I was wrong. Very wrong.

It got to the point where I was spending more time preparing reports, returning emails, phone calls and meetings with "President Micro-Manager" than I did in actually leading the team and operating the Club.

Finally, I asked if we could have a confidential conversation. A date and time was set. It came down like this...

"Mr. President (I wisely left out the "Micro-Manager part.), I have a few very serious questions to ask you. Actually, they are rhetorical in nature — so you really don't have to answer them. But I would like you to ponder them in your own mind. And, I'm asking these rhetorical questions with the greatest sincerity and respect. Also, please don't respond at all until I'm finished. Please just hear me out."

Here were my questions:

"Mr. President, do you think you are qualified to be the GM/COO at The Olympic Club in San Francisco? Or, qualified to be the GM/COO at The Los Angeles Country Club? Qualified to be the GM/COO at Cherokee Town & Country Club in Atlanta? Congressional? River Oaks? Medinah? Ocean Reef?" Seeing that he was letting me continue uninterrupted with an expression that conveyed just about as much emotion as any one of the faces on Mount Rushmore — I kept right on going.

"Of course, Mr. President — again, my questions are indeed rhetorical. But I can tell you that if I were asked if I felt I were qualified to be PRESIDENT of any of those clubs...even with my years of GM/COO experience...I'm afraid my answer would be, "NO."

"On the other hand, if asked about my being capable to be GM/COO at any of those clubs, my answer would be, "YES."

"However, I don't care about any of those other clubs. Because the only one that I do care about is this club, right here and now."

"And, I am very happy that YOU are indeed qualified to be a great president right here and now — as I am not. HOWEVER — I am indeed very qualified and proud to be your GM/COO, right here and now. And — (Here it comes!) — with much respect, sir — YOU, are not."

"Mr. President...what I am trying to convey, is that both of us have roles that each is capable and proud to fulfill. Succinctly stated, my role is to report to you and I am happy to do so. Deeper still — with the greatest respect — sir, please back off a bit and allow me do the job. Frankly, I feel overly micro-managed."

He remained silent and stoic. No sign of emotion whatsoever. His face as solid as a rock carved into the side of a mountain.

So what the heck, I figured I may as well finish strong!

"Respectfully, sir ... I need to ask for a little more breathing room in my being the top operations professional/leader of this club. I will continue reporting directly to you, I am accountable to you in getting the results we both know we need, and I'll seek your advice when need be — However, I'm asking for the chance to perform without the overly micro-management environment that I sense now. It simply cannot go on."

"Thank you for your time, and for hearing me out."

I then stood up and offered my hand.

Well, Mr. President Micro-Manager did let me get through my entire bit. He sat there a moment, stood up, and shook my hand.
He thanked me for my candor and said he understood. He then left the office.

That was it.

From that moment on, the micromanagement ended and I enjoyed another 4 or 5 years at this great club.

He finished out a very productive 2-year term as President and, I believe, more effective in that role than he may have been otherwise. And, I know for sure, I finished as a more effective GM/COO than I might have otherwise.

And at my next club in Rancho Mirage, CA, I never experienced even a moment of micro-management in six wonderful years there.

I have nothing but the fondest memories of both Exmoor and Thunderbird Country Clubs. In fact, my wife Kim and I will always have a little "Exmoor Blood" in our veins! We left lots of friends and loved ones there.

Severe Micro-Managing is a very delicate subject to breach. Some otherwise effective GM/COO's allow their performance, and even career's, to be negatively impacted when it occurs. Others simply tread water in hopes of outlasting their term. Some just wind up leaving either through the front or back door.

All those who have been in top positions of leadership within the private club industry have either personally experienced being subject to attempts of Micro-Management or have heard stories.

By the way — ever since that eventful day years ago, I've always wanted to go to Mount Rushmore.

But, somehow, I feel like I've already been there.

MONEY TALKS
AND PLUTONIUM CLUB LEADERS KNOW
WHAT THEY ARE TALKING ABOUT

While every board member may have his or her own particular area of focused interest in club operations, they all share a common interest in the financial condition of their club.

One of the basic obligations club management has to every board member is to MAKE SURE that s/he is always in an informed position to respond appropriately to their fellow members who understandably cast questions their way along the lines of, "Hey, you're on the board. How is the club doing?"

THEN – AFTER MANY MORE WEEKS OF DATA MINING, PROJECTIONS, ANALYSIS, CHARTS, AND REPORTS ... THE ULTIMATE FINDINGS ARE PRESENTED BEHIND CLOSED DOORS IN EXECUTIVE SESSION.

Successful club managers know that the answers given to address the understandable interests from members (Owners) about club finances is perceived as a direct reflection on how the leadership (Board and Management) are going about the business of monitoring revenue/expenses and protecting their assets.

Depending upon the unique "club culture" that prevails, different clubs have different perspectives.

During "The Salad Days" of strong economic times, it may seem that some members are not much more than casually interested in the numbers (other than perhaps how many croutons should be on a Caesar salad).

During more challenging economic times, the interest in numbers can understandably become more serious.

Nonetheless, regardless of economic times, whatever they might be—

ALL CLUBS function better when their board members are fully informed.

ALL SUCCESSFUL CLUB MANAGERS make it their personal/professional business to ensure that the leadership of the club is right on top of all finances.

No "ifs," "ands," or "buts."

Successful club managers definitely do not have the luxury of suggesting that their club is not doing all that well and is often subject to micro-management because their board is not on top of things. Phooey.

Effective boards are on top of things simply because their management team is.

Successful managers are not people who don't have problems. Successful managers are people who manage problems well.
Newer board members (correctly or not) may initially look upon the opportunity to review the finances of their club in great detail as a primary reason for accepting a position on the board. However, once actually there:

They should be able to quickly pick up on the fact that the board has confidence in their GM/COO when it comes to the numbers.

They should be able to see a consistent pattern of accurate, meaningful summaries of current situations being routinely presented by the GM/COO.

They should become immediately privy to constantly updated cash flow charts and projections.

They should be able to comfortably answer any financial questions from fellow members knowing that their information provided and analyzed by management is both timely and accurate.

Board members need to have confidence that all dues, assessments, fees and income derived from sales are being used to offset ONLY the club's legitimate operating expenses – and not to ever subsidize waste or poor management.

In the eyes of board members, the financial statement is more than a record of dollars and cents. It tells them whether or not their management team has business acumen.

Do not make the mistake of assuming that a financial statement which indicates a dramatically improved bottom line does not require any sort of explanation from management.

Do not make the mistake of thinking that a significant unfavorable variance to budget can somehow slip by with no explanation.

Do make certain the entire board is exposed to a professional analysis of every financial statement. That professional analysis should be provided by the GM/COO.

It is not necessarily the financial statement results (be they good or bad) that dictate the tone at board meetings, but rather, the confidence the board has in the management team to:

- Fully understand and convey how those numbers came about.
- Professionally know the difference between timing issues or trends.
- Make the necessary decisions to stay on track over the long haul.

Then, of course, the whole process repeats itself. And each time it does, there MUST be a clear, unmistakable pattern of management consistently being proactive in keeping the train on track headed towards the desired goal.

Preliminary monthly financial statements should be on the desk of the GM/COO for scrutiny and analysis before distributed to the board — including the president and treasurer.
It is management's job to be on top of things, and they will not be in a great position to address any concerns if they are seeing the preliminary numbers for the first time right along with the board members.

The GM/COO and Club Controller should scrutinize together every line item, making sure they are accurate and that no "timing" issues are allowed to needlessly create perceptions that are not on solid ground.

Also, as a professional courtesy, once the GM/COO and Controller are confident in the accuracy of the numbers, the President and Treasurer should be made privy to any highlights prior to distribution to the full board. There should NEVER by any surprises at that level at any board meeting — NEVER.

It is highly recommended that at the board level a club focus on the actual YTD results as they compare to budget...not on the minutia of every 30-day swing.

There will always be isolated ebbs and flows that are due to timing issues and other influences that can sway a 30-day report one way or the other. But unless a clear trend is indicated that is going to impact the entire fiscal year — it is best to stay focused on the bigger YTD picture.

No sense on stamping on ants if elephants are approaching!

Department heads and mid- management are expected to spend the appropriate amount of time every day paying attention to operational details.

The board should not have to!

In light of the ripple effects of recessionary challenges, a club deserves the full attention and focus of their Board of Directors to be unwavering in dealing with concerns like these:

What is the optimum place to set our Initiation Fee structure?

Do we need to revisit our Long-Range Plan?
Should we be looking at new membership categories to better position our club? Or, perhaps do we have too many?

Should we completely update some of our longstanding club rules to better reflect the times? Do we really need as many committees and board members as have been cast in stone for decades?

What policies need to be changed? Do our bylaws need updating?

What plan do we have to address future capital needs if Initiation Fee income is unreliable?

What are we going to do to have the average age of our members be in a desired range?

Are we fully engaging the entire family? Do we have a meaningful Strategic Plan in place that truly reflects who we are as a club and where we want to go? Are we reviewing and tweaking it to remain relevant?

Fully discussing serious policy issues like these, and then effectively communicating them is the highest and best use of board time and talent.

Conversely, time spent debating whether there should be 5 or 7 croutons on a Caesar salad is perhaps not. Perhaps a bit tongue in cheek, but you get the point.

If the answer is a confident "Yes!" — There is no need for a board to become overly involved in operations.

If the answer is otherwise, this is NOT a sign to begin micro-managing operations. It is a sign that the potential of identifying a top GM/COO be explored.

Many very fine clubs do not even distribute the detailed monthly financial statements at a board meeting.

However, they must be confident that the YTD numbers are tracking close to plan, and that for any significant variance an explanation is always provided and proactive plans are in place.

NOW THEN — WHILE ALL OF THE ABOVE-BOARD POLICY CONCERNS ARE IMPORTANT, IT IS MANDATORY THAT THE #1 OPERATING QUESTION BE ANSWERED FAVORABLY. THAT QUESTION IS — "DO WE HAVE THE RIGHT GM/COO IN PLACE?"

They know that there is no sense in having the full board become stuck in minutia. Watch it! Those croutons can get you every time.

Instead, stay focused on the long-range desired goals of their club and the policies that will keep their club on track.

A meaningful GM/COO's presentation always analyzes the financial condition of the club. Always.

However, this definitely does NOT imply that the duration of any meeting is elongated by the redundant verbal presentation of what has already been provided to the board several days ago, in a very direct and accurate Executive Summary.

It is mandatory that an "Executive Summary" that offers a succinct overview of all club operations be professionally prepared, and in the hands of every board member a few days prior to any board meeting.

A cover letter from the GM/COO discussing any unusual numbers (favorable or otherwise) and commenting on the statement highlights should be included.

Make sure that all members of the board have had adequate time to thoroughly review all numbers, and will hit the ground running, being already familiar with the overall picture rather than to start from ground zero.

If management appropriately sends financial numbers prior to the board meetings, but inappropriately does not include competent analysis, more problems can be created than if nothing were sent in advance.

A financial statement without spot-on GM/COO analysis will always raise more questions than it answers.

> REMEMBER, CONFLICT CANNOT BE AVOIDED, BUT IT CAN ALMOST AL-WAYS BE RESOLVED! AND THE TIME TO RESOLVE CONFLICT IS BEFORE THE MEETING; AVOID HAVING IT THROWN ONTO THE TABLE DURING THE MEET-ING. YOU WILL FIND THAT, FOR THE MOST PART, 90% OF HOW WELL ANY MEETING GOES IS DETERMINED BEFORE THE MEETING EVEN TAKES PLACE!

Do not expect the club treasurer to assume what properly is management's responsibility.

Perhaps it is a good idea to have the treasurer report on any individual member delinquent accounts or major changes in financial policy, but — the basic numbers that are the direct result of budgeting and day-to-day operations in all club departments are the responsibility of management.

Capiche?

(Psssst. Oh, and by the way — uh, about those croutons...the answer is 7.)

NOMINATING COMMITTEE IS RENOWNED FOR SELECTING QUALITY.

NATIONAL CLUB ASSOCIATION
DEBUNKING THE INDUSTRY'S
5 MOST HARMFUL MYTHS / MISCONCEPTIONS

INTRODUCTION

Many people misunderstand the purpose of private clubs; it is not to keep people out, but to create a community built on shared values. **HENRY WALLMEYER**, President and CEO of the National Club Association, has educated officials on Capitol Hill, members of the media and many folks from outside our industry about private clubs and why they, like any small business, are important to the economy and their communities. **NCA is a primary advocate and source of relevant information for private clubs.** We recommend that all clubs belong to and support NCA. The ABC's of Plutonium Club Leadership would not be complete in the absence of NCA or of the quality of leadership Henry provides. Here, he succinctly offers insights as to the true value of clubs. To learn more about the NCA, please visit nationalclub.org

MYTH 1: CLUBS DISCRIMINATE
There are many different types of private clubs, including golf clubs, athletic clubs, social clubs, racquet clubs, yacht clubs, beach clubs and hunting clubs. There are even private clubs for magicians, comedians, writers and thespians. They all share one common denominator: they provide an opportunity for people with a shared interest to pursue that interest.

That's why clubs rely on referral programs for membership, to ensure that new members mesh with the current culture.

Over the past century private clubs have evolved—and, frankly—improved, just like America has.

- Today, clubs don't discriminate but they are selective in admitting members.
- They have established bylaws or policies that require new members to be nominated and sponsored by existing members.
- Private clubs are exclusive and value the privacy of their club and members.

We live in a time when tens of millions of Americans use social media to keep in touch and socialize with friends and loved ones. In the past, people didn't use technology to do these things; they actually got together and had in-person relationships, and private clubs were one of the earliest and most important way they did so.

Americans' Constitutionally-guaranteed right of freedom of association allows clubs to establish a variety of different criteria as a basis for membership. For instance, there are women-only clubs, men-only clubs, and clubs that build their membership around religious affiliation, political leanings or family heritage.

But, more often than not, many clubs are simply a place for community, recreation and engagement among neighbors, classmates, friends and colleagues. A true home away from home.

MYTH 2: CLUBS ARE JUST ABOUT GOLF

Sure, most private clubs (85%) offer golf as a primary draw for members. But private clubs are so much more: from tennis and swimming to dining and fitness, there are a wide array of experiences and types of clubs to suit all interests. The only limit on clubs' focus is the limits of members' interests and imagination.

ULTIMATELY, THE PRIVATE CLUB EXPERIENCE IS PRIMARILY ABOUT FRIENDSHIP. CLUBS ARE SAFE, WELCOMING PLACES WHERE PEOPLE COME TOGETHER TO CONNECT, PLAY, AND DINE WITH PEOPLE WHOSE COMPANY THEY ENJOY AND WHOSE INTERESTS THEY SHARE.

In urban areas, city and athletic clubs reign, offering social programming for "clubs within a club" for literature, politics, bridge and wine, as well as myriad athletic facilities and sports leagues.

Dining experiences run the gamut too, from upscale formal dining to casual pubs, in a plethora of facilities that offer spectacular rooftop views, sunsets over the golf course, and fun gathering places for families and friends.

MYTH 3: SINCE THEY ARE PRIVATE, CLUBS ONLY BENEFIT THEIR MEMBERS

Private clubs are small businesses, and like other small businesses they benefit the community in many ways. The most obvious benefits are economic.

Private clubs favorably impact the U.S.A. economy year after year by...
- Providing more than half a million jobs across the United States.
- Contributing more than $3.75 billion in taxes.
- Adding $21.5 billion to the economy.

Many private clubs are also very philanthropic and community-oriented, much like their members.
- Clubs rally behind their members who host charity events, golf tournaments, food drives, toy donations and other initiatives in support of good causes that impact the community.

Many clubs also have caddie scholarship programs, foundations and offer scholarships to the youth of our country.
- For instance, The Union League of Chicago has a culture that values members' engagement in public life. The club's programs, committees and policies reveal a commitment to understanding and advancing public policy issues and community life. For more than 95 years, the Union League of Chicago has served as an affiliate member of the Boys & Girls Clubs of America, serving the after-school development needs of at-risk youth in Chicago.

Clubs also provide a great place to work.
- According to Club Benchmarking, the average club spends between 52 and 60 percent of total operating revenue on labor.
- Salaries at private clubs tend to be much higher than comparable positions at area businesses.
- Employee turnover is much lower, with about half of private clubs reporting less than 15 percent rate of turnover according to a recent National Club Association/McMahon Group survey.

As a result, jobs at private clubs tend to be highly sought after. For instance, the Detroit Athletic Club is one of only three organizations to be recognized every year for the last 18 years as one of Metro Detroit's Best and Brightest Companies to Work For.

MYTH 4: CLUBS ARE NOT ENVIRONMENTALLY FRIENDLY

Clubs with golf courses have hundreds of acres of land. This sounds like a lot of watering, fertilizing and mowing, and it's precisely why many clubs work with certified agronomists — plant and soil scientists who develop innovative practices and technologies to improve sustainability and protect the environment.

> THE ENVIRONMENT IS CENTRAL TO THE MISSION AND SUCCESS OF PRIVATE CLUBS, PARTICULARLY THOSE THAT OFFER GOLF. AS SUCH, PRIVATE CLUBS TEND TO BE VERY PROACTIVE WHEN IT COMES TO SUSTAINABILITY AND, IN FACT, CLUBS ARE MUCH MORE ENVIRONMENTALLY-FRIENDLY THAN THE TYPICAL HOMEOWNER.

A recent National Club Association/McMahon Group survey of private clubs found that 74 percent pursue sustainable practices, and the typical club spends nearly $50,000 each year to promote sustainability.

Like many environmentally-friendly businesses, private clubs use a variety of traditionally sustainable practices and environmentally safe products and recycled materials in their operations.

In an integrated and far-reaching approach to resource management, Army Navy Country Club in Arlington, Va., constructed a LEED Silver Certification clubhouse.

Many clubs also practice hyper-local food sourcing and advanced environmental programs:

- The Jonathan Club's rooftop garden in Los Angeles, annually produces $100,000 worth of ingredients.
- Medinah Country Club's USDA-certified chicken coop and organic garden and maple syrup program, which taps trees on the Illinois property.
- Pine Valley Golf Club (the #1 rated golf club in America according to Platinum Clubs) was certified in 1999 by the Audubon International's Audubon Cooperative Sanctuary Program for Golf.
- Congressional Country Club (the #1 rated country club) was certified in 2011.

MYTH 5: CLUBS ARE RELICS OF THE PAST

The majestic architecture and storied pasts of many clubs belie the modern nature of today's private club. But it's that modern nature that is attracting so many Gen Xers, Millennials and junior members.

> INSIDE THE DOORS, TODAY'S PRIVATE CLUB IS MORE REFLECTIVE THAN EVER OF THE VALUES AND INTERESTS OF MOST ACTIVE AMERICANS. IT'S MORE FAMILY-ORIENTED AND FOCUSED ON FUN, HEALTH AND WELLNESS.

Clubs are helping members balance fun and family by offering more social activities for families, children and guests. The entire family can enjoy a wide range of offerings, including pool-based activities, game nights, themed parties and other family events.

Many clubs offer junior sports camps for children to play golf, tennis or swim. Coffee-shop cafes, youth rec rooms and spa amenities also make clubs a destination to serve all members of the family.

Examples of clubs' focus on family abound. Denver Country Club has a family focus on youth training for team sports and Palo Alto Hills Golf & Country Club provides families with fitness and kid's yoga classes, cooking lessons, magic shows and a "tween" dance social.

At the Country Club of Fairfax (Va.), its Wine and Golf program has increased women's play by providing a low-stress introduction to golf that includes on-course instruction and coaching, fun, and a focus on meeting other members (and drinking wine).

ALL the above are just a few examples from thousands of clubs across the United States.

Clubs have always provided recreational outlets for active members through golf, tennis, sailing, swimming, and other activities. However, today's private club is more committed to promoting members' health and wellness as well. That may include exercise studios, spas, physical therapy, private trainers and nutrition programs, and it extends to the clubhouse menu, with many clubs offering healthier food choices.

In short, private clubs have expanded their offerings to better reflect Americans' modern lifestyles.

Thank you, Henry, for all that the National Club Association does for the private club industry and for the steady hand of Plutonium Leadership you represent.

IDEAS
COME BY GETTING YOUR ENTIRE TEAM TO THINK PLUTONIUM THOUGHTS!

Just think.

The answers on how to grow and improve anything are NOT found in file cabinets in HR.

Sure — we need things like: policy manuals — employee handbooks — new employee orientations — organizational charts — job descriptions — SOP's — performance reviews — bonus systems — mission statements — core values — etc., but great ideas that can grow and improve things are not inside file cabinets. They are inside the heart and mind of creative people who are encouraged to take all of the available information and:

- *Evaluate* — where we are now,
- *Envision* — where we want to be,
- **THINK** about creative IDEAS on how to get us all there, and ultimately
- *Transferring* ideas into action!

True leaders convey in a compelling way the reasons why none of us should be overly content about "HERE" — and light a fire in the mind and heart of everyone to unceasingly think about creative ideas to propel us "THERE."

Knowing that it is impossible for people to be creative and defensive at the same time — true leaders establish a culture where everyone breathes the same air in an atmosphere of positive expectations where sharing thoughts and ideas thrive.

THE RESULT? Everyone is always THINKING about creative DEAS to continually drive things toward being: Easier — Healthier — Faster — Error Free — Worry Free — Understandable — Agreeable — Efficient — Organized — Professional — Personable — FUN!

The collective knowledge and experiences of an entire team — if not applied — is no better than an individual with a total lack of knowledge. What you don't know, can hurt you. What you do know, and don't apply, hurts as well.

THE JOB OF A PLUTONIUM LEADER IS TO MAKE EVERYONE AROUND THEM SUCCESSFUL.

A leader's success is measured in their ability to use knowledge and — if you are really thinking —their ability to motivate others to put their knowledge to work for all those around them.

THERE ARE NO BUDGET RESTRAINTS.

Thinking is even for the frugal, as it costs nothing. But, not thinking can get pretty pricey.

It does not necessarily take money to make money. What it does take is IDEAS. And, ideas only come from those who are thinking. No team grows any bigger than the size of their ideas.

IDEAS MAKE THE WORLD GO 'ROUND.

As you begin to think about the things around you, you will find that the ideas will begin to come. And, many situations that you thought were out of control will now have not one, but several solutions to them that may put them very much in control.

Do not be discouraged when told new ideas are impossible.

This can be one of the first positive signs of a truly great idea. Really great ideas are impossible. That is what makes them such great ideas to start with!

Flying was an impossible idea, but a great one! Handheld devices were impossible ideas, also great ones!

- It is much better to think about new ideas, and to fail occasionally, than to think about nothing, and succeed all the time.
- Team productivity is similar to a computer in that if you change the input, you automatically change the output.
- Don't just react to the world around you with no more than "knee-jerk" responses.
- Develop your skill to THINK — from thinking comes new ideas.
- With these new ideas comes the need for further thinking.

Now then — DO NOT simply take the above ideas and file it for future reference.

Instead: send it to your entire team — call a meeting — throw it in the middle of the table — and establish a culture where everyone breathes the same air in an atmosphere of positive expectations where sharing thoughts and ideas thrive.

What do you think?

NEW MEMBERS
HERE'S THE MOST EFFECTIVE WAY TO ATTRACT THEM

There is a new Sheriff in town. Try this for openers.

THE CONCLUSION

"The club's Entertainment Committee should be dismantled and then absorbed and ran as an offshoot of (get ready for this) – THE MEMBERSHIP COMMITTEE."

Case closed. Oops. Some may think we opened and closed that case a bit too fast?

Not really. Because after looking at the facts, it is a foregone conclusion.

Let's start with a basic premise to build our case upon. A premise is a position upon which an "argument" is based, from which a logical conclusion can be drawn. It's only logical...that a solid premise be established.

THE PREMISE

In order to remain viable, clubs must be successful in retaining existing members and attracting new ones. How are we doing so far? Any dissenters out there? I didn't think so.

Prior to presenting below the "Seven Entertaining Facts for the Membership Committee" – we submit as evidence the following obvious "dots" that require no expert testimony and are easily connected.They compel us to be drawn towards the conclusion above that we opened with.

1. Existing members want to have fun at their club.
2. Existing members have non-member friends.
3. Potential new members have friends who belong to your club.
4. Potential new members would enjoy having fun at their friends' club.
5. Existing members enjoy entertaining friends. So —
6. Connect the dots!

It's only logical to conclude that *in order to remain viable – everything possible should be done to enhance the probability of members inviting and entertaining their friends at the club.*

"Suddenly, when looked upon in this light – club events and parties that have traditionally been handled by an Entertainment Committee, are more accurately nowadays acknowledged as being a vital outreach and function of Membership."

THE UNDENIABLE

Nowadays – inspiring members to "showcase" their club is a Plutonium priority!

And the most effective way to do this is by consistently creating events that are renowned throughout the community as being so much fun that non-members actually covet the potential of receiving an invitation, and members are compelled to extend them.

No stone can be left unturned in creating entertaining opportunities where members consciously invite groups of friends to consistently great social events over the course of the calendar year, enabling their guests to meet the membership and become enamored with the club.

Is your club spending heavy amounts in printing brochures and marketing material that is soon forgotten? Consider the far greater ROI if this money were reallocated to generating consistently creative club event experiences that members and guests simply never forget.

"THE SUCCESS OF ACHIEVING THIS SORT OF ENVIRONMENT IS PIVOTAL IN REACHING YOUNGER GENERATIONS!" Your events MUST be conducive to not simply having a few members inviting that same-oh-same-oh non-member couple again and again! NO!

Plan everything so that it is easy to invite "two, four, six, eight who do we appreciate" guests every time! Make your own little party of it! And, rub elbows with several hundreds of other members and their guests doing the same.

If a club has an earned reputation of throwing the greatest parties in town - the compounded ripple effects of sustained initiation and dues income dwarf the cost of subsidizing creative invitations, innovative decorations, spot-on props, staff attire, professional lighting, ingenious execution, outstanding food, enthusiastic service --- and, not to mention the hottest bands/entertainment possible!

Doesn't just reading the above paragraph prime your own pump? Wooo—hooo! Lots of fun here! Every Plutonium club party creates a visceral member/guest experience that leaves a very positive memory and compels a perpetual anticipation of "I can't wait for the next one!"

But, behind all the above "fun" – due diligence has uncovered seven factors that must be brought to light in order for our foregone conclusion to come to life. Here they are…

SEVEN ENTERTAINING FACTS FOR THE MEMBERSHIP COMMITTEE

1) Guests MUST be encouraged!

What generates turnout for parties is the anticipation of being around fun people.

Doing a nice job in coordinating dates, themes, props, bands, menus, and then communicating it all is very important. But what really gets people pumped to attend is knowing that fun people are going to be there.

This is why the #1 question the receptionist gets when members call to ask about a club event is what other names are already on the reservation list. You don't think so? Just ask your receptionist!

The best way of making sure fun people are going to be in attendance is to make every planning decision based upon a favorable answer to this question: "If we did this, would it increase the probability of more guests, and the next day proclaiming that it was the most fun they have ever had?" (Well, that is, since the last time they were invited to your club.)

2) Pricing policies discouraging attendance MUST be eliminated!!

Membership/Entertainment MUST be funded by dues! PLEASE do not throw a wet blanket on the entire process by being beholden to demanding that each event "pay for itself."

In pricing your events —just go ahead and anticipate ALL of the expenses, divide the estimated attendance into the cost, and that's your ticket price. This means that the entire cost of each event is the responsibility of only those members who actually attend the event.

It sounds logical. It's not.

This drives up the ticket price resulting in many members simply getting out of the habit of attending because they are viewed as cost prohibitive — particularly if they were to consider inviting guests. To offset this, an overemphasis is made to keep the costs down which results in a reputation for consistently ho-hum events — that are perceived as being overpriced to start with.

3) Plutonium club events are perceived full of value.

Forget thinking that every party should pay for itself! Nonsense. VERY short-sighted.

Instead, establish an annual budget that funds ALL entertainment, decorations, invitations, postage, etc. – and then establish a "market value" price for each individual event. This means that the entire membership shares the fixed cost of offering to the entire membership an exciting social calendar.

It also means that club parties are routinely viewed as great value by the vast majority of members — especially as opportunities to entertain guests. Lots of them! Furthermore, the emphasis is on how can we yet further enhance our reputation for consistently throwing the greatest parties in town, that are of great value to our club.

Price each event guided by what the "perceived value" will be by the membership.

For example – supposing that the menu is a fixed. That leaves variables that include a wide range of entertainment, props, themes, bells and whistles. All of these should positively impact the perceived value.

Adjust your pricing accordingly. Not to cover the cost of the event, because that is done by dues.

Instead, adjust your pricing as to what the perceived value is to a typical member when they look at what they are getting in return. And, then, blow their mind...knock it out of the park.

You want them to see LOTS OF PERCIEVED VALUE not in just members showing up themselves...but, in routinely showing up with 4, 6 or more guests as well.

The committee and management must be focused on creating exciting events and building enthusiasm for them — NOT on stewing about balancing the individual per person/per event budget. Complete folly.

All income generated from an event goes directly to F&B. There is no direct "income" credited to Membership/Entertainment as this is strictly a budgeted expense department — exactly like Golf Course Maintenance - Administration - etc.)

4) The entire entertainment year MUST be planned well in advance.
Make sure there is no conflict with other club functions. Check the local community calendar for any conflicts that members may have to make a decision as to which to attend (local charity events, etc.). Be aware of school dates and events that may impact participation (Graduations, homecoming, etc.).

The best bands may not be available if you wait. "Book 'em, Danno!"

5) Every event MUST be communicated again — and again — and again…

- Send a refrigerator magnet to the full membership with all the annual party dates and themes, along with a letter sharing the exciting details of every event. Earn the reputation of your club throwing the most outrageously fun and creative parties in town.
- In every newsletter (print and electronic) systematically repeat all the remaining dates and themes. Include actual pictures of members and guests at previous club parties having the time of their lives.
- In every promotion always state, "Your guests are enthusiastically welcome!"
- For every major event, display a first-class poster(s) and send a separate, highly creative, snail-mail invitation 2-3 weeks out.
- On the bottom of every ala carte check presented — include a reminder about the date and theme of your club's next outrageously fun event!

6) Members MUST perceive some degree of "ownership."

The more members who "perceive" that their fingerprints are on an event — the better. Their job is to promote "their" party to fellow members. Definitely not to plan the details or execution. Leave that to the professionals!

Consider the committee being involved in a "phone chain" or text "blast" personally from them to their individual contacts.

7) The professionals MUST be allowed to make it all happen.

Once the committee has approved annual dates and themes that are presented by management - from that point on, the club professionals should do the lion's share of all else. (Hear them ROAR!)

- Your professional Director of Membership should play a significant role in working side by side with the Event/Catering management team. Why? Because the net bottom line purpose of creating and offering outrageously great club entertainment is all about membership.

All of which brings us right back to…Yes, there is indeed a new Sheriff in town and s/he is not taking any prisoners! But they are looking to round up a posse of new members!

THE CONCLUSION

"The club's Entertainment Committee should be dismantled and then absorbed and ran as an offshoot of (and now you know it's true!) – THE MEMBERSHIP COMMITTEE."

OPERATIONS ARE SUCH THAT ALL FEEL PRIDE.

ONE THING THAT NO LEADER CAN AFFORD
PLUTONIUM CLUB LEADERS MAY BE ACCUSED OF MANY THINGS — BEING BORING IS NOT ONE OF THEM!

FACT: MOST INDIVIDUALS (OR ENTIRE ORGANIZATIONS FOR THAT MATTER) DON'T POSITION THEMSELVES TO BE FIRED, PROMOTED, OR TO QUIT.

QUESTION: HMMM — THEN WHAT'S LEFT?

ANSWER: INSTEAD OF ANY OF THE ABOVE, THEY SUPPRESS THEIR OWN CREATIVITY AND DRIVE — SEEMINGLY CONTENT TO PERFORM AT WHAT COULD BE CALLED "ADEQUATE" YET NOT VERY EXCITING LEVELS.

There is no Olympic swimming event where gold medals are handed out for excellence and record-breaking performance in the dog paddle. Or, for endurance in treading water while keeping one's head above it.

Do a quick mental exercise by picturing in your mind your favorite dynamic and memorable leaders that had a positive impact in the world or, better yet, your own professional and personal life.

Allow your thoughts to cover the various arenas where these individuals cast their sphere of influence. (i.e.: Business — Sports — Political — Humanitarian — Entertainment — Science — Religious — Social Justice — Education…)

To make it even more relevant — put aside these general categories, and think in the specifics of your own personal family & friends or professional mentors & associates who stand out as great leaders.

You will easily be able to associate a plethora of descriptive words that embrace almost all of the people that come to your mind. Words like: Passionate — Charismatic — Engaging — Creative — Encouraging — Inspiring — Appealing...

One word that never comes to mind when describing a leader is: **BORING.** *zzzzzzzzzzzzz ...*

PLUTONIUM LEADERS INJECT EXCITEMENT INTO PROJECTS, PROGRAMS & PEOPLE!

When looking for the right individuals to head up projects, deliver programs, or to lead people — "flat liners" need not apply.

> **THOSE WHO HAVE THAT INNATE ABILITY TO LIGHT UP AN ENTIRE ROOM JUST BY WALKING OUT OF IT — SHOULD JUST KEEP ON WALKING!**

When I graduated from high school, I thought my favorite subject was physics. I just loved every aspect of seeing how physics was involved in every activity in the cosmos including my own day to day life.

It was EXCITING!

So, upon entering college, I excitedly signed up for physics.

It was BORING!

Q: How was what I thought my favorite subject jettisoned from one end of the cosmos right into the black hole of the other?

A: Because my high school teacher was passionate about his subject. He brought it to life. He was: Charismatic — Engaging — Creative — Encouraging — Inspiring. He made it exciting!

The college professor was a masterful expert in his field of study. But he was lifeless. He was a "flat-liner." He made it boring.

From this experience I learned a great insight into Plutonium leadership.

> **IN ORDER TO LEAD YOU MUST NOT ONLY TEACH, BUT YOU MUST INSPIRE. YOU NOT ONLY TEACH WHAT TO DO AND HOW TO DO IT, BUT YOU MUST ALSO INSPIRE A FLAME OF DESIRE TO WANT TO DO IT.**

"An automobile goes nowhere efficiently unless it has a quick, hot spark to ignite things, to set the cogs of the machine in motion. So, I try to make every player on my team feel he's the

spark keeping our machine in motion. On him depends our success."
  —Knute Rockne, Legendary Notre Dame Football Coach

Just as soon as you finish reading right here and now — picture in your mind the people who you have known throughout your entire life that have had the most positive and encouraging impact.

You will find that the names that come to your mind are all people who had high expectations of you. They were hardly boring! They enthusiastically knew you could do it. And, so do you.

Just remember that in order to bring projects and programs to life — Platinum Leaders inspire people to perform at exciting levels. There is nothing boring about it at all!

Pretty exciting stuff, isn't it? Plutonium Club Leaders know of no other way. It's just the way they are wired. The way you roll.

ORIENTATION FOR NEW BOARD MEMBERS
AKA: HOW TO AVOID DISORIENTED LEADERSHIP

THE QUESTION: If you just had to come up with one answer, what is the singular most important committee at your club?

Since no two clubs are exactly alike, the potential answers may seem to be wildly variable from one club to another. Yet, there is a fixed answer that is universally correct.

During criminal investigations and looking for responsible individuals it is often said, "Follow the money." In looking for the correct answer to what the most important club committee is, rather than following money — let's follow the decision-making process.

Ultimately, decision making authority and responsibility rests firmly on the board room table. But the BOD's is not a committee. A committee only recommends. A board makes decisions.

In following the decision-making process at clubs — let's connect a few dots:

- Ultimate decisions are made at the board level.
- The board as a whole, is made up of individuals.

Ah-ha! We are getting closer to our answer! Now we can ask the question, "Where do those individuals come from?"

THE ANSWER: The singular most important committee at any club is — The Nomination Committee. This is the committee that recommends the individuals that make up the board.

(A very close second is The Search Committee. Mistakes made by either of these committees can have negative ripple effects lasting for years.)

OK. Now that we have identified the two most important committees — let's say that each has done a great job in recommending quality individuals to serve the club. They are full of up-side potential.

Hopefully, a new GM/COO will serve for many years, growing and developing in all of them. But, being a paid professional club executive — other than a very brief initial learning curve, this individual can and must very quickly hit the ground running and providing meaningful leadership.

By design, board members come and go and serve for limited terms. They really don't have the luxury of having many years to grow and develop in their decision-making role. While there is still a learning curve, in order for then to make informed decisions, there must be an accelerated process, right from the get-go to quickly bring them up to speed.

A RHETORICAL QUESTION: By a quick show of hands — is there anyone out there who wants disoriented new board members making decisions at your club?

A FIRM ANSWER: No.

All PLUTONIUM PRIVAE CLUB LEADERS have a very structured and meaningful "NEW BOARD MEMBER ORIENTATION" program in place. The program includes private meetings, written documents/reports and a tour of the entire facility.

Each club needs to structure and annually update the specific steps that best reflect the current times, as well as the culture and traditions of their own uniqueness. The important thing is to make sure your club is up to speed and provides every new board member an opportunity to hit the ground running with relevant facts and information, providing them a foundation of knowing their role and contributing right from their first meeting.

Ideally, an actual "New Board Orientation Handbook" is personally presented by the club president and GM/COO during a private meeting/lunch where all areas are discussed. This is followed by a thorough, complete tour of the entire club property. They should see everything including employee areas, back of the house, maintenance facilities — everything!

The GM/COO should arrange in advance and personally serve as "tour guide."

An effective tour has a very detailed timeline moving from one area to another where each department head is given the opportunity to describe what they do and to show the facility/tools they have to work with.

The staff takes great pride in doing this and new board members are always enlightened, as they otherwise never would have had the opportunity to be so. They come away with a new perspective and appreciation of the many moving parts and complexities of club operations.

The following is an actual table of contents used by a model "best practices" club. *It is not intended to be all-inclusive.* However, it does give a nice template for any club to augment, customize and update from year to year.

New Board Member
Orientation Handbook

TABLE OF CONTENTS

MISSION STATEMENT   *3*
Now That You Are A Director   *4 - 6*
Meetings & Responsibilities   *7 - 9*
Board Meetings & Between Board Meetings   *10 -13*
Representing the Membership   *14*
Working with Board Members & Management   *15 - 16*
Club Operations & Budget   *17 - 22*
Committee Position Descriptions   *23 - 32*
Board Meeting Procedures   *33 - 34*
Background Information to Review Prior To Your First
Official Board Meeting as a New Director   *35 - 38*
Current FY GM/COO Executive Summaries   *39 - 50*

Current FY Board Minutes   *51 - 65*
Last FY Auditor's Letter   *66 - 69*
Bylaws/Club Rules/Core Values   *Attached*

BECOME FAMILIAR WITH
Club Management 101   *70 - 73*
Components for a Winning Club   *74 - 76*
Understanding Club Food & Beverage   *77 – 80*

PEOPLE ARE IN THE RIGHT PLACES — DEEP AND WIDE.

PEOPLE
PLUTONIUM CLUB LEADERS MAKE SURE THE RIGHT ONES ARE ON THEIR BUS.

THE WHO is considered one of the most influential rock bands of the 20th century, selling over 100 million records worldwide, and performing to sold-out performances since the mid 1960's.

Their original classic line-up consisted of lead singer Roger Daltry, John Entwistle on bass, drummer Keith Moon, and guitarist Pete Townshend. Over the years, Daltry and Townshend have remained the core of the group and have had continued success by carefully selecting various other top musicians to join them on an as-needed basis.

Their most notable "replacement" has been drummer Zak Starkey who has recorded and performed with them since 1994. Of interest is that Starkey is the son of one of the most recognizable drummers of all time - Ringo Starr of The Beatles.

"Magic Bus" was one of their most memorable songs. It was written by Townshend and released in 1968. To this day, in live concerts, Daltry will sing out, "... now I've got my Magic Bus." And an approving crowd thunders in return:

"Too much - Magic Bus! Too much - Magic Bus!"

I recently sent a short note of admiration to a respected fellow Plutonium Private Club Leader for successfully steering a "small" club (with annual gross revenues of $30'ish million!) through several challenges.

I got the immediate insightful response shared here.

In large measure, it was through their leadership in concentrating on getting the right people in the right places that resulted in an enjoyable position of strength across the board of operations, approved capital improvements within a master plan, and (most importantly) membership satisfaction.

"Michael, I appreciate your note. It truly has been a great year and we continue to push to get better each and every day. We are now in a very strong position and hitting on all cylinders. The reason is that I finally have all the right people on the bus. It makes all the other things we do much easier."

To some, an operational turnaround may appear as if by "magic". But as my esteemed Plutonium Club Leader friend alluded - there is no magic involved at all. None. Instead, it is all attributable to leadership remaining focused on simply having the right people on the bus.

Over the years, no matter the industry, when engaged for management consulting, clients would seemingly ALWAYS have me there for all the wrong reasons. Not to worry - I ALWAYS knew that going in.

At the conclusion of an assignment while making a final presentation and offering written "actionable" recommendations, I oftentimes would hear the likes of: "Wow! You are spot-on! How is it that you were able to so quickly identify and make meaningful recommendations that will help us solve our "XYZ" problems?"

And it mattered not the "problems" that they initially thought they brought me in for.

I'd simply tell them the truth. And, since it is no secret - you can listen in right now.

The reason I am able to identify very quickly and to make meaningful recommendations is because I know ahead of time why I am here. And I know ahead of time that the "problems" you contacted me about are really just illusions or symptoms — because you most likely have none of those problems.

Why?

Because it ALWAYS comes down to people. You have "People Problems." And, as a result of that, symptoms eventually start to bubble to the top. I do my homework ahead of time in becoming familiar with your business model. But, upon arrival, I start looking for those individuals with overinflated egos and/or those people who are simply either the wrong ones, period — or, perhaps, even the right ones, but — in the wrong places — or both! Providing that a business model is fundamentally viable — when it comes to actual operations —

NO problems actually exist except people problems.

> **TO PROVE MY POINT — ASK YOURSELF THIS QUESTION AS YOU PONDER ALL THE "PROBLEMS" YOU THOUGHT YOU HAD AND THAT YOU BROUGHT ME IN FOR : "IF (AS IF BY MAGIC) I HAD ALL THE RIGHT PEOPLE IN ALL THE RIGHT PLACES, WHO WERE REALLY FOCUSED AND EXCITED ABOUT WHAT THEY DO — WHAT THEN WOULD HAPPEN TO ALL THOSE "PROBLEMS" OF OURS?"**

The short answer is that they would all go away.

Bottom line: "answers" to so-called club "problems" seldom are necessarily remedied solely by things like SOP's — regimentation — org charts — annual reviews…blah, blah, blah. Oh, sure ☐ these things are important. But — in the absence of the right people in the right places — they mean nada! Zero. Empty. Null. Void.

When you think you have club operating problems, don't allow your focus to be diverted by illusions or symptoms. Instead, take a very clear look at the people on your bus. There is no magic involved here. Just make sure you have the right people in the right places on your bus.

POSTSCRIPT: THIS IS VERY MPORTANT!

Of course — simply having the right people in the right places in a vacuum is not enough in the absence of solid leadership at the top (and a viable business model to start with). The purpose of this specific offering in The ABC's of Plutonium Private Club Leadership is to point out that having the right people in the right places IS a function of solid leadership — and, that is where you start.

Oh, yeah — about that business model. Just remember two things:

1. You can't make up for a bad business model by volume. (Unless it is DUES!)

2. Even a viable business model is going nowhere without the right people on the bus.

BUT WHO IS DRIVING THE BUS? In this case, don't casually glance in your rearview mirror. Nope. Pull the bus over and look right into the mirror. You're driving, aren't you? I mean — that is you, is it not?

No way around it! You've got to ask: "Who is driving this bus?" Plutonium Private Club Leaders must consistently steer in the direction of:

- Hiring the right people and putting them in the right places.
- Developing, motivating and mentoring them.
- Culling the herd when necessary.

If you are truly in the driver's seat, making sure the bus is polished, always in good repair, with the right people in the right seats, and your GPS locked in on achieving consistent membership satisfaction — then sing out, "... now I've got my Magic Bus!"

An approving crowd will thunder in return — "Too much - Magic Bus! Too much - Magic Bus!"

> BUILDING AND MAINTAINING EXEMPLARY MANAGEMENT TEAMS IS ACCOMPLISHED BY IDENTIFYING TALENT, MENTORING THEM, AND MONITORING ACCOUNTABILITY FOR TERRIFIC RESULTS WITH A STYLE OF LEADERSHIP BASED UPON POSITIVE SUPPORT AND EMPOWERMENT, RATHER THAN FEAR OR MICRO-MANAGEMENT.

PERFORMANCE REVIEWS
ARE AKIN TO RATING CHICKEN WINGS
AND, ARE OFTEN COUNTER PRODUCTIVE

Check the box on the review form: "Potentially Damaging"

HEY! Who doesn't like great chicken wings! And – who doesn't like rating great employees?

Hmmm…where are we going with this analogy?

Rather than your having to read through all the "set-up" verbiage (believe me, it's coming) — let's just jettison right to the "Executive Summary" premise: Whoa! Doesn't that depend upon what those desired results might be?

Sure.

But there can only be two pursuits worthy of the entire process:

1. A formal documented process to "rate" overall great performance and to show appreciation. Or …
2. A formal documented process to "rate" overall poor performance and think this is the way to improve it towards someday really being great.

Oh — perhaps a third underlying reason for annual performance/appraisal reviews is to be able to file something in H/R that shows how astute management is in monitoring employee performance and coaching and counseling those who are not performing where they should be. Really?

However, if the desired intent is to achieve the first two above — it is a good idea to really stop and ask yourself if your annual performance appraisal system is truly accomplishing either? Is it? Really? Do these annual meetings really drive results? Is the ROI of time and effort effective? Think about it.

The whole process is usually wrapped around 'rating' employees in various criteria, converting the ratings into some sort of numerical scale, and then averaging it to an overall score.

Management *(weak)* then *(usually)* dwells on the areas of less than the highest possible rating and coerces the employee to "agree" that these less than perfect areas will now form the basis upon which "their" goals will be established for them in the next rating period.

Of course, if it seems that progress towards these "goals" was indeed achieved by the next rating, little time will ultimately be invested there. Why not? Because management is interested in moving forward and improving future performance ratings (right?). Why waste valuable time in expressing appreciation and accolades for past performance!

More times than not, a preponderance of the time is spent dwelling on yet new areas of less than perfect rating and yet again coercing agreement that these areas will now become "goals" for still the next rating period.

A perfect rating is NEVER forthcoming! Why not?

Obviously, because this would be a clear indicator of management not being able to do their job. Their job is to focus on continuous measurable improvement. Right?

And – so it goes. If the very top rating in a scale is, let's say, 30 — even the greatest performing employee will be rated only in the high 20's. If a perfect rating is 10 — even the very best employees will only be rated 8.5'ish. If a perfect rating is 5 — the best of the very best can expect no more than 4.6'ish. Huh?

If the very top rating is deemed unrealistic and can never humanly be attained, not really — then why not lower the rating scale to where it truly acknowledges the pinnacle of great performance! Nah — this would only lower our standards and take away a management tool by which to motivate great employees to improve their performance! Get it? No, not really.

- *Consistent great performers* are generally internally motivated and do not walk out of annual performance reviews inspired to do better. Instead, they are personally/professionally already driven to excellence and, frankly, find annual appraisals/reviews somewhat of a nuisance — in fact, slightly insulting.

  (You don't think so? Point blank ask them and plead that they tell you the truth!) *Keep in mind — these are your greatest employees telling you this!*

- *Inconsistent poor performers* could care less! All that matters to them is that the box at the very bottom of the printed review is checked. Then they walk out of the annual review meeting with not a care. You know — the box that confirms "Overall Performance Is ..." either "Satisfactory" or "Adequate."

  (Think about it. They know the truth is that their job is secure if either of these is checked.) Keep in mind — your so-so employees all know this!

They go home that night and proudly proclaim, "Honey, I'm home! And look at this box that is checked right here! Looks like I made it through another year being 'satisfactory' and I'm even in line again for the blanket 2.24% annual cost of living increase! Aren't you proud of me?"

What applies for one great employee may not for another. Some produce overall great results while appearing quiet and focused. Others are friendly and even somewhat gregarious. Some have a natural gift for numbers and are valued for creating organized reports. Others create dynamic boardroom presentations. While still others might have the gift of inspiring everyone.

All great employees have their own unique criteria that simply works — uniquely so, for them. There is no *"one size fits all"* when it comes to producing great results.

OK. But what does this have to do with chicken wings?

A major publication in Atlanta recently had the cover headline: "The Ultimate Chicken Wing SmackDown! This "SmackDown" is an annual tradition (hmmm — somewhat akin to an annual employee review?).

A scale of 1 to 30 was used to rate the chicken wings from over 100+ restaurants that all claimed to have the greatest in the city. Each wing was rated in five criteria: flavor, exterior texture, interior texture, value and overall experience.

There was no "one size fits all" in rating these chicken wings. Some were smoked. Some were lathered in Buffalo sauce. Others covered in lemon pepper. A basil and garlic approach worked for some — teriyaki great for others. Some broiled. Others fried. Still others, baked. Even a unique fish sauce-flavor ultimately made the final top 12.

While reading "The Ultimate Chicken Wing SmackDown" article, I could almost hear a drumroll as the overall points were disclosed and the ratings counted down to proclaiming the greatest #1 chicken wing in Atlanta!

Finally — arriving at the greatest chicken wing, I could not help but notice that the rating was only a 27 points out of a perfect rating of 30. That's right — the greatest chicken wing in this entire major city still had room for improvement! I suppose that a perfect rating of 30 would NEVER be forthcoming!

(Hmmmm — just imagine for a moment if **YOU** were a chicken wing and had just been proclaimed to be the very best of the best! Ahhhh — spread your wings with pride!)

So how does the greatest performing chicken wing in the city *(YOU!)* feel when called into the office for your annual review/rating with the boss?

Would management focus on the 27 highest-rated points in the entire city? Or, will they most likely dwell on the criteria of where needs for 'continuous improvement' have been identified and then coerce you to "agree" that these 3 will form the basis upon which your "goals" will be established until the next rating period?

Ahhh — your wings have just been clipped. How does this make you feel? Perhaps just a tiny bit discouraged? Just a tad less enthused to be creative?

Anything less than a glowing review tends to somewhat discourage enthusiasm and diminish the creativity of even top performers — while poor performers are encouraged to learn that their job is 'safe' as long as their overall performance is confirmed as satisfactory or adequate. For them — that's a successful annual review.

> "ALMOST ALL ANNUAL PERFORMANCE REVIEWS ARE NOT ONLY A WASTE OF EVERYONE'S TIME — THEY OFTEN ACHIEVE EXACTLY THE OPPOSITE OF DESIRED RESULTS."

And, never forget that *it is impossible for a winning team to be both creative and defensive at the same time.* Think about it.

ONWARD!

Outstanding Plutonium Level Leadership consists of 3 closely interwoven talents that are consistently exhibited.

1. The talent of being able to instinctively identify talent in others. You know it when you see the kind of talent that enables a team to consistently hit targets that others cannot even see. Translation: Hiring the right people and giving them a seat on the team bus.

2. The talent of mentoring and monitoring accountability for terrific results within the wheelhouse of the combined talents of all those on the team. Translation: Having the right specific people in the specific right places to thrive due to their own unique talent, while wasting no time in "culling the herd" whenever necessary for the good of the team.

3. The talent of consistently exemplifying a palpable positive leadership style based upon appreciative support and empowerment, rather than fear or micro-management. Translation: The success of the team is a direct result of successfully blending individual talents into a collective, creative, positive culture that could not exist otherwise. Positive thinking begets creativity.

- None of these things should be happening only once every 365 days in a formal meeting where employee performance review/ratings are documented and filed for future reference in a file cabinet in H/R.

- ALL of these things should be happening every day, many times each day, and seldom require a formal meeting! Every daily interaction should in itself buttress and exemplify the perpetually on-going process of building the team as a whole and as individuals.

The higher one goes up the ladder of executive leadership, the more ultimate success revolves around talent:

- Identifying it in others (and, being comfortable in your own skin as well).
- Knowing what to do with it.
- Providing positive energy leadership that perfectly blends unique individual talent into dynamic cohesive winning teams.

Think about it. We just described Super Bowl and World Series winning teams. Why should your approach to leadership be any different? Go ahead — give reasons why not. Those that can easily offer reasons (excuses?) for anything less than being consistently in contention for championship rings are perhaps themselves in the wrong league and need to go back to the minors for training, coaching and counseling. Just stop by the H/R office — there you will find the proper forms to fill out.

Developing job knowledge (what people know) and technical skills (what they can do) are necessary entry level necessities. These kinds of things can be taught or learned through repetition or training.

But, at top executive levels it comes to innate unique talent that naturally comes and manifests itself in spontaneous reactions to people, circumstances and situations leading to success. This cannot be taught or learned. It is all but hard-wired.

Can these talents be continually polished and refined? Sure. But only if that is just the way someone is wired from the get-go. Talent, in itself, is not enough without positive leadership orchestrating it. Every day.

"IN GENERAL, ARE OUR ANNUAL PERFORMANCE APPRAISAL / REVIEWS POTENTIALLY A WASTE OF EVERYONE'S TIME? IS IT POSSIBLE THAT THEY POTENTIALLY CONTRIBUTE TO ACHIEVING EXACTLY THE OPPOSITE OF DESIRED RESULTS?"

So ask yourself — If your heartfelt answer borders between a "maybe" or a flat-out "yes" — then make the necessary executive decision to simply reevaluate the whole deal.

For some, it may result in only tweaking a bit here and there. Perhaps you feel your system is working well for your needs. If so — congratulations and keep it up. For others — you just might come up with an entirely different approach.

- In any case — *Plutonium Club Leaders earn their wings, every day!*

PEOPLE AND PROCESS
IT'S A BALANCING ACT

Nowadays, in a highly automated business world, there is a tendency to focus on converting industry relevant data into ratios, KPI variance reports with a few graphs and charts thrown in. Basically, the focus is on PROCESS.
At the club, there are basically two groups of people: Members and Staff.

> HAVING THE RIGHT STANDARD OPERATING PROCEDURES (AKA: PROCESS) IN ANY BUSINESS IS IMPORTANT. BUT — HAVING THE RIGHT PEOPLE IN THE RIGHT PLACES IS MANDATORY IN THE BUSINESS OF OPERATING A HEALTHY PRIVATE CLUB FULL OF LIFE.

It ALL comes down to people — members and staff that combine to bring things to life at a club.

It was near the end of an orchestrated interview process for the GM/COO position at a truly great private club when one board member went off script and said a very important question needed to be asked before wrapping things up. It went something like this:

"I think all of us at this table are completely comfortable with your ability to work closely with our members. What I want to know is, how do you treat the employees? How do you interact and get along with them?"

The candidate smiled warmly and laughed right out loud. The answer went something like this:

"With the greatest of respect, the question itself is reason to smile and laugh. Why? Because the very question suggests that a person might treat and interact with people differently based upon their position at the club, or life in general. That person is not me. At this table we have officers of the club and a search committee representing a cross-section of your entire membership. How have we treated and interacted with each other all throughout this entire interview process? I'll be bold in offering that you've seen forthrightness, honesty, and industry expertise laced with appropriate moments of shared laughter and smiles. Well, that is exactly how I treat and interact with every member of the staff I am honored to work with and serve alongside. *I treat every person with exactly the same consistent approach."*

The club president smiled and said he didn't know how he felt about being treated just the same as a pot washer. The candidate shared a smile back and said, "Well – I suppose the pot washer may not be used to being treated like a club president either — but, my guess is everyone will quickly get used to it."

And yes, this candidate was offered the position with no dissention.

The point of sharing this true story it is to convey the importance of focusing on people, rather than overemphasizing process.

We could take the most detailed and meticulously prepared Standard Operating Procedure book, complete with a lengthy table of contents, broken down departmentally with color-coded indexed tabs. Next, let's bind it in leather and gold stamp your embossed club's name and logo on the front. Next, we take this beautiful piece of work and place a copy on the desk in the GM/COO's office, another on the boardroom table and also place a copy in the employee lounge.

> A PROPOSED CANDIDATE FOR BECOMING A MEMBER OF A FINE CLUB GOES FAR BEYOND JUST MAKING SURE THEIR CHECKS WILL CLEAR. A VIBRANT CLUB NEEDS VIBRANT MEMBERS — WHO NOT ONLY TAKE PRIDE IN BEING A PART OF SOMETHING SPECIAL, BUT APPRECIATE ALL THE PEOPLE THAT MAKE IT SO.

> CLUB EMPLOYEES ARE NOT JUST SIMPLY HIRED. INSTEAD, THEY ARE HAND-PICKED AND SELECTED. THEY, TOO WILL QUICKLY LEARN THAT THEY ARE INDEED PART OF SOMETHING SPECIAL AND TAKE PRIDE IN PROFESSIONALLY TREATING AND INTERACTING WITH A DESERVING MEMBERSHIP — AND, EACH OTHER!

Guess what? Without the right people in the right places it means nothing. It means just about as much as that nicely framed organizational chart on the wall. It is lifeless.

Private club operations that generate consistent remarkable member experiences are simply a byproduct (yet, a highly predictable one) of where the focus really needs to be — specifically, on all the people involved.

When it comes to club operations, it starts with the GM/COO and goes up, down, around and throughout the entire team.

EVERY CLUB IS UNIQUE and there is obviously no "Silver Bullet" where one size fits all. But, as a general guideline, Plutonium Leaders know that private clubs are an honorable calling for which to both belong as well as be employed. Private clubs offer the highest and very best opportunity to continually bring out the greatest quality of people and highest level of service available.

> **PLUTONIUM CLUB LEADERS HAVE A GREAT PROFESSIONAL PASSION FOR THE INDUSTRY AND ENJOY SEEING CLUBS DOING THINGS 'RIGHT.' BUT, EVEN A GREATER PERSONAL AFFECTION FOR THE PEOPLE THAT BRING IT TO LIFE — MEMBERS AND STAFF.**

It's like a balancing act, alright. A mix of two groups of people and a process adhered to. Not layered one on top of the other. But, instead, a perfect circle — well, that is, if you do it right.

POOR PERFORMERS
ARE NEVER UNWITTINGLY "REWARDED" BY PLUTONIUM CLUB LEADERS

WEAK MANAGEMENT — avoids confrontation and effectively dealing with poor performers. They are very bad at it. As a result, the poorest performing employees are unwittingly actually rewarded! This is no good at all.

PLUTONIUM PRIVATE CLUB LEADERS — seek daily opportunities to consistently identify and reward great performers. And, they are very good at it! That's more like it.

We have all seen the ripple effects of poor performance that can become toxic to the performance of an entire team. We've needed to personally acknowledge and deal with it. We've all had to mentor direct reports in telling them that they need to acknowledge and deal with a poor performer of their own.

Yup — poor performers do need to be acknowledged and dealt with. But, who would think those poor performers would be "rewarded?" Regardless — they often can be. How?

HERE ARE JUST A FEW WAYS POOR PERFORMERS ARE UNWITTINGLY REWARDED:

- *Weak management placates them to avoid conflict.* (Some are happy about that.)

- *Weak management tries to play amateur psychologist.* (They enjoy the attention.)

- *Weak management quietly corrects their errors.* (So, what's your point?)

- *They are sent away for special training programs.* (Great! An extra paid vacation!)

- *They are routinely given easier tasks to handle.* (Gee. That was easy!)

- *They are assigned jobs that allow lots of freedom.* (Not my job, man.)

- *Less is expected of them.* (As long as "Satisfactory" is checked — the annual review form is good. Right?)

- *They get "promoted."* (So they can become someone else's problem?)

- *They are given nothing to complain about.* (The good old "squeaky wheel" tactic.)

- *They continue to get paid.* (That's why they stay.)

- *Top performers are asked to help them complete their work.* (Super. Let 'em.)

- *They oftentimes get overtime.* (Why work faster if it pays more to not?)

- *They are seldom asked to do any extra work.* (Great! Cuz they're not looking for more.)

OF COURSE, IF THE POOREST PERFORMERS ARE BEING UNWITTINGLY REWARDED — THE HIGHEST PERFORMERS ARE SIMULTANEOUSLY BEING UNINTENTIONALLY PUNISHED. HOW COULD THAT BE?

They get an annual across-the-board annual salary increase. (Poor performance has not been formally documented. So, they are entitled to at least that cost of living increase. Right?)

- Management spends little time with them. (Because they perform with little or no direct supervision.)

- They are expected to work harder and faster. (Because they always meet expectations — don't they?)

- They may feel taken for granted. (Because they never complain that they need anything.)
- *They may get less opportunities for ongoing professional training.* (They're just too productive to be sent away!)

- *All additional or leftover work from others lands on their desk.* (They can handle it.)

BOTH LISTS COULD GO ON AND ON. AND IF THEY DO...

- *They are also subject to higher expectations.* (If their performance fell to merely "Satisfactory" — they'd hear about it!)

Q: What might "rewarded" poor performers think about the top performers?

A: Most will think they are fools. Behind the scenes there will be collective smirks.

Q: What might "punished" top performers think about themselves?

A: A few may ultimately also begin to think of themselves as fools. Some may openly smile less.
If this type of unhealthy reward/punishment scenario is allowed by weak management to exist …

Two scenarios have the chance to play out:

1. The weakest performers will plan on being "rewarded" with a job where they can hang around for years.

2. The strongest performers will ultimately take their talent and career elsewhere — a place where great leadership acknowledges and rewards great performance (This should happen every day — not just annually).

If weak performers are somehow allowed to hang around while strong performers move on — what does that leave weak management with?

This is contrary to the focused mindset of Plutonium Private Club Leaders! In fact, think about it — this is where fertile ground sets the stage for "Sacred Cows" that can find comfortable pastures to graze for years.

Yes — in an era of "political correctness" – H/R coaching and counseling and proper documentation — there still exists the responsibility of Pluto-

> YOUR HIGHEST AND GREATEST RESPONSIBILITY TO THE TEAM IS TO DECIDE WHO IS ON THAT TEAM. PLUTONIUM CLUB LEADERS GO THROUGH WHATEVER PROCESS THEY MUST — BUT KNOW WHAT TO DO WITH ULTIMATELY POOR PERFORMERS.

nium Leaders to make the decisions necessary for the team to succeed! To win the Super Bowl! To win the Word Series!

They deal with it. They don't reward poor performers with grazing pasture on their watch. They make the decisions necessary for the team to win.

POTENTIAL FOR PERFECTION
PLUTONIUM LEADERS ARE ABLE TO SEE THINGS AS THEY ARE — AND THEN, TAKE THEM TO WHERE THEY CAN TRULY BE

DEFINITION OF A GENIUS: "Someone who sees a target that no one else sees — and hits it!"

> JOHN HARBOTTLE WAS A VERY FINE MAN. HE WAS ALSO QUITE ARGUABLY AMONGST THE FINEST OF UP-AND-COMING GOLF COURSE ARCHITECTS OF RECENT TIMES. BOTH HIS PEERS (WHOM HE RESPECTED GREATLY) AND RENOWNED CLIENTS LOOKED UPON JOHN WITH APPRECIATION FOR HIS PERSONAL APPROACH AND HIS PROFESSIONAL DEDICATION.

John began his professional career in 1984 working on construction and design with the legendary Pete Dye. When asked about the value of that early experience, John said, "Pete gave me the opportunity to work in both the office and in construction. He showed me the importance of spending time in the field and of using a talented construction crew to perform the work."

This is my favorite story of a man who truly exhibited the inner vision that allowed him to see the potential for perfection, and the ability to bring it to life. In my interactions with him, I learned to pay close attention, ask sincere questions, be quiet when need be, and to usually expect a memorable lesson to unfold right before my eyes.

To set the stage for telling my favorite story — it is germane to quickly share 3 things that happened over just a few months in early 2012.

1. *FEBRUARY* - Unbeknownst to me, John had written a recommendation regarding our experience of working together on a Master Plan project. Inadvertently, it happened to be shared with me long afterwards.

2. **APRIL** - Completely unrelated to the above, I wrote a recommendation for John to be included in his LinkedIn profile.

3. **MAY** - John was 53 years of age.

Here we go. But this time, with a bit more background and depth in in exactly what happened in each of these months.

FEBRUARY — 2012: Here is the recommendation that John wrote that I had no knowledge of.

The above has NOTHING to do with me. Zero. Nada. Don't waste any time at all in thinking it might. Instead, it is shared solely as a tribute to John as a man who would go out of his way to help others (in this case - me).

He did not have to say any of the above. I did not ask him to. I had no idea he had even written these comments until months later. God just wired him to have the heart to always reach out.

"I have been in the golf business for most of my life and have worked with some of the best clubs in the world. Michael Crandal is as fine a general manager as I have met. My relationship with Michael began several years ago at the Thunderbird Country Club in Rancho Mirage, CA. I found Michael to be very bright, energetic and a positive person. He is a pleasure to work with and a first-class individual. He has my highest recommendation. I wish him the best." --- **John Harbottle**

APRIL – 2012: Here is the recommendation that I wrote while having no knowledge whatsoever that John had authored the above about me just two months earlier.

MAY – 2012: It was with a broken heart that John's wife sent me an email informing me that her beloved husband had died of a very sudden and completely unexpected heart attack. He was waiting between flights - in transit between two major course renovation projects.

"John is head and shoulders above so many of his peers. While I was GM/ COO at Thunderbird Country Club (Rancho Mirage, CA) we retained John to work closely with management, the Golf Committee, and ultimately the Board of Governors to create a long-range Master Plan for our 50+ year old course. John's expertise, love for what he does, and his communication skills (including GREAT listening) was evident in each step of the process that culminated in something the entire membership embraced. I've worked with and around many solid people in my career — John easily distinguishes himself as being amongst the very best of the very best. His vision for what the course could be and what the membership wanted was orchestrated perfectly. And, yes — on time, on budget." – Michael Crandal, CNG

NOW THEN — KEEPING ALL THE ABOVE IN MIND
HERE'S MY FAVORITE STORY.

John was always so gracious in allowing me (as a club GM/COO - definitely NOT a Superintendent) to sort of "tag along" with him during many rides on the course. And all the while, he gently responded to all of my "naïve" questions about how and why things were done to a golf course.

While I felt like Beaver Cleaver hanging around with his older brother Wally — John never treated any of my "stupid" questions as such. Never. He always responded with, "That is a good question. Let me explain."

Well - there was one time (actually 3 times, but all in the same scene) where he could not explain. On this particular day, John was working on a major renovation project — I believe on the 6th hole at Thunderbird Country Club with our great Superintendent, Roger Compton.

I'd eavesdrop while John and Roger would converse in hopes of my learning something. But, due to my lack of technical expertise in agronomy and golf course design/renovation — they may as well have been talking in secret code. Little doubt that most of it was all way over my "suit-and-tie/administrative" head.

The three of us are standing near the 6th green when John suddenly hops in a cart and asks if I'd like to come along.

We drive down the fairway, back to the tee, my "Jerry Garcia" tie flopping this way and that in the desert air.

John parks the cart, stands up on the seat and wanders back to the green we just left. The entire time, he is shaking his head in a steady negative slow motion. Finally, he sits back in the cart while still looking down the fairway. He seemed focused - so I refrained from asking any more stupid questions.

We drove back slowly. In silence. Back at the green - he and Roger reconvene, while both pointing to this or that. Back in the cart.

No conversation. Back to the tee. John slowly turns the cart around facing down the fairway and coasts to a stop.

Again, he is standing up on the seat. He intently looks for 3 seconds and then again starts to slowly move his head from side to side in a slow negative fashion.

Back to the green. In silence again. He and Roger chat a bit. Back in the cart. Silence.

And, for the third time, he stands up on the seat, peering without blinking — staring back to the green that rises a bit down the fairway. Again, he begins moving his head in a slow-motion unconscious "No-No" fashion.

Back in the cart. Silence reigns. We again arrive at the 6th green area.

This time he goes directly to Roger and moves without hesitation. This time he is animated and quickly points to this and that areas around the green. He confidently measures off paces from point A to point B. He then points again to imaginary lines, followed by a few more very confident measured paces.

He turns to me and says, "Let's go!" This time he drives faster back to the tee. In fact, full speed!

Still no words are said - even though I am brimming with questions as to just what the heck is going on and what the big deal is, etc.

Back at the tee he quickly wheels into position to again face the green. In one fluid motion, he jumps up on the seat, and immediately starts to grin — and then smile broadly. He is still smiling as his head begins nodding up and down in an affirmative confirmation.

I CAN'T STAND IT ANYMORE, SO I ALL BUT BLURT OUT, "JOHN - EXPLAIN TO ME JUST WHAT THE HECK WERE YOU LOOKING FOR? WHAT?"

HE ANSWERED ... "I NEVER KNOW WHAT I AM LOOKING FOR, BUT I DO KNOW IT WHEN I SEE IT. I DIDN'T SEE IT BEFORE. NOW I DO. IT WILL BE PERFECT!"

While he is doing this - I keep thinking that something strange must be going on, because I am looking at the same golf hole he is and nothing has changed. NOTHING! It all looks the same to me (perhaps the desert heat is getting to him and John is seeing things?).

I SENSED A GENIUS AT WORK.

The cart heads back at full speed, with John still smiling, while nodding up and down the entire time. I grab my tie to keep it from repeatedly slapping me in the face.

Back at the green, John leaps out before the cart has even come to a full stop. He was like The Lone Ranger, dismounting his horse Silver from a full gallop.

He pulls out an envelope folded in half from his back pocket, and creates a quick diagram on it — points to here and there — confidently paces off along some sort of imaginary lines — and then says to Roger as he hands him the envelope, "Have Andy (our heavy equipment operator) make these changes according to these specs and I'll see you in the morning."

Roger rubs his chin - digests what he sees on the envelope, slowly starts nodding up and down, smiles broadly, shakes John's hand, and suddenly - our work for that day was over.   The next morning - as usual, Roger had the work done exactly as directed. And, even I could now see that the hole was brought to life!

We all smiled, as indeed - **IT WAS PERFECT!**

So now you know my favorite story of a man who truly exhibited the inner vision that allowed him to see the potential for perfection, and the ability to bring it to life.

John was only 53 years of age. In all his interactions with me, he exhibited the following — Philippians 2:3-4: "Do nothing out of selfish ambition or vain conceit. Rather, in humility value others above yourselves, not looking to your own interests but each of you to the interests of the others."

PRESIDENT ALWAYS LOOKS GOOD
PLUTONIUM CLUB LEADERSHIP KNOWS NO OTHER WAY — JOB #1

When any search committee extends a career opportunity — they are basing that action on the prediction of their final candidate's success. **Period.**

And depending upon what specific industry and level of position, some may think that the very definition of "success" would be wildly variable depending on the job. Nope — indeed, it is fixed.

Q: Huh? How can that be?

A: Because everyone, no matter what — has the same job (KPI) where success is mandatory.

Q: Hmmm — and just what might that be?

A: "YOUR JOB IS TO MAKE YOUR BOSS LOOK GOOD."

If you're offended by the simplicity of this, just ask yourself this question: "What happens to those who fail in that endeavor?"

No matter how talented, knowledgeable, skilled, or articulate you may be — it's going nowhere if you don't grasp that your real job is to make your club president look good.

That's the bottom line why you were hired. It is why any of us have ever been hired. And, truth be known — every person you have ever personally extended a job opportunity was based on your predicting that candidate would reflect well on you (in other words — make YOU look good).

- You may have never really thought about it in this exact way. But — think about it right now. It is the truth. It had better be!

A basic tenant of leadership is that one can only be as good as those s/he surrounds themselves with. Therefore, it is imperative that you hire people who ultimately will make you look good.

If this seems superficially way too self-serving — ask yourself, *"How successful am I going to be if I make just enough "bad" hires that are ultimately incapable of making me look good? Or, what happens if I fail to get rid of poor performers that compromise the team?"*

- If you allow yourself to be surrounded by folks who don't really understand what they were hired for, what their job really is — by default, immediately — YOU are incapable of making *YOUR* boss look good. And, that means, *YOU — ARE NOT — DOING — YOUR — JOB!*

To complete the circle, using the position of GM/COO as our example — PLUTONIUM PRIVATE CLUB LEADERS know that this is how it all comes down:

1. The search committee selects a new GM/COO based on a prediction of that final candidate ultimately making them look absolutely brilliant.

2. The club president (your new boss!) wants the board, and search committee, to look good.

3. Your boss (the club president) cannot look good unless the GM/COO (that be YOU!) successfully champions her/his vision and having it looking good in the eyes of the membership.

4. But, the GM/COO is only capable of making the club president look good if their direct reports (meaning ALL department heads and key staff) are doing the same to them.
5. The department heads are incapable of making their boss (YOU!) look good unless all of their staff is successful in doing their jobs — making their boss look good!

In fact, leadership is only as good as those "good" hires surrounding them in every department who know what their real job is. This applies to the newest hired hourly wage seasonal employee as well as veteran management. This is a perennial truth.

Looking up the organization chart, the job of a successful GM/COO is simple: make the club president look good. The only way this can happen is where the real joy of operations and management comes in. At EVERY level of management — decision makers focus on three key things:

1. Hiring the right people and putting them in the right places.
2. Developing, motivating and mentoring them.
3. Culling the herd when necessary.

Of course, while all this is going on —there must be a vibrant and supportive environment where everyone (vertically and horizontally) knows what their real job is and feels great about doing it.

Building and maintaining exemplary management teams is accomplished by identifying talent, mentoring them, and monitoring accountability for terrific results with a style of leadership based upon positive support and empowerment, rather than fear or micro-management.

To put a ribbon around this: A vibrant and supportive environment thrives throughout the club! The department heads appear to be a collection of superheroes straight from the pages Marvel Comics, dedicated to making the totality of club operations look exceptional. By default, the GM/COO truly appears as "Captain Marvel" in making the club president look good. Thus, the entire board has no need of micro-managing, and looks very good to an appreciative membership.

> REMEMBER, WHETHER JUST ACCEPTING A NEW POSITION OR ENJOYING THE ONE YOU HAVE HAD FOR MANY YEARS — A HALLMARK OF PLUTONIUM CLUB LEADERSHIP IS THAT EVERYONE KNOWS WHAT THEIR REAL JOB IS AND WHY THEY WERE HIRED IN THE FIRST PLACE.

Most importantly, at the very tip-top of the organizational chart — THE MEMBERS — they believe that life at their club is far, far, far more than just good. In fact, it is the best there is! Hands down.

Let's not forget about that search committee. Wow! It now looks like they really were brilliant!

PRIVATE CLUB RADIO
PRIVATECLUBRADIO.COM

The Private Club Radio Show is the industry's weekly source for education, news, predictions, product spotlights, trends, and other current developments in the world of private clubs. PCR is the most awarded podcast in the golf industry, having received a 2017 Communicator Award of Distinction as well as a Pazzie Award.

Each week, Gabriel Aluisy hosts and conducts a great interview with guests who have the opportunity to share their story and answer questions related to their field of expertise. Guests range from association presidents to GM/COO's, and from industry experts to product manufacturers and club vendors.

PCR was created by Gabe and is recognized as a tremendous asset and ambassador of goodwill for the industry. Just a quick look at the guest list of past shows is enough to establish credibility. The most instantly recognized and respected names in Private Clubs are insightfully interviewed by Gabe each week. For Example:

Jackie Carpenter/Private Club Advisor — *Rick Coffey*/MobiCom — *Rick Coyne*/Private Club Marketing Association — *Ray Cronin*/Club Benchmarking — *Henry DeLozier*/Global Golf Advisors — *Steve Graves*/Creative Golf Marketing — *Dick Kopplin/*Kopplin, Kuebler & Wallace *Bill McMahon*, Sr./McMahon Group — *Jeff Morgan*/CMAA — *Peter Nanula*/Concert Golf *Bill O'Brien*/Troon — *Gregg Patterson*/Industry Icon — *Norm Spitzig*/Master Club Advisors *Henry Wallmeyer*/National Club Association — *Harvey Weiner*/Search America

Oh, by the way, the most popular guest in the history of Private Club Radio was inadvertently omitted above. We'd like to correct this by humbly mentioning the name of *Michael Crandal, CNG.*

Every Monday, *Private Club Radio* releases yet another great interview. These are collectively proving to be a "Must Listen" experience every week for all serious leaders in the industry.

Keep in mind that the full library of great interviews is continuously (24/7) available and can easily be forwarded to industry peers, as well as shared with both BOD and key club staff.

We've all copied and shared industry print magazine articles relating to important issues at our respective clubs. Private Club Radio expands that concept to new heights.

So, tune in to Private Club Radio every week where Gabe interviews the most dynamic leaders in the private club industry. You can find the podcast on iTunes, Spotify, Soundcloud, Google Play and wherever podcasts are heard.

QUALITY IS NEVER LEFT TO CHANCE.

QUALITY AND SERVICE

There are two words that are ceremoniously thrown about the market place in universal fashion. They are the two most redundant words found in print, electronic, and in verbal sales pitches.

This is so much the case that they are all but rendered meaningless. And, in an absence of a clear definition, they are indeed just that: meaningless.

The purpose here is to be very clear in offering a meaningful definition of these two words (hold on, they're coming).

When presenting to groups of leaders (Providers) from variable backgrounds, I will ask them to share what they focus on the most in order to differentiate themselves from others in the marketplace. Invariably — regardless of product or industry — the same two words will ultimately surface as the top two.

What is interesting, is that when polls are given to potential customers/clients (Consumers) asking them what is most important to them — the same two words reign here as well.

Gosh - it looks like we have a winner here! Everybody agrees. Everybody expects. Everybody demands. Of course — the two words are: **QUALITY & SERVICE.**

Fine. It looks like everybody knows those two words. The problem is that when directly asked what those two words mean - next to nobody knows!

If nobody really knows a clear definition of **QUALITY & SERVICE** — how is it possible to know if either of these words is really happening or being delivered?

So, let's be very clear in accepting meaningful definitions of these two words. Here we go:

QUALITY is: "Conformance to requirements." Sounds easy enough, doesn't it? And it would be, but we are not done yet! Those words alone are still unclear. So, let's be really clear about the "Q" word!

"QUALITY IS CONFORMANCE TO REQUIREMENTS — THE REQUIREMENTS OF THE CONSUMER!" (OF COURSE, IN OUR WORLD OF PRIVATE CLUBS, THIS MEANS MEMBERS AND GUESTS!)T

In order for communication to happen, there must obviously be a transmitter and a receiver. Again, in our world of private clubs, the transmitter is Management & Staff, while our intended receiver of Members & Guests.

It is easy for CEO-types or marketing firms to focus on only the transmitter. Oftentimes they believe in THEIR own mind that what THEY are transmitting is quality stuff — and their job is over. Guess what? It's not. A recent survey proved it.

- 80% of CEO's believe they are delivering a "superior" customer experience. However...
- Only 8% of their customers agreed!
- 60% of customers rated "satisfied" on surveys — PRECEEDING their defection!

Obviously — in the mind of the consumer — "superior" experiences are definitely NOT rooted in fancy slogans, eye appealing logos, or catchy taglines that come from the marketing department.

Those things are nice, and may even win Addy Awards — but, not necessarily win the hearts and minds of consumers.

Of critical importance is not necessarily the intended transmission. Instead it's all about the heart and mind of the consumer (Members and Guests!) since they are who will define whether or not quality was received at all. Now that we have a meaningful definition of QUALITY...let's go on to define that next word: SERVICE.

SERVICE IS: "A MANAGED OR ORCHESTRATED PERCEPTION, LEFT ON THE MIND OF THE CONSUMER, ABOUT THE MANNER IN WHICH WE GO ABOUT OUR BUSINESS."

CPA-types and bean counters oftentimes have difficulty in getting their intellectual arms around the monetary value of SERVICE because they can't:

1. Inventory it.
2. Account for it on your balance sheet.
3. Find it as a line item within every department.
4. Locate it in the chart of accounts.

Yet, it is priceless. Without it, any business becomes irrelevant in the marketplace.

There are several key concepts in our definition of service. Let's break 'em down:

- *"...managed or orchestrated..."* — This implies that it can be controlled. It means that it is a function of management. It means that it can be presented in an orchestrated fashion. It means that it is not random. It means that it is intentional.

- *"...perception..."* — Here is where it comes to life in the expectations and feelings of those receiving it. Perceptions cannot be kept in inventory simply to be requisitioned whenever needed. Perceptions are delivered very much in "real time" right on the spot at the very moment of need. Perceptions form impressions, expectations and feelings.

- *"...the mind of the consumer..."* — Here we have the piece de resistance! The mind of the consumer! The all-important consumer! The intended "receiver" of all communications! Here (in the mind of the consumer) decisions are made!

> AT EVERY MEMBERSHIP EXPERIENCE ENCOUNTER, IT IS THE MEMBER WHO MAKES THE FINAL DECISION IN THEIR OWN MIND REGARDING ALL KINDS OF PERCEPTIONS THEY DEEM AS THEIR OWN PERSONAL REALITY.

Was a transmitted message received at all? If so, did it conform to my personal requirements? Was I truly blown away? Do I want to experience this again, or not at all? Was I under or overwhelmed? Do I want to share this with family and friends?

From this point on, whenever you see the word QUALITY or SERVICE - define them in the terms offered here and see if there is some new meaning that your team can wrap their arms around.

Some folks may have had several other words come to mind in addition to **QUALITY & SERVICE** and understandably wondered why they were not shared above as well. And, indeed, you'd be right in pointing out many other words of significance. But our focus here is the top two words.

However, as a quick follow up to the points above — there are indeed two additional words that are always right in the mix. Let's touch upon both quickly right now.

VALUE - is always in the top responses. This word is in the back of every member's minds when a dues increase or assessment is proposed. It comes to mind when signing any transaction at the club. Yes, perceived VALUE is indeed a "Mission Critical" component of membership satisfaction and a mandatory mind-set of favorable membership experiences.

> IT IS IMPORTANT TO NOTE THAT VALUE IS COMPLETELY DRIVEN BY PERCEIVED QUALITY & SERVICE! IF PRESENT, THE CORRESPONDING PRICE POINT (VALUE) IS ACCEPTED BY THE MEMBERSHIP. BUT, IN THE ABSENCE OF EITHER — THERE IS NO PERCEIVED VALUE AT ALL — IN AT ANY PRICE.

> SO IMPORTANT IS CONSISTENCY, THAT IF NOT RELIABLE, YOU HAVE NOTHING! PUT THE WORD "INCONSISTENT" IN FRONT OF QUALITY & SERVICE AND, ANY FAVORABLE PERCEPTION OF VALUE IN THE MIND OF THE MEMBERSHIP IS EMPTY, NULL, AND VOID - AGAIN, AT ANY PRICE.

CONSISTENCY - Yikes! This is so very, very essential! This represents the hands down most treasured desire of members — especially when having confidence in entertaining guests. Nothing worse in the eyes of the membership than having up and down experiences where they never know what to expect the next time. Reliable consistency is a must! Mission Critical. Mandatory for Plutonium Club Leaders to strive for, maintain and constantly monitor.

QUESTIONS
A GM/COO PLUTONIUM CANDIDATE CONSIDERS
ASKING THE SEARCH COMMITTEE ARE THE SAME QUESTIONS
EVERY CLUB SHOULD ASK OF THEMSELVES

PREFACE

While the below is presented as potential questions a GM/COO candidate might opt to ask of the search committee…frankly, **these are questions that EVERY BOARD AT EVERY CLUB should be asking of themselves!** For right now, let's pretend we are a fly on the wall as the search committee concludes a formal interview with a GM/COO candidate.

Things seem to be winding down. A few search committee members start gathering and straightening papers before them as they share seemingly ad-lib comments while thanking a candidate for spending time with them (kind of like what you see on TV as the local news team gets ready to end a broadcast).

Get ready. Here it comes.

Before any of the group actually stands, the room draws quiet, as one of them (as if on cue) looks the candidate right in the eye and says, "Do you have any questions for us?"

Now THEY had better be ready. Because a Plutonium candidate IS prepared!

Below, in no particular order of importance or priority, is a list of 10 questions from which you might consider asking a few of.

They cannot be listed in degree of importance or priority, as only a very seasoned executive will be able to ascertain if any of them are even appropriate at all.

As the interview unfolds and a Plutonium candidate begins to sense the general culture of the club and roles of those around the table — only then will s/he be able to identify which, if any, of the following questions are strategically appropriate.

Are you ready? OK. Let the silence last only a heartbeat as you look around the table at each person in the eye and say, "Thank you for asking. Yes. I do have just a few."

Elbows will then come back on the table.

Keep in mind, regardless of how 'well' the interview itself seemed to go - often what can distinguish candidates is not just offering answers, but their ability to ask meaningful questions. Trust me on this one. It proves a candidate knows what they are talking about. HEY! It also means a candidate had darn well better know what they are talking about! Because now that s/he has opened the barn door — there is no turning back now!)

HERE WE GO — 10 POTENTIALLY VERY MEANINGFUL QUESTIONS.

1) QUESTION: "Does the club have debt, and if so, what plans are in place to eliminate it?"

- *WHY ASK? Their answer lets you know all kinds of things.*

If there is no debt at all - it tells you all kinds of GOOD things! If there is debt, that in itself is not a knock-out punch by any means.

But if their debt is rising, or there is no real plan to systematically reduce or eliminate it - it tells you that there may very well be a day of reckoning, where a significant unplanned balloon payment looms or a dreaded assessment is a future necessity.

Hmmm — what happens if this comes down while you are on the job? You couldn't possibly be held as a scape goat for this could you? Nah. Of course not! Such nonsense never happens in clubs! We all know that! Forget this question...I'm sorry I even brought it up. What could I possibly have been thinking?

2) QUESTION: "Does the club have a Capital Reserve Plan in place and a means to fund it?

WHY ASK? This lets you know if the club takes seriously the importance of protecting their physical assets. Their responses will give you a picture of their approach to funding depreciation (a very real cost...are they ignoring it?).

It may shed light on the potential existence of behind the scenes deferred maintenance. It may also offer insight as to the inadequacy of Initiation Fee income and/or how they allocate it.

If Initiation Fee income is allocated to operations rather than capital - you may safely deduct that dues are artificially low, and not sufficient to truly support the level of quality and service the membership expects.

Hmmm ... what happens if Initiation Fee income is suddenly reduced and in order to avoid raising dues or having an operating assessment, the new GM/COO is forced to reduce quality and service? I mean, I'm just askin'…

3) QUESTION: "Does your club have a meaningful Strategic Plan in place that is well communicated and updated on an on-going basis?"

- *WHY ASK? A professionally orchestrated Strategic Plan is mandatory. But, just having a 3-ring binder sitting on the shelf collecting dust is meaningless!*

Imagine if in answer to your question, a member of the board points over to a book shelf and says proudly, "Oh sure we do. It's been right over there for years."

All things else considered, any club that has a meaningful, professionally prepared, Strategic Plan that is routinely monitored and updated by club leadership is a highly desired place of employment. Why? Because a solid Strategic Plan will engraft many of the questions posed here and will directly identify procedures and policies to systematically move the club forward.

This is a great place for a dedicated GM/COO to be ▢ playing a significant and meaningful role in keeping the board informed and dialed in to the importance of consistently reviewing and moving into the future with confidence.

4) QUESTION: "Ideally your club has many long-term employees that are highly regarded and appreciated by the members. However, there are isolated instances where a few may fall into the category of "Sacred Cows"… without going into any details, does your club have many of these that are somewhat concerning to the board?"

- *WHY ASK? Every club has a few "Sacred Cow" employees that may no longer be as productive as the membership deserves. The real question here is, does this club know that? Do they care?*

Be careful here — you DO NOT want to imply that if you are the new GM/COO you will all but immediately take steps to eliminate the very employees that the membership loves. No way! You DO want to know how the board views staff performance. Do they "get it" when it comes to what it really takes to maintain quality service. Tread lightly here…but you do want to know.

5) QUESTION: "How well attended is your club's annual biggest member/member golf event?"

- *WHY ASK? This offers insight into how well the membership interacts and gets along.*

Ideally, this event should be a big deal! Something that there is a waiting list to get into every year. In fact, you want to hear that those who participated the previous year are given priority for the coming year. A thriving member/member event tells you a great deal — so does an under subscribed or declining event.

6) QUESTION: *"Does your club have a "Legacy' class of membership, or by whatever name - an approach to encouraging generational membership? If so, is it getting the results the board wants?"*

- *WHY ASK? Any club's greatest source of potential new members is the existing membership.*

Membership in a club is based on relationships. Business. Friends. But the strongest relationship is family. A truly "built-in" pipeline of membership continuity is based on family relationships. If a club has a very weak approach to generational family memberships - what does this tell you about this club? On the other hand, if there are many members with strong family ties up and down - this is one indication of a strong club.

7) QUESTION: *"Does your club have a major member/guest event that is one of the highlights of the year? If so, can you tell me a bit about it?"*

- *WHY ASK? A solid club takes pride in annually hosting a major event enabling members to showcase their very best efforts and aspects of the entire operation.*

As they respond to this question, look for a sparkle in their eyes and a sense of pride as they describe what they do. The more sparkles you see the better. This indicates a vibrant club. No sparkles? If they are not all that proud in belonging to their club, uh - why would you be proud of managing it?

8) QUESTION: *"What significant changes in member expectations has your club experienced over the past 10 years?"*

- *WHY ASK? Here you learn what they are looking for going forward.*

Obviously, if there are new challenges that they are aware of, these are predictably the same areas they are looking for a new GM/COO to help in addressing. And, it perfectly positions you to identify in your own mind and heart if you are just as perfectly aligned to deliver the goods or not.

Now then — what if they say that they really have not noticed any changes in member expectations over the past 10 years? Yell at the top of your lungs, "FIRE!" Run! Get out! Head for the nearest exit!

9) QUESTION: "Does your club have 'Waiting Lists' to either get in or out? If so - what is your club's policy/philosophy towards them?

- *WHY ASK? There are obviously desired "correct" answers whether or not lists exist at all - but, what you really want to know is their feelings towards them! Their response here will tell you volumes about where they are coming from. Listen closely.*

10) QUESTION: "Looking forward, let's say your new GM/COO has been leading your club for 2 years and has just received a stellar performance review from the people sitting here at this table today. Tell me, what are the key accomplishments that made your review such a strong one?"

- *WHY ASK? OK. If there was one singular, very best question that would yield you the very best information about the club - this is it.*

This one cuts through all the haze. It tells you exactly the potential that they want to see in the ideal candidate who would ultimately make them look good if this person was hired as their next GM/COO.

Of course, you would only consider hand-picking a few from the above questions that you deem as the most appropriate given the tone of the interview itself and the cards already tipped on both sides of the table.

But, no sense in even considering any of the above until you have asked those below. First impressions are important, so come right out of the chute fast and furious as you take your seat. Ready? Take a deep breath and let's get it on!

"Once I start this job, what kind of discount do I get in the golf shop? I know y'all support a family/career balance. You wouldn't expect me to work weekends or holidays, would you? I'm glad to hear y'all have family memberships. Does this mean my kids can use the pool? I never spend more than the approved budget. So, what is the monthly budget for competitive dining? And I, of course, like to keep the club's dry-cleaning bills down by always having appropriate business attire — so what type of clothing allowance is there? I suspect you are always open to looking at potential new members...so can I bring my pals over for my regular Saturday morning tee time? I'm glad you are impressed with my college background. Any chance we could have my class reunion here this fall? Toga! Toga! Toga! And, oh, by the way, where does the GM/COO park? And, yah know, I really do prefer a coupe rather than a sedan. And, while not a deal breaker— candy apple red is my favorite color. — And..."

POSTSCRIPT: If responses to any of the above legitimate questions draw out "bad" answers - this is not to suggest that that club should be dismissed out of hand. Far from it!

While your questions may indeed expose some serious shortcomings - those may be the very same reasons that they are now seeking a great new GM/COO in order to address them! And — thank goodness you are interviewing, because you are just the kind of professional they need to help them pull out of any death spirals!

In some cases, "flaws" to some, can just as easily be "opportunities" to a candidate with great strengths in those areas when coupled with a board that is seeking professional leadership to help them. On the other hand — enough negative answers may send strong signals of "buyer beware!"

LASTLY - Think about this. Let's say there were "X" number of candidates who were interviewed and all of them gave similar superb answers to every one of the questions posed to them. Further, let's say that at the end of the interview process all but one said, "No. I have no questions. You have already been generous with your time and have pretty well given me enough information about your club. I do hope to hear from you."

BUT - there was that one who said, "Thank you for asking. Yes. I do have just a few." And then they asked 2 or 3 meaningful questions and were able to engage in some meaningful follow up conversation.

Hmmm — all other things being equal — who gets the offer? Toga! Toga! Toga!

REMEMBER: *These are questions EVERY BOARD AT EVERY CLUB should be asking of themselves on an ongoing basis! That is called INTROSPECTION. Something that all Plutonium Private Club Leaders routinely do.*

RESTAURANTS SERVE NOTHING BUT EXCELLENCE.

RESPONSIBILITY
IS ULTIMATELY OWNED BY PLUTONIUM CLUB LEADERS. BUT, THEY ARE MASTERS AT DELEGATING AUTHORITY (AND APPROPRIATE LEVELS OF RESPONSIBILITY) TO DEVELOPING STAFF, AND GETTING THINGS DONE

Weak MANAGERS look for excuses to not delegate. Plutonium Club Leaders actively look for opportunities to appropriately delegate. This is a very distinct line between the two.

Here are the ten most common "excuses" weak managers use to not delegate effectively.

1) Folks around here don't really want to accept responsibility anyway!

Does it seem that whenever you assign someone a job – BINGO! They ultimately drop it right back in your lap? If so, some sort of delegation is indeed going on here - but, in reverse.

> DON'T BLAME YOUR STAFF. YOUR STAFF IS YOUR RESPONSIBILITY. THAT MAY SOUND LIKE A NEW CONCEPT TO SOME. BUT, TRUST ME ON THIS ONE. OK. ADMITTEDLY, WE DON'T KNOW EACH OTHER ALL THAT WELL. SO WHY DON'T YOU JUST ASK YOUR BOSS INSTEAD?

Weak management may have trouble delegating - and instead inadvertently create an unhealthy culture where their staff sure as heck does not! This results in "Upward Delegation" where the staff actually piles added responsibilities on their boss.

- With proper delegation, you just might be surprised how eagerly many on the team will anxiously accept responsibility, deliver great results and open new doors of opportunity that otherwise might never have existed.

2) I guess it is something that never really occurs to me. Really?

What this truly translates is that you think you are way too busy personally making sure things get done and that it is a waste of your valuable time in developing others by involving them. With that kind of thinking, no wonder delegation never really crosses your mind. Heck — you are too busy making sure things get done around here. Right?

3) Doing everything shows everyone just how indispensable I am around here!

Oftentimes a personal sense of "needing to be needed" is what derails an otherwise successful professional career. The fact is that nothing will make anyone indispensable — because no one is. Get over it (and yourself).

4) I can get things done better and faster than anyone else.

The problem here is that short-run expediency, oftentimes comes at the expense of long-range effectiveness. By continually doing the job yourself, you are only ensuring that you will have to do the job again when it reoccurs. And, brace yourself - that will happen again, and again, and again...until somebody eventually has seen it all just one too many times.

Suddenly your fast pace will start moving in slow motion with more and more activity with less and less results. Gee — I wonder why?

5) Speaking candidly - nobody here has the experience or depth of competence that I do.

If your staff is that incompetent — what are you paying THEM for? If you are responsible for an incompetent staff — what is the club paying YOU for? Connect the dots...or your board soon will.

6) To be frank, I really want the folks around here to like me. I really do. No sense in my needlessly telling anyone what to do.

If a fear of being disliked is a primary motivator - then perhaps a career as a clown in the fantasy world of a circus might be a great place to park your emotions. However, fear had better strike out when reality is the pitcher.

It is indeed nice if employees like you. And, nice as well if you like them. However, what is crucial in the real world is that your staff slowly gains a deeply earned respect for you (and, each other).

7) I don't want to be seen as losing control of my job.

THERE IS A GREAT AND HUGELY IMPORTANT DIFFERENCE BETWEEN CONFIDENCE AND ARROGANCE. ARROGANCE HAS NO PLACE IN PLUTONIUM LEADERSHIP. HUMILITY IS NOT JUST A BIG DEAL — IT'S HUGE!

Playing BIG cheese — BIG wheel — BIG boss —or BIG anything — will prove a bigger than big roadblock in any career path. Everyone respects a leader who at their core exhibits confidence that is balanced with humility.

No one respects (or, for that matter, even likes) any individual in a position of leadership who seems too big for their britches...commonly known as Control Freaks.

8) Dependence upon others might be perceived a sign of weakness.

This irrational idea is perhaps to some degree linked to the fact that all of us were once babies. In fact, babies are totally helpless and their entire world is in a state of complete dependence on others to do all the things for them in order to survive.

But — as we start growing up, it is not too long before we start hearing, "Do it yourself — you're not a baby anymore!" So - grow up!

Plutonium Club Leaders embrace the fact that you cannot have everyone depend on you, nor do you want them to. Grasp the reality that you cannot depend solely on yourself while ignoring your team. We are all adults around here. We ALL need to grow up.

Plutonium Club Leaders understand that their job is to help everyone around them to grow and be successful together. Forget about childish behavior

VERY SIMILAR TO PLANNING - DELEGATION CAN INITIALLY BE TIME-CONSUMING. BEING TOO BUSY TO DELEGATE IS LIKE BEING TOO BUSY TO PLAN.

exhibiting a core of weakness — instead, do your part in growing a strong team and being a part of that team.

9) Frankly, I'm too busy to delegate.

This mentality ties back to #2. It must be understood that effective delegation is indeed an ongoing process — not just an occurrence, such as flipping a toggle switch and being done with it. It does take time.

Some situations may indeed take investing time in deciding who to delegate to, sometimes actually teaching people, and then even more time in checking back, being available, and monitoring performance. But, as time is invested in the right people at the just the right moments — your time as an executive will begin to open up like it never possibly could have otherwise. Weak management may indeed feel they are too busy doing everything themselves. The truth is, if they don't know how to appropriately delegate their upward career path is stifled. DOA.

10) Deep down - I actually want to do it all by myself. I just do.

An easy trap to fall into is filling our days with trivial tasks that should be delegated to others while enabling them to learn and grow. At the same time, freeing time to further develop the entire team.

Weak management keeps doing their old job - but with their new title. This is common when a department head finds themselves for the first time in a new GM role. It is a natural tendency to migrate towards an old comfort level.

Doing your old job well obviously helped position you for the new job you now have. But that is the point — you now have a new job.

RETURN ON INVESTMENT OF BEING A MEMBER
"PROFIT" IS DEFINED IN TERMS OF MEMBERSHIP SATISFACTION

In what other business could it be said that the board of directors, the customers and the shareholders — were all one and the same?

THERE IS A SUBTLE DIFFERENCE IN THE PURPOSE BETWEEN A DEFINITELY "PROFIT ORIENTED" ENTERPRISE, AND A DISTINCTLY "BENEFIT ORIENTED" PURSUIT WHICH EXISTS IN A PRIVATE, MEMBERSHIP-OWNED CLUB.

Just imagine the potential conflict of interests between those three groups as various business decisions (both policy and operations) needed to be made. It would be impossible to operate and to keep all concerned completely satisfied. Yet this is exactly the scenario that exists in a private member-owned club.

BOARD AND MANAGEMENT HAVE VERY DIFFICULT MULTI-FACETED ROLES.

The very definition of "profit" is vastly different in the "real world" – and the world that exists only in the sanctity of a private club. There are few comparisons between the business world and the world of operating a private club. These two worlds spin on a different axis.

Profit can only accrue for the membership in the form of: Increased satisfaction. Perceived added services. Perceived higher quality in both the products and services offered.

In a club operation, "profit" is defined in terms of membership satisfaction. Not by an absence of red ink on the operating statement.

All private, member-owned clubs lose money on departmental operations. This is true no matter how elite, prestigious, successful, or exclusive the club might be — or think they are. If this were not the case, there would be no need for dues — as the membership (owners) would simply live off of the profit from operations and even be justified in expecting a dividend check at the end of the fiscal year.

THE ONLY THING PRIVATE CLUB DUES ENTITLE MEMBERS TO IS THE PRIVILEGE TO HAVE THE CLUB FACILITIES AND STAFF MADE AVAILABLE TO THEM SHOULD THEY CHOOSE TO UTILIZE IT   AT AN EVEN FURTHER COST.

People don't join private clubs expecting a check from the club to appear in their mailbox every month. No, they expect to pay dues. Not dues that in any manner subsidize waste or mismanagement, but dues that must be available to offset very legitimate operating expenses.

YOU ARE CORDIALLY INVITED TO...

A strong membership base at a successful private club must have its roots established by its current members expending personal "invitations" to qualified candidates — not by routinely accepting casual "applications" from non-members.

Brochures, mailings, open houses, social media and websites are not necessarily going to consistently attract the type of potential members who understand the long-range commitment needed to truly foster and maintain the character and tradition of a fine private club.

A successful club is built upon common interests, families and friends from within, not by opening its doors to anyone outside whose initiation fee check will probably clear.

Clubs that resort to mass mailings may experience instant results, but results with no real long-range depth. They may find themselves having to engage in yet another membership drive every three or four, years to solicit new members whom none of the current members may even know.

A private, member-owned club is not "successful" simply because it is able to pay its bills. A successful club is one whose members truly enjoy their fellow member's camaraderie and are willing and able to pay the dues to support it. Just because a membership drive attracts a few who are able to pay dues does not also mean — financial ability aside — that the desire to do so can prevail over time.

Who would want to belong to a club where every member paid their dues, but didn't know each other or frequent the club? Financially, this club might appear to be a success. But it would be like a cardboard cake covered with frosting on the **outside.** It looks good – but there is nothing of substance *inside.*

FORE!

In broad general terms, a quite private, member-owned country club in the moderate seasonal temperate zone, with 18 holes can reasonably expect to accommodate 18,000 to 22,000'ish rounds of golf each year. This exact same golf course, if open to the public, might expect to see 2 or 2.5 times that amount.

Since the market at a private club is limited, so too is the income from potential greens fees.

Members want to be able to come to their club on a Saturday morning (perhaps even without a tee time) and have a reasonable expectation of finding a game with a few fellow members, and teeing off on their own course within an hour of arriving at the club.

Only a highly skilled and well compensated golf course superintendent should be entrusted with making sure the condition of the course is the very best it can be. Yet, no matter how close to perfection their professional expertise — even after crediting sales from green fees and cart rentals — *golf operations at a private club will still annually lose deep into six figures just by operating a private golf course.*

Ironically, this same golf course may be a club's greatest asset, and quite often the pride of the membership.

MONDAY OUTINGS?

Many private country clubs are frequently approached with requests from outside groups who would like to host large corporate and charitable golf outings. Even though these events may generate significant positive cash flow, the majority of private clubs, more times than not, decline altogether or limit the acceptance of these requests simply because they do not care for the wear and tear on their property.

Members want as few rounds of golf played as possible *(except for their own, of course)*.

HAND ME MY 7-IRON, PLEASE.

A private member-owned country club may strive to have a well-developed caddie program. Strangely, the stronger and more successful the caddie program, the deeper the red ink flows. Every caddie used means a loss of potential golf cart rental revenue.

Still — a dynamic and reliable caddie program is deemed an absolute essential necessity by many very fine private clubs. In fact — their very reputation and quality "brand" is renowned due to their caddie program.

A BANQUET HALL?

A private, member-owned country club with 300 to 600 members, offering a full range of first-class food and beverage options, including banquet facilities for the exclusive use of the members and their guests, will most likely generate in the neighborhood of $2.5-ish million in annual sales.

This exact same facility, if opened to the public, might expect to do three or five times in sales.

But the majority of private clubs, more times than not, decline altogether or limit the acceptance of these requests — simply because they do not care for the wear and tear on their facility or staff.

In fact – **THE MEMBERS PAY DUES** in order to have the facilities and staff available to **THEM** for the special events and times of **THEIR** lives to be shared in **THEIR** private club.

A PRIVATE, MEMBER-OWNED CLUB WILL QUITE OFTEN OFFER MENUS AND HOURS OF OPERATION THAT, WHILE MAKING A GREAT DEAL OF SENSE IN TERMS OF ATTEMPTING TO BE ALL THINGS TO ALL MEMBERS, ARE INDEED NONSENSICAL WHEN ANALYZED BY FOOD & BEVERAGE PROFESSIONALS.

Imagine being the one who informs a member that they cannot use THEIR club because it is instead being utilized by non-members to host an event that precludes members to have access to their own club. Oh, really?

LET'S MAKE SOME SENSE OUT OF ALL THIS.

This creates even more potential for red ink, yet it has an even greater potential to serve members in such a manner that they feel proud of their club.

On one hand, the routine demands on the kitchen and service staff might not appear to be all that different from what is needed at a nicer family restaurant. *(You'd be wrong about that.)*

On the other hand, a highly skilled, well compensated Executive Chef and culinary team is mandatory in order to handle not only the limited demands of a family restaurant, but to also simultaneously orchestrate special membership dining experiences, private parties, and club events to rival the Four Seasons or luxury cruise ships. (You got that right!)

This diversity and ability to serve the members is of great value, and is a source of pride for a membership.

LOST IN SPACE?

A private, member-owned club will frequently have a spacious clubhouse with lots of infrequently used space. Contrary to a retail operation that has industry standard ratios between facility square footage and sales, a clubhouse often presents a plethora of non-revenue producing square footage.

> SPEAKING FROM A STRICTLY FINANCIAL STANDPOINT, THE PURPOSE OF PRIVATE CLUB OPERATIONS IS TO CREATE SUCH A HIGH LEVEL OF PERCEIVED VALUE AND VISCERAL RETURN ON INVESTMENT, THAT A MEMBER IS RECEPTIVE TO PAYING DUES FOR THE PRIVILEGE OF BELONGING.

Yet, this space must be furnished, maintained, insured, "staged" and often even staffed just in case a member might want to show their club to a guest. Members understand that major capital improvements need to be on-going in order to attract new members. They also know that funding depreciation is key in avoiding deferred maintenance.

> HERE IS A QUICK MATH EXAMPLE TO SHOW THE IMPORTANCE OF DUES TO A CLUB. FOR EVERY 300 MEMBERS, A MONTHLY DUES INCREASE OF $25 WILL GENERATE A TOTAL OF $90,000 TO THE BOTTOM LINE - (300 X $25) X 12 = $90,000

Initiation income should be earmarked for capital improvements and for fully funding an on-going Capital Reserve Plan.

Dues income is earmarked to subsidize day-to-day departmental operations, which, by design – run at a financial loss.

DO THE MATH.

Now ask any public golf course operator the number of additional rounds s/he would have to see to NET that same amount. Then ask a good restaurateur the number of additional dinner guests s/he would have to serve to NET that same amount

Once you get those answers, keep in mind that the members of a vibrant private club are not interested in numbers like that at their club. Instead – they want it private. For their exclusive use. When they want it. How they want it. And, they are able and willing to pay dues for it.

The purpose of the club staff and facility is to consistently deliver incredible member experiences. To drive usage. To remain relevant in the lives of members. NOT to increase departmental revenue.

YOUR TABLE IS WAITING.

A member wants to know that, oftentimes on the unintended spur of the moment (akin to the concept of not having a tee time), they can rely upon taking guests to their club on a Saturday night and be greeted warmly, by name, and not be told they have to wait in the bar for an hour for a table.

Much less being handed a flashing vibrator or being summoned on their cell phone when they can be seated. Oops! I forgot — cell phones may be frowned upon in the clubhouse! My mistake!

They also want to know that the dining room will not be packed to the gills, like the public restaurant down the street.

STAFFING LEVELS

Always higher simply because (speaking in general terms) the club prides itself in being ready to serve when the members desire to be served — instead of the Maître d' or Golf Starter deciding when they are ready to serve. The availability of the club and staff is of value to a member.

People join a private club to have use of its facilities and to be part of a special group. A part of something special going on. Plutonium club leaders make it special.

THE RETURN ON INVESTMENT IN BEING A MEMBER UNDER PLUTONIUM CLUB LEADERSHIP IS REALIZED IN: PERSONAL ENRICHMENT. CULTURAL GROWTH. GOOD HEALTH. MAKING NEW FRIENDS. ENJOYING FAMILY TIME.

Years back, the primary motive to join may have been in the hopes of gaining business contacts. While this activity will always, and perhaps should, exist to some minor extent – of greater and greater major incentive is to recognize that Membership at a private club is an ideal quality environment in which to spend time and enjoy activities with the entire family.

This represents the greatest R.O.I. yet!

SACRED COWS ARE NOT ALLOWED TO GRAZE

SANCTUARY
COUNTY CLUB

PREFACE

Before reading this tongue-in-cheek bit of whimsy — here is a quick Executive Summary statement of fact: "Member-owned private clubs are indeed private spaces, are not open to the public, are governed by private rules, and are legally protected by the right of association."

While every club can decide just how "Politically Correct" they might want to be, just for fun — the following is an example of a club that just may have taken things a tad bit too far. Let's see what is happening there!

In order to not discriminate — perhaps private clubs should eliminate all initiation fees — I mean, not everyone can afford those and that's unfair! Right?

And, those dues — they got to go as well.

Of course — for tax purposes, nobody should be able to deduct their dues! (Oh — that's right, nobody is paying any.)

While dining at the club there will be two sets of menus handed out in order to not further discriminate — the exact same menu items of course, but one with Men's prices and the other Women's (Women's pricing will be 83.65 cents per every one dollar on the men's menus).

And — Menu-caid is offered to all those who cannot afford the menu prices at all (gives a whole new meaning to un-priced menus).

Also — waiters will receive an automatic service charge of 18% while waitresses get 21.5%.

And, you know — not everyone can afford Big Bertha drivers! So, those will be banned too. How embarrassing to be the only one on the tee without one. Size does matter and those with smaller drivers — well, that might keep some from taking up the game.

And, what about those carts? Such privileged folks should have to walk like everyone else!

And — what about all those Beemer's in the parking lot? Some potential golfers may be too embarrassed to take up the game if having to drive a Chevy to the club. Not fair!

To avoid this auto class warfare — no personal cars allowed! Everyone must UBER to the club!

The reclaimed real estate that used to be a parking lot can now be converted to a natural habitat for spotted owls and vegetation (or, in states where it is legal — perhaps cultivating medical marijuana fields).

Forget about Sanctuary Cities — why not become a Sanctuary Country Club! To make sure we are all paying our fair share and playing by the same rules.

WELCOME TO SANCTUTARY COUNTRY CLUB!

Where there are no initiation fees — no dues — gender and transgender neutrality — all member's clubs are the same size — where the "No Carts Today" sign is posted everyday — where no personal ultimate driving machines are allowed — you are surrounded by spotted owls, otherwise threatened species and thriving free range vegan delights!

WOW! There are plenty of potential members who would pay a great deal to belong to a club like this! Oh yeah, I forgot — it's "free."

SERVER COMPENSATION
FINDING A WAY TO LINK PERFORMANCE TO COMPENSATION

PREFACE

The basic thrust presented here is to move towards compensating the F&B service staff on strictly an hourly base while at the same time clearly establishing expectations and rationale that is directly linked to performance.

One of the most common "problems" in member-owned private clubs is being able to directly link the hourly wage of F&B servers to performance. This is true not only from a management viewpoint, but it's also an irritant for a service staff that can see no clear-cut performance expectations or understandable rationale as to how they might better themselves going forward.

For decades, private clubs offered very low hourly wages while supplementing server income with various formulas to distribute the service charges from sales to payroll checks. These formulas vary wildly from one club to another. The base service charge percentage varies from club to club and oftentimes within the same club between regular ala carte dining, club events, member parties and sponsored banquets.

Some "pool" all service charge income and then the accounting department has to unravel the equation by dividing the number of staff, the hours actually worked, and often in what outlet and meal service (breakfast/lunch/dinner).

Others opt to not "pool" the service charge income, but instead allocate it directly to the specific server who presented the check.

If the service charge is not pooled — then those servers working breakfast or lunch are at a seriously disadvantaged level of compensation, simply because the check averages (and resulting service charge income) are dramatically less than those serving dinner.

Add to this the fact that large banquet menu prices tend to be higher than regular ala carte — thus, the resulting service charge income is greater even though all servers know that it requires greater skill and more work to be scheduled in ala carte than buffets or banquets (not to mention that it takes just as much work and skill to serve breakfast as dinner — maybe even more).

If the service charge is pooled — servers know that the more staff that is scheduled, the less income they will get, simply because it is divided amongst more people. Thus, depending of course on the specific formula a club might embrace, there is a chance that servers opt out on the schedule if it looks to them that staffing is going to be heavy.

Then, there is the added work in the accounting department when the same server is scheduled to work in both ala carte and banquet during a pay period — another "moving part" is thrown into the equation if the club has the policy of different methods of compensation when a server works in different outlets.

It also frustrates employees who find it next to impossible to budget their income when it may vary wildly from one pay period to another, even when the same number of hours are scheduled.

ALL OF THE ABOVE SCENARIOS (OR OFFSHOOTS OF THEM) BY DESIGN HAVE ALL KINDS OF UNNECESSARY MOVING PARTS. EVERY PAY PERIOD THE ACCOUNTING DEPARTMENT HAS TO MAKE CALCULATIONS THAT REQUIRE EXTRA TIME AND WORK. NOT TO MENTION THE CONFUSED SERVERS WHO FREQUENTLY COME TO THEIR OFFICE BECAUSE THEY CANNOT UNDERSTAND THEIR PAYCHECKS.

So much for all the work, confusion and still no clearly established expectations and rationale that is directly linked to performance. What to do?

REMOVE TWO UNNECESSARY MOVING PARTS:

1. Take service charge income completely out of the equation.
2. Disregard entirely what meal period or outlet a server is scheduled.

FOCUS ON TWO OBJECTIVES:

1. Establish individual hourly wages that apply whenever or wherever they are scheduled.

2. Establish performance expectations that directly link to individual hourly wages.

ONE OF THE MOST COMMON "COMPLAINTS" HEARD FROM MEMBERS IS THAT, "THE STAFF NEEDS MORE TRAINING." FRANKLY — MORE TIMES THAN NOT, IT IS NOT TRAINING THAT IS LACKING — WHAT IS REALLY MISSING IS A MEANS OF COMPENSATING THE STAFF IN A WAY THAT SERVERS CAN CLEARLY SEE THE VERY BASICS OF WHAT IS EXPECTED OF THEM, AND HOW IT DIRECTLY LINKS TO THEIR PAYCHECK.

"Training" on how to serve from the left and pull from the right only goes so far. Way short of all the little "MANDATORY" things that members really want to experience at their club.

NOTE: Take a look at the "MANDATORY" performance levels below, and just imagine what the members would think if the entire service staff performed at this level — at a minimum! If all staff were to all perform at just this level — suddenly, the membership feels that the team is better "trained." But what has really happened is that the staff now knows that their performance is directly linked to their compensation in a way that they understand, and can connect the dots.

Below are the basics of a compensation program you are encouraged to "tweak" so that it best fits into your own club's culture and circumstances.

Every club is different, while the concept of the below is the fixed. The variable is you must identify specifically what the ideal entry hourly wage for new hires needs to be in order for your club to attract/retain quality staff (in keeping with your budget guidelines).

THE STARTING RATE YOU ESTABLISH IS KEY! ONCE YOU ESTABLISH YOUR NEW HIRE HOURLY RATES — EVERYTHING ELSE SPINS OFF THIS, AND YOU NEED TO ADJUST ALL OF THE FOLLOWING NUMBERS TO REFLECT THIS STARTING RATE. THE STARTING RATE OF $12 BELOW FOR A NEW HIRE WITH NO EXPERIENCE IS STRICTLY FOR ILLUSTRATIVE PURPOSES.

Your club may need to be much greater or slightly less. Figure that out, and then start from there. You may find you will have to run through the entire format, tweaking again and again until finally landing on what will make perfect sense for you.

DO NOT get hung up on the minutia of details or tweaking of the numbers that you will have to unravel to ascertain if the concept works at all for you and your club. Just work through it to see if you are able to identify the dollars and if the entire concept even works at all for your club.

The point is, just get started. Try it — you might like it!

CONCEPTIONAL F&B SERVER COMPENSATION

NEW HIRE EXPERIENCE LEVELS/STARTING RATES

1. Zero = $12 p/h (Arbitrary. You MUST identify the best starting point for your club.)
2. Some = $13 p/h
3. Strong = $14 p/h

At the end of 30 days, all new hires MUST have proven themselves by being rock-solid in all the below **MANDATORY PROFICIENCIES.**

If they are not, management MUST decide to either replace them or to increase their proficiency levels within a matter of only one more pay period and then reevaluate.

ONLY those servers who consistently exhibit the MANDATORY PROFI-CIENCY levels are subject to further employment and potential wage increases. F&B Server compensation rates are based upon three foundations:

1. NEW HIRE EXPERIENCE LEVEL. (Zero / Some / Strong)
2. PROFICIENCIES. (2 levels: MANDATORY & MASTER)
3. CLUB LOYALTY. (Here we factor in years of service to the members.)

LOYALTY AKNOWLEDGEMENT: Only Master Proficiency and Super Stars are subject to Loyalty Acknowledgement.

One of the pleasures of belonging to a private club is coming to rely upon a loyal staff that members enjoy seeing and that actually become a meaningful member of the club's extended family.

Loyalty is recognized by management to reflect the policies of the club in making sure a proficient and loyal staff is maintained over the years.

After 2 years of service: + 25 cents to current Master Proficiency = $15.25
After 4 years of service: + 50 cents to current Master Proficiency = $15.50
After 6 years of service: + $1.25 to current Master Proficiency = $16.25
After 8 years of service: + $1.50 to current Master Proficiency = $16.50
After 10 years of service: + $2.00 to current Master Proficiency = $17.00

SPECIAL SUPER STAR STATUS: This category is strictly at management discretion after 2 years of service. Those very few unique performers who demonstrate tremendous reliability, contagious great attitude, enjoy the respect of staff and the confidence the membership. NOTE: Super Stars earn $1.50 p/h recognition above Master. $15.00 + $1.50 = $16.50.

MANDATORY — Non-Negotiable "MUSTS"
Understands the priority of CONSISTENCY in service.
ALWAYS gets the name of members before approaching table.
NEVER asks members for their name or account number.
Is comfortable with all basic functions of the P.O.S. system.
Is familiar with the entire menu and knows all specials / soups of the day.
Is able to quickly tell guests all available sides, dressings, specials, etc.
Always exhibits a great attitude with members and all staff.
Has a "Sense of Urgency" in appropriate pace of service.

NOTE: All servers who achieve Mandatory Proficiency level will have a base hourly pay of $14.00

MASTER — In addition to all Mandatory
Models the priority of CONSISTENCY in service.
Always addresses all members by name. Makes sure new hires know member names before approaching tables.
Ability to train new hires on all aspects of P.O.S. system.
Is confident in both ala carte and banquet service.
Flexible in scheduling. With advance notice, is usually available for breakfast, lunch, or evening.
Can be relied upon for "opening" and "closing" procedures.
Has respect of members & staff to serve as "MOD" when called upon.
NOTE: All servers who achieve Master Proficiency level will have a base hourly pay of $15.00

PROFICIENCY LEVELS

LAST TIME: DO NOT get hung up on the minutia of details or tweaking of the numbers that you will have to unravel to ascertain if the concept works at all for you and your club. Just work through it to see if you are able to identify the dollars and if the entire concept even works at all for your club. The point is, just get started. Try it — you might like it!

SHAKESPEARE
SURE KNOWS HIS CLUBS!

(All the Drama, Tragedy & Comedy one can take.)

If the Finance Committee explains McDonald's making money every day and the club does not by saying *"it's Greek to me"* — they are quoting Shakespeare.

If senior members often talk about the club's *"salad days"* — they are most likely NOT talking about Greek Salads, or menus — but, they ARE quoting Shakespeare.

If resigning members say their leaving is *"more in sorrow than in anger"* — they are quoting Shakespeare.

If they *"vanished into thin air"* — quoting Shakespeare helps explain what happened to long waiting lists after 2008.

If the bridge ladies say they won't *"budge an inch"* when a 32-cent increase is suggested in the luncheon price that has been in place for 7 years — they are quoting Shakespeare.

If slow play could be addressed by playing *"fast and loose"* — all players should agree that Shakespeare knew what he was talking about.

If you have ever been *"tongue tied"* at a board meeting — you were at least trying to quote Shakespeare.

If the club president is a *"tower of strength"* — s/he must know their Shakespeare.

If you have been *"hoodwinked"* — Shakespeare feels your pain!

If the kitchen is *"in a pickle"* and behind — Shakespeare would not mind waiting for his clubhouse sandwich.

If you have *"knitted your brows"* during committee meetings — even Shakespeare would tell you to stop it! Unicorns may be in. A unibrow is out.

If the board explains a dues increase by having *"made a virtue of necessity"* — they are not only smart, but quoting Shakespeare as well.

If your handicap committee insists on *"fair play"* — they are quoting Shakespeare.

If after board meetings everyone gets *"not a wink of sleep"* — they should try reading Shakespeare in bed.

If your club books weddings and therefore *"stood on ceremony"* — Shakespeare is your best man.

If you say you *"laughed yourself into stitches"* at some point every day at the club — better there than a hospital — but, regardless, you are quoting Shakespeare.

If the morning after club parties the same members are always saying that they had *"too much of a good thing"* — don't worry — they are just quoting Shakespeare.

If you have "seen better days" or have been living in a *"fool's paradise"* — if not for quoting Shakespeare how could you ever have explained it?

If members expect reasonable dues as a *"foregone conclusion"* — they are quoting Shakespeare.

If you present operating budgets *"as luck would have it"* — you'd better start learning how to prepare a Zero-Based Budget instead. But, until then, you are quoting Shakespeare.

If the band has played *"Last Dance"* and club staff says it is "high time" to go — they are quoting Shakespeare.

If your executive summary explains the *"long and short of it"* — little did you know you were just quoting Shakespeare.

If the membership committee has a legacy membership requirement of being *"your own flesh and blood"* — they are quoting Shakespeare.

If the culinary team says their new special is *"a dish fit for the gods"* — they are quoting Shakespeare.

If you have reciprocal arrangements with clubs from *"all corners of the world"* — your club is not only one that apparently does not cut corners — but, also one that quotes Shakespeare.

If the Rules Committee suspects *"foul play"* — you can suspect that they are quoting Shakespeare.

If the members complain of *"teeth set on edge"* — quoting Shakespeare will do you no good whatsoever!
When it comes to financing major club projects, if you remember it is good to *"neither a borrower nor a lender be"* — you're smart and also remembering the words of Shakespeare.

If policies seem to be made *"without rhyme or reason"* — at least Shakespeare gave the club a way to explain why.

If when announcing a dues increase by saying *"give the devil his due"* — it would be wise to blame Shakespeare for saying that rather than you!

If the *"truth were known"* — it would be amazing to know how often we use the words of Shakespeare and did not even know it. Well, now you know! Be amazed!

If you'd think *"what the dickens"* while having a member plead that 4 raw steaks, 2 bottles of house wine, and a banana crème pie picked up in 15 minutes surely must apply to their F&B Minimum…you'd be thinking like Shakespeare.

If you explain the difference between a tip, service charge and gratuity by saying, *"it's all one (and the same) to me"* — you'd be wrong. But, right in using another quote from Shakespeare.

If the kitchen uses a *"laughing stock"* as a base — that's one way to keep the members (and Shakespeare) smiling.

If you can describe one member as the *"devil incarnate"* — be grateful there is only one, and keep on quoting Shakespeare.

If just one member says the GM/COO must be a *"blinking idiot"* — *"tut tut"* — *"the truth will out"* and until it does — quoting Shakespeare may make them feel better.

Finally, if you decide after reading all this to wish Michael Crandal, CNG "were dead as a doornail" and hope to *"bid me good riddance"* and "send me packing"

Well — that's fine with me because *"all's well that ends well"* and this all just proves that there is indeed way too *"much ado about nothing"*.

I'd like to remind you that *"discretion is the better part of valor"* — and also remind you that I'd be quoting Shakespeare if I did. (BTW – I just did.)

Just remember that *"there's method in my madness"* and Shakespeare could not have said it better!

STRATEGIC PLANNING IN TWO QUESTIONS
ANSWERED BY THE RENOWNED NORM SPITZIG!

INTRODUCTION: If you ask 100 people who know anything at all about the private club industry to list the top 5 luminaries of leadership, many names may come and go — BUT the name **NORM SPITZIG** remains a fixture. Norm's command of the little nuances as well as the big picture is highly regarded as a fellow Plutonium Private Club Leader! www.masterclubadvisors.com

Question #1: Norm, how would you define strategic planning in the private club environment?

Norm: A strategic plan goes beyond a list of planned programs and tasks. A plan becomes "strategic" when it identifies outcomes the club is working toward, and then, based

> *"SIMPLY STATED, STRATEGIC PLANNING IS THE PROCESS OF DETERMINING WHERE AN ORGANIZATION IS GOING, HOW IT WILL GET THERE AND HOW IT WILL KNOW IF IT HAS SUCCEEDED."*

on an assessment of the club's operating environment, the community where it is located and its own abilities and resources, selects the best possible approaches for achieving those outcomes.

A meaningful strategic plan addresses the necessity of making decisions:

- *Personnel.* What levels are needed to accomplish the mission? The professional expertise demanded of key positions? A plan means nothing unless the right people are in the right places.

- *Funding.* What is it going to take at various levels of membership to make this happen?
- *Advancing the overall mission.* Is every decision, of which there are many, aligning perfectly in support of where we want to go?

- *A process for evaluating results.* Just having something in a 3-ring binder collecting dust is a waste of time and space! RESULTS are what matters and there must be an established on-going process to consistently monitor the progress.

A private club strategic plan itself can serve as a tool to support conversations with current members, as well as a marketing tool for attracting new members.

- Yet, as we all know, the very term "strategic planning" makes some people wince. They have images of (or past experience with) months of rigid process, extra work, endless meetings and retreats, flip charts and magic markers, drafts and redrafts – all to produce a binder-bound document that collects dust until the next time someone says: "I think we need to do some strategic planning."

To be successful, the strategic planning process must be focused, specific to your club, enjoyable, and actionable. It MUST be wrapped up with "specific deliverables" clearly mapped out that capture: the Mission, Vision, Values, Goals, and Strategies developed and agreed upon by the Strategic Planning Committee as being second to none.

IN SHORT, A STRATEGIC PLAN SERVES AS A VITAL TOUCHSTONE FOR ALL BOARD DECISIONS, STRATEGIC AND TACTICAL, OVER AN EXTENDED PERIOD OF TIME.

The strategic planning process itself, when combined with the endorsement of the plan as a living document by a club's Board, is critically important to informing, guiding and directing the actions of current and future Boards of Directors.

Question #2: What specific methodology is necessary for developing a strategic plan that achieves all of the things you've pointed out? What are the steps/ingredients that must be included in a successful recipe for success?

Norm: A private club's strategic plan is developed by addressing, in a thoughtful and articulate manner (and sometimes, but not necessarily, using member-at-large focus groups and/or member surveys), the following issues:

- *Vision:* What does the club need to be, ideally, in the coming five to ten years?
- *Values:* What set of core guiding principles, if followed over time, will produce a community of members who are active, vibrant, financially responsible and socially compatible?
- *Mission:* What is the fundamental purpose of the club?
- *Evaluation:* What are the club's strengths and weaknesses? What are they key opportunities, critical success factors and external threats?
- *Goals:* What outcomes or results with the club work toward in order to successfully carry out its mission? How should these goals be prioritized?
- *Strategies:* What general approaches and methods will a club use to achieve each goal? What are the risks involved? How can a club manage or mitigate them?

Thank you, Norm! As one of the most respected voices in the industry — honored to have your PLUTONIUM LEADERSHIP insights.

TRADITIONS ARE RESPECTED WHILE THE BAR IS CONTINUALLY RAISED

TEAM BUILDING
THE "IT'S SHOWTIME" PHILOSOPHY

INTRODUCTION:

An undeniable trait of a Plutonium Private Club Leader is the ability to build and maintain great teams. And, none do it any better than ALAN JACOBS. His "business" side of things is spot-on. Balanced with incredible creativity that simply makes being on his team – well, FUN! Here to prove it — Alan tells us all below what time it is. "It's SHOWTIME, baby!"

"It's Showtime!"

THIS AGE-OLD ENTERTAINMENT AD-AGE AND ANALOGICAL APPROACH TO TEAM BUILDING BEGINS WITH THE ESTABLISHMENT OF BUILDING AN ORGANIZATION SIMILAR TO THAT OF MAKING A MAJOR BLOCKBUSTER MOVIE. UNDERSTANDING THAT WE ALL WANT THIS "MOVIE" TO BE HIGHLY-PROFITABLE, OSCAR-WORTHY AND AWARD-WINNING.

Of course, our film is shot every day —on location — right at your club!

In preparing for the live shoot, there are many people involved and everyone must know their roles. Let's take a look at the credits as they would roll up the screen.

THE MEMBERS — are The Producers of the "movie" in providing the vision, funding and budget.

THE GM/COO — is The Director who "makes it all happen".

THE STRATEGIC PLAN — provides the background for The Plot as it unfolds.

CASTING — is coordinated by the HR Director.

THE PRINCIPAL ACTORS —are The Department Heads.

THE SUPPORTING CAST — is comprised of All Employees of the club.

ON LOCATION SUPPORT — is an ensemble of coordinated efforts who all do their part enabling those in any scene to perform flawlessly. The Designers, Technical Staff, Administration/Finance, Editors, PR/Marketing, Support/Logistics, Extras and Vendors all play vital roles in the overall success of making the "movie".

AUDIENCE/CRITICS —are, of course, the Members & Guests who buy the "tickets" to the show.

Everyone has important roles and specific responsibilities to work together as a Team to make the best movie possible. This entails a highly communicative, strategic and collaborative effort to create a successful "movie".

The Director has the responsibility of:

> **"IT'S SHOWTIME!" REQUIRES PASSION, A CULTURE OF BOTH EXCELLENCE AND FUN, ALONG WITH THE UNDERSTANDING THAT THE SHOW MUST GO ON!**

- Identifying the best possible Oscar-winning talent.
- Motivating them to play their specific roles to perfection.
- Creating synergy to effectuate the "script" and vision.
- Delivering the movie within budget.
- Achieving the "business" aspect of Show Business.

It is extremely important to create a culture of "same-page" understanding; where everyone respects and appreciates not only their parts, but those of all others.

A Plutonium Director shares the "whole picture" with everyone involved rather than simply doling out just a "limited scene" morsel of what it is all about. Plutonium Directors fosters a participative and collaborative Team effort and a culture where people can "improvise," contribute their expertise, share suggestions and creative ideas in a constructive way to help produce the best possible product.

An environment prevails where every member of the cast, crew and support team knows that they are part of something special. Greater and expanded role opportunities based on initiative, drive, gained experience and proven performance is known to all.

Since so many players are involved, and pivotal to the success of the movie — it is essential to hire properly, provide clear expectations, tools, resources and the necessary orientation and training to then hold people accountable. *"It's Showtime!" requires everyone to remember that they are always "on camera!"*

Thank you, Alan! Your PLUTONIUM LEADERSHIP insights are respected and you are high esteemed by all your peers!

THE TENNIS PLAYERS ARE VERY CONCERNED ABOUT RUMORS OF FREE "ARNOLD PALMER'S" BEING ELIMINATED TO SAVE MONEY. HORRORS! THIS CANNOT BE! THEY START MEETING MONDAY NIGHTS, SECRETLY IN A DOWNTOWN CITY CLUB.

TENNIS, ANYONE?
PLUTONIUM PRIVATE CLUB LEADERS ANSWER WITH VIBRANT PROGRAMMING REACHING MEMBERS OF ALL AGES.

INTRODUCTION:
What a privilege to have fellow Plutonium Leader, John Embree (CEO for the USPTA — United States Professional Tennis Association), share his personal insights on the vital relevancy of tennis and creative programming in providing great member experiences for all generations. The title here should more appropriately be "TENNIS, EVERYONE!" as John serves up a Plutonium "ACE." John.Embree@uspta.org

THESE ARE CHALLENGING TIMES FOR PRIVATE CLUBS, PARTICULARLY COUNTRY CLUBS.

It is no secret that golf is waning, baby boomers are aging out, and millennials would rather try different activities than make the huge financial commitment to join a club.

The conundrum that traditional, well-established private clubs face is trying to balance two groups with different demands and expectations:

1. Their existing stable membership of "older" members and what they expect and are accustomed to seeing and experiencing at their club.

2. A potential "younger" generation of members whose expectations of what a club should look like and their desired experiences may be diametrically opposed to the modus operandi.

What these two demographic groups demand may very well be conflicting. Against that backdrop:

- Clubs are beginning to recognize that tennis should no longer be treated as a "step child" as it has in so many instances in the past.

- No longer can a club afford just to hire a ball-feeder or an inexperienced teacher in an effort to save a few dollars.

- No longer will club members accept their tennis facility to sit dormant most of the day or just be a lesson factory for the teaching staff, with few other programs to capture interest.

- Members expect the same level of customer service that the golfers get with their PGA professionals, or the highly engaged food and beverage staff that must deliver exceptional customer service in the restaurants and during special functions.

Mediocrity cannot be the norm in tennis any longer. The tennis program has to have life, positive energy, activity, and enthusiastic participants, and that can only be a by-product of an educated and outgoing staff. Great things just don't happen. Great people make them happen!

Tennis operations and member experiences are driven by the personality of the professional staff, NOT by the facility. For many clubs, the golf course itself is the product that drives participation. But in tennis, the program is the product that drives participation.

PLUTONIUM CLUB LEADERS REALIZE THE INVESTMENT IN THE TENNIS STAFF IS FAR MORE IMPORTANT THAN THE FENCES AND WINDSCREENS. IN SUM, TENNIS IS PRO DRIVEN — WHILE GOLF TENDS TO BE MORE FACILITY DRIVEN.

Young families seek wholesome recreation that can not only engage their children but the adults as well. While country clubs have always had a family focus, there are so many other opportunities for families today to spend their hard earned, discretionary dollars elsewhere that there has to be a premium on making the club tennis program the absolute best that it can be. Absent that, parents will take their children to those programs which offer the experience that they desire and most importantly, where their friends are hanging out.

Making tennis an anchor for your club is sensible on so many levels. Unlike so many traditional sports that have seen participation decline over the past ten years (especially golf), tennis has held its own.

My intent is not to pick on golf because I am an avid golfer myself. However, golf has not embraced fundamental changes to how it is played. It continues to be difficult to learn, is incredibly time-consuming when time is at such a premium, is expensive as all get out, and is viewed by most in the younger generation as my "father's game" — not cool.

On the other hand, tennis administrators and industry leaders have worked hard to make the game more appealing to all ages. If your tennis facility is not embracing some or all of these activities, then you are clearly missing out.

- Smaller courts with modified equipment for young kids.
- Shorter scoring formats for adults.
- Gender-neutral play occasions.
- Team competitions.
- Cardio Tennis (incorporating fitness workouts on the tennis courts with music) is now one of the fastest growing fitness activities in America!

There are also several other new off-shoots of tennis that are getting a strong foothold, gathering momentum and developing membership enthusiasm around the country. I refer to them as the "4-P's" — here they are: *Pickleball — Platform Tennis — Padel — Pop Tennis*

1) PICKLEBALL. This is a "tsunami" that is captivating to not only senior players but folks of all ages. If your senior members have not inquired about implementing pickleball at your club, it will come. Pickleball has over 3 million players at the moment but is growing in leaps and bounds each and every year.

There is a nationwide network of ambassadors that travel to private and public facilities and even city governments to make its case why pickleball should be a part of the fabric of the community. In all but a very few cases — it must be a vital component of successful private clubs in the future.

One of most compellingly attractive draws of Pickleball is that it is highly social by nature. Participants, mostly seniors, flock to the courts and don't mind sitting for a round of play until it is their turn to step on the court. Players rotate on and off the court during a 2-3 hour period. If they are not playing, there is plenty of time to engage with others who are in attendance, including eating and drinking beverages of their choice.

Pickleball is now seen as being complimentary to tennis, as tennis court time can be filled when it is typically not in high demand. Golfers who desire another outlet at their club see pickleball as a viable option. Seniors who have stopped playing tennis, because of injury or fitness, can satisfy their craving for a more active pursuit by joining a pickleball program.

2) PLATFORM TENNIS: Whereas pickleball has just come on the scene in the last 10-15 years, Platform Tennis has been around for decades. Originally started in the northeast by tennis players before indoor tennis was an option, they sought to play a game outdoors in the winter that incorporated aspects of tennis and squash. Thus, Platform Tennis was born.

While the northeast and mid-west are the hotspots, the sport is seeing growth in the south, Denver and northern California. The season typically runs from October through March and provides surprising cardio benefits, even when played in the dead of winter.

Q: Why is it called platform tennis?

A: Because the court is constructed on a platform above ground level so that propane heaters can be installed below the court surface in order to melt the snow and ice.

As crazy as it sounds, Chicago now boasts the largest single league of men and women playing with over 5,000 players! And you know how rough Chicago winters can be! Hard core players think platform tennis is the best game on the planet (and —I am one of them).

Platform Tennis is incredibly social (because of the proximity of all the players on a small court that is enclosed by a taut chicken wire fence), physically demanding at the higher levels and incredibly strategic.

Platform Tennis courts are expensive ($70,000- $90,000 per court) but that pales when you consider that the best facilities in the country have a paddle "hut" that serves as a warming escape. Truth be told, these buildings are no longer bare cabins with heaters as they were 20-25 year ago. Rather, they are large clubhouses boasting kitchens and full-service bars, adorned with televisions and fireplaces, locker rooms and showers, plus expansive viewing of the courts.

It has amazed me to see one club try and outdo their competition down the street with the most lavish and beautiful building, but that is what members are now expecting. If done correctly, the club will be able to create an entire new membership activity that is self-sustaining and extremely active.

3) PADEL: Not yet a big sport in the USA but it is coming! Be proactive and get ahead of the game. This is a very viable addition to what the better private clubs will be offering to their members in the future. There are only 20 courts total in America as of this writing, but new padel-centric facilities are on the drawing boards in various locations. Many clubs are evaluating the feasibility of building padel courts to augment tennis.

LIKE PLATFORM TENNIS:
PADEL COURTS ARE SMALLER IN SIZE, ALUMINUM IN STRUCTURE BUT ENCLOSED BY GLASS WALLS.

UNLIKE PLATFORM TENNIS:
PADEL CAN BE PLAYED YEAR-ROUND, OUTDOORS OR INDOORS. BE ON THE LOOK-OUT FOR PADEL!

LIKE PICKLEBALL AND PLATFORM TENNIS:
THERE IS A STRONG SOCIAL COMPONENT TO THE GAME WHICH CONTRIBUTES TO ITS SUCCESS. A MEANINGFUL SOURCE OF TREMENDOUS MEMBERSHIP INTERACTION AND GREAT MEMBER EXPERIENCES!

During a fact-finding mission to Madrid in December of 2017, I was shocked to learn that there are almost twice as many padel players in Spain as there are tennis players. In addition, padel courts outnumber tennis courts by almost 2 to 1. Visiting clubs throughout the city, I was incredulous to see stand-alone padel clubs that were thriving, and tennis clubs that had more padel courts than tennis courts!

Though born out of South America (Argentina), Spain may now be the padel capital of the world. The game is seeing massive growth in Europe and it won't be long before padel gets a foothold in the USA.   Again – be proactive. This can (will) be a tremendous draw for new members in the foreseeable future.

(#4) POP TENNIS: This is starting to get a great deal of traction. Originating from the beaches of Southern California, the game began as paddle tennis. However, because of branding confusion with platform tennis (called paddle by its enthusiasts and not to be confused with padel), the leadership of Pop thought it would be best to rebrand the game. It was a smart decision. Besides, the sound that the low compression ball makes when hitting a POP tennis paddle is a popping sound — very distinctive!

A more dramatic and strategic change took place several years ago when the leadership took a bold step to alter the size of its court to match those of a 60-foot blended line tennis court. In doing so, Pop can now be played on over 18,000 blended lined courts across the country. What an ingenious way to tap into an incredible infrastructure of ready-made courts!

CONCLUSION: Remember that call to action back in the 70's and 80's when tennis was on the forefront of everyone's mind, when the tennis boom was at its apex, when it was considered "chic" to wear their tennis warm-up suits to the grocery store or to cocktail parties, when Hollywood glamourized the sports in movies and television?

While those days of tennis being the "cool" sport may be in the rear-view mirror, **tennis in today's world of private clubs remains a viable family activity that is uniquely positioned to be the cornerstone of a favorable membership experiences for decades to come.**

IT ALL STARTS WITH PLUTONIUM CLUB LEADERS RECOGNIZING THE VITAL IMPORTANCE OF HIRING A POSITIVE ENERGY TENNIS PRO, WHO HAS AN ACUMEN FOR CREATIVE PROGRAMMING AND A STAFF THAT IS HELL-BENT ON CONSISTENTLY PROVIDING INCREDIBLE MEMBER EXPERIENCES. WHEN THAT HAPPENS — TENNIS, THE ENTIRE PROGRAM AND THE CLUB CAN THRIVE.

With the addition of the aforementioned activities that can enhance a club's menu of offerings to all generations — an energized membership will be using their club on a more frequent basis and help establish the vibe of a club destined for success.

The advantage is yours and the ball is clearly in your court!

THRIVING
NOT JUST SURVIVING

Today's fast paced, changing and diversified nature of membership expectations, drives home the need for club leaders not satisfied with just surviving, but instead, thriving during uncertainty. Just good enough - no longer is.

Effective boards and top management cannot simply react to change. Instead, they proactively stay ahead of the curve.

One of our greatest strengths, or weaknesses, is that people over time can seemingly get used to just about anything. What may have started as a passing thought, a flimsy cobweb - with constant repetition over the years - will ultimately develop into habits that can serve as strong cables to either strengthen or shackle us.

Clubs that are overburdened with by-laws, club rules, or top-heavy committee structured governance models from yesteryear, find it difficult to proactively reflect new demographics. They feel shackled in making necessary decisions that may require breaking some of the old habits that have been practiced for years.

Thriving clubs - protect cherished traditions of longtime members, while making ongoing decisions conducive to newer members getting into the habit of joyfully spending time at the club.

Club dynamics have shifted dramatically from proudly pointing to a 3-ring binder, 2nd from the top shelf, 4th folder from the left and feeling comfort in knowing that they have in place a strategic plan.

Fundamental strategies that just seemed to work for many years - no longer do so. Some may need to be scrapped altogether.

Outdated by-laws, club rules, and committee structured governance models may need to be revisited. Oh, and about that 3-ring binder that is pointed to every so often...

The bottom line? Changing demographics and expectations are now a greater factor in how thriving clubs develop and execute long-range strategic planning, as well as even day to day operations.

In order to not simply survive, but to thrive - forward thinking club leaders are expanding options from just 'Long Range and Specific' - to 'Short Term and Broader.'

Reviews, updates and tweaks are now, by necessity, somewhat ongoing.

In years past, even traditional, successful clubs would update their strategic plan only every couple of years in efforts to keep in line with long-term goals. Today, club leaders that are proactively leaning into the curve are reviewing and making ever-so-slight course modifications every 3 or 4 months.

That doesn't mean the entire plan is thrown away at every turn! The foundation of the plan always remains the lens through which decisions are viewed.

But it is necessary to examine the strategic direction by updating, revisiting and continually tweaking to ensure all the necessary factors are in place and still appropriate for reaching long term goals and values.

Planning now must be capable of revision on extremely short notice. Building flexibility and adaptability into club operations is now critical. And, yes, relevant by-laws, club rules, and governance models need to be up to speed heading into the curves.

Anticipate the gravitational forces of change and have the flexibility to adapt and pull a new generation of members into your club.

Thriving clubs in this new era know it's not enough to just be aware of how fast things are moving around them. Club policy makers (Board) and operation decision makers (Management) must anticipate the need for change and oftentimes flat-out initiate it.

Thriving clubs have the agility to shift focus and change direction on a dime, without hesitation. At the same time, they have the steadfast commitment to protect traditional club values.

Hey! Nobody said it was easy. That's why you are needed in a position of leadership at your club - to not just survive, but to thrive.

THREE CLUB
MANAGERS WALK INTO A BAR ...

PREFACE

Take your career seriously. Take family and friends seriously. Take your relationship with God very seriously. But - never be one of those types that takes themselves way too seriously. Remember – *if you do take yourself too seriously, nobody else will.*

In this light, just have some fun with this. Smile! Relax! Now then — on that note — let's get started!

Three club managers…*C, G* and *E-flat* walk into a private club asking about a major career.

The club career manager looks up and says, "Sorry, we don't serve minors!"

So, *E-flat* leaves, while *C* and *G* have an open fifth between them.

After early career years over few drinks, the fifth is diminished and *C* is flat out cold!

F comes in and tries to augment the situation, but is not sharp enough. *F*-bombs in the attempt!

D is dull of hearing. (And learning.) So, knowing s/he too is not all that sharp, morphs into career plan *B*, and heads towards the restroom muttering, "*G* whizz. Excuse me. I'll just be a second."

A second later, *A* comes in. But the club manager is not convinced that this relative of G is not a minor lateral career move. So — they have a staff meeting to decide.

Then the club manager notices *B-flat* hiding at the end of the bar and says, "Get outta here! You're the seventh minor I've found in this bar tonight." The bar clears.

However, without missing a beat — *E-Flat* comes back the very next night! But this time holding a brief case apparently full of solutions and dressed in a business suit.

The club career manager says, "Now you're looking sharp! Come on in, this could be a major development. Perhaps even worthy of "Idea Fair" submission at Conference."

Strangely enough though, under the glare of a micro-managing conductor, E-flat is fresh out of ideas and takes off the business suit (and everything else!) and soon is standing au naturel in the middle of the boardroom.

E-flat is exposed! An empty business suit. Holding an empty brief case as well.

Eventually *C* sobers up and realizes in horror that s/he is not only under a boardroom table — but, under *A* rest as well!

C is brought to trial. Found guilty of contributing to the diminution of a minor. Sentenced to 10 years of D.S. without Coda silence. At an upscale correctional facility. Taken away in chains.

Ten Years After, upon release (but, without a song), C became an unchained melody.

By this time our original club manager has become a *GM/COO* with other blue notes of distinction behind his/her name like: *CCM, MCM,* and *CCE* from *CMAA.*

In preparation for that next staff meeting and last career movement, the *GM/COO, CCM, MCM, CCE* takes down copious notes of *A, B, D, E-Flat,* and *F* — and take no prisoners (or ex-cons like *C*) — until the music finally stops and it's time to take a bow at the end of a brilliantly conducted club management career!

TOXIC EMPLOYEES
THEY GOTTA GO! IT'S A PRIORITY.

"I AIN'T WORKIN' HERE NO MORE."
-Johnny Paycheck

I'd like to point out that over the last 20 years of my career I've never had to fire even one person. However, I have (from time to time) accepted a few resignations. Ahem.

In every work week, we have many things atop our morning desk demanding attention. And, using a deck of cards as an analogy — we are wise to not simply keep a messy pile spread face down and then randomly pick one to begin working on.

Instead — we shuffle the ever-changing deck before us every day, look at the face value of each card, and then we prioritize by leaving in our hand what represents our greatest ROI in time and decision making.

There is nothing random about it at all.

For illustrative purposes, let's say Wednesday morning we have successfully identified our current top ten priorities. Unencumbered, we start with #1 and then systematically begin moving through all ten. (Whew! Are we good, or what?)

That would mean that after cleaning our desk at the end of the day, on Thursday morning we would have ten new top priorities where we'd again start with #1 and then systematically begin moving through another ten. (See. I told you how good we are!)

Q: Right? Why not?

A: Well, it turns out that Wednesday was pretty hectic with meetings, a few unforeseeable situations, and an incoming email that required your immediate response in the form of a detailed report.

The fact is, of our original top ten priorities, we only got through 5 of them on the day before — plus another opportunity that wasn't even on the list, but raised its head with a real sense of urgency to it.

Since we only got through the top five — does that mean that all the remaining cards (starting with what used to be #6) will now all in lock-step move up to become the new top priorities?

Q: No! Why not?

A: Because EVERY day, we again shuffle that ever-changing deck, look at the face value of each card, and leave in our hand what for the moment are our new priorities.

And, by the way, all those meetings, unforeseeable situations, emails, etc., don't just happen on Wednesdays, do they?

Almost moment to moment, every day is a new day with new priorities of its own.

OK. Now let's go back to my opening, where I said that I like to point out that over the last 20 years of my career, I've never had to fire even one person, but (from time to time) I have accepted a few resignations.

In every deck there are a few "jokers" that need to be discarded.

While the vast majority of the team performs "off the charts" and is dedicated to continuous improvement — face it, there are indeed (from time to time) a few that ultimately need to sit across the desk and hear those famous words:

"You're fired!"

Now then — because the deck is always being reshuffled with coaching, counseling, training, and documentation — habitual underperformers may take a while until ultimately landing on your desk and into your hand as a top priority of your day.

When that day comes — deal with it! Never procrastinate or put it off. When it is in the best interest of all concerned — **fire them!**

Actually —you can't really fire them at all!

Q: Huh? Why? Why not?

A: More than likely they've already quit many times and have just been bouncing around the deck for some time now. One day, or more than likely over the course of many days —they just flat-out quit.

- *They quit* improving.
- *They quit* being proactive.
- *They quit* supporting the team.
- T*hey quit* making their boss look good.
- *They quit* making their job performance a priority.
- *They quit* taking personal responsibility for what happens.
- *They quit* focusing on the reason for everything: Membership Satisfaction.
- *They quit* creating an environment where their team loved making them look good.

So, when that day comes, directly acknowledge the fact that they have quit, and indeed ain't working here no more. If it has gotten far enough up the ladder to land on our desk — it has gone on for far too long.

You can't fire someone who has already quit! But - today is the day - call them

> **THE REST OF THE TEAM MAY NOT HAVE THE AUTHORITY OR RESPONSIBILITY TO DO WHAT THEY HAVE ALL KNOWN FOR WEEKS NEEDED TO BE DONE. BUT — YOU DO!**

into H/R or your own office, have your ducks in order along with any final checks - and, formally accept their resignation! Right there. On the spot.

PLUTONIUM LEADERS owe it to the team to eliminate any toxic employee who somehow slips between the cracks and has quit. It has nothing to do with you, or the toxic employee who has to go. Instead — YOU owe it to the team to eliminate what they can't. Time to cull the herd!

It's a priority.

TRAINERS TEACH
PLUTONIUM LEADERS INSPIRE

High performing teams are built around great leaders — not on training programs.

Other than the preparation of military troops for combat or performers in

> **TRAINERS TEACH: WHAT AND HOW? LEADERS INSPIRE: PRIDE AND CARE!**

a 3-ring circus, I've never embraced the word "Training" in the realm of providing leadership to men and women applying their collective creativity and drive to build a winning team in a business environment.

TRAINING — is something that is best suited for programming circus animals and pets. It focuses on repetitive drills with the objective of conforming behavior to respond to directives in a certain manner.

A circus is a company of performers that may include trained animals, clowns, acrobats, trapeze acts, tightrope walkers, jugglers, and stunt-oriented artists. Are you getting a visual? Do you see your career in this light?

In the absence of caring leadership — just going to work every day can be akin to going past Checkpoint Charlie into a cold war zone, or getting your ticket punched to perform in the center ring of a circus.

The most common consumer complaint hurled at poorly managed service related businesses is that of a perceived lack of training. Frankly, training (good or bad) is not the problem that causes consumers being treated as an intruder who is interrupting employees between coffee breaks and paychecks.

- An employee who doesn't KNOW — indicates a lack of training. An employee who doesn't CARE — indicates a lack of Plutonium leadership from the top.

And, THAT is the problem. So we're gonna change those stripes on that tiger! Sure we are.

In fruitless efforts to coach and council individuals who just don't seem to care, it seems that many well-intended companies have designed elaborate training programs (with all kinds of acronyms) in hopes of "programming" good customer service techniques into their people.

> **PLUTONIUM LEADERS CREATE DYNAMIC TEAMS BY:**
> **SELECTING THE RIGHT PEOPLE AND PUTTING THEM IN THE RIGHT PLACES.**
> **DEVELOPING, MOTIVATING, AND MENTORING THEM.**
> **CULLING THE HERD WHEN NECESSARY.**

Yes, people can be trained in the necessary skills to have a "can do" understanding of a job. And — they might even pass a written test to prove that they know the right answers. BUT —

- *"Without a caring "will do" attitude of enthusiasm towards any job — all the training programs and acronyms are DOA.*

Leadership is not a "program." Instead, it is the palatable presence of individuals who are driven by mentoring, encouraging and presenting themselves as a great role model with a positive energy that simply proves contagious. Everyone on the team truly feels that they are part of something special. This results in a sense of pride of being on the team and to care about others.

Of course, there is a need for "trainers" to teach entry level employees what needs to be done, and how to do it. But — a greater need is for leaders who inspire, encourage, mentor, develop and have the ability to consistently elevate positive expectations of every individual and, thus, the team as a whole.

Yes, leaders care about WHAT important things that need to be done. Yes, leaders care about HOW things get done. But — above all, leaders take pride in and care about the people who make it all happen.

The old economic law of supply and demand seems to apply to products, but not necessarily to service and caring. Consumer demand for better service does not create a supply of caring people capable of delivering it.

A heart-felt plea (demand) for executives dedicated to providing dynamic and caring leadership does not create a supply of dynamic and caring leaders. Instead — it has tended to create a supply of candidates dedicated to posturing and preening, in hopes of being interviewed for high paying jobs.

> "GOING TO WORK FOR A LARGE COMPANY IS LIKE GETTING ON A TRAIN. ARE YOU GOING SIXTY MILES AN HOUR, OR IS THE TRAIN GOING SIXTY MILES AN HOUR — AND YOU'RE JUST SITTING STILL?"
> J. PAUL GETTY

This makes the point. Go ahead and get on the train. But, don't think you have arrived just because you have been offered a seat.

Sure — put all the programs and acronyms in place. Just never forget this one: GLIPWC

(Great Leaders Inspire People Who Care.)

PLUTONIUM CLUB LEADERS DO THIS EVERY DAY.

UNBELIEVABLE STORIES ABOUND OF GREAT STAFF ANTICIPATION.

UNPLANNED CAREER MOVES
THE #1 REASON FOR THEM

When embarking upon a club management career, there is an accepted "learning curve" of progression — supervisory, department head, director of "this or that", general management — and ultimately to a COO or CEO position.

The next logical step is an appropriately timed move to a larger operation, with greater annual gross revenue and still more opportunity to utilize professional expertise gained over the years.

And — as it says on the back of every shampoo bottle: "Repeat as necessary."

There are applaudable career moves advancing up the food chain via promotions within, or at more pivotal times, perhaps a move to a larger club altogether.

However — once firmly established in a career — "unplanned" changes will draw no applause from club search committees or retained search firms (instead, perhaps a hushed silence).

For many years, the average tenure of a GM/COO hovered at less than 3 years. And, any current improved longevity is the direct result of two factors:

1. The advent of great executive search firms that specialize in the club industry and in making sure the best possible "match" is made between a club seeking leadership and available talent.

2. The incredible advance of professional education offerings made available through CMAA is creating far more talented club leaders.

Q: OK. So now we know why early planned moves are good, that unplanned moves are not, and why top GM/COO tenure is slowly improving. But…what is the #1 reason for top GM/COO derailment that is unplanned?

A: The short answer is — board-approved unrealistic operating budgets.

THERE ARE ALL KINDS OF OTHER GENERAL CATALYSTS THAT MIGHT COME INTO PLAY: SACRED COWS/ POLITICAL ASSASSINATIONS/UN-FOUNDED RUMORS/FLYING SAU-CERS/ALIEN ABDUCTION/DATING THE SPOUSE OF THE VICE PRESI-DENT, AND OF COURSE, "CASPER THE GHOST" GM'S, ETC.

(Another thing — right behind this reason for why GM/COO's may personally start looking is micro-management. We deal with that elsewhere.)

When looking strictly at operating performance — the #1 specific conundrum is when management is held accountable for achieving an impossible mission: meeting unrealistic operating budget expectations that engraft dues income grossly inadequate in offsetting legitimate operating expenses.

The result from is a nice little "set-up" jab — followed by a solid "knock-out" punch.

THE "KNOCK- " — THE NECESSARY DUES INCOME TO SUSTAIN AP-PROVED CLUB OPERATING EXPEC-TATIONS IS DISAPPROVED! (BOO!)

THE "SET-UP" — ALL OF THE EX-PENSE LINE ITEM NICETIES THE MEMBERSHIP EXPECTS FROM CLUB OPERATIONS ARE APPROVED! (AP-PLAUSE!)

In situations like this, the attitude of the board seems to be, "Our membership expects us to operate at a certain level, but dues cannot go up! We are going to approve this budget and management will just have to make it work." (Hushed silence.)

And, please, no clucking of tongues suggesting that no capable GM/COO would ever allow this scenario to happen on their watch! That absolute position suggests that any GM/COO who has ever lost a great position was incapable to start with. Not true.

In recessionary times, a plethora of very capable club managers have experienced what they themselves thought to be impossible on their watch. It happens. Don't ever let anyone tell you otherwise. Don't tell yourself that it could never happen to you.

Q: Looking ahead — what's the best way to deal with this?

A: The strongest proactive management tool available to avoid this scenario is in developing the expertise to truly create realistic Zero-Based operating budgets, and then in a compelling way, presenting them at the Finance Committee and ultimately Board level.

CMAA is leading the way by continually enhancing professional education offerings focused on the vital importance of financial expertise (RMS, Club Board Professionals and Club Benchmarking are all great resources).
Let's wrap this up by stressing the importance of solid financial/business acumen in building a successful club management career:

- *ASPIRING YOUNG GM/COO's* — If you make it your business to develop expertise in creating/presenting realistic Zero-Based budgets, you will be favored by future search committees and sought by retained search firms. (Applause!)

- *SEASONED GM/COO's* — You already know that your polished financial expertise in creating/presenting realistic Zero-Based budgets is a deterrent to unplanned changes, and encounters with search committees or search firms tend to be on your terms. (Standing Ovation!)

VISITORS COVET MEMBERS EXTENDING INVITATIONS.

VISION
HOW PLUTONIUM CLUB LEADERS SEE THINGS.

Plutonium Club Leaders — Visualize possibilities, and then bring everyone into the big picture. Plutonium Club Leaders continually focus on building a winning team capable of being on the very top of their game...NOT the problems that losing teams dwell upon in the bottom of the cellar. (AKA: Show me a poor leader who thinks good enough is good enough, and I'll show you a philosopher.)

Philosophers? See difficulties. They almost always have to have someone else draw them a picture. When they do —the dots seldom connect, the picture is too small, and the big picture is seldom seen at all.

Plutonium Club Leaders— Have a proclivity of being proactive problem solvers! Solving them before they ever have a chance to happen.

Philosophers? — Have a tendency to be reactive problem presenters. All too often, perhaps even unwittingly, being a part at the root of the very problems they lament about! (Go figure.)

Plutonium Club Leaders — Present EXCITING new ideas! Hey, let's go this direction! Let's try this! I bet this has never been done before!

Philosophers? — Offer BORING old excuses. Been there. Done that. But we don't have the budget. But —we've always done it this way. Yeh, but...yawn.

Plutonium Club Leaders — Step up and say, "We can handle that!" And then, turn up the heat and prepare the entire team in making it happen.

Philosophers? — Step aside and say, "That's not my job." And the truth is... they are more than likely simply not up to the job. Philosophers spend their time reactively putting out fires — not proactively turning up the heat.

Plutonium Club Leaders — Seek answers for every potential problem. And then act upon them. Just thinking about great ideas is not enough. It's all about execution!

Philosophers? — Cast doubts on every potential answer, and are unable to effectively put any solutions into action. Hmmm...this just doesn't seem to add up, does it? Do the math.

Plutonium Club Leaders — Eyes are focused on every green, not on any nearby sand traps.

Philosophers? — Are distracted by sand traps that they see surrounding every green. They cannot seem to get out of their "Bunker Mentality."

CLOSING PLUTONIUM THOUGHTS:

When having to deal with proven, dedicated, unmovable, negative folks who are seemingly "wed" to losing attitudes...always remember the reality of "Pig's Law"...

PIG'S LAW: Don't fight with pigs, as you just get dirty...and they love it!

OBEY THE LAW! And remain focused on continually building winning teams and individual winners who want to be perpetually on top of their game.

KEEP YOUR EYE ON THE BALL --- You cannot change the world, and every individual (little piggies as well) has the right to approach life from the perspective s/he chooses.

Don't spend **excessive** time trying to make those who choose a negative (philosophical) frame of mind see things the winning way you do.

No sense at all in putting the efforts of an otherwise winning team on the back burner due to the somewhat annoying sounds heard from cellar-dwellers.

KEEP YOUR EYE ON THE BALL and, who knows...that next pitch coming your way just might be right up in your strike zone, right down the middle of the plate.

KEEP YOUR EYE ON THE BALL — and it's a whole new ball game!

WAIT STAFF SERVICE IS NOTHING BUT THE BEST.

WAIT STAFF SERVICE
SHOULD BE ORCHESTRATED BY BEING UNDER THE GRAVITATIONAL PULL OF THE CNG BLACK HOLE THEORY

THE CNG BLACK HOLE THEORY: This is like in an epic science fiction movie, where when in deep space, a gravitational pull becomes so strong that it simply pulls everything to the center of it. Same theory applies in a first-class dining room.

Everyone, the ENTIRE front of the house service team...all the time, keep your head up...surveying the entire area...whenever a member even enters the room...it matters not if it's your table or not — **IMMEDIATELY** start feeling the gravitational pull, move towards the table they are headed for, and pull a chair for them!

This only take 5 seconds and conveys a strong perception that the service team is collectively awesome. (Just imagine the visual impact of a table of six being seated, and quite suddenly, seeming out of the blue...all six chairs are being pulled. OMG!)

THE CNG BLACK HOLE THEORY should happen multiple times all over the room throughout the entire dining experience!

NEVER ASK A MEMBER FOR THEIR NAME OR MEMBERSHIP NUMBER! NEVER EVER EVER!
Before going to any table, MAKE SURE you already know their name! Ask a senior member of staff, look it up, do whatever you have to do...but, NEVER ask the member! Always address them by their name.

FIRST THING AT EVERY TABLE

Greet the member by name! This is a commanding first impression you give that you are indeed in control. Now – prove it! Address them by name several times throughout the entire time they are seated at your table.

THE CNG BLACK HOLE THEORY applies whenever moving through the dining areas. When passing by any member you know by name — if it is your table or not — greet them by name and move on! **(Guests will be shaking their heads, "Wow! This is incredible!")**

WATER SHOULD BE SERVED ALMOST IMMEDIATELY!

Always from a bar tray (or, ice/water service to table if glasses are pre-set). Never just carried by hand. Always from the right side. When refilling – always "pour to the table' – using side towel to shield from splash. OK. Let's be honest. The chances of spilling on a guest are minimal. However - the elevated perception of service is maximal. Hmmm - is that even a word?

COCKTAIL NAPKINS

When approaching a table for a cocktail order…have a bar tray to write on… bring cocktail napkins with you…place them from the right-hand side of each guest having ordered something.

 This not only saves you time when actually delivering the drinks ... it also serves as a visual confirmation to all the staff that drink orders have already been taken. Note: This applies only on hard surface tables! No napkins on tablecloth.

ALL BEVERAGES ARE SERVED FROM YOUR BAR TRAY

Serve from the right-hand side of guests with your right hand. Ladies first. Even if just serving one drink from the bar, use your bar tray. It is ALWAYS a good idea to have a side towel with you.

EVERY TABLE GETS A COMPLIMENTARY SMALL APPETIZER

This should be served fairly quickly after orders have been taken, menus cleared, and before any of their food order is delivered. They are available for immediate pick-up in the kitchen. This buys you more time, keeps the table busy…and, again, another "touch point" where you are in control. Never on your heels.

NEVER, EVER, NEVER...ASK A TABLE WHO ORDERED WHAT!

Always know where each plate is to go. Be in control of the order. BOOM! Everyone is served exactly what they ordered without having to ask a single question. Why? Because you are in control.

ALL FOOD IS SERVED FROM THE LEFT-HAND SIDE OF EACH GUEST.

Again – ladies first. Place each plate so that the entrée is at 7:00 PM...as if on the face of a clock. This means guests aren't spinning their plates in order to get to the entrée. Also, it means we consistently do things right.

THE CNG BLACK HOLE THEORY applies every time you see a teammate serving their table, and you have 30 seconds — go right over and help! This blows guest's minds when suddenly 2, 3 or even 4 servers surround their table and in a matter of seconds it's over! If it is your table – just make sure you quietly confirm to all teammates exactly who gets what.

ALL PLATES ARE CLEARED FROM THE RIGHT-HAND SIDE OF EACH GUEST

Again – ladies first. For a smaller table, your bar tray may work. Otherwise, bring a large tray and tray-jack nearby and clear to that. **NEVER scrape plates in sight of guests.**

WRAP UP: While all the above can/should be massaged to fit your own unique approach to ala carte dining service, the basic conceptual approach of THE CNG BLACK HOLE THEORY to member dining experiences can be used as a foundation to build upon team success.

SERVICE is a managed/orchestrated perception left on the mind of the member/guest about the way you go about your business.

By uplifting the perception of orchestrated service, "suddenly" the plate presentation, as if by magic, is better...the food tastes better, and the overall dining experience is elevated. All achieved by simply having the front of the house staff collectively fall into a black hole. Go figure.

Of note...all the above is FREE! It requires no greater staffing or equipment purchases. Just a matter of consistency and organization. Yield to the gravitational pull of **THE CNG BLACK HOLE THEORY!**

WORKING YOUR WAY TO THE TOP
EXAMPLES OF HARD WORK, BUT ALSO HOW PLUTONIUM LEADERSHIP SKILLS ARE USED IN DEVELOPOING YOUNG TALENT WITH POTENTIAL

PREFACE

Although every word here is true and accurately reflects exact happenings in my early career life — the lesson here is definitely NOT about me. Instead — it is about the power of hard work being behind any successful career. It also portrays how appropriate delegation of just the right balance of added responsibility and authority to the right people at the right time can serve to develop those yearning to be exposed to new challenges. OK? — Let's begin.

I began a lifelong career in club management at The Carriage Club in Kansas City, MO. Just 2 weeks shy of my 21st birthday, I was sworn to secrecy as a big part of my new job was to show the wine list and follow through with actual service (shhhhhh — don't tell anybody I wasn't of legal age in the "Show-Me-State" to do so).

BTW --- JUST AS AN ADDED TIP. WHEN YOU SEE THESE WORDS PRINTED ON AN INVITATION: "BLACK TIE OPTIONAL" — THEY ARE JOKING. TRUST ME ON THIS ONE. JUST TAKE THE HIGH ROAD, AND BE DONE WITH IT.

My official title was Main Dining Room Captain. Six nights a week you'd find me heading off to work in a formal tuxedo — complete with ruffled shirt and "Tony Orlando" oversized bow ties.

My wonderful mentor — the then undisputed dean of old school formal Maitre'd's in Kansas City, Bob Rohovit, took me to school. I started as his student — but, due to his leadership, slowly became an expert at classic tableside preparation and service techniques.

Ahhh, remember the days of grandeur on gueridons! Lamb Racks on Flaming Swords — Steak Tartar — Crepes Suzette — Cherries Jubilee — Bananas Foster — Caesar Salad — Steak Diane — Chateaubriand — Dover Sole, etc.

On the management side — I hired, trained and scheduled a staff of 6 "Bus Boys." This was my very first team!

- I learned so very much from Bob in all aspects of fine ala carte dining operations. He was/is one of my greatest mentors. Although I did not recognize it at the time, he was truly a Plutonium quality leader.

377

In time, I began thinking that it might be "smart" to have my ala carte support team that reported to me be "cross-trained" to also be able to be scheduled for club banquets and events. And since if my idea proved successful, it would make the Banquet Manager's (Ken Holman) job easier — I lobbied for, and soon gained Ken's support in thinking that my experiment might be a great idea!

However, I also opined that it would be confusing for my team to report to two different supervisors (me and the Banquet Manager).

By working hard and getting prior approval from Bob, my responsibilities of Main Dining Room Captain were soon extended to encompass the duties of Assistant Banquet Manager as well.

And, it was here that Ken took me under his wing and exposed me to the finer touches needed in booking, staffing and orchestrating private parties and special events.

- I learned a great deal from Ken about banquet and catering operations.

Moving forward, since the task of getting areas set-up and turned over for each event involved the Housekeeping staff — I successfully lobbied to assume responsibility here as well. My team was expanding, right along with my areas of responsibility and authority.

- I did not know it at the time, but I was being groomed by effective delegators and leaders around me.

BTW --- JUST AS AN ADDED TIP. WHEN YOU SEE THESE WORDS PRINTED ON AN INVITATION: "BLACK TIE OPTIONAL" — THEY ARE JOKING. TRUST ME ON THIS ONE. JUST TAKE THE HIGH ROAD, AND BE DONE WITH IT.

Then, down the road a bit, I positioned myself to begin taking the beverage inventory and figuring COGS %'s weekly flash reports for Bob.

You bet I was working hard. But I didn't want a new job. I wanted to learn and build a career —right where I was.

If you consistently excel and distinguish yourself at all the little things right now — BIGGER things will take care of themselves.

During a very rare occasion that I took time off, I noticed in the Kansas City Star newspaper that The Carriage Club was seeking an experienced person to prepare the weekly payroll and quarterly tax reports.

I knew nothing about accounting. And, that is precisely why I contacted the GM (Bill Barrington) to secure an appointment. I told Mr. Barrington that I wanted to talk about the club's search for an experienced person to prepare the weekly payroll and quarterly tax reports.

He started smiling - and then asked if I knew of someone I could recommend. Yes, I did — ME!

He stopped smiling - and I instantly knew I'd better explain fast.

I quickly admitted that I had no experience, but I did have a desire to learn and the willingness to work hard. I explained that I would not allow this added responsibility to affect the performance of my other duties. I made it clear that the opportunity to learn would be my total compensation. The only real "cost" would be that the club invest the time to teach me the needed technical skills. He was grinning!

- Four weeks later, I was preparing weekly payroll and quarterly tax reports! I successfully created the opportunity to develop new skills, very marketable skills!

The very best way to position yourself for that next BIG job is to succeed at the one you have! That is the secret: SUCCEED at the job you have! That MUST be your main focus. If you are successful in what you have on your plate right now and seek out more responsibilities…tomorrow will take care of itself!

With this recipe, the results are highly predictable:

- You will leave behind you a trail of goodwill and solid recommendations.

- You will find your new job presents still more areas to be exposed, add polish and succeed again! Seek more responsibilities and authority. Then consistently succeed.

- You will find that your tomorrows will indeed rise on the horizon before you at the right times, and open up to the right places.

Again - here is a meaningful quote by Bob Burdette found in Elbert Hubbard's Scrap Book. It is worth repeating again and again and again and — even right here in The ABC's of Plutonium Private Club Leadership!

"Whether you handle pick or wheelbarrow or a set of books, digging ditches or editing a newspaper, ringing an auction bell or writing funny things, you must work.

Don't be afraid of killing yourself. Men die sometimes, but it is because they quit work at 9:00 p.m. and don't go home until 2:00 a.m. It's the intervals that kill you.

Work gives you appetite for your meals; it lends solidity to your slumber and gives you perfect appreciation for a holiday. So, find out what you want to be and do, take off your coat and make dust in the world. The busier you are: the less harm you are apt to get into — the sweeter will be your sleep — the brighter your holidays, and — the better satisfied the whole world will be with you."

X-TRA ATTENTION IS GIVEN TO ALL MEMBERS AND GUESTS.

XTRA ATTENTION AND PERSONAL CARE
THIS IS THE VIBE PLUTONIUM CLUB LEADERS USE TO CREATE MEMBER EXPERIENCES

While every facet of a private club has a direct impact on those members who may be utilizing any particular department at any given time — Food & Beverage operations represent the only place where 100% of the membership is served.

Not all members golf, play tennis, visit the spa, shoot skeet, use the marina, go to yoga, swim, play cards, or attend club events. However, all members do indeed eat and drink.

> YOU CANNOT PRIORITIZE THE VARIOUS OPERATING DEPARTMENTS OF A PRIVATE CLUB. WHY? JUST ASK ANY MEMBER WHAT THE MOST IMPORTANT AREA OF THEIR CLUB MIGHT BE AT ANY GIVEN POINT IN TIME, AND THEY WILL BE HAPPY TO TELL YOU THAT IT IS THE ONE THAT THEY ARE EXPERIENCING AT THAT VERY MOMENT.

"Everything that happens at any moment at the club is Priority #1 to someone — and every one of them must be treated as such." Bud Gravette, Past President - Thunderbird Country Club - Rancho Mirage, CA

While ALL departments are "Mission Critical" – it must be acknowledged that F&B is the: Most visible — Most utilized — and oftentimes — (Need we say it?) — Most scrutinized — area of the entire club.

Plutonium Club Leaders leverage these facts into their team's advantage. Consistent and personal F&B experiences are where the greatest return on investment can be leveraged toward: increased retention levels, a means to encourage guests, and enhancement of new member referrals.

MEMBERS TREASURE PERSONAL EXPERIENCES.
We are selective in our surroundings. Every form of life must ingest food in one form or another in order to maintain life. We humans are the only form of life that somehow derives pleasure not only from the act of eating but also from the environment/ambience of where we decide to eat.

- *Where better than a familiar clubhouse?* We care about who surrounds us. Our enjoyment is further enhanced by surrounding ourselves with family, friends, and like-minded people to share the time with us.

- *Where better than at the club?* We like what we see. How our food is presented adds further enjoyment. The saying that people "eat with their eyes" is proven by the great appreciation we have for a culinary presentation that immediately makes us stop, just to enjoy the visual stimulation before even taking a first bite. It matters not whether it is a full-blown holiday buffet, a classical dish, or simply a half sandwich and a cup of soup.

- *Nobody does it better than the club's culinary team.* We appreciate the manner and spirit in which we are served. Equally important to quality food preparation, plate presentation, and accompanying beverage of choice is the manner and spirit in which service delivers every component of an enjoyable meal to the table. We are not only aware of those around us, but we also care about those who serve us.

Many of the club's loyal service staff have been there for years and care deeply for the members.

A GREAT STAFF TAKES IT PERSONALLY. (In fact— EVERYTHING at the club is personal!)

"You're almost like a personal chef for each individual member, which is fun." Kenneth Hogh, Executive Chef - Ridgewood Country Club - Paramus, NJ

Plutonium Club Leaders are warmly open to change but covet consistency.

THREE KEYS THAT PLUTONIUM CLUB LEADERSHIP LEVERAGES INTO FAVORABLE PERSONAL EXPERIENCES FOR THE MEMBERSHIP:

- *CONSISTENCY* with THE QUALITY VIBE

- *CONSISTENCY* with THE SERVICE EXPERIENCE

- *CONSISTENCY* with THE EXPECTATIONS THAT PLUTONIUM CLUB LEADERS ESTABLISH!

Does anyone see a pattern here?

> **"YOU MUST HAVE CONSISTENCY! IT ALL STARTS THERE. CONSISTENCY IN FOOD AND STAFF. A FRIENDLY STAFF AND GUEST RECOGNITION ARE KEY INGREDIENTS."**
>
> **JULIANA MANION-COPLEY, CO-OWNER**
> **COPLEY'S ON PALM CANYON, PALM SPRINGS, CA**

Achieving consistency in great member experiences is contingent upon developing a club staff that takes things personally. It ALL comes down to selecting and maintaining a professional staff that takes things personally.

> **OUTSIDE OF PRIVATE CLUBS, WE ARE ALL SO USED TO IMPERSONAL EXPERIENCES THAT WE'VE BECOME DESENSITIZED TO THEM. IT HAS BECOME WHAT WE EXPECT AND DON'T EVEN KNOW IT!**

To prove it — let's take a look at two very representative, yet very different, dining experiences: Dining at a restaurant vs. Dining at the club.

1) AT A PUBLIC RESTAURANT after finally being seated:
In an effort to "up-sell" at every table, your server appears with a memorized script delivered in one deep breath. It goes something like this: (Take a deep breath.)

"Hello. My name is Rhetoric, and I'll be your server tonight. The chef's special soup du jour is Warhol Tomato. This is a nostalgic potage served room temperature in a vivid red and white can, that is ceremoniously opened tableside. This evening's fish is Skinhead Idaho Trout. This trout is line-caught under a rainbow with the skin and head removed. Tonight's dessert is Strawberries Manilow served with a medley of the pastry chef's greatest hits."

Then, once the opening lines are finished, there is a slight intake of air, followed by: "Could I start the table off with an appetizer? Perhaps Goldie Lox & Three Bagels."

Then, while everyone at the table is sitting in stunned silence: "May I offer you something from the bar while you make up your mind?"

Here is where the eyes glaze over, they tilt their head 45 degrees, and smile in the general direction of the salt & pepper shakers in the middle of the table.

Suddenly you realize it is your turn to say something. While you do not yet know what you are going to order for dinner, after listening to this performance, you do know you'd like (need?) a drink!

You meekly offer, "Yes, please. Bring me a scotch on the rocks. As a matter of fact, make that a double!"

Without missing a beat: "Wonderful! Would you like me to make that Macallan's 64 year-old Lalique Cire Perdue?" (Cha-Ching.)

2) AT YOUR PRIVATE CLUB *after being warmly greeted and immediately seated:*

"Good evening Mr. & Mrs. Petersen! It is always so nice to see you both at the club. Jimmy called from the valet to let me know you'd just arrived, so we've taken the liberty of chilling a bottle of that chardonnay you both commented on liking so much at the wine dinner last week. There were two bottles left, so we set one aside for you to enjoy again whenever you might like. I did want you to know that it is available for you. On the other hand, Mr. Petersen, would you prefer your usual Dewar's on the rocks with two lemon twists?"

> **WHILE THESE TWO EXPERIENCES SUGGEST MANY DIFFERENCES — THERE REALLY IS ONLY ONE. THAT ONE MAKES ALL THE DIFFERENCE. THE FIRST EXPERIENCE IS AN IMPERSONAL ONE. THE OTHER ACCURATELY PORTRAYS THE DIFFERENCE A PERSONAL INTERACTION MAKES.**

These types of highly personal interactions and exchanges should be consistently happening in: EVERY department. EVERY opportunity throughout the entire club property! EVERY day. EVERY time. EVERY team member.

Hmmmmm…does anyone see a pattern here?

THIS is what makes a private club different! Wonderfully so.

YOUNGER MEMBERS, YES THEY SEE

YOUNGER MEMBERS LIKE POP
UP EXPERIENTIAL EVENTS

Traditional is out. More impromptu, one of a kind, trendy - is in. To stay relevant, retailers stay attuned to changing trends and consumer preferences.

Nowadays, many private clubs are embracing the need to modify traditional offerings or face obsolescence.

Past experiences can give perspective on enjoying our present experiences.

From the perspective of younger generations of members, the internet, smart phones, and a plethora of instantaneous social media options that they are used to impulsively acting upon IS their life experience. They've never known otherwise.

New/younger members are not necessarily traditional.

- The traditional club newsletter? Goes unread (tell me otherwise).
- Routine club events? Deemed uneventful.
- Committing to advance reservations? No, because something better may pop up.

Q: The solution?

A: Create a growing trend of 'Pop-Up's - out of the ordinary, all but "catch 'em off guard" unique dining/social opportunities.

- No printed invitations, or even email blasts.
- Pop-Ups are all real-time messages — both text and visual stimulation.
- Very short bursts of information.
- A limited quick window for response.
- A small cap for total attendees.
- Absolutely no more than 2 weeks away (in some cases – 72 hours).

A sense of urgency is created to attend an event that almost seems secret - a "can't miss soiree" of one sort or another. And — better hurry! Reputation of being quickly filled!

Pop-Ups revolve around perceived truly unique experiences:

- Dining in crazy different club locations (even the roof).
- Presentations/food never before seen on regular menus.
- Novelty themes outside the norm. Perfectly executed!
- Table-side personal visits with the Executive Chef & culinary team.
- Always, the unexpected. (A marching high school band, unannounced — right down the middle of the venue! Just in and out with no explanation whatsoever. Whud duh?)

It is VERY important that Management be empowered to make changes/additions on the fly. This is no time to get bogged down in committee structure. Simply no time for that. Creative, opportunistic energy that leverages any/all current new approach creating a memorable experience at the club.

Successful Pop-Ups help create a younger, loyal following who will all but immediately respond to the next text message offering yet another unique experience at their club. There MUST be a pervasive sense of, "Fun things happen spontaneously at my club."

And, why not transfer the same unexpected "you gotta be kidding" Pop-Up experience to golf! (Not to mention ... the fitness center - pool - etc. etc. etc.) Something like...

Appearing one night only!
FIRE-FLY NIGHT GOLF
"Definitely NOT a Fly by Night Experience!"

EXECUTION?
- Portable fire pits down the entire line of practice range tees.
- Glow in the dark golf balls.
- Bug Juice' cocktails with pulsating light ice cubes.
- Fog machines.

- Illuminated targets down range.
- Don't forget the sound effects.
- Don't stop the creative juices of your team!

Sound crazy? Of course it is! And that is exactly why when your text message goes out, that your reservations radar screen will immediately light up and start blinking wildly.

Hmmm…are 'traditional' clubs having trouble fully engaging a new generation?

Start building a tradition of crazy Pop-Ups and they will come!

YOU'RE ON A FIRST-NAME BASIS
PLUTONIUM CLUB LEADERS EMBRACE HORIZONTAL RELATIONSHIPS RATHER THAN VERTICAL

INTRODUCTION

My highly esteemed colleague and Plutonium Club Leader, Robert Sereci (GM/COO at Medinah Country Club) said this far better than I could. So – with his gracious permission — **ROBERT** — you're on! linkedin.com/in/robertsereci

Some time ago, I was visiting a friend and fellow club manager and I noticed everyone addressing him as Mr. Upthere (a fictionalized name). I asked him if that was a club cultural requirement or his personal preference.

He honestly replied that it was his idea. Being curious, I asked him why?

He stated that asking his employees to refer to him by his surname created an atmosphere of professionalism, as well as establishing a mutual feeling of respect and authority. He further explained that while he does care for his employees, he believes that there is a clear-cut difference between his position and everyone else's, and by using his first name it would place everyone on the same level, thus, his status as GM would be diminished, hampering his ability to gain respect and lead.

Before I begin, please allow me to state, unequivocally, that while there is no right answer and no hard and fast rule for this issue, my inner self in my professional position does not allow me to comfortably adopt Mr. Upthere's philosophy.

Just like every club has a different culture, club managers have different philosophies. But what, or who, ultimately is responsible for the club culture? Is it the club manager or the members? Most often we use the "club culture" as a reason for how we address our employees and how they address us. While changing membership culture is exponentially harder and involves the collaboration of club boards and membership, the employee culture is entirely in the hands of the club manager.

So, if you personally prefer that employees call you by your last name, then go for it.

So, what do I believe? Below is a memo that I addressed to my entire team here at Medinah Country Club.

Dear Associates;

In all my years of leading various teams of associates, I have always taken pride in my horizontal approach to management as opposed to vertical. In other words, I place myself side-by-side with my teammates as opposed to being at the top of the heap looking down on my subordinates as if I am king and you are my subjects.

Because most of us here at the club will spend more time with each other than we do at home with our loved ones, I think of our team as a close-knit family. We're in this thing together and I want every one of you to know that I look at each of you as a partner.

It is for this reason that I ask each of you to please call me "Robert."

I know it's important to all of you to refer to our members using their surnames, but like I said, I'm your partner and not a member.

If you feel uncomfortable with this level of informality, then by all means refer to me as Mr. Robert or maybe Senior Roberto. But I would prefer that you don't call me Mr. Sereci.

I want everyone to feel as comfortable with me as I do with you.

Trust me; your respect to me comes by way of your performance and the professionalism that you practice with our members. To me, respect comes by way of actions and not established by putting a Mr. in front of a name.

So, the next time our paths cross, let's have a handshake, a Medinah wave or a gentle fist bump followed with: "Hello, Robert."

Thank you for all you do for me and for our club!

With warm and friendly regards,

Robert

Of course, I expect our members to call me Robert also, even though I refer to them with their surname unless instructed to do otherwise. I'm the linkage between our club employees and the members. I'm the guy in the middle fighting for both sides. It's a mutual relationship that is not divided by the formality of a name; it's Robert from top-down and bottom-up.

It's very important to me that both parties see me as a partner without the distance of formality. I like to think of myself as the net that defines the two sides of a tennis court, depicting the arena between two participants.

Let me ask you: Do you address your friends as Mr. Friend? Or do you say howdy Robert, or whatever their first name may be?
I want my associates to rely on me and trust me as they would a friend, rather than think of me, and possibly avoid me, as an adversarial force (a.k.a. Boss).

The respect I receive from my staff does not come simply by way of entitlement or just by virtue of position. I earn their respect by behaving in a manner that earns their trust. Don't we all trust our friends?

Hi, I'm Robert, and you are?

> *Thank you, Robert, for sharing this tremendous insight. Spot on. Your focus on Horizontal relationships rather than Vertical is pure Plutonium.*

ZEE CLUB — ZEE CLUB — ZEE CLUB!
IS THE PLACE TO BE!

Will private clubs exist in 25 years? How about 50 or 100 or 500? Spoiler alert...of course they will! That is not the question you or I or anyone else will need to answer. The real question - the critical question - you'll need to answer is, "will *my* club be around in 100 years?" That answer, I'm sorry to tell you, is no. But before you toss this book in the waste bin and lament the hours you spent reading, only to reach this sad and dark conclusion, allow me to explain.

Since the beginning of time, humans have longed for connection. We've gathered together. We've built communities. We've searched for our tribes from the African serengeti all the way to the virtual world online. Just take a look outside your door. Power lines, telephones lines, fiber optic lines and more have all been built to connect us to one another. You've even got a device near you right now that connects you to the entirety of human knowledge that you can unlock with your fingerprint or face.

So for anyone to tell you that private clubs won't exist, or golf is dead, or no one likes to go out anymore, or millennials aren't interested in a dying industry is simply fear mongering or peddling ignorance. Because as long as a few folks with shared passions or a love of sport wish to connect, they'll find or build a club to do it. It's our most basic inclination.

But will *your* club exist? I firmly believe it will not. At least not the way it does today. As a plutonium club leader, you'll need to accept that. No, embrace that!

See, in addition to connection, humans love progress. We love evolution. We love to push the boundaries and test our limits. When I was a kid, I loved to watch the Olympic Games. In 1988, I remember watching the athletes break all kinds of unimaginable records. Shattering world records even. It was incredible. Then, in 1992 athletes came and broke those records. In 1996, they did the same. Over and over and over every year, they ran faster, jumped higher and traveled further. That's why I loved to watch after all.

If you glean nothing else from this book, I hope you'll take away the fact that you hold a great responsibility to push your club to be more than it is today. Your job is to take the great club you already have and make it something unimaginably more. Plutonium leaders don't accept the status quo. They are proactive. They think nimbly. They act decisively. They have a vision of what's to come.

WHAT YOUR CLUB WILL NEED TO MAINTAIN ITS PLUTONIUM STATUS

Now, here comes the real advice that I feel I'm uniquely qualified to give. The reason I think I am is because I've asked a lot of questions. I'd be shocked if there is an individual in the industry that has asked as many questions as I have in the last few years. I've interviewed hundreds of experts on *Private Club Radio*, both inside and outside the industry. I've visited hundreds of clubs, attended dozens of conferences and all the while, if you can believe it, spoken very little. Instead, I asked questions and listened. You might hear my keynotes for 90 minutes but the rest of the the conference I spend listening. You might hear my show for 30 minutes a week, but the majority of my day is spent asking questions. I ask questions of my clients, my team and those I admire. It's my superpower. I'm really, really good at it. Now I've got a few answers, and I'd like to share them with you.

I believe there are three critical ways clubs must evolve in order to remain relevant and become "your members very favorite place to be."

- Focus your efforts on connection
- Take security seriously
- Find ways to engage members even when they can't walk through the door

FOCUS ON CONNECTION

Ask yourself, "what ways can I create more member collisions?"

As stated above, humans crave connection. Outside of food and shelter, it's the next most important human need. The opportunity to be the place to make connections is the secret sauce that makes a great private club.

In a world that is increasingly lived online, the next generations will have very little chance to connect one on one with real, oxygen-breathing humans. Clubs will become a sacred space to forge those bonds. That's where the true value of the club is. It's not the golf course or that new outdoor dining space you just built. Those are the means to an end. The end game is connection.

The number one reason members resign is not financial. It's not because they age out either. It's a lack of meaningful connection. I've been to clubs where the members are too old to golf, yet still come every day. Why? Because the club is fulfilling their desire to connect and form bonds with other like-minded individuals.

How can you introduce members to each other? How can you "break the ice" for new members and get them sewn into the fabric of the club? How can you forge more social interaction? How can you encourage more business connections? That should be priority number one as you think about the long-term vision of your club.

TAKE SECURITY SERIOUSLY

Ask yourself, "what am I doing to make my club a safe haven?"

Every time I turn on the news (which is rare), I'm greeted by horrific story after horrific story. I hear about mass shootings, car jackings and various other misdeeds. I wholeheartedly believe that it's purely media sensationalism and that the world is actually getting much safer. However, I would be blind to deny that there is a pervasive feeling, especially amongst Americans, that the world is becoming an increasingly unsafe place. Clubs need to capitalize on this and spin it for their benefit. The ones who do will succeed.

Many clubs are behind a gate. That's a selling point for them. However, many others are not. I've walked right into clubs in Manhattan and other major cities without so much as a second look. I could walk into just about any golf course around the world without even being greeted at the front door. Yes, even Platinum level clubs! That scares me a bit if I'm being honest.

The most important, most affluent, most influential folks in the community and their families are frequently members or guest of our clubs. If there was ever a target, it's them. We need to take their protection seriously. I'm talking about physical protection *and* cyber protection. Data breaches have happened and will continue to happen because that data is extremely valuable. Every clubs should take an audit from a professional organization and consider security a vital part of their master plan.

THE CLUB IS NOT 4 WALLS

Ask yourself, "how can members feel they are part of the club without even walking through the front door?"

I have an American Express® platinum card. Just about every month, Amex emails me and tells me about all the benefits I may not even know I have. For instance, they tell me that I have a $200 baggage credit with the airlines when I travel. I have access to hundreds of airport lounges around the world. I have a $20 UBER credit each month. On and on it goes. I rarely need to ponder why I spend $495 on my annual fee each year. I have the reasons explained each month. It's magic.

Our world will become more and more online-experience based. If your club is going to exist in 100 years, members will need to interact with it from outside its walls. You can start doing some things right now to get you there. For instance, I've suggested my clients, especially city clubs, live stream their events. When there is an author, speaker, comedian or entertainer that comes to the club, let folks access this online. It's easy and affordable. At a minimum, a private Facebook group for the members will give them exclusive access. I'm traveling as I write this. I am going to miss some of my club's events because I can't physically be there. How cool would it be if I could log on and participate?

Does your club have an ongoing email series like the AMEX example above? Why not? You probably have a reciprocal club network, strategic partnerships and more. Showcase them. Let your members know that dividing golf rounds by monthly dues is not how membership value is measured.

If you don't have these benefits, get out there and form some relationships. My friend Stuart Finlay in Wales has approached hotels in the area and secured discounts for his members at all their locations. What a great value add for members who travel! Go to your local sports teams, theaters, theme parks, and other attractions and work out some deals for exclusive, behind-the-scenes access. Once you have these relationships in place, get the email series up and running. Don't forget, you can even use email to introduce members to each other. Showcase one each month so that they all know how special and connected each one is.

TIME FOR ACTION

Now it's time to take what you've read and put it into action. If you can manage to accomplish these three key differentiators during your tenure as a Plutonium club leader, your club won't exist in a few years. It will be something utterly and completely more remarkable. You'll shatter today's "world records." It will truly become your members very favorite place to be. Godspeed.

AN EPILOGUE (OF SORTS)

ALL THINGS MUST PASS. EVEN GREAT CAREERS OF PLUTONIUM PRIVATE CLUB LEADERS.

All who have built enduring successful careers within the private club industry, become aware of the fact that they serve at the pleasure of the current board. Always have. Always will.

> **GOLF COURSE SUPERINTENDENTS, EXECUTIVE CHEFS, GENERAL MANAGERS, LOCKER ROOM MANAGERS, HEAD GOLF PROFESSIONALS, CONTROLLERS AND OTHERS, ALL SERVE AT THE PLEASURE OF THE CURRENT BOARD.**
>
> **AND — STATING THE OBVIOUS — AS ANY BOARD CHANGES, OFTENTIMES THE DYNAMICS BY WHICH THEY MEASURE SUCCESS AND MAKE DECISIONS DO AS WELL.**

While established traditions and proven relationships will always matter - new traditions and new relationship slowly evolve and ultimately become what is relevant and accepted as today's news.

Over time, new boards introduce new priorities that can come to overshadow old relationships and understandings. Familiar names and faces of dedicated employees of many years can "suddenly" become viewed as yesterday's news.

Nonetheless- while the past is valuable as a guide post, it can be very dangerous if used as a hitching post. Over passing time, the definition of remaining relevant to the lifestyle to a new generation of club members evolves and can change dramatically. In fact, it always has.

After years of what can only be defined as true "servant leadership" and heartfelt dedication, of giving far beyond what could ever have been asked by members, committees, boards or even fellow staff - as if without notice, it can somehow slip into the past.

It might start with a committee meeting or two taking place in a member's home, rather than at the club where they were always held. Oh - and, somehow you were not formally made aware of the meeting. But, informally, rumors begin to be quietly shared.

Then comes a concerned neighborly phone call from a highly esteemed professional peer, who wants you to know that the board of your club is having a meeting at their club.

And, when that day happens, as intellectually all know it invariably can - the very souls of the men and women who have performed admirably over decades are inevitably touched.

A few weeks or even a few months may pass, where all seems "normal." Yet, every so often the subtle signs and nuances become more and more undeniable.

In the mind of the current board - the thrill is gone.

And, even though there has been no formal announcement, or even acknowledgement - it is now you who is making personal calls to your highly esteemed professional peers and neighbors — wanting them to know the "news" — and, if for no other reason than a "professional courtesy" — you want them to hear it from you first.

Then, "THAT DAY" does come where it is all formalized. Where a young club president or committee chair sums it all up by stating that they are "going in a different direction." One that does not include you.

Within hours close friends share THE letter. You know, the one e-blasted to your entire membership that thanks you for all those years of heartfelt dedication and of giving far beyond what could ever have been asked of anyone.

It is comforting for you to read that you are leaving on the very best of terms to "seek other professional opportunities." (If only you knew what they were.) It's nice to also see that you just might be spending more time with family. (You've got to explain this to them as well.)

There is an all but immediate support and understanding from a multitude of caring neighbors and appreciative peers who "get it," and are quick to offer a supportive arm around what they know are only temporarily slumped shoulders of a highly esteemed brother or sister.
Recently there were massive layoffs at ESPN, and one of their premier anchors, Scott Van Pelt, ever so eloquently lamented the ripple effects of loss felt by peers.

"This was a very difficult day in our neighborhood," Van Pelt said to the camera. "People we care about, some of our neighbors, who have been here a long time, lost their jobs.

"They are our friends — and yours. We value them, because they are valuable. We care about them, because they are worth it. Because of circumstances beyond their control, they will no longer be part of our block, our neighborhood, even as they remain our friends, and always will be."

YOU WILL READILY FIND THEM IN THE PGA, GCSAA, CMAA, HFTP, ACF, PCMA AND OTHERS. BECAUSE WE'VE ALL BEEN LIVING IN THE SAME NEIGHBORHOOD FOR YEARS AND HAVE BECOME FAMILIAR WITH ONE ANOTHER.

WHETHER IT WAS AN OCCASIONAL HANDSHAKE, OR JUST A CARING FRIENDLY NOD UPON EYE CONTACT AND A GENUINE SMILE AT CHAPTER MEETINGS OR THE ANNUAL CONFERENCE - THERE IS A BOND OF MUTUAL RESPECT, AS WE ALL ARE LIVING AND WALKING DOWN SIMILAR CAREER PATHS IN THE SAME NEIGHBORHOOD.

BUT — NOW, THERE IS A SENSE OF LOSS AS THE WORD SPREADS THROUGHOUT THE NEIGHBORHOOD THAT ONE OF OUR ESTEEMED HAS LOST THEIR JOB. AND, EVERYONE KNOWS THAT ONCE "THAT AGE" IN YEARS IS REACHED - THE CHANCES FOR MEANINGFUL INTERVIEWS ARE SIGNIFICANTLY DIMINISHED.

Let out a deep breath - and take in remembrances of every day of a job well done. Days that stretched into years, all contributing to a rewarding career well spent!

Look up! And when blue skies again appear, it will be you who is ready to offer to others those words of encouragement that you needed to hear back when your day came. Soon, you will become the one to offer a supportive arm around the temporarily slumped shoulders of a highly esteemed brother or sister in the neighborhood — just down a bit on the same career path you walked.

Life goes on. It will be alright. There are plenty days of great "shelf life" ahead - beyond what once was seemingly all-important - but can no longer be.

It's a new day. Go out and make some news - all of it good!

None of us are dealt a pat-hand in life. And, should anyone dare think that life owes them a living, or a career for life - think again.

In our bouts with temporary blindness and sorrow, we oftentimes look to yesterday or tomorrow. Forget past trials and sorrows. There was, but is, no yesterday -but there can be plenty of meaningful tomorrows.

IT IS UP TO EACH OF US TO CHOOSE HOW TO PLAY OUR CARDS, WHATEVER THEY MAY BE, AT ANY POINT IN OUR LIFE, TO THE BEST OF OUR ABILITY. OUR HAND MAY BE CONTINUALLY CHANGING, BUT OUR DESIRE TO CONTINUALLY PRESS ON AND TO HELP THOSE AROUND US SHOULD BE CONSTANT. IN FACT, BOTTOM LINE — THAT IS WHAT PLUTONIUM LEADERS DO BEST: HELP OTHERS.

During all the years since time began, TODAY has been the friend of man. Today is the future. Today is the day.

We can't change the past. But we can tarnish the present by worrying about the future. Even a simple pleasure like a good meal cannot be fully appreciated, if one is always thinking about the next course.

A glass filled with mud will become clear if drops of pure and clear water are continually added to it. Keep the mind out of the mud. Stick with those thoughts and subsequent actions that are pure and clear.

Amuse yourself with those who are so consumed with what their future holds that the first thing they do each morning is to read their horoscope. They simply must have some sort of advance warning of what kind of day they will be having that day!

Then, after learning first thing in the morning that they are sure to have a rotten day, they prove their horoscope accurate by having just that. What a predictable self-fulfilling prophecy.

This makes about as much sense as on a Wednesday morning, looking up Tuesday's horoscope to remind yourself of what kind of day you had yesterday. Really?

We author our own horoscope every day. Our future is not in the constellations in the sky, but - with reliance on God's guidance - in your own mind and heart.

With your own two feet planted firmly on the ground, and with God's guidance, it is YOU who decide what your position in life will be. The positions of the stars in the heavens above have nothing to do with it.

> YOUR FUTURE IS NOW! NEVER CARRY DISAPPOINTMENTS FORWARD, ONLY THE KNOWLEDGE LEARNED FROM THEM. YOUR HAPPINESS DEPENDS UPON YOU, AND YOU CAN BE AS HAPPY AS YOU WANT TO BE. HAPPINESS IS NOT THE RESULT OF SOMETHING THAT HAPPENS TO YOU. IT IS THE RESULT OF A POSITIVE STATE OF MIND THAT THRIVES ON BEING ALIVE TODAY, RIGHT NOW!

The greatest use of time is in making the most of the little joys and successes we experience every day. Life is full of these!

A baby's smile. The wind in the trees. Dinner with a friend. Receiving an unexpected card from a loved one. Coming to a heartfelt understanding. Spending time in prayer. Enjoying a brisk walk. Holding hands with your spouse. Listening to your favorite music. Attending a good meeting. Building a snowman with the kids. Cleaning the garage. Calling an old friend. Reading a thought-provoking book (oh, say, this one).

Yes, life is full of successes. Just open your eyes and look!

The world out there thinks success lies in getting what you want, or at least what you thought you wanted. But true success lies in being content with what you have and finding happiness in sharing it with others.

Accept the cards dealt to you in life, play them to the very best of your ability, and know when to fold and walk away to new things.

Your outlook towards life- this very day - right now - serves at the pleasure of your own mind and heart. Not that of any board of directors.

You are still that exact same person with a deep sense of true "servant leadership" and heartfelt dedication towards giving that goes far beyond what could ever be asked.

One door closes. Many doors of other opportunities can open.

Knock - knock. Who's there?

It's still YOU!

There is a whole new world out there. Welcome to the neighborhood! It's a beautiful day.

And – here's one last thought:

Q: Are you wondering if your mission here on this earth is finished?
A: If you are alive – it's not.

Have fun along the way!

REGARDLESS, DUE TO A BRILLIANT RECOMMENDTION MADE BY A MAN AT A PREVIOUS BOARD MEETING LINKING REBUILDING OF THE GREENS TO THE FIRST MEANINGFUL DUES INCREASE IN YEARS --- IT PASSES, WITH MINIMAL DISSENT.

SPECIAL TRIBUTE

JOHN SIBBALD
June 20, 1936 - June 27, 2016

You are about to read insights into the man who had the single greatest positive impact in private club management, approach to effective governance, and improving the longevity and compensation of management.

His name is John Sibbald.

SPECIAL TRIBUTE: HERE IS A HEARTFELT TRIBUTE TO A LUMINARY IN THE PRIVATE CLUB INDUSTRY AND A GREAT PERSONAL FRIEND OF MANY YEARS. JOHN'S STORY IS QUITE RELEVANT TO THE INDUSTRY AND THE VERY CONCEPT OF THIS BOOK. A LITTLE HISTORY IS IN ORDER. HERE WE GO!

John Sibbald passed away in Atlanta, GA after several years of battling various ramifications of Parkinson's disease. All through his professional life, John presented the striking image of a gentleman who had that knack of gaining the attention and quickly establishing rapport with those seated around a board room table. This was evidenced in his being retained by the board of directors and search committees of 1,000+ private membership country/city/yacht clubs in the United States and abroad.

His giant footprint on the private club industry is responsible for an enormous positive ripple effect that lasts to this very day. His contributions to the industry were HUGE, enduring, and more profound than many of the younger GM/COO's of today would even be aware — yet are the beneficiaries of.

Hmmmm...lots of accolades here. But, so far, no real substantiation.

So – let's quickly just race through.
John's early background starting with college in the late 1950's until he founded his own business, John Sibbald Associates, in 1975. Let's go.

- 1958 –– Bachelor, University Nevada
- 1958 -1964 –– Captain United States Army
- 1964 –– Master of Arts, University Illinois
- 1964 -1966 –– Office manager - Hewitt Associates, Libertyville, Illinois
- 1966 -1969 –– Corporate personnel manager - Pfizer Inc., NYC, New York
- 1969 -1970 –– President, Chief Executive Officer - Re-Con Systems
- 1970 -1975 –– Vice president Booz, Allen & Hamilton, NYC/Chicago

Immediately after college, John's career revolved around the human resources industry with ever-increasing positions of responsibility. He learned the basics with Hewitt Associates, at their corporate headquarters near Chicago, and then parlayed that to a move to New York City as an executive with Pfizer. Seeing the leadership talent John possessed, it was one of Pfizer's clients that actually lured John to become President and CEO of Re-Con Systems.

At every early step in his career he added to a growing reputation of being a young executive with the keen ability to identify talent and then place them in the right positions to succeed. It was this reputation that caused Booz, Allen & Hamilton to lure John to join them in their New York City offices as a Vice President in charge of their executive personnel division. John was subsequently promoted to head up their office in Chicago.

- This brings us to 1975

At the age of 39, John knew he was ready to leverage all his professional expertise and personal contacts in the corporate world to successfully open his own executive search firm.

John Sibbald Associates was born in Chicago, with an office in the Sears Tower and then later near O'Hare International Airport, to enable quick trips to major corporation clients around the country.

John's reputation got his foot in the door with several major corporate players and soon he was retained by the like of Ralston Purina, Monsanto, Anheuser-Busch, Barry Wehmiller and Johnson Wax to recruit top talent to their company.

While unplanned, more and more of his anchor clients were based in St. Louis. So, in 1979 John opened a second office in St. Louis while he was personally still based in Chicago.

But his major clients preferred to deal with him directly, so the Chicago office was closed and John Sibbald Associates moved to St. Louis in 1996.

John Sibbald Associates was gaining traction in the corporate world and he deepened his personal/professional relationships with many top corporate executives from various industries around the country.

John took note that the top decision-making executives of the major corporations that retained John Sibbald Associates would, for privacy and convenience reasons, often arrange to meet with John not at their corporate offices at all. Instead – there were many meetings taking place at the major private country and city clubs where the executives were members.

A shift in the focus of John Sibbald Associates was initiated innocently enough while conducting a retained search for an anchor client, the Johnson Wax Company.

At the successful conclusion of a particular key search, Sam Johnson, president of Johnson Wax, asked John an off the cuff question, "Being president of this company is my easy job. My tough job is being president of the Racine Country Club in Racine, Wisconsin. Do you think you might be able to find a great general manager for me?"

Before giving an immediate answer, John suddenly sensed the gaping hole need in the private club industry that could be filled by professional executive search expertise that the corporate world already embraced and sought. He quickly remembered the dozens and dozens of private clubs he had already visited in the normal course of meeting with his corporate client executives.

Suddenly – the dots began to connect.

IN THE CORPORATE WORLD, THE TOP EXECUTIVES ARE ROUTINELY DIRECTLY INVOLVED IN HIRING OTHER TOP EXECUTIVES. BUT, IN PRIVATE CLUBS, GENERAL MANAGERS ARE NOT HIRING OTHER GENERAL MANAGERS. NO – IT IS THE PRESIDENT AND BOARD MEMBERS THAT DO THAT. AND, WHILE PERHAPS BEING CAPTAINS OF INDUSTRY IN THEIR OWN FIELD – THEY GENERALLY MAKE LOUSY HIRES FOR THE WRONG REASONS IN THEIR OWN PRIVATE CLUBS. JOHN PERSONALLY SAW SIGNS OF THAT DURING HIS TRAVELS.

John smiled as he looked Sam Johnson in the eye and said, "Yes. I'll find you a great general manager."

John already had strong personal/professional relationship with many top executives from various corporations from around the country – almost all of which surely belonged to private clubs or were oftentimes on the board.

In other words, John had a good feel for the need of professional executive search in private clubs, had personally visited many across the country, and had already established a relationship of trust with many decision-makers.

Keep in mind, up to this time, no private clubs retained outside professional expertise in their hiring of management. None. It was all done by board members who had little concept of even what the job itself was, not really, nor what to look for in a potential candidate even if they could find one.

- Written club manager position descriptions were not commonplace. And, if a club did have one, it usually was copied from elsewhere and not reflective of the real job needed at that specific club.
- Annual reviews were not routine.
- Performance expectations were not clearly identified.
- Many club managers did not even attend board meetings. And, if

they did, were excused after giving their report.
- The golf professional and superintendent routinely reported to their committee chairman – not to the club manager at all.
- Employment contracts were a rarity.
- And, not surprisingly, the average tenure of a club manager hovered around just slightly over two years.

John continued doing executive searches for corporate clients with a private club sprinkled in here and there as a new client. At first slowly, then quickly, his reputation within the private club industry began to spread – with both club members and club managers.

In a few short years, John Sibbald Associates shifted its entire focus to the needs of private clubs.

During an interview with a business publication, when asked why he transitioned his business from the corporate world to private clubs, John said, "At first, finding club managers was the frosting on the cake. But that eventually became the cake itself!"

John Sibbald Associates grew to become the premiere company in the country hired by country clubs to recruit general managers, clubhouse managers, assistant managers, head golf professionals and directors of golf.

During the peak years, John Sibbald Associates was oftentimes conducting 16—18 searches at any given time, with as many as 26 searches at one time.

Over a 30-year span, John Sibbald Associates placed more than 1,500 Club managers in the world's most prestigious private clubs and exclusive resorts.

Still today, many accomplished GM/COO's owe a great debt of gratitude to John Sibbald —— even if they never met him. He laid the groundwork for those in the industry today.

He gave many a start in the business and placed countless in the finest jobs. John knew how to match personality, flair, ability and overall talent with the right opportunity. He laid the groundwork for those in the industry today — both for candidates as well as search firms.

John Sibbald did more, much more, than just place qualified candidates at clubs. He revolutionized the private club industry.

JOHN SIBBALD'S IMPACT ON THE PRIVATE CLUB INDUSTRY:

John's impact on the career of a GM/COO and the private club industry as a whole has left an enormous ripple effect that lasts to this very day.
Championed "Retained Executive Search" being applicable to the Private Club Industry:

While certainly not inventing the executive search business, he definitely pioneered and transferred it successfully from the corporate world to the private club industry.

Largely due to his early role and increasing influence in the industry:

1. *THE AVERAGE TENURE* of his placements far exceeded the theretofore norm of slightly more than two years, and

2. *THE BASE PAY AND TOTAL COMPENSATION PACKAGES* gradually became more competitive, ultimately being amongst the top in the hospitality industry as a whole.

He personally elevated the compensation of those in the club management profession <u>exponentially</u> across the country, at a far greater accelerated pace than would have otherwise happened...if at all.

In the corporate executive search business, the client is typically billed a percentage of the accepted annual base compensation. But since John was in most cases actually negotiating the final mutually agreed starting salary, he felt this presented a perceived conflict of interest. So, contrary to the corporate world, in serving his new market niche, he introduced a flat fee for his professional services. (FYI: Fees ranged from $18,000 to $75,000 for a search with the average in the $25,000 to $30,000 range.)

John did not simply want to 'place' club managers. He wanted to enhance the probability of general managers and private clubs both being successful. So, John personally championed the following to the private club industry:

- The creation of a board approved, specific, written General Manager position description for each club client.
- Each position description included the mention of an annual performance review and what the criteria would include.
- A formal, again board approved, written job offer spelling out the basics of compensation and severance protection.
- A written employment agreement requiring signatures of both parties.

Yes, many of these things nowadays appear simply routine. And, over the years several very fine search firms that specialize in private clubs do terrific all-encompassing jobs and continue to uplift the industry.

But, keep in mind – none of these things were routine prior to John Sibbald introducing them to the world of private clubs. He made it happen. He was the pioneer.

John conceived and founded the 'Platinum Clubs of America'

What private clubs are the most distinguished and highly respected in the county? And, by what criteria could they possibly be measured? And, by whom?

While there are no 'perfect' answers, John Sibbald wanted to establish a means to answer all the above in the best manner possible. He started by surveying 5,000 general managers, presidents, directors, and owners of private clubs. All were asked to rate quality of membership, tradition and culture, amenities, governance, quality of management and staff.

They were asked to rank the "very best" clubs, and those that are the "best managed and most successful" in five categories: city clubs, full-service country clubs, golf clubs, athletic clubs, and yacht clubs.

This was an exhaustive and extensive effort that resulted in the most reliable acknowledgment of private club excellence possible. A Platinum Club is equitable to AAA Five Diamond Award in Hotels & Resorts.

The survey is still viable today, and has been conducted every three years since 1997. And – John started it all.

To this very day, a "Platinum Club of America" designation is one of the most highly revered hallmarks of the industry – equitable to AAA Five Diamond Award in Hotels & Resorts.

The Private Club Leaders Forum

John began publishing this in the early 90's. It was the first publication of its kind. Inside the pages was club and industry information for management, presidents and staff. Simply stated, Club Leaders Forum promotes excellence in private club leadership.

When it was first introduced, it had a following that actually outpaced Club Management Magazine, the official publication of CMAA.

The Club Leaders Forum is still published twice a year and remains one of the most meaningful and valuable sources of relevant private club information available. Yes. There are today very strong sources of industry information. But John's was the first entry in this field. He planted the seeds before anyone else.

The Board of Director's Self Audit

John wanted to revolutionize the governance of private clubs.

He knew that without strong governance and a board that really knew what their job was and what to expect from a general manager – would only result in continued job turnover due to poor performance or potentially strong managers leaving on their own.

To help move the ball down the field, he authored The Board of Director's Self Audit, made it available to clubs across the country, and was a relentless champion of educating the BOD's of private clubs on truly effective leadership models.

This was the first instrument that provided club boards, of all types and sizes of clubs, with a standard and comprehensive form by which to assess their club's overall condition.

This booklet covers three major areas: (1) Structure. (2) Operations. (3) Human Resources.

There are 52 very direct questions, specifically targeting and resulting in a comprehensive self-evaluation of what the board should really be doing and how to go about it. Answers are weighted as to Mission Critical importance, and at the end a candid assessment is given as to what the total score says about your club.

It is a brilliant document that John personally authored in 2001. It has stood the test of time and is just as impactful and relevant today as it ever was.

The Career Makers

John authored this hardbound book that focused on the top 150 top executive recruiters in North America. This book became a business "best seller" and was widely accepted as the "Bible" of those in the executive search business as well as for executives looking to better their careers.

John based his findings on a nationwide survey of America's public and private companies. The Career Makers is the only guide available to rank executive recruiters, in what areas they specialize, and how candidates can work with them to build careers or recruit top talent for their organizations.

John was an entrepreneur at heart.

EARLY ACCOLADES:

John Sibbald Associates was the first (and, obviously, then the only) search firm to have been endorsed by the Club Managers Association of America.

Boardroom Magazine named John Sibbald Associates the "Top Executive Search Firm of the Year for Clubs of All Types" in 2001, 2003 and 2005 – the first three years the award had been given.

In addition to this, Executive Recruiter News cited John Sibbald Associates as one of the Top 50 executive search firms of a total 2,500 recruiting organizations serving all industries in the United States.

HALL OF FAME FOLKS

We have all heard the saying, "You are judged by the company you keep." Well, here is just a short list of some very recognizable names that used to work with John Sibbald Associates and made significant contributions of their own to the private club industry:

- *Dan Denehy* served JSA as vice president of their executive search division for 8 years. Dan leveraged this experience and his own strong expertise to found his own firm in January of 2010: Denehy Club Thinking Partners. In February of 2012, Dan's firm became a Strategic Alliance Partner of the National Club Association. Dan is a highly regarded and respected leader in the private club industry. As of this writing, he has brought on Kirk Reese to further strengthen his scope of influence. Great move!

- S*cott McNett* was a vice president in the executive search division for 6 years and 4 months. Of note is that Scott was the co-owner and manager of the South Hampshire Racquet Club in St. Louis. Today, he is a principal with the respected firm of GSI Executive Search. A solid Plutonium Club Leader in every respect.

- *Teri Finan* served JSA as vice president of communications. Among other accolades, Teri was editor for the Private Club Advisor for 3 years and Club Management Magazine for 5+ years. Teri is currently Director of Communications with the highly regarded Club Benchmarking. Few have as much historical background in the club industry as Teri.

- **W.R. "Red" Steger** was with JSA as a senior vice president of the executive search division. Red was a past president of CMAA and was GM with River Oaks Country Club for over 25 years.

- **Norm Spitzig** worked with JSA for a short time and to this day holds John in highest regard. Incidentally, on the back of the Club Board's Self Audit, is a terrific full-page article, The 12 Hallmarks of Great Private Clubs. Guess who wrote it? You guessed right! Norm's epic article first appeared in the April/May 1998 issue of Club Leaders Forum.

- **Carol Jeffers** was John's most trusted and relied upon associate during the early years. She handled some of the firm's most demanding searches for great clubs with poise and purpose. Of note was the fact her sincerity and elegant professional presence won over the confidence of boards and the search committees of clubs that "back in the day" did not even allow women members and treated the wives as "guests of their member/husbands." She was undaunted.

John was a pioneer even in this respect. Long before the emphasis on "women's equality in the workplace" — John recognized Carol had talent and went with it. John asked me to speak at Carol's memorial service many years ago in Chicago. I was honored to do so.

And — special mention simply must be made of…

- **Kathryn Sibbald.** She joined her then husband's efforts in 1986 as managing partner in supervising the recruiting and consulting activities. Her efforts exponentially enhanced to productivity of JSA. I personally saw the organization and enthusiasm she brought to every aspect she became involved with. Much of the ultimate success of JSA can be attributed right here.

PERSONAL CLOSING NOTES:

You may be interested in knowing that while Parkinson's definitely compromised John's stamina, he remained a gentleman with that quick smile and always optimistic outlook.

My wife (Kim, who happens to manage the Cherokee Town Club here in Atlanta) and I shared a glass of wine with John just a few months before he passed. We met in the home of his son and first wife, who surrounded John with love and genuine care at a time it mattered most.

> *I TOLD JOHN THAT EVEN THOUGH I HAD LED TWO CLUBS TO PLATINUM CLUB STATUS, THE FACT WAS THAT I THOUGHT OF MYSELF MORE AS A PLUTONIUM CLUB MANAGER RATHER THAN MERE PLATINUM. JOHN HOWLED WITH LAUGHTER, AND TOLD ME HE THOUGHT I WAS DEFINITELY RIGHT ABOUT THAT!*

While sitting with John we swapped some old stories about some of the real characters we both know in the business. And, boy, do we ever know some characters, and the stories that go with them. Laughter and broad smiles prevailed!

We did talk about how The Platinum Clubs of America and The Club Leaders Forum are now in good hands and would continue serving the industry well. John did not mention any of his accomplishments in the private club industry. Instead – knowing I might not get another chance — I was the one who initiated and presented to him, all of the history and facts of his efforts to better the profession of club management.

I wanted him to know that his contributions to the industry were HUGE, lasting, and more profound than any of the younger GM's of today would even be aware.

Let me just say that I "really poured it on" and substantiated every one of my points of admiration and appreciation.
John was very touched. Appreciative. And, of course — while still being a gentleman – smiled while agreeing to all the above as fact.

And – the fact is: he was the man who has had the single greatest positive impact in private club management, the approach to effective governance, and improving the longevity and compensation of management.

He is also the friend, who over a glass of wine, just a short time prior to his death — smiled broadly and gave me his blessing to go ahead with my idea of a PLUTONIUM Private Club Leadership concept. He thought it was great.

His name is John Sibbald.